Southeast Asia

Thailand, Cambodia & Vietnam

The Solo Girl's Travel Guide

Alexa West

"If you want to live a life you've never lived,
you have to do things you've never done."

Every girl should travel solo at least once in her life.

You don't need a boyfriend, a travel partner or anyone's
approval to travel the world. And you don't need a massive
bank account or an entire summer off work.

All you need is that wanderlust in your blood and a good
book in your hands.

If you've doubted yourself for one moment, remember this:

Millions of girls travel across the globe all by themselves
every damn day and you can, too.

You are just as capable, just as smart, and just as brave as
the rest of us. You don't need permission- this is your life.

Listen to your gut, follow your heart, and just book that
ticket already!

TheSoloGirlsTravelGuide.com

Table of Contents

Let's Spill Some Tea Real Quick…

Hey, I'm Alexa.

I started The Solo Girl's Travel Guide series not to make tons of money or become famous on Instagram. I wrote it for my best friend Becky when she came to Thailand for her honeymoon and for my childhood friend Kelsey who was backpacking with her girlfriends around Southeast Asia. I began these guides for my real-life girlfriends all over the world.

All with the goal of showing them the REAL Southeast Asia in a short amount of time on a modest budget.

A true SEA vacation should be equal amounts culture, street food, and tan lines. And that's exactly what this guide is!

What this Guide is not…

- An overwhelming deep-dive into Asia's history
- A 5-hour read with historical dates and ancient facts
- An advertisement for hotels that pay other travel guides to write about them.
- A book written by some man who doesn't even live here…
-

Speaking of men, since the success of The Solo Girl's Travel Guide, I've had many dudes ask me, "Yeah, but why a girl's guide?"

Um, because we have tits. And for some reason, that's enough for the world to treat us like toys. We constantly have to ask ourselves questions like….

- Are there drugs in my drink?
- Is that dark alley filled with serial killers?
- Am I going to be kidnapped and sold to the highest bidder?

The answer is usually no, but for us girls, "usually" doesn't cut it. In order to be wild and carefree, we've got to feel 100% safe.

And I've never found a travel guide to take my safety into consideration…so, here we are.

1

Take it from me: a girl who has been traveling solo around the world for almost 10 years straight. I know these countries inside and out. Go into your vacation knowing that I'm leading you to the BEST, the SAFEST, and the TOTALLY WORTH it spots.

Let your hair down and tell your mom not to worry. I've got you.

Oh, and once you've bought this book…we're officially friends. **I'm here if you need me, just write me on Instagram @SoloGirlsTravelGuide**

TheSoloGirlsTravelGuide.com

Is this how you feel about planning the biggest trip of your life?

I can help.

Want to make sure you've planned the best vacation ever?
√   Itinerary Checks

Trust me to plan the whole trip for you?
√   Full-on Itinerary Planning with your Bucket List

Don't want to lift a finger?
√   Total Trip Planning Concierge including Reservations and Flights

Find trip planning services and itinerary checks at
TheSoloGirlsTravelGuide.com

How to Budget for Southeast Asia

How much money should I bring?
How much will I spend?
What is the least amount I can spend and still see it all?

When it comes to traveling Southeast Asia, there are 3
spending routes you can take:

 Budget - $30 per day
Stay in hostels, eat local, take the minibus, and drink beer
from convenience stores.

 Balanced - $80 per day
Spend the night in a hostel and eat street food one night, then
check into a beachfront resort and sip tropical cocktails the next.
Or just stay middle of the road the whole way through – not too
fancy but comfortable.

 Bougie - $160+ per day
Infinity pool resorts, private boat tours, and quick flights from
one beach to the next.
All 3 of these options are possible, easy and will offer you the
trip of a lifetime – as long as you plan it right.

Daily Expenses

Cost	Price in USD
Street Food	$1.50
Local Restaurant	$4.00
Hamburger	$8.00
Bottle of Beer	$3.00
Cocktail	$5.00
1 Night in a Hostel	$8.00
1 Night in a Private Room	$30.00
1 Night in a Resort	$110.00 +
Day Tour	$30
1 Hour Flight	$25 - $150
7-Hour Bus	$28

Tips to Spend Less in Southeast Asia

- Visit during "low season" when accommodation and flights are cheaper
- Go to the ATM just once a week – the ATM fees are up to $6-$8 per transaction
- Get a Sim Card to download Grab Taxi or Pass App
- Drink beer from 7-Eleven or hole in the wall bars, rather than clubs
- Haggle at markets and when street shopping! Start your haggling at half price and work your way from there.
- Avoid Tuk Tuk drivers and fixed-rate taxis
- Eat street food

Your biggest expenses will be

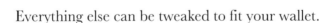

- ✓ Alcohol
- ✓ Partying
- ✓ Organized Island Tours

Everything else can be tweaked to fit your wallet.

Got all that?

Good. Now to the fun stuff…

Thailand

Introduction: Thailand 101

Come for the beaches and stay for the food: Thailand is about to blow your mind.

Over 30 million tourists come to Thailand each year; many of them solo girl travelers just like you. And it's easy to understand why. While this tropical paradise is only slightly larger than the state of California, it boasts impressive geographical diversity offering jungles, beaches, and cities for you to explore.

Fly into the sprawling capital city of Bangkok where old culture meets new. Spend the day sightseeing at the Royal Grand Palace and unwind in the evening with a cocktail at a rooftop bar with glittering views of the city.

From Bangkok, head north towards Chiang Mai where you'll encounter a region covered in jungle terrain home to elephants, waterfalls and rolling hills. Next, make your way to the southern peninsula where you have two coasts to choose from - both lined with warm turquoise water and dotted with white sand islands. There are nearly 1,445 islands in Thailand and over 2,000 miles of coastline!

You can scuba dive with Giant Manta rays in the Andaman Sea, stroll with elephants in the jungles of Phuket, rock climb on the limestone cliffs of Railay, and go swimming with Whale Sharks off the coast of Koh Tao. The vacay possibilities are endless…and that's kind of a problem when you have a limited amount of time to see and do it all!

Each region offers a different kind of holiday…yet, a similar holiday. A phenomenon that we in Thailand like to refer to as "Same Same but Different". Meaning, each region is going to offer white sand beaches, coconut shakes underneath the palm trees, snorkeling with colorful fish and all the Pad Thai you can eat. The difference, though? Them vibes!!!

The key to planning the best vacation is to set your travel goals and then budget your time. And that's what I'm here to help you do.

Whether you've got a passport full of stamps or you are planning your first trip alone, put Thailand on the top of your Bucket List and let's plan the best vacation ever.

Thailand Weather

When to Visit & Where

Rule of Thumb:

Bangkok – November - March
Chiang Mai – October - April
Krabi & Phuket – November -March
Koh Samui & Koh Phangan – February - July
Koh Chang – November- April
Hua Hin- October -March

Thailand is hot year-round- just some months are stickier than others.

December to April is considered the dry season with temperatures starting at 77°F (25°C) and increasing to about 102°F (35°C) towards the end of the season. Expect around 60% humidity during this season.

Mid-May to September is the rainy season. The temperature will stay pretty steady around 86°F (30°C) but the rain can be unpredictable. Some weeks it will pour and some weeks you won't see more than a couple hours of rain. To save disappointment, expect a couple hours of rain every day in the afternoon during rainy season. Also, humidity can get pretty intense at around 80%.

Wettest Month: September
Hottest Month: April
Most Ideal Time to Visit Thailand: November- February or "High Season"

Note: "High Season" is when Thailand experiences the highest rates of tourism. In other words, this is the season with the best weather and thus, the most visitors taking advantage of the beaches and bars! This also means, however, that prices are higher when it comes to hotels and flights!

So, if your window for your epic Thailand adventure falls outside of High Season- don't worry about it, darling. Take advantage of the lower prices, emptier planes, and embrace the rain! In the end, you'll still get a tan.

Want more trip planning info?

Want advice and tips?

What to know what I pack?

Want to travel like me?

TheSoloGirlsTravelGuide.com

Fun Thai Fact
"Koh" means "Island" in Thai.

Top 10 Thailand Experiences

1- Elephant Nature Park – Chiang Mai

2- Loi Kratong Lantern Festival, Chiang Mai

3- Bicycle the Green Lung, Bangkok

4- Wat Phra Yai Temple, Koh Samui

5- Krabi Sunset Cruises, Railay Beach

6- Songkran Water Festival, Chiang Mai

7- Wat Po, Temple of the Reclining Buddha, Bangkok

8- Ang Thong Marine Park Boat Tour – Koh Samui

9- Starz Ladyboy Cabaret Show, Koh Samui

10- Thai Cooking Class, Anywhere!

Top 10 Thailand Beaches

1- Sunrise Beach, Koh Lipe

2-   Phra Nang Cave Beach, Railay

3-   Bottle Beach, Koh Phangan

4-   Lamai Beach, Koh Samui

5-   Long Beach, Koh Lanta

6-   Emerald Cave, Koh Muk

7-   Coconut Beach, Khao Lak

8-   Lipa Noi, Koh Samui

9-   Secret Beach, Koh Samui

10-   Tri Trang Beach, Phuket

Thailand Culture Norms

Girl, you're grown. I know.

But I'll just leave these here in case you're interested....

Thai Do's & Don'ts

Do...

Cover your Shoulders & Knees in the Temples
Modesty is required inside spiritual spaces. Wear a long skirt or buy a Thai shawl to wrap around your waist and/or shoulders when you visit the temples.

Wai
To show respect to your elders, monks, and friends, put your hands in prayer at your chin and give a slight bow of the head- this is a wai. You'll start to love it.

Smile
In tense or unfair situations, argue with a smile. Thais don't like to "lose face" or get embarrassed. You're much more likely to resolve an issue with a smile.

Tip Your Salon Lady
Massages, pedicures, haircuts- these kinds of services definitely deserve a tip. 15-20% should do it.

Don't...

Disrespect the King
This one is a super don't. Thailand loves their king- he was a great man who did a lot for this country. Speaking disrespectfully about him is unheard of.

Touch a Monk
No one- not me, not you, not the Pope- can touch a monk. No handshakes, no selfies and no hugs. Instead, smile and wai.

Touch People's Heads
Even kids. The top of a person's head is sanctified in this spiritual country. Thais will try to keep their head lower than yours to show respect, not because they want a pat.

Show the Bottom of your Feet
In Thailand, feet are seen to be lowly as they are connected to the ground where human suffering occurs. Don't step over people sitting on the ground, don't point the bottom of your feet towards Thais while sitting cross-legged, and *don't don't don't* rest your feet up on a chair or on a seat in the bus.

Wear Bikinis in Public

I know you're on vacation, but Thai People are not. Save your banging bod for the beach or pool and cover up while you walk around town.

Hook Up in Public

Vacation romances are half the fun of traveling. Holding hands and some kissing is cool – but save the make out sessions for a private space.

Try to Buy anything Illegal

If you go looking for trouble in Thailand, you'll find it. While you might meet travelers with stories of getting high and taking trippy substances, they are all lucky they didn't get caught. Just because drugs are readily available, doesn't mean they're risk-free. Law enforcement is heavily cracking down on partying in Thailand (but often looks the other way for Full Moon Parties). Respect the laws of the country.

Tip Taxis or Servers

I mean, you can if you want to. But typically, Thais don't tip. In some situations, tipping is actually quite awkward.

Activities to Avoid in Thailand

Just because you *can* do it, doesn't mean you *should* do it…

Ping Pong Shows

More traumatizing than entertaining, Ping Pong Shows are where women stick objects and animals inside themselves and perform tricks on stage. If you're out of touch, you may get a rush from how shocking this is to watch. But if you're plugged into reality, you'll likely be horrified for these exploited women who feel that Ping Pong shows are their only opportunity for work. There will be plenty of Thai hawkers inviting you Ping Pong shows while you walk around touristy areas- just ignore them and walk along. Purchasing a ticket is perpetuating a disgusting industry.

Tattoos of Buddha

Buddha is sacred in these parts. So much so, that in neighboring Myanmar, a backpacker was jailed for having a tattoo of Buddha. That is quite unlikely to happen to you in Thailand, but it goes to show how disrespectful it is.

Riding Elephants

What may seem like a 'Bucket List' activity is actually an industry bred out of animal cruelty and torture. Instead of riding elephants, find an elephant sanctuary that allows you to feed, trek and bathe in the river with elephants rescued from the circus, work camps and elephant riding tourist centers around Thailand.

Tiger Temples or "Sanctuaries"

Those cute baby tigers that you're about to take a photo with…do you ever wonder where they come from? Tigers are essentially farmed, taken from their mothers at 2 weeks old, and given to tourists to bottle feed. And that's only the beginning…

Some Tips Before You Go!

Beer, Wine & Alcohol Sale Times
Alcohol is sold between 11am-2pm & 5pm-11pm. This goes for all supermarkets and convenient stores. However, if you can find a little Mom & Pop shop- they'll hook you up 24/7.

The Tour Companies actually have Great Deals
Walking around any tourist area in Thailand, you'll see plenty of tour companies with books of jungle treks and floating market tours. For day trips, these companies are pros at giving you great experiences for great prices. As far as multi-day trips, you'll save a couple bucks by planning those on your own.

Toasties
Curry is good but 7-11 Toasties are better. Grab one of these sandwiches from the fridge section of 7-11 and hand it to the 7/11 staff who will cook it for you. The ham and cheese croissant is my favorite! Warning: these treats are addictive!

Bumble
Find a sightseeing partner with another traveler or link up with a local who knows all the best spots in the city. This is a very date-friendly country. Just avoid Tinder…it's more popular for illicit dating…

Ask for "No Sugar"
Thai's love processed sugar. They put it in fresh fruit smoothies, coffee, and even will scoop a tablespoon into your soup. I find myself asking for no sugar nearly every time I order something – no matter what it is. If you like your food fresh, don't feel weird doing the same.

Cheap Flights with Air Asia

When flying in and around Thailand, check out Air Asia. Cheap, convenient and safe – just know that you'll have to pay extra to check a bag.

Carry Passport Photos

If you're country hopping, get cheap passport photos made in Thailand and carry them around in your wallet. This will save you time and money during border crossings.

Download Local Apps

This city is connected to some awesome apps that will make your trip a lot easier and a lot cheaper if you use them!

❖ **Grab Taxi -** Grab Taxi is like Uber but tends to be cheaper and have more cars available. Some Grabs are actual Taxis, and some are private cars. You can pay cash on the taxi meter or pay by card

❖ **Eatigo -** This city-wide food app offers insane food deals up to 50% off all around the city. Why not plan your day around food?

❖ **Line -** Most Thai locals use Line as their messenger app in place of WhatsApp. You can make calls and text with fun little stickers on wifi.

Keep in Mind

ATMs in Thailand spit out your money first and your card second, resulting in many a forgotten card.

Okay enough of all that. Let's get to the fun stuff!

Chapter 1: Bangkok

I'll admit it. I wasn't impressed with Bangkok the first 12 times I visited. It felt big and busy and overwhelming- because it is.

For years, I stuck to the heavily trodden tourist path with high prices, jaded locals and fellow travelers who were just as clueless as I was. Because that's easy to find.

I never knew about the vibrant floating markets. I didn't know about the glamorous sky. I had no idea where to get the most authentic Thai food in town. And I certainly hadn't a clue that there were so many hidden temples off the beaten path. Then I moved there.

Bangkok is the city with unlimited possibilities.

When you visit, stay at an upscale hotel where you can spend your days with Thai massages and cooking classes, then hop from one glamorous rooftop bar to the next at night. Traveling on a budget? Stay on Khao San Road where you can mingle with other backpackers in cozy guest houses and rowdy hostels, go on day trips to the Grand Palace, and spend the night wandering night markets sampling the most delicious $1 bites. A trip to Bangkok is completely customizable for any and every budget. Don't skip this city. You'll later be able to tell other Bangkok haters that they don't know what they're talking about.

From the Airport in Bangkok

First things first- let's get you into town…

From Suvarnabhumi Airport (BKK/SVB)

Option 1: Metered Taxi

Destination: Sukhumvit, Khao San Road, and beyond!

Where: You will find metered taxis on level 1- one level below the Arrivals Hall

How Much: The taximeter operates by distance with a metered fare. On this journey, you'll also pay a 70 Baht freeway tax and a 50 Baht airport tax. In total, the ride will cost somewhere 250-600 baht depending on the location of your accommodation

- ❖ Sometimes taxi drivers will ask you if you want to take the freeway instead of the main road- as it really does save a lot of time sitting in the horrid Sukhumvit traffic.
- ❖ Avoid the private Taxi kiosks inside the airport! If someone is yelling "Taxi, taxi, where you go?"- keep on walking! These companies offer flat-fare (instead of metered) taxi rates. Their prices will easily be twice as high.

How Long: Typically, 45 minutes to 1 hour, depending on traffic

Option 2: Skytrain Airport Link

Destination: Sukhumvit and beyond

Where: Access the Airport Link inside the airport on the basement level by following the signs that hang outside the arrival gate. The link makes several stops, two of which connect to the BTS and MRT.

- ❖ Makkasan for MRT
- ❖ Phaya Thai for BTS

How Much: You'll pay between 15-55 baht depending on the stop.

How Long: The sky train departs every 15 minutes and takes 25 minutes for the whole distance, beginning to end.

Times of Operation: The Airport Link runs from 6am-Midnight.

Option 3: Take a Bus
The Airport Express runs on 4 different routes throughout the city towards major hotels.

Destination: Sukhumvit, Khao San Road, and beyond!

Where: You'll find the official Airport Express Counter on level 1 near Exit 8. The busses are big and air conditioned!

How Much: 150 baht per person

How Long: Typically, 45 minutes to 1 hour, depending on traffic

Times of Operation: Buses leave every hour from 5am – Midnight

Fun Thai Fact
One-tenth of the entire population of Thailand lives in Bangkok.

From Don Mueang Airport (DMK)

Option 1: Grab Taxi

Saving you the hassle of navigation.

Destination: Anywhere.

Where: Easy Peasy. Go out of departures,and on to the pick-up curb. Order a GrabTaxi and wait.

How Much: GrabTaxi Prices similar to metered taxi prices. You'll see the price even before you order.

Option 2: Metered Taxi

Destination: Sukhumvit, Khao San Road, and beyond!

Where: You will find metered taxis on level 1. Walk out of the arrival gate all the way to the left end of the hall where you'll see the line for metered taxis.

How Much: The taximeter operates by distance with a metered fare. You'll pay a 50 Baht freeway and airport tax of 50 Baht. In total, the ride will cost somewhere 250-600baht depending on the location of your accommodation

- ❖ Sometimes the taxis will ask you if you want to take the freeway instead of the main road- as it really does save a lot of time sitting in the horrid Sukhumvit traffic.
- ❖ Avoid the private purple Taxi kiosks in the airport! If someone is yelling "Taxi, taxi, where you go?"- keep on walking! These companies offer flat-fare (instead of metered) taxi rates. Their prices will easily be twice as high.

How Long: Typically, 45 minutes to 1 hour, depending on traffic

Option 3: Take a Bus

The cheapest option!

Destination: Sukhumvit Road, Khao San Road and the BTS/MRT

Where: Walk through the arrival gate and walk outside (Level 2). You'll see signs advertising Bus A and Bus B- usually with a beaten down red bus in front of the signs.

How Much: The bus fare is around 30 baht per person and the buses leave every 30 minutes, 24 hours a day!

Pro Tip: Make sure you have 100 baht notes or smaller- as the ticket lady cannot break big bills!

Bus A and Bus B stop near stations for the BTS and MRT along Sukhumvit Road. You can hop off and connect to the BTS or MRT, or head to your hotel by jumping in a Taxi.

Here are the BTS and MRT stops made by airport buses:

Bus A1
BTS Mo Chit > BTS/MRT Chatuchak

Bus A2
BTS Chatuchak > BTS Mo Chit > BTS Saphan Kwai > BTS Ari > BTS Sanam Pao > BTS Victory Monument

Bus A4
Yommarat > Lan Luang > Phan Fa > Democracy Monument > Wat Bowonniwet > **Khao San Road** > Sanam Luang

The bus attendant will announce the stops, but don't be shy to confirm which stop is yours by asking the ticket attendant or other local riders around you.

How Long: Typically, 45 minutes to 1 hour, depending on traffic

Airport Pro Tip

Take 10 minutes and purchase a Sim Card with internet data before you leave the Airport. It's a time and stress-saver!

You can get plans that last for 3 days, 1 week, 1 month, etc., starting as low as $8. This will be a big help in getting to your accommodation and getting around the city for the rest of your trip.

Accommodation in Bangkok

Heads Up

Compared to hotels in Bangkok, AirBnb offers some incredible properties for a fraction of the price. Many AirBnbs feature condo properties that have a gym, pool, and kitchen in fantastic locations!

That being said, the hotels that made it on this list score above and beyond the rest in terms of value for money, location, and experience that will match every traveler's budget.

Bodega Bangkok Party Hostels

Owned by the most handsome trio of American brothers from small town Wisconsin- this centrally located hostel never disappoints. These boys know how to throw a party, so if you're looking to play drinking games, socialize, and join in on late-night bar crawls around the city, this is the place to stay. They offer walking tours, bicycle tours, and have multiple locations in Chiang Mai, Krabi & Phuket making them a one-stop shop for countrywide fun and advice. Oh, and they're dorm beds will put you into a blissful sleep coma. So comfy.

Ps. If you're in Bangkok during the Songkran Festival, you MUST stay at Bodega to properly experience the madness.

Style: Dorms
Starts at: $10 USD / 300 THB
Where: Sukhumvit - BTS Asok - Take a 10 min walk or a 10-baht motorbike taxi from there
Address: 120/15, 96/13 Soi Sukhumvit 23, Khlong Toei Nuea

New Joes $

Arriving late? Sometimes your bus or flight gets in to Bangkok around midnight. No problem. New Joe's will sort you out with their 24-hour reception. This place has been a backpacker favorite for years with their cheap double rooms, daily housekeeping, drink specials for guests, wifi and killer location. Situated in a safe pedestrian alley tucked just behind Khao San Road, you're enough close to the party but far enough for a quiet night's sleep.

Pro Tip: Try to book online days in advance- they book up quick. If they're fully booked online, however, try just showing up. They usually have some rooms saved for walk-in customers.

Style: Private Rooms
Starts at: $12 USD / 440 THB
Where: Take a taxi to Khao San Road and enter into the alley behind D&D Hotel
Address: 81 Chakrabongse Rd, Talat Yot

The Yard $

"A social hostel, but not a party hostel", the Yard is truly one of a kind. As the name suggests, there's big grassy yard where you can lounge with a book or join in on some yoga. There's also a multimedia room to watch movies, a shabby chic bar on site for meeting other travelers, an amazing Burger restaurant out front, and the trendy Ari neighborhood to explore. With the BTS, the MoChit Bus + Train station and the popular Chatuchak Market nearby- this place is top choice for convenience if you want to explore Bangkok and then move on to other destinations in Thailand. Oh, and they have free bikes!

Style: Dorms + Multi-bed Privates for Sharing
Starts at: $15 USD/ 550 THB
Where: Sukhumvit – Ari BTS – Walk towards Soi 51
Address: 51 Phahon Yothin 5, Khwaeng Samsen Nai

Rainforest Guest House and Café $

It can be a struggle to find a private room at a decent price on Sukhumvit Road- but I've got one for you. Rainforest is a quaint guest house with clean, but simple rooms. Here, you've got a comfy bed, safe space, and friendly reception. Not to mention, they make some amazing coffee and smoothies in the café lobby. Just steps from the BTS, massages, and the center of Bangkok- it's a great choice when you want a little bit of privacy without spending above your budget.

Style: Privates
Where: Sukhumvit Road- BTS Thong Lo
Address: 764/11 Sukhumvit 32-34 (Next to Rex Hotel), Bangkok 10110
Starts at: $20 USD/ 800 THB

Mad Monkey Hostel $

Staying near Khao San and want to party your face off? Mad Monkey is notorious for wild nights and lazy hangovers by the pool. Yes, I said pool! This dorm is pretty luxurious. The bar is massive, the beds are comfy and the food...hands down some of the best western food in Bangkok. The big plus to staying at Mad Monkey Hostel is that they've also got locations in Cambodia and The Philippines – so if you're trip is headed that way, they can help sort you out.

Also, if you're looking for a private room but still want social vibes – they've got really nice options with private bathrooms, as well.

Style: Dorms
Starts at: $12 USD/ 350 THB
Where: Take a Taxi to Khao San Area/Prasumen Road
Address: 55 Phra Sumen Rd

Khao San Palace $$

Luxurious with 5-star service? Not exactly, but on a backpacker's budget, this place is a pretty sweet deal. Khao San Palace is smack dab in the middle of the ultimate party and shopping street, plus they've got a rooftop pool for those super-hot Bangkok days. However, be warned: if you're looking for a quiet nights' sleep, you won't get it until 2am when the bars close and the music shuts off.

Style: Privates
Where: Khao San Road
Address: Khao San Road
Starts at: $29 USD/ 1000 THB

Dang Derm in the Park $$

Party like a kid, hotel like an adult – Dang Derm offers the best of both
worlds right on Khao San Road. This brand-new hotel lets you relax in a
clean, air-conditioned room with plush beds, modern décor and a TV with
all the western channels. It's exactly what you need after a day of
sightseeing, bargain shopping, and partying – all of which you can do right
outside the lobby steps. Their hotel sister offers a rooftop pool just 3-minutes
down the road with party music and backpackers, if you're looking to
socialize with the younger crowd. Afterwards…you can escape back to your
adult bed.

Style: Privates
Where: Khao San Road
Address: Khao San Road
Starts at: $32 USD/ 1100 THB

Shanghai Mansion $$

You'll feel like a Bond girl staying in the Shanghai Mansion. This place
screams Asian glamour with brightly painted walls, velvet lounge chairs,
lanterns to set the mood, dark wooden canopy beds, and deep bathtubs that
will make you want to strip down to everything but pearls. There is much to
see, eat, and photograph in Chinatown and this hotel puts you smack dab in
the center of it all. Not to mention, free mini bar and walking tour. Get it,
girl.

Pro Tip: Chinatown is located near Hua Lamphong Train Station and is
just a quick taxi ride away from Khao San Road.

Style: Privates
Starts at: $55 USD/ 1900 THB
Where: Chinatown (Yaowarat)
Address: 481 Yaowarat Rd, Khwaeng Samphanthawong

The Salil Hotel Sukhumvit 57 $$$

Hello, luxury. Stay in one of the swankiest areas in Bangkok at this ultra-
chic hotel. The Salil Hotel gives you close access to the sexiest rooftop bars
on Sukhumvit, including its own rooftop pool and bar. Go out for a night of
live music and wine, then head back to your hotel where they've got a gym,
boutique shop, café and some seriously chic rooms. Take a

bath, slip into your robe and slippers then lounge in a bed that feel like floating clouds. Bonus: each room has a desk space if you need to do a little work in-between play time.

Style: Privates
Starts at: $88 USD / 3070 THB
Where: BTS Thong Lo
Address: 24 Ban Kluai Nuea Alley, Khwaeng Khlong Tan Nue

Galleria 10 $$

Social pool, prime location, trendy rooms and the best damn breakfast in the entire city of Bangkok- what more could a girl ask for? Perhaps a welcome coconut brought to you by a cute bellboy? Done. Galleria 10 will treat you like a queen, plus they've got a fabulous rooftop bar & pool with yummy food and fancy drink specials. With social events and parties throughout the week, this place is ideal for solo girl travelers.

Style: Privates
Starts at: $90 USD/ 2800 THB
Where: Sukhumvit- BTS Asok
Address: 172/ 10, 155/10 Sukhumvit Rd

The W Bangkok Hotel $$$

It doesn't get any fancier than the W. Your wish is your command with top tier service from the most accommodating hotel staff in town. The W will arrange tours, hotel transport, room service, special requests- anything you want. Visit the spa, gym, rooftop, and certainly don't skip the bar where you can mingle with all sorts of interesting people from around the world. This is the high life, girls.

Style: Privates
Starts at: $180 USD/ 6,239 THB
Where: BTS Chong Nonsi
Address: 106 North Sathorn Road, Silom

Inn a Day $$$

Guaranteed to be the most memorable stay in Bangkok- Inn a Day will leave you speechless. The rooms feel like a modern-day art gallery. Go to sleep with views of the regal Wat Po from your bed and wake up with a coffee on your patio while watching the water taxis zip by. With its close proximity to the Grand Palace, Reclining Buddha, Saranrom Park, Wang Long Market, and Khao San Road- this is the ultimate sightseeing hotel.

Style: Privates + Multi-Private Rooms
Starts at: $100 USD/ 3500 THB
Where: Near Tha Tian Pier near Khao San Road
Address: 57-61 Maharat Rd., Phra Borom Maha Ratchawan

Sightseeing in Bangkok

Amphawa Floating Market
There are 5 floating markets in Bangkok; Amphawa being my top pick for the perfect balance of humans to stalls. In other words, less crowded than others and more space for you to explore.

Wander over to the board walk and boat vendors will paddle over to you offering soups, grilled meat, coconuts, beverages and more right from their boat. You'll be given a tiny stool to enjoy your treats while you gaze out at the mesmerizing sights.

When you've had enough to eat, take an hour-long boat tour along the river, which stops to visit temples and a zany petting zoo; rent a bicycle to tour the town; shop til you drop with plenty of clothing and souvenir stalls; or stay until nightfall to go firefly watching on the river. All of these activities will be available to arrange once you show up to the market- just keep your eye out for ad signs.

PS. Boat tours are 50 baht per person in the public tour or 500 baht for a private tour.

Entrance Fee: Free
Open: Friday – Sunday 8:00am-7:00pm
Location: Amphawa- 50km from Bangkok

Wat Saket – The Golden Mountain
For the most pristine views of Bangkok, you're going to want to head over to Wat Saket where you'll journey up a 300-step winding staircase to the top. Along the way, gong the drums and ring the bells that line your path. Once you reach the top, prepare for a breathtaking 360-degree view of the city.

Bonus: At the base of the temple, you'll find an ancient cemetery tracing back to the Ayutthaya period (1350- 1767 AD) covered in vines and mystery.

Entrance Fee: $.60 USD / 20 THB
Open: Daily 9am - 5pm
Location: Near Khao San Road - Between Boriphat Road and Lan Luang Road, off Ratchadamnoen Klang Road
Address: 344 Khwaeng Ban Bat, Khet Pom Prap Sattru Phai

Wat Po –Temple of the Reclining Buddha

This 46-meter long Buddha glistens in gold as it lounges on its side in a pose that is scarcely seen around the world. Just as impressive as the golden Buddha itself, are the monks' ceremonies that take place at Wat Po. Listen to the echoes of Sanskrit mantras as you wander the meticulously adorned temples with smaller Buddha statues galore. Purchase a bowl of gold coins where you can make a wish as you drop each coin into the 108-bronze bowls that line the temple- each drop ringing with an enchanting chime.

Bonus: Wat Po is also known as one of the best places to get a traditional Thai massage at their Thai school.
Entrance Fee: $3 USD / 100 THB
Open: Daily 8:00am – 5pm
Location: Maharat Road
Address: 2 Sanamchai Road, Grand Palace Sub District

The Grand Palace & Wat Prakeaw

What used to be the home of the King Rama I and his harem, guarded by combat-trained female sentries, is now the most popular tourist attraction in Bangkok. Prepare to spend hours exploring this royal compound with over 100 golden buildings featuring over 200 years of royal and governmental history.

Head to the Outer Court where you'll find the main attraction- The Emerald Buddha (Wat Prakeaw). With French-inspired structures, ancient thrones and sparkling rooftops, the entire scene is captivating. Hire a guide inside the walls to get the full story.

Entrance Fee: $15 USD / 500 THB
Open: Daily 8:30am- 3:30pm
Location: Khao San Area
Address: Na Phra Lan Road, Old City near Khao San Road

The Green Lung of Bangkok

Easily, one of the best (and most surprising) days you'll have in Bangkok! You wouldn't expect to find rivers, jungles, and a national park in the big city…but that's exactly what this is!

The Green Lung is a massive peninsula just over the river from Sukhumvit that takes you back in time 30 years. The land is preserved, the locals have kept their customs, and the markets are as authentic as it gets.

Climb aboard the local ferry (5 baht) that zips you across the river for a day of exploring. Upon landing at the pier, you'll be greeted by bicycle vendors that will rent you a bike, give you a map, and send you on your way.
On the map, you'll find these FREE adventures:
- Siamese Fighting Fish Gallery
- Sri Nakhon Khuean Khan Park and Botanical Garden
- Glittering Golden Temples like Wat Rat Rangsan, Wat Bang Kobua, and Wat Kong Kaew
- The Floating Market - Talad Nam Bang Nam Peung (only on the weekends

You'll ride down small village roads between palm trees, flower fields, roadside food stands and wooden houses on stilts, passing other bicyclists and the occasional car – it's a very safe and slow journey.

You can easily ride for 4 hours or 1 hour – this road loops around for a customizable escapade.

Pro Tips for The Green Lung

- Wear sunscreen
- Bring small bills for local vendors
- Start early – around 9am for the best weather
- Bring a shawl or wear something that covers your shoulders for the temples.
- Stay at Bangkok Tree House Eco Hotel for a fully-immersed getaway

How to Get There

Option 1: Go to BTS Khlong Toei and take a taxi to Klong Toey pier. Here you can take a longtail boat (100 baht) or a water taxi (10 baht) across.

Option 2: Go to BTS Bang Na and take a taxi (5 baht) to Wat Bangna Nok Pier. Get on the water taxi that takes you directly to the gorgeous Wat Bang Nam Phueng Nok – so easy.

Pro Tip: Option 2 is cheaper with more of a Thai crowd and drops you in the center of all the attractions. Go left for the floating market and go right for the park and fighting fish.

Fun Thai Fact
There are over 35,000 Buddhist Temples in Thailand

Areas to Explore in Bangkok

Khao San Road

Having a wild night on Khao San is a rite of passage when you come to Bangkok. If wild isn't your scene, you can still enjoy everything Khao San has to offer during the day. Countless stalls line the winding streets selling clothing, jewelry, luggage, electronics, souvenirs and knick-knacks galore- all at super reasonable prices.

There are massages to be had, both street food and restaurant dishes to be eaten, and people watching to be done. Once nightfall rolls around, the entire road turns into one entertaining circus filled with tipsy backpackers from every walk of life.

How to Get There: Stay in the area or take a taxi from BTS Victory Monument (less traffic this way)

China Town / Yaowarat

If you're hungry for out of this world seafood, go to China Town or "Yaowarat". If you're looking for exotic herbs and spices, go to China Town. If you're wanting to take photos of bizarre dark alleys with vendors selling an array cured meats, go to China Town. If you're looking for Eastern medicine being sold in the spirit of ancient tradition, go to China Town. You could easily spend a whole day walking the streets lined with food stalls, taking photos of historic buildings that date back to 1902, or getting a taste of the Thai-Chinese culture fusion.

In terms of temples, there's Wat Traimit- a temple that is home to the world's largest Gold Buddha, and Wat Mangkol Kamalawat- the principal Buddhist temple for religious celebrations in the area.

Pro Tip

China Town is right next to the train station Hua Lamphong. Make a visit before catching your train!

How to Get There:
- ❖ Option 1- Take a water taxi to Ratchawong Pier and walk a couple hundred meters to Yaowarat Road and Sampeng Lane
- ❖ Option 2- Take a Taxi

❖ Option 3- Take the MRT to Hua Lamphong Station and take a taxi towards Yaowarat Road

Victory Monument

Honestly, most Thais don't even know what the monument at Victory Monument is all about. The answer: it's an ode to the Thai military. However, this monument is not what makes Victory Monument such an inviting destination. Actually, Thais and Farang know Victory Monument as a street shopping haven with tons of makeup stalls (my favorite), Thai clothing stalls, food stalls, and collection of mini malls while also being a major traffic hub for the city. While there aren't as many minivan travel options as there used to be, Victory Monument is conveniently located on the BTS and is where you can find important public buses- including the airport bus.

How to Get There: BTS Victory Monument

Pro Tip

Many entertainment hawkers will offer you a "free five-minute" peek of a male strip show but remember that nothing is ever free in Thailand. They'll likely find a way to pinch some money off of you.

How to Get There: BTS Silom

Fun Thai Fact

There is an ultra-rich community of Thai's we call "Hi-So," as in "High Society." Recently, photos appeared in the news of a Hi-So girl in Bangkok who called an ambulance to come put a band aid on her toe after she broke a toenail.

Soi Cowboy

Soi Cowboy is certainly not everyone's cup of tea- but for some, it's totally fascinating. I'll leave the morality debate out of this one and let you decide where you stand. But if you're curious, read on.

Bangkok's most popular Red-Light street is wild with women and ladyboys who line the street in scantily clad outfits, pulling men into their clubs to watch the girls dance (usually with their tops on) and have a drink.

The neon lights and loud music usually kick off around 9pm, and if you're not easily shocked, it can be quite a "cultural" experience to pop into one of the clubs for a drink. The drinks serve as your cover charge (usually 100-175 baht each).

You'd think that this street would feel super sketchy and unsafe- but it doesn't. The girls are nice, the street is brightly lit, and there are tourists from all over the world hanging out to watch the madness. And when you've had enough, the safe haven of Terminal 21 Shopping Center is just across the street (3-minute walk).

How to Get to Soi Cowboy: MRT Sukhumvit Station or BTS Asok. Located 100 meters from Terminal 21- between Asok Road and Soi 23

Silom

Silom area is home to Patpong- the other Red-Light district which is full of Ping Pong shows, male strip clubs, and if you've got the eye to spot em- drug dealers. While this may sound super scary and unsafe, it isn't. This is simply just another side to Bangkok that may or may not intrigue you.

At night, Silom is brightly lit with a large market where you can buy scarves and souvenirs or take it easy at one of the bars that line the street offering mixers at great prices. Worth a look-see!

Fun Thai Fact
Thailand used to be named "Siam." On May 11th, 1949, Siam was officially renamed as the Kingdom of Thailand.

Shopping in Bangkok

Siam

This cosmopolitan shopping area has your favorite retailers from home like Forever21, H&M, & Uniqlo alongside the upscale Siam Paragon that boasts Armani, Chanel, and Dior. Spend a day in air-conditioning with a movie at the Paragon Cineplex or some fun at the musical bowling alley. Paragon has a great food court and gourmet grocery store in case you get hangry. PS: There's an iHop in the basement!

Open: Daily 10:00am – 10:00pm
How to Get There: BTS Siam/ Chit Loem

Terminal 21 Shopping Center

Mimicking an international airport, each floor of Terminal 21 is themed like a different city around the world. Paris has a MAC store and H&M, Tokyo and London have tons of Thai clothing boutiques, Istanbul has a NYX makeup store, and San Francisco is home to the most amazing food court around- seriously...best food court in the city. Get out of the heat for the day with a movie on the top floor, Los Angeles.

Open: Daily 10:00am-10:00pm
How to Get There: BTS Asok

Khao San Area

It's time to learn the art of haggling on Khao San. The vendor says 200 baht for those elephant pants? Nah, you can get them for 150 if you're confident. Find anything you want on Khao San from gorgeous dresses and handmade jewelry to tailored suits and fake IDs. Keep your eye out for Suzy Walking Street, which is a cut-through alley between Khao San and Soi Rambuttri that offers hippie-esque jewelry, art and tattoo shops.

Open: Stalls open up roughly around 9am and stay open past midnight
How to Get There: From Sukhumvit, take the BTS to National Stadium and then hop in a taxi.

MBK Center

Within this massive mall stacked with floor after floor of electronics, gadgets, clothing, and more- there is one floor that stands out from the rest!

When you've lost, broken or had your phone stolen, head to phone heaven on the 4th floor of MBK. 1st hand and 2nd hand phones are displayed in case after case- it's just a matter of finding a vendor you want to work with. Get a replacement or a Chinese off-brand phone that is just as good and twice is cheap. You can also get your phones and tablets repaired here!

Afterwards, check out the clothing floor, the furniture floor, the camera floor and so on. Once you've worked up an appetite, head outside to the food market and get your grub on!

Open: Daily 10:00am – 10:00pm
How to Get There: BTS National Stadium

Chatuchak Market

Clear your schedule for the day, lather on the sunscreen, and prepare to shop til you drop! JJ Weekend Market is the biggest outdoor shopping market that you ever did see. Handmade purses, vintage records, essential oil infused soaps, souvenirs in bulk- you're about to hit the jackpot.

This market is divided into sections- some with clothing, some with high-end & handmade leather bags, some with furniture, some with animals...anything and everything you could want can be found at Chatuchak.

Pro Tip

If you see something you like and think, "Oh, I'll come back for it later"- you won't. You're going to get lost in in the winding corridors of stalls and restaurants, but if you shop with a 'life is short' attitude and you'll have no regrets.

Open: Friday 6:00pm-Midnight/Saturday & Sunday 9:00am - 6:00pm
How to Get There: BTS Mo Chit (Exit 1) or MRT Kamphaeng Phet (Exit 2) or Take a taxi from Khao San
Pro Tip 2: Getting off at MRT Chatuchak is actually a super inconvenient walk!

Fun Thai Fact
His Majesty King Bhumibol Adulyadej was actually born in Cambridge, Massachusetts in the United States. The King was highly educated, with an engineering degree from Switzerland.

Things to Do in Bangkok

Visit Erawan Shrine

While you're out and about for a day of shopping near Siam center, take a moment to find peace at the Erawan Shrine. One of the most beautiful shrines in Bangkok with glittering gold statues and fresh flowers placed by gracious followers every day, this shrine represents the daily connection between Thai people and Buddhism precisely.

Open: Daily 6:00am-11:00pm
How to Get There: BTS Chit Lom (Chidlom)- Exit 1

Thai Massage

While you can consider Thai Massage as a form of relaxation, it's actually a centuries old spiritual practice. You'll be bent like a pretzel, squeezed like a lemon and walked on like a pretty little doormat- but it feels so good in the end. Thai massage releases toxins from your body and leaves you feeling like a new, more flexible, woman. No oils here, in fact, you'll be provided clothing to wear during the process. You'll see Thai massage parlors everywhere!

Price: Starting at around $6 USD / 200 baht per hour

Bangkok Comedy Club

See a different side of Bangkok culture as you join expats living in Bangkok and travelers from around the globe for a night of humor and beer at the Comedy Club. The comedy club invites world-class comedians to debut improv and standup bits that never disappoint. Afterwards, the whole club gathers downstairs at The Royal Oak Restaurant and Bar with good vibes and great cocktails.

Price: Starting at $12 US / 400 baht
How to Get There: Phrom Phong BTS – head towards Soi 33/1 and look for Royal Oak Restaurant (the club is upstairs)
Address: 595/10 Sukhumvit Soi 33/1

Bangkok Forensic Medicine Museum

Bangkok Forensic Medicine Museum, also known as Siriraj Medical Museum, is made up of 4 museums in one, exhibiting the bizarre side of nature, medicine, and death. Get up close and personal with diseased specimen, common parasites, dissected human organs, real-life embalmed bodies of the deceased, and even a mummified cannibal who loved to eat children. Oh, Thailand.

Open: Monday - Saturday 09:00 to 16:00
Price: $1.20 USD / 40 baht
How to Get There: Take the water taxi to Prannok Pier
Address: 2 Wanglung Road Khwaeng Siriraj, Khet Bangkok No

Watch a Muay Thai Boxing Match

Thai Boxing is a national treasure all across Thailand. From the ceremonious music to the gambling crowds to the high paced action in the ring- it's an all-around exhilarating experience. Don't be alarmed when you see kids in the ring- they've been well trained and can hold their own. You can buy tickets from your hotel in advance or jump in a taxi and have them drop you off.

The two most popular stadiums for watching Muay Thai:

❖ **Rajadamnern Boxing Stadium:** Built in 1945, this is a classic Muay Thai stadium with lots of locals!
Fight Times: Monday, Wednesday, Thursday & Sunday starting at 6:00pm
Ticket Price: Starts at $30 USD / 1000 baht
Area: Just north of Khao San

Address: 1 Ratchadamnoen Nok Rd, Pom Prap, Khet Pom Prap Sattru Phai, Krung Thep Maha Nakhon 10200

❖ **Lumpinee Boxing Stadium:** The most popular with tourist companies and easy to access via the BTS + Taxi
Fight Times: Tuesday-Friday fight at 18:30 & Saturday fights at 4:00pm & 8:00pm

Ticket Price: Starts at $30 USD / 1000 baht
Area: Just north of BTS Mo Chit
Address: No.6, Ramintra Rd, Anusawaree

Cooking with Poo and Friends

"Oh, here's just a little something I learned how to whip up while in Thailand". This cooking class is great for anyone with just a few days to spend in Bangkok! They'll pick you up at the conveniently located meeting point- Emporium Sweets next to BTS Prom Pong at 8:30am- where you'll be whisked away with your Thai chefs to shop in the local morning market to buy all of the ingredients you'll be cooking with that day. You'll learn how to prepare a 4-course Thai meal and then…you get to eat it. Win-win. Book ahead via their website.

When: Daily! 8:30am – 1:00pm
Price: $45 USD /1,500 baht per person
Location: Klong Toey Slum (not as scary as it sounds, I promise)
Visit: cookingwithpooandfriends.com

Go on a Bicycle Tour

Some of the best Bangkok adventures are not available by foot. After all, this city is massive. But on two wheels, you can access off-the-beaten path temples, small-town neighborhoods, and rural pockets of the city that would otherwise be unreachable.

Link up with the amazing crew at 'Follow Me Bike Tour' for an unforgettable local experience. There are tons of bike tours to choose from including jungle tours, street food tours, night tours and more. Tours range from 4-8 hours with entertaining guides and all gear provided.

When: Daily! Times depend on the tour!
Price: Starting at $40 USD 1,300 baht per person
Location: Sathorn Soi 9, 126 (33/6)
Visit: followmebiketour.com

Where to Eat in Bangkok

Bangkok Cafes

Caturday Cat Cafe

In my next life, I want to be a cat at Caturday Cat Café. All day, these cats get to lounge around on humans' tables, chase feathery toys, eat healthy treats, get lots of love- and when they've had enough, nap in skyscraping cat towers. Meanwhile, the lowly humans sip on Matcha Tea Frappes and eat wasabi french-fries. There's no minimum fee or any rush to push the human guests out the door. Meow.

Open: Daily 12pm-9pm
How to Get There: BTS Ratchathewi (Exit 2)
Address: 115 Phayathai Rd

Kai Zen Coffee Company

Nitro Cold Brew on tap and Cold Drips galore - these guys aren't messing around when it comes to that caffeine fix. They've got signature coffee drinks like the Cherry Cola Cold Brew that will blow your mind and of course, all the café classics made with quality roasts. Additionally, you'll find awesome Paninis, sandwiches, and an incredible Breakfast Burger.

Open: Daily 8am-6pm
How to Get There: Ekkamai BTS - hop in a quick taxi
Address: 582/5 Tai Ping Tower Between 26-28 Ekkamai Rd.

Unicorn Café

Become one with your inner unicorn. Literally, put on a Unicorn onesie, eat rainbow waffles with ice cream, sip on Cotton Candy Italian Sodas, and let the glittery pink atmosphere permeate your soul! This is every little girl's dream come true! Bring your camera for the most Bangkok selfies ever.

Open: Daily 12:00pm – 8:00pm
Price: 35 baht per hour
How to Get There: Bangkok BTS Chongnonsi
Address: Soi Sathorn 8

Brunch in Bangkok

BKK Bagel Bakery

Photo Credit: BKK Bagel Bakery

New York Bagels in Bangkok? Believe it, sister. Handmade fresh every day, these bagels are the real deal. BKK Bagel Bakery also cures their own meats and cheeses in house, which means that it would be a shame not to try a bagel sandwich. The 'Lox, Stock & Bagel' with house-cured salmon is a life changer- just sayin'.

Open: Monday- Friday 7:30am-5:00pm / Saturday-Sunday 8:00am-5:30pm
Where: BTS Chit Loem then hop in a quick taxi
Address: 518/3 Maneeya Center, Ploenchit Road

Atelier
The most 'Real Housewives'' Brunch spot in Bangkok, visit Atelier every Sunday from 12pm – 3pm to feel like a bougie bitch. Feast on an extensive array of fresh seafood, including King crab, prawns, shucked oysters and mussels, along with a selection of gourmet salads at the salad buffet. There's also a hot buffet which includes a spread of both international, Thai, and Indian specialties. Order a glass of champagne to feel especially fabulous!

Pro Tip: Get up to 50% off when you book online @ Atelierbangkok.com

Open: Sunday 12pm-3pm
How much: $55 USD / 1,900 baht for all you can eat!
How to Get There: BTS Asoke
Address: 2nd Floor, Pullman Bangkok Sukhumvit, 30 Sukhumvit 21 Asoke Road

Roast

Gourmet brunch with all the fixins can only be found at Roast. Undoubtedly the most popular spot for brunch in BKK, this place is worth a visit if you don't mind opening your wallet for western prices. You'll find dishes from home like Huevos Rancheros, Crab Cake Benedict, and Roast Breakfast with Smoked Salmon all looking like they're fresh from the Food Channel. PS. Roast is super vegetarian friendly!

Open: Daily 10:00am-10:00pm
How to Get There: BTS Phrom Phong
Address: 1st floor, The Helix Quartier, EmQuartier

The Clubhouse Sports Bar and Grill

A hair of the dog is sometimes just what you need. No matter how early you order that Bloody Mary, no judgments will be passed as there are probably a handful of other patrons with a morning drink at The Clubhouse Sports Bar and Grill. With sporting events constantly streaming on their screens, pick and team and pay tribute to the cause by getting a little tipsy.

Open: Daily 9:00am-1:00am
How to Get There: Asok BTS
Address: 21/1-3 Soi Sukhumvit 23, Sukhumvit Road, Klongtoey-Nua

IHOP

You heard right! The International House of Pancakes has made its way from the USA to the BKK. When you need fluffy pancakes and sweet tea, head to the basement of Siam Paragon to get your fix. This location is a bit swankier than you're used to, however, with water features all around and top-tier service.

Open: Daily 10am-10pm
How to Get There: Siam BTS
Address: Siam Paragon

Soi 2 Khao Man Gai

My absolute favorite place for breakfast in all of Thailand and hell, even all of Asia is located in the neighborhood of Bearing. From around 8am-11am (or once food runs out), there is a little Khao Man Gai (chicken and rice) street food stall that sells the best Khao Man Gai I've EVER had. Ever.

For 35 baht, you get a big plate of what I call "sushi-grade" steamed chicken, rice and chicken broth soup on the side. Grab a cup of ice and pour yourself some water, sit down on a plastic chair and eat breakfast with the locals. Afterwards, wander south on Sukhumvit to the market of Samrong to continue your local adventure.

Open: Daily 8am-11am (Best to get there before 10am just to be sure)
How to Get There: Bearing BTS Exit 3 – walk towards 7-Eleven and take a left on Soi 107. Walk a couple blocks to Soi 2.

Lunch in Bangkok

Green House Hotel
The best Penang Curry in all of Bangkok is at Green House Hotel. Order with shrimp and white rice for a mind-blowing meal. Strangely enough, they also have the best hummus I've ever found in Bangkok, served with pita bread! Both their Thai selection and Middle Eastern menu far exceed expectations while keeping their prices relatively low for the area (especially when it comes to imported beer).

Open: Daily 10am-3am
Address: 84 Rambutri Road
How to Get There: Rambutri Road is located right next to Khao San

Suzy Wong's Beer and Buns
If you're staying in the Khao San area, make it a priority to eat lunch at Suzy Wong's. Bahn Mi, buckets, and new best friends- this place has everything to offer. You'll find lots of BBQ here- BBQ pork, BBQ bacon, BBQ chicken. No one's complaining. The half-covered outdoor atmosphere is great for people watching and socializing.

Open: Daily 10am-3am
How to Get There: Suzie Walking Street, Khao San Road

Im Chan
"Eat where the locals eat" is always a good motto to live by while traveling. Im Chan serves the lunch rush full of Thai office personnel and shop workers who want traditional Thai food fast. With a menu full of pictures and English to go with them- you can eat just like the locals. Food is cheap, dishes are made to order, and location is central- what more could you ask for?
Open: 7am-10pm
How to Get There: Phrom Phong BTS
Address: Sukhumvit 37 Alley, Khlong Tan Nuea

Cabbages and Condoms
"Our food won't make you pregnant." Yep, that's the actual slogan of C&C. If you want to make a difference while in Thailand and keep others like you from getting pregnant, support a restaurant with a cause. C&C contributes revenue towards family planning services in Thailand. A little contradictory however- the atmosphere here is quite romantic with twinkling lights

dangling from lush trees in an intimate garden. Maybe that's why they send you home with condoms.

Open: Daily 11am -10pm
How to Get There: Asok BTS- Exit 2
Address: Sukhumvit 12 Alley, Khwaeng Khlong Toe

Terminal 21 Food Court

Back home when you hear the term "food court" you think of subpar Chinese joints and fast food. Not in Thailand. Here's how it works: got to the top floor of Terminal 21 shopping mall, stand in line where you'll exchange cash for a prepaid food card, and then go crazy. They have some of the best street food options like Khao Man Gai, Stewed Pork Leg, and Mango Sticky rice. Best of all- it's all cooked in such a clean (and air conditioned) environment. When you're done, take your card back to the counter to retrieve what you didn't spend.

Open: Daily 10am-10pm
How to Get There: Asok BTS – Terminal 21 Shopping Center, 5th floor

Pro Tip

Don't show up during the 12-1pm lunch rush and expect to find a seat.

Dinner in Bangkok

Thip Samai

Photo Credit: Brady Weeks Photography

The best Pad Thai in Bangkok! You won't see Pad Thai like this anywhere else. Made fresh, traditionally seasoned and then wrapped in a scrambled egg blanket- it's everything you could ever ask for. They also sell fresh-squeezed orange juice that you'd be a fool for not trying. I'll warn you that there will be a line, but the wait is worth it.

Open: 5pm-Midnight

How to Get There: Head towards Khao San Area
Address: 313 Th Maha Chai, Banglamphu

Vertigo Grill and Moon Bar

On your last night in Bangkok, treat yourselves to a Sex in the City style dinner with steak, lobster, and champagne at Bangkok's most glamourous rooftop restaurant. Sitting 61 floors high, Vertigo Grill and Moon Bar gives you spectacular views of one of the most glamourous metropolises in Asia. The dress code is smart-casual so no flip flops or tank tops. Have fun getting dressed up and playing the "international woman of mystery" game.

Open: Daily 6pm-11:30 pm
Where: Banyan Tree Hotel
Address: 61st Floor, 21/100 South Sathon Road

Soei

Want to try real Thai food? Let the man himself, P'Soei, cook for you. Dishes like Goong Chae Nam Pla (sort of like Wasabi shrimp ceviche) and Yam Kai Dao (Thai fried egg salad) will change everything you thought you knew about Thai food. This is certainly a must-try spot for anyone that has a foodie soul. The feel of the restaurant is very personal as P'Soei has photos from his days of playing Rugby all around the restaurant and even a couple photos of that time the famous foodie, Andrew Zimmern, stopped by.

Open: Daily 10 am – 9:30 pm (Closed on Saturday)
How to Get There: Sanam Pao BTS – then hop in a taxi
Address: Near the corner of Phibun Whattana Yaek 6 and Rama VI Soi 34. Moo Baan Piboon Whattana neighborhood (you can find this place on Google Maps)

Best Beef

Imagine this: fresh plates of prawns, sliced beef, pork tenderloin, garlic bread, veggies, and more brought to you to cook at your table on a charcoal grill as you order. Sounds pretty good, right? What if I told you that this was an all-you-can-eat situation spanning 2-hours for 269baht? And then, what if I told you that for 439baht, you could get 2-hours of all-you-can-eat AND all-you-can-drink beer and cocktails. You're sold, aren't you?
Open: Daily 4pm-12am
How to Get There: On Nut BTS – go straight out of Exit 2, walk for 5 minutes and look for the huge sign
Address: 1490/2 Sukhumvit Rd, Khlong Tan

Tacos and Salsa

Guacamole, Tortilla Soup, fresh ceviche…do I have your attention yet? Tacos & Salsa is widely popular (i.e. make a reservation for weekend nights) amongst expats who crave tastes from home in the form of frozen margaritas, mariachi music and of course, tacos and salsa. The owner is a Mexican female who is really kicking ass at what she does by putting out great food and creating a vibrant atmosphere that has created a loyal following. It's definitely worth tasting what all the fuss is about.
Open: Daily 11am – 11pm
How to Get There: BTS Phrom Phong BTS or BTS Asok – Walk 5 minutes
Address: 21/3 Sukhumvit Soi 18

Street Food & Night Markets in Bangkok

Not-So-Fun Fact: The Bangkok government has pledged to "ban" street food in Bangkok despite the city being internationally ranked for the best street food in the world. Don't worry- I know the best kept street secrets in BKK and will help you find them.

Soi 38

Don't let anyone tell you that Soi 38 street food doesn't exist anymore- it does. The street food has just gone underground. Walk onto Soi 38 any time after 5pm and you'll find an old parking garage converted into a food hawkers site with tons of stands, stalls, and places to sit! Tastes dishes from the north, south, and central regions. They've also got Chinese, Japanese, and hotpot! Plenty of vegetarian options, too.
Best Time: Sunday-Monday 5pm-10pm
Where: Near BTS Thonglor- Road 38

❖ **Food to try**
> Mango Sticky Rice
> Crab Fried Rice
> Massaman Chicken Curry

Suttisan Market

To feed the two towers full of Insurance Company workers, this market offers traditional Thai dishes morning, noon and night. In the morning, you'll find coffee stands, boat noodles and fresh fruit vendors. The afternoon has the best Khao Man Gai and lots of "point and pick" curry pots. In the evening, take the chance to try the best Tom Yum Soup you'll ever have in your life is located at a small Isaan (Northern Thai) restaurant just next to the bridge stairs by the MRT Exit 3. The Sunday Evening Market offers whole chicken, grilled shrimp, lots of curry, and even…fried bugs.
Best Time: Daily 8am-1pm & 5pm-9pm
How to Get There: MRT Suttisan

Rod Fai Market Srinakarin (Train Market 1)

You may have heard of the market where trains pass through on the tracks and the vendors scramble to get out of the way, yes. This is it. But the heart and soul of this market is so much more. The Warehouse Zone offers a collection of old electronics, Japanese memorabilia, vintage car collections, and more whacky finds. And the Market Zone has over 2000 stalls for buying modern clothes mixed with hippie everything. It's the biggest market with the most to eat, see, and buy, yet is relatively untouched by the backpacker community with its off-the-beaten-path location.

Best Time: Thursday-Sunday 5pm to 12am
How to Get There: BTS On Nut is the closest station but requires a taxi journey from there.
Address: Srinakarin Road Soi 51 - behind Seacon Square Mall

❖ **Things to try**
   Vintage Soda (look for a VW van)
   Kao Moek Gai (Muslim Rice and Chicken)
   Banana Roti
   Beef Kebab

Talat Rot Fai Ratchada - Train Market 2

Guys, it's about to get real. Come hungry because the street food at this trendy Thai market never ends. Rows and rows of seafood, Thai salads, bite sized snacks, sushi and ice-cold walking beers await. Each section of the market offers a different niche. When you've had your fill, there are live music bars stacked in old shipping containers that surround the market. Sit down, order a bucket of beers on ice, bring your snacks, and soak up the best people watching.
Best Time: Tuesday-Sunday 5pm-11pm
Where: MRT Thailand Cultural Center Exit 3- Ratchadaphisek Road

❖ **Things to try**
   Massive Seafood Platters for $10- you'll see em
   Thai Fried Chicken Wings
   Mini Cupcakes
   Seafood in a Bag (you get to eat with plastic gloves!)

Khao San Road

Hangovers are best cured with Khao San street food starting in the AM. Smoothie stands with fresh fruit, soups that speak to your soul, and in my opinion- the best Pad Thai in Bangkok. And the morning street food rush is only the beginning. As night falls, vendors bring their carts round to offer wild and wonderful fare that goes perfectly with a cold walking beer.
Best time: All day – every day
Where: Khao San Road & Rambutri Street

❖ **Things to try**
   Scorpion on a stick
   Fried egg rolls

Bars in Bangkok

Teens of Thailand

Photo Credit: TOT

The only proper gin bar in Thailand, TOT is for you girls who appreciate a fine, handcrafted cocktail made with gourmet ingredients by some Thai dudes who know what they are doing! This intimate speakeasy is filled with hip vibes and a laidback creative Thais. TOT is near Hua Lamphong Train Station and is a perfect stop off before a night train journey.
PS. TOT isn't closed, their entrance is just super low-key. Push those wooden doors open.

Open: Daily 7pm to 1am
How to Get There: Take a taxi to Soi Nana in Chinatown or take the MRT to Hua Lamphong and take a 5-minute walk
Address: 76 Khwaeng Pom Prap, Khet Pom Prap Sattru Phai

Wishbeer
For the best ciders and craft beers in Bangkok – there is only one place to go and that is Wishbeer. Frequented by both local Thais and international expats, Wishbeer is a favorite of all beer drinkers in Bangkok, but still relatively unknown by backpackers They've got ciders and craft beer on tap and in the bottle – but it will cost you western prices. Expect to pay, at the

very least, $8 per beer. When you are craving those hops bad enough though, $8 sounds like a steal. With burgers and finger food – Wishbeer is a great place for dinner, too.

Open: Daily 5pm-12am
How to Get There: BTS Prah Khanong – go down Alley 67 and look for the almost hidden entrance on the left.
Address: Soi Sukhumvit 67

The Iron Fairies

Imagine Peter Pan's Neverland meets Sex and the City- that's what you get at The Iron Fairies. This popular local spot draws in crowds with their weekly line-ups of live music, Thai hipster bands and Monday's open-mic night. If cocktails are your thing, The Iron Fairies is the place. Dim lighting, intimate seating, and a collection of interesting characters- this place is pretty sexy.

Open: Daily 6pm-midnight
How to Get There: Thonglor BTS – Exit 4
Address: 402 Soi Thonglor, Sukhumvit 55 Rd.

Sky Train Jazz Bar

Get rooftop views without rooftop prices at Sky Train Jazz Bar. It's not swanky or elegant- but rather, a hole in the wall bar with a staircase that leads you to what feels like a secret terrace decked out with patio furniture and 100-baht beers and spirits. While Sky Train Jazz Bar intended to be a jazz spot…there's not actually jazz music here. However, this makes for a quiet spot to enjoy some good conversation while watching the lights of Victory Monument's traffic circle.

Ps. For real live jazz music, check out Saxophone Bar!

Open: Daily 5pm-1am
How to Get There: Victory Monument BTS – Exit 4
Address: Soi Rangnam

Craft

That first sip of craft beer from home after spending a few weeks sipping Singha might just bring a tear to your eye. With 40 taps and lots of bottles, prepare to geek out on beer here. The vibes here are super laid back with a backyard tailgate vibe and lots of expats. Friday nights you can catch some live music- usually along the tunes of acoustic folk and blues. But wait, it gets better! On site, you can get your taco fix with the Slanted Taco Stand catering to Craft guests. They've also got a menu full of bar food that is to die for.

Open: 12pm - midnight
How to Get There: BTS Asok- Exit 4. 10-minute walk.
Address: 16 Soi Sukhumvit 23 Khwaeng Khlong Toei

Havana Social

If you want cigars, mojitos, and empanadas, I can tell you where to go. But first, you'll need to find the telephone booth on Soi 11 which serves to "recreate the Pre-Revolutionary era of Cuba" when each speakeasy was hidden. Sometimes you need to punch a passcode into the phone to get in (which can be found on Havana Social's FB page and other times a bouncer will sneak you in). Friday & Saturday at 10pm is the best time to go for social vibes and live music.

Open: Daily 6pm-2am
How to Get There: BTS Nana – Exit 2. Look for the little alley in front of Fraser Suites
Address: Sukhumvit Soi 11

Rod Fai (Train Market 1 & 2)

If you're looking for vibrant atmosphere and adventure, there are so many unique bars at both train markets. There are bars with live music, hip hop bars, bars serving out of the back of vintage trucks, open-air rooftop bars where you can look out on to all of the action- and the drinks here nearly half the price of the trendy city bars. These markets are where groups of Thai friends gather for a cheap and tipsy night out.

❖ **Rod Fai Srinakarin (Train Market 1)**
Open: Thursday-Sunday 5pm - 12am
How to Get There: BTS On Nut is the closest station but requires a taxi journey from there.
Address: Srinakarin Road Soi 51 - behind Seacon Square

❖ **Rod Fai Ratchada (Train Market 2)**
Open: Thursday – Sunday 6pm- Midnight
How to Get There: MRT Thailand Cultural Center – Exit 3

WOOBAR @ The W Hotel

Don't waste your sexy dress on Khao San Road. Save it for the swankiest spot in all of Bangkok…the W Hotel. **Thursday nights,** WOOBAR hosts "Ladies Love Bubbles" from **8pm-10pm.** Come meet yourself a man who wears matching socks and most likely has his life together.

400 baht: Includes a welcome cocktail and 2-hour free flow bubbles.
800 baht: Includes 2-hour free flow bubbles, red wine and white wine.
1,100 baht: Includes 3-hour free flow bubbles, red wine and white wine til 11pm.

*except every 2nd Thursday of the month.

Open: Daily 9am-2am
Where: BTS Chong Nonsi
Address: 06 N Sathon Rd, Khwaeng Silom

Sky Bars in Bangkok

Octave

Photo Credit: Octave

'Holy shit' is the only way to describe Bangkok's #1 sky bar- Octave. The 360 ° view of BKK's city skyline, the playful EDM beats, the breezy sunset- it all feels so surreal and euphoric at the same time. Happy Hour is every day from 5-7pm with killer cocktails for 220 baht. You can easily snag a table if you show up at 5pm but reserving a table ahead of time is a smart move, too. FYI: there is a dress code. Come looking polished instead of wearing your elephant pants.

Open: Daily 5pm-2am
Happy Hour: Daily 5-7pm
How to Get There: Thong Lor BTS – Exit 3- Rooftop of the Marriot Hotel
Address: 57 Sukhumvit Rd, Klongtan-Nua

Brewski
Brewski is a laidback rooftop bar with beautiful views and beautiful brews. You can get a variety of craft beers on tap for around 300 baht. They serve you a fancy bowl of peanuts to munch on while you peruse their tapas menu. Every day they offer a 'Pint of the Day' happy hour and along with rotating food specials like Taco Tuesday and Pulled Pork Thursday.

Brewski doesn't get too crowded so you can rock up and find a seat with no problem. There are a few large tables for big groups and some intimate spaces that offer a bit more of a romantic experience.

Open: Daily 5pm-1am
Happy Hour: Daily 5-8pm
How to Get There: BTS Asok– Exit 4- Rooftop of the Radisson Blu- 30th floor
Address: 489 Sukhumvit Rd Tan

Bar9

Affordable, comfortable, and open all day! Smack dab in the thick of Siam's shopping district, Bar9 is a great place to kick your feet up after your BKK shopping spree. Bar9 has one of the best Happy Hours in town with a 2-for-1 special on wine, draft beer, and classic cocktails. After 5pm, you can get some serious dinner discounts (up to 50%) when you make a reservation online. **Tip:** make your reservation on your phone during happy hour and then you can redeem your discount reservation once dinner service opens up.

Open: Daily 8am-1am
Happy Hour: Daily 12pm-5pm
Where: BTS Siam – Rooftop of the Novotel - Behind Central World
Address: 220 Petchaburi Road, Ratchathewi

Above Eleven

Salsa Ladies Night on Wednesdays, Live Jazz on Thursdays, and a live DJ every night in-between- Above Eleven knows how to throw a good party. The cherry on top is the 360° view of BKK's glittering skyline where you can get cozy on comfy couches while enjoying an incredible Japanese Peruvian Fusion menu and signature cocktails. The semi-casual dress code is an excuse to get dressed up- who doesn't love that?

Open: Daily 6pm -2am
Happy Hour: Daily 6pm-10pm
How to Get There: BTS Nana– Rooftop of the Frasier Sweets
Address: 38/8 Soi Sukhumvit 11

CRU Rooftop Champagne Bar

Visiting Bangkok solo? Lover of wine and all things bubbly? CRU is calling you, girl. With a circular bar situated smack dab in the center of the rooftop, it's super easy to meet and mingle with other guests, travelers, and expats. While the price tag might be a little higher than other establishments (think $20 per glass), the views and ambiance are certainly worth it if you're after a sophisticated night with sophisticated strangers.

Open: Daily 5pm-1am
Where: BTS Chidlom – 55th Floor of Central World
Address: 22 Centara Grand at CentralWorld, 999/99 Rama 1 Road

Lebua Tower Sky Bar

Have you seen the movie, The Hangover 2? In the film, the traveling misfits find themselves 63 floors up on top of Lebua Tower, a hotel bar overlooking the entire city, including clear views of the river and river taxi boats puttering through. As Lebua is a bit of an older bar, the layout isn't designed to accommodate big crowds of people – yet, since the iconic movie was released….big crowds come! My advice: Go before 6pm. Go at 5pm before the main bar opens, where you can have a drink "Distil" – their secondary bar. Here, you can meander on the terrace which gives you equally great views as the main bar but without the crowd. And now you can say that you've been to the Hangover Bar.

Open: Daily 6pm-1am
Where: Saphan Taksin
Address: Lebua at State Tower 63rd Floor, 1055 Silom Road

Clubs & Live Music in Bangkok

Sing Sing Theatre

Sing Sing Theatre - or 'the Bangkok Moulin Rouge' as we like to call it- is a super solo girl friendly club. Replace grinding dudes with singing ladies swinging from the ceiling, spectacularly performed live music, and themed parties under dim lights- and that is Sing Sing Theatre. It will be a fantastical night where the excitement is enough to keep you there until closing.

Open: Tuesday-Sunday 9pm- 2am
How to Get There: Located between BTS Phrom Phong and Thonglor – next to Quince Restaurant
Address: Sukhumvit Rd - Soi Sukhumvit 45

Beam

Beam is known for their hypnotic visuals, dancing lights, and Asia's first "body kinetic" dance floor that helps you literally become one with the music. Get ready for international DJs spinning deep house or EDM beats in a warehouse setting that will transport you to another world. When you need a break, meander downstairs into the lounge known as the Dalmatian Room for some mellow music and comfy seats.

Open: Wednesday- Saturday 9pm-2am
How to Get There: BTS Thong Lo
Address: 1/F, 72 Courtyard, Sukhumvit Soi 55 (Thonglor)

Saxophone Bar

Enjoy live jazz music in a relaxed atmosphere with beer that comes in Tuba-shaped mugs at Saxophone Bar in Victory Monument. This chilled out spot is the epitome of a dive bar that fills with local musicians and patrons, well off the beaten tourist path. Tip: Some of the best seats are upstairs where you can sit on the floor and peer down at the stage.

Open: Daily 6pm-2am
How to Get There: BTS Victory Monument – Exit 4 – make a U-turn and walk until you see a small pub street on the right
Address: 3/8 11 Phayathai Rd, Thanon Phaya Thai, Ratchathewi, Bangkok 10400

Mustache Bar

Mustache Bar is known for being Bangkok's #1 after-hours bar. When every other bar is closing down, Mustache is just warming up. To stay open after hours, they keep a low profile from the outside, but inside is this underground college-party vibe with a killer sound system- perfect for tossing back some beers while socializing amidst revved up DJs spinning some dance-worthy tunes. You'll find that the patrons here are mostly expats and western English teachers who are blowing off a little steam from the workweek- come make some friends.

Open: Officially 6pm-12am but the party tends to rage until sunrise
How to Get There: MRT Thailand Cultural Centre – 20-meter walk down Soi 7 Ratchada
Address: Ratchada Soi 7

Fun Thai Fact

It was two Thai brothers that inspired the term "Siamese Twins" as they were conjoined at the chest when the country was named "Siam" in the 1800's.

Spas in Bangkok

Yunomori Onsen & Spa Bangkok

All of the baths! Detox your system by spending the day hopping from one hot bath to another in a calming, warmly lit atmosphere. Relax in the outdoor open-air garden bath, detoxify in the CO_2 soda bath, or get some "me time" in the individual teakwood bath. There is a spa on sight where many guests indulge in a 2-hour Thai massage or body scrubs to make their skin glow. If you don't know already, a traditional Japanese bath is communal- but separated by gender. I promise, it's not as awkward as it sounds.

Open: 9am – Midnight – Book 48 hours in Advance!
Entrance Fee: $13 USD/ 450 baht (services not included)
How to Get There: BTS Phrom Phong – 1km away so you can a taxi or Tuk Tuk without being totally ripped off.
Address: A-Square 120/5 Soi Sukhumvit 26, Klongtoey

ZenRed Hair Salon

THE #1 expat hair salon in Bangkok is ZenRed. Blonde, red, Balayage-they know what they're doing. Asian hair and western hair are very different- and they know it. With a salon full of professionals who have trained in London with a combined experience of 40 years doing western hair... you can trust them not turn your hair blue (trust me, it happens). They also do styling, Keratin treatments, extensions and more.

Open: When: 11:00am – 9pm
How to Get There: 5km from Sathorn and Silom- Easiest to take a Taxi from BTS Asok or BTS Sala Daeng
Address: Monopoly Park Mall, Rama III, 59/27 Industrial Ring Road

Su Esthetic Home Spa

The humidity, the sand, the dust- it all messes with your skin if you stay here long enough. Make sure you go home with a glow by getting a professional facial or body scrub at Su Esthetic Home Spa. This Korean-style spa is super girl-friendly with staff that make you feel instantly comfortable. Plus, their prices aren't bad either. The neighborhood is filled with a great selection of little restaurants to recharge afterwards.

Open: Daily 9:30-7:00
How to Get There: Phrom Phong BTS- Exit 4 – Make a U-turn and walk 10 minutes and head up Soi 26
Address: Soi Thanphuying Phuangrat Praphai, Sukhumvit Soi 26

How to Get around Bangkok

BTS/MRT

From 5am-midnight, hop on the most convenient form of air-conditioned travel that ever did exist. Everything is in English, easy to understand, clean, and safe. Taking the BTS or MRT is often much faster than taxing a taxi on the congested roads of Sukhumvit.

Taxis

Always use the meter in a taxi! The driver will try to give you a fixed rate (that's 3x the price) and will justify by saying things like "Oh so much traffic" or "Very far" but he's just trying to make an extra buck. Once the meter is on, you can trust that he'll take you where you need to go.

Grab Taxi

Skip the taxi headache and order a Grab Taxi who will run the meter honestly, use GPS to find your location, and will drive much safer and slower than the taxi drivers who just don't give a shit. Sometimes the Grab Taxi is not a taxi, but a personal car like Uber. Grab Taxis are all around you so don't hesitate to take this safer option! There is even a Grab Van for airport transfers!

Tuk Tuks

Tuk Tuks are a fun experience but they are not for long distance journeys-more so for a day of sightseeing around Khao San Road or a 5-minute ride from the BTS to your hotel.

Buses

These old school busses are the cheapest form of transport in Bangkok and a fun way to see the city! Your hotel can help you sort out which bus goes where. It's a leisurely ride so don't use them if you're in a hurry!

Chapter 2: Chiang Mai

Elephants, jungles, and temple hikes- this gem of a city in the north of Thailand is loved and adored by all who visit.

Easy to navigate thanks to the ancient square fortress that surrounds the "Old City" and convenient to walk, Chiang Mai is a dream to just throw on a pair of shoes and explore. Inside and outside the fortress walls, you'll find accommodation for all budgets, lots of shopping nooks, and a little bit of partying, too.

Amenities here are a pleasant balance between the comforts of home and the exciting novelty of Thailand. You've got cafes with handcrafted coffee, bistros with western sandwiches made with local ingredients, and Thai food infused with northern flavors. There is ALWAYS a foodie adventure to be had.

It's easy to see why Chiang Mai is currently the 'digital nomad' center of the world. Prices are cheap, the city is safe, and meeting other travelers is a breeze. Many people come here for a quick vacay…and end up turning Chiang Mai into their second home.

Bring your sunscreen. Chiang Mai is a whirlwind of outdoor adventure.

Getting into Chiang Mai

From Chiang Mai Airport

Finally, an airport that is actually in the city! Only 10-15 minutes from the center.

Option 1: Take a Grab Taxi
With so many guesthouses in Chiang Mai, the most hassle-free way to get from the airport is to just program your route into GPS and let a car pick you up at the curb.

How much: 50-160 baht depending on your hotel

Option 2: Airport Taxi
If you don't have data on your phone, take a standard taxi.

Where: There are two taxi Kiosks in the airport terminal where you can organize your ride, or simply walk outside the airport to the left, and wait for someone to yell "taxi!"
How much: 160-baht flat charge per car
Pro Tip: Confirm the price with the taxi driver, "160-baht, Na?" – just so they know that you know the correct price.

Option 3: Take a Songthaew
In Chiang Mai, Songthaews are trucks where you sit on little benches in the back. You tell the driver your destination, and he takes you to your location, as he drops other riders off one-by-one. The driver will tell you when it's your stop OR you can press the little buzzer if you see your stop.

Where: Walk to the outside gates of the airport, where you'll see a little covered bus stop with Thai people waiting. A Songthaew will pull up here every 20 minutes or so.
How Much: 40-60 baht per person
Time: Songthaews stop operating just before midnight

From Chiang Mai Train Station

The train station is located about 3km outside the city center- super convenient.

Option 1: Public Transport

When you walk outside, you'll be bombarded by a line of Thai men offering tuk tuks, taxis, and Songthaews. You've just got to pick your price point.

Songthaew: 40 baht (although, they might push you to 60 baht)

Tuk Tuk: 150 baht

Taxi: 200 baht

Option 2: Grab Taxi

Important: The public transport drivers don't like Grab Taxi encroaching on their territory at the Train Station. Simply, cross the street and go to a local café before you call your Grab to avoid conflict. Be discrete.

How Much: 80-200 baht depending on your hotel's location

For my Chaing Mai Train Guide, visit my blog at TheSoloGirlsTravelGuide.com

Fun Thai Fact

Chiang Mai means "New City"

Areas to Explore in Chiang Mai

Old City
The confines of Old City are surrounded by an ancient fortress wall and moat with ties to 13th century royal rivalries. All throughout the old city, you'll see historic temples, crumbling and worn away, standing right next to a brand new 7/11. You'll never tire of wandering Old City's streets amongst cafes, guest houses, restaurants, and the popular Sunday Night Market. This is the heart of Chiang Mai.

Nimman
Outside the Northeast Corner of the Old City is Nimman- the Digital Nomad Zone. Here is where waves of international expats have come to settle down for a few months or a few years. You'll find tons of western food, lots of vegan options, and the giant shopping mall called Maya Mall that satisfies the western and vegetarian palate.

Loi Kroh Road + Night Bazaar
Home to the daily Night Bazaar, Loi Kroh Road comes alive as soon as the sun starts to set. This street is lined with stalls selling souvenirs, street food vendors, and bars with bar girls playing pool with old white dudes. It's an entertaining place to have a wander.

Accommodation in Chiang Mai

Pro Tip: Remember to check out AirBnbs, too!

Stamps Backpackers $

Stamps is the ultimate party hostel in Chiang Mai. Not only are they located right next to the biggest nightlife spots in the city, every night offers a social scene in the lobby bar where they've got a fridge of craft brews and local beer fully stocked. When 10pm rolls around, a group heads out to party and get a little wild.

Style: Dorms
Starts at: $8 USD / 280 baht – Minimum 2-night's stay
Where: North Eastern Side of the Old City
Address: 1/11 Chaiyapoom Road Soi 1

Bodega Hostel $

Unsurprisingly, the Bodega Boys have done it again. Led by Daniel, the youngest Bodega brother, this party hostel in Chiang Mai is always buzzing with backpackers. A good balance between chill and party, you can take a couple days of rest in their 4-bed or 8 bed dorms where you get a decent amount of privacy and then emerge in the evening to play beer pong in the garden foyer or go on a pub crawl adventure with the crew. And just like their Bangkok location…their beds are the most comfortable dorm beds on earth.

Style: Dorms
Starts at: $9 USD/ 300 baht
Where: Southeast Corner of the Old City – 5-minute walk to everything!
Address: Ratchamanka Alley 3

Love CNX Guesthouse $

You can tell by the attention to detail that Love CNX is owned and run by a super savvy woman! Bee, the Thai goddess herself, personally designed this modern guesthouse that is quiet and comfortable with a trendy feel. Grab a refreshing Iced Honey Lemon Tea (my favorite drink in Chiang Mai) from the café lobby or go across the street for some of the best smoothies in town. You can also rent bicycles next door for just a couple dollars per day.

Style: Privates
Starts at: $20 USD / 679 baht - Minimum 2-night's stay
Where: Old City
Address: 104 Ratchapakhinai Rd A. Muang

Lamphu House Chiang Mai $$

My vote for the best solo girl hotel in Chiang Mai is Lamphu House. Dreamy beds, a fabulous pool, and amazing location within walking distance to Tha Phae Gate, right next to the big Sunday Night Market, and surrounded by some of the best restaurants in the city. After you're done exploring, go collapse on a lounge chair by the pool.

Style: Privates
Starts at: $38 USD / 1300 baht

Where: Old City
Address: Phra Pok Klao 9 Alley

Arch39 Art & Craft Hotel _{$$}

Make a couple friends? Traveling in a group of 3 or 4? This is the ultimate sleepover room! With two bunk beds- one accessible via a rock climbing wall and one with its own staircase- and one big double bed below...this place feels like a big kid sleepover party.

Style: Shared Privates
Starts at: $64 USD/ 2000 baht
Where: Nimman Area
Address: 21,21/1-2 Maneenopparat Soi 2 Road, Sriphum

Jomkitti Boutique Hotel $$$

You just can't beat great service. For a pampered stay with a free mini-bar, complimentary luxury taxi to the airport, and professional staff- this is it. The hotel is brand new, the rooms are sparkling clean with modern amenities, the pool is magical, and the breakfast – omg

Style: Privates
Starts at: $107 USD/ 3,630 baht
Where: Center of Old City
Address: 100, 102, 104 Rachamanka Road, Phra Sing

Shopping in Chiang Mai

Saturday Walking Market

Scarves, paintings, lanterns, and silver jewelry line the streets of the Saturday Market- but, you'll have to elbow your way through the crowd of people to have a look. The market is laid out on one very narrow street where you can expect to be shoulder to shoulder with other tourists. The saving grace is the outdoor food court with sit-down tables. If you don't mind crowds- go for it. If not, wait til Sunday…

Open: 5pm – 10pm. Get there around 4:30 to beat the crowds.
Where: Wualai Road just outside the Old City
How to Get There: Walk or take a Grab Taxi to the Southern Gate Wall. You'll see the crowds!

Sunday Market

Right in the center of Old City is the Sunday Walking Street. With two wide lanes, you can take your time strolling around while you visit stalls with handmade jewelry, artisan soaps, and little souvenirs. The street is lined with a couple of Buddhist Temples that open up into day-time food markets with every Thai food under the sun. When your feet are tired, there are rows and rows of comfy chairs for 150-baht foot massages. Go crazy.

Open: 5pm – 10pm. Get there around 4:30 to beat the crowds.
Where: Ratchadamnoen Road stretches from Tha Phae Gate and Wat Phra Singh temple.
How to Get There: The road is huge, and you can intersect it at many junctions. It's easiest to start at Tha Phae Gate.

Warorot Market

A true Thai Flea Market- Warorot Market is a 3-story facility divided into sections selling teapots, dried fruit, skin care, fabrics, live amphibious creatures, and oh so much more. The few blocks that surround Warorot are lined with stalls selling random things like flashlights and fishing nets across the street from big beauty stores and cheap clothing stores. Go have a wander and sample some food along the way.

Open: 4am – 6pm.
Address: 90 Wichayanon Rd.
How to Get There: Hop in a red Songthaew for 40 baht

Malls

There are 7 malls in Chiang Mai; each one a little different than the next. Here are the top 3...

Maya Mall: Located in the Nimman Area, Maya has an amazing food court in the basement, popular stores like NYX Makeup & American Eagle, has a modern movie theater with the latest releases and an open-air rooftop with bars and live music.

Central Festival: About a 20-minute Grab Taxi from the Old City, Central Festival is where you go to restock on the basics from home. There is an H&M, Zara, Uniqlo and a few more trendy stores. The basement has a collection of Thai teas, dried fruit, and small-business shops.

Central Kad Suan Kaew: This old-school Thai mall is more of a cultural experience than a shopping-spree destination. Conveniently located in the Nimman area, it's worth a look if you want to grab an ice cream at Dairy Queen or a Starbucks coffee. There are tons of low-priced Thai clothing stores, but the sizes are targeted towards slim Thai girls with no boobies.

Things to Do in Chiang Mai

Elephant Sanctuaries

Photo Credit: Meagan Daniel Photography

The original Elephant Sanctuary in Chiang Mai is called 'Elephant Nature Park', run & founded by a Thai woman named Lek. This little lady crusader has rescued injured, old, and abandoned elephants from street begging, overworked logging jobs, and tourist-fed elephant riding establishments.

Visiting the park truly is a once in a lifetime experience. You get to interact with the elephants, taking long walks, hand feeding them fruit, and even bathing with them in the river- without disrupting their schedule or exploiting their existence. To visit, book your tour weeks in advance. In the event that this sanctuary is all booked up, then check out Elephant Jungle Sanctuary, Ethical Elephant Sanctuary or Hug Elephant Sanctuary.

Major Key to Look For: If an elephant park offers elephant rides, they are not a sanctuary.

Elephant Nature Park Info
Starting at: $77 USD / 2,500 baht
Open: Everyday- Time depends on your Tour
Where: Mountains in Chiang Mai

How to Get There: Free pickup from your hotel in Chiang Mai
Doi Suthep Temple

Photo Credit: Brady Weeks Photography

You can see the glittering temple of Doi Suthep 1,600 meters below in the city center. Once you get to the base of Doi Suthep, you'll find a road buzzing with small shops selling scarves, trinkets, and waffle hotdogs (yum). Climb up the 300 or so steps to the temple, with little Hmong Children lining the stairs trading photos for cash. Expect towering golden temples, the scent of incense burning, and the little pockets of Buddhist statues where locals go to pray. Once you've had your spiritual moment, visit the breathtaking viewpoint where you can see the entirety of the city while watching planes taking off the airport.

Entry Fee: $1 USD / 30 baht
How to Get There:
- Experienced motorbike drivers can enjoy the windy drive up the mountain, stopping at a café at the base of the mountain afterwards
- Order a Grab Taxi
- Take a 50-baht Songthaew from the Northern Gate Market– corner of Manee Nopparat Rd & Changhuak Rd
- Set off on a gorgeous yet challenging 2-3-hour hike starting at the base of the Chiang Mai Zoo where you'll pass Wat Pha Lat Temple and waterfalls along the way.

Doi Kham Temple

Also known as Wat Phra That Doi Kham, this temple is totally worth the 30-minute adventure south of the city center. Standing at 17 meters high with a uniquely draped golden shall, this is easily one of the most impressive Buddhist Temples in Thailand. Off the beaten path, you can expect a more local crowd who comes to pray for good student grades and lucky lotto tickets. As with many temples, you'll find stalls with local Thai snacks and souvenirs outside the temple on the top of the hill.

Entry Fee: Free
How to Get There:
- If you're an experienced motorbike driver, slap on a helmet and drive up the steep winding mountain.
- Order a Grab Taxi who will drive you to the top of the mountain. You can take a Songthaew back down the mountain into town.
- Hike from the base of the mountain up a 20-30-minute natural staircase. You can find the entrance where the Songthaews hang out.

Temple Tip: At the base of the mountain, you'll see stalls selling strings of flowers to give as an offering to Buddha (and supporting small entrepreneurs)-starting at 1 baht.

Wat Rong Khun – The White Temple

Right out of a Disney movie, this whimsical 20th century Buddhist Temple is a one-of-a-kind artistic tribute to Buddhism, the afterlife, and eastern mythology everywhere you look. To get there, you'll have to take a full-day trip to Chiang Rai, a town about 3 hours north of Chiang Mai. Tours include a private driver and usually, some extra trips to Doi Kham or a boat ride on a local river. Ask your hostel or hotel to help you book!

Temple Entrance Fee: 50 baht
Full-Day Tour Prices: Starting at $55 USD/ 1800 baht

Gibbon Experience

Become one with your inner monkey as your climb through the trees on wooden bridges, zipline through the canopy, and repel down to the floor. The 2 ½ hour tour includes the canopy tour, lunch and a waterfall walk. It's an exhilarating experience led by professionals who no stranger to the occasional 'fear of heights' freak out.

Starting at: $130 USD/ 4,199 baht

Tour Times: 6:30am, 8am, 9am, 12:30pm
Where: Mountains in Chiang Mai
How to Get There: Free pickup from your hotel.

Chiang Mai Cabaret Show

You've never seen anyone more glamorous than a Thai Ladyboy- and damn, do they know how to put on a show. Iconic musical impersonations with wardrobes that are to die for and choreography straight off Broadway, this Cabaret show is incredible. Your entrance fee comes with one free drink, too. What a bargain.

When: Daily 9:30pm
Entrance Fee: $11 USD / 350 baht
Location: Anusarn Market, Night Bazaar
How to Get There: Head towards the night bazaar & Loi Kroh Stadium

Sticky Waterfalls

Take a nature stroll through bright green bamboo trails until you reach Sticky Waterfalls, also known as Bua Thong Waterfalls. Grab onto a rope start climbing up the 500-meter cascading falls! It's not too intense, don't worry.
PS. Food & drink is not allowed inside. Just water bottles.

Entrance Fee: Donation Box
Where: 60km in the Mountains of Chiang Mai
How to Get There: 1.5-hour ride via motorbike or hire a Songthaew/Taxi and haggle a price depending on how many people are in your group (maybe 120 baht per person round trip).

The Thai and Akha Cooking School

Thai Style Cooking with a sprinkle of Akha Hill Tribe Flair, this cooking class offers a unique local experience off the tourist path. During your cooking class, you'll prepare 11 different dishes, including a combination of soups, desserts, appetizers and entrees in an outdoor Thai kitchen! You'll learn each step of the process, including shopping for ingredients at the local market (morning class).

Starting at: $30 USD / 1000 baht
Class Times: Every day at 8:30 & 4:30
Where: Northeast Corner of the Old City
How to Get There: Free pick-up and drop-off from your hotel!

Grand Canyon Water Park

There is a massive manmade gorge just 20 minutes south of the center which has been turned into a Thai-style waterpark with a floating obstacle course, water slide, and massive blob that catapults you into the air. There is a restaurant on site, lockers, and lounge chairs to catch some fun.

Entrance Fee: $10 USD / 300 baht
Open: Everyday 10am – 7pm
Where: Grand Canyon Chiang Mai
How to Get There: Take a tuk tuk for about 600 baht each way.

Not So fun Thai Fact

At the start of the 20th century Thailand had over 100,000 Asian elephants. Today, it's estimated that there are just around 4,000 elephants left, of which just 1,500 live in the wild.

Want to help those numbers increase? Say no to elephant riding establishments. Support elephant sanctuaries.

Where to Eat in Chiang Mai

Chiang Mai is a street food city! But there are a couple really great restaurants scattered around the city, so here we go...

Funky Monkey Cafe

Try the 'No Ice' Smoothies, the croissant Sandwich, or the French Toast for breakfast. Then come back for lunch and have the Hummus Plate or the Green Chicken Curry. This family run business keeps prices low, ingredients fresh, and taste on point!

Open: 7am – 8pm
Address: 67 Ratchapakinai Road

Blue Diamond Breakfast Club

Wake up slowly as you sit in a tranquil botanical garden with a waterfall feature and cool breeze. Sip on freshly squeezed juice and snack on vegan muffins or vegetarian omelets. Before you go, check out the Blue Diamond storefront where you can take home organic jam or homemade donuts for a yummy afternoon snack.

Open: 7:30am – 8pm
Address: 35/1 MoonMuang Road, Soi 9

Three Little Pigs Soul Kitchen

Soul food done right! Come get yourself a deep bowl of Biscuits and Gravy, Fried Chicken and Waffles, or a good ol' Breakfast Sandwich. Don't be surprised if you come with the intention of eating brunch and are then swayed by their BBQ and burger options, though. It happens with no regrets.
Open: 7:30am – 8pm
Address: 242 Manee Nopparat Rd

Lert Ros

You guys! You cannot come to Chiang Mai and not eat at Lert Ros. Lert- the man himself- is manning the grills every night with massive grilled fish, shrimp, beef, and pork that come with amazing sauces- it's all about the sauces! Order a hot bowl of Tom Yum Soup and a side of Som Tom Salad and you're set for life. Plus- the food is cheap! Walk away spending around 360 baht for 2 people (with beers, duh).

Open: Sunday-Saturday (closed Monday) 12pm-9pm

Address: Soi 1, Ratchadamneon Road

Ginger & Kafe

This upscale Thai bistro with vegan & vegetarian options offers a rustic yet elegant oasis in the middle of Chiang Mai. Here's your chance to try elevated Thai dishes with a twist on the classics. Try hand-tied dumplings with sweet plum sauce, colorful fresh spring rolls with Thai mango and shrimp, or chicken satay skewers with peanut sauce. The dishes here is plated so beautifully that they are sure to wind up all over your Instagram.

Open: Friday-Thursday 10am-11pm
Address: 199, Moonmuang Road, Tambon Si Phum

Maya Mall Basement Food Court

Food courts in Thailand offer the best street food style dishes prepared in the cleanest kitchens for the best price- and Maya Mall's food court is no exception. They've got all the best Thai dishes – vegetarian stalls included- but the real star of this place is **Wrap Master**…the best burritos in town starting at 80 baht…try their chips and salsa, too!

Open: Daily 11am - 9pm
Address: 55 Huay Kaew Rd

Salsa Kitchen

 Crunchy corn tortilla tacos, legit enchiladas, and some damn fine margaritas, The Salsa Kitchen hits the spot when you're in the mood for Mexican. The ambiance is a relaxed sit-down space with attentive service. And the best part- food portions are huge, so you can expect to take some food to go.

Open: Daily 11am - 11pm
Address: 26/4 Huay Kaew Road

Tong Tem Toh

Isaan is the largest region in Thailand and also the poorest. As Isaan workers migrated to the big cities for work, Isaan restaurants started to pop up everywhere! You can experience Northern dishes at this family-owned and operated Isaan restaurant in Nimman where steamed fish, grilled pork, and traditional fried morning glory are the stars. 10 extra points for ambiance and service!

Open: Sunday 11am-11pm, Monday 9am-9pm, Tuesday-Thursday 11am-9pm & Friday-Saturday 11am-11pm
Address: Nimmana Haeminda 13

Night Markets in Chiang Mai

Chiang Mai Gate Night Market
From the grill to the wok- everything Thai can be found at this quaint night market sitting over the moat with about 30 stalls total. With plenty of tables and chairs, you can collect dishes from several stands and create a feast! Stock up on beers at the 7/11 across the street!

Open: Daily 6pm - 11pm
Address: 87 Bumrung Buri Rd

Chiang Mai Night Bazaar
Snack on crispy spring rolls or coconut ice cream as you wander the streets of Chiang Mai Night Bazaar. Head into the food court for the full spread of Chinese-inspired noodles, Mango Sticky Rice and every Thai curry you could ever imagine. When you're done, walk it off as you browse through an endless line of souvenir stalls with soft scarves and tiny carved elephants.

Open: Daily 6pm - 11pm
Address: Between Loi Kroh Rd and Tha Phae Rd

North Gate Night Market
Once the sun starts to set, this little night market comes alive. From the best Khoa Kha Moo in the city to authentic middle eastern Roti- there's tons to eat here. You'll also find lots of fresh fruit and vegetarian options! Afterwards, head towards the massage shop at the back of the market and embrace your food coma.

Open: Daily 6pm - 11pm
Address: Manee Nopparat Rd.

Nightlife in Chiang Mai

Zoe in Yellow

The party starts here. At around 9 o'clock, the collection of bars that make up the Zoe in Yellow court start to fill up. There is a big courtyard with picnic tables, some smaller establishments where you can pull up a stool at the bar, and a couple bars with a dance floor. By midnight, the partiers spill into the middle of Zoe for a mingling session before they migrate to the next location together.

Open: Daily 9pm-midnight
Address: Rajvithi Road

Spicy

Next up, the crowd moves to Spicy- the warehouse nightclub with a live DJ, lazer lights, and a dance floor. Beers are a bit overpriced and the place gets super packed- but if you're looking for a bit of flirty fun, here is where you'll find it.

Open: Spicy opens at 9 but the real party doesn't start til after midnight.
Address: Chayaphum Road

Living Room

End the night at Living Room. With a bit of a dingy college party feel, this 'underground' after-hours club has two pool tables, a smoking area, and a college-esque bar pumping mingle music. The catch? This place closes its metal gate outside to appear closed as bars are not allowed to be open past 2am. **Ps**. Your admissions ticket counts for 1 drink.

Open: 9pm-5am
Address: 5, 95 Sithiwongse Rd

Club Mandalay

Imagine the hit TV show 'The Voice' with the big stage, the professional lights, and the passion that pours out of the singers! Mandalay's show is full of energy with Thai singers covering English songs from Rock Classics to Modern Gaga. Get a table, order a bottle, and know that the 200-baht cover is totally worth it. Bring your ID to get in.

Open: 10pm-2am
Address: 5/3 Moon Muang Rd Lane 2

Spas in Chiang Mai

City Nails
City Nails does it all- simple gel nails, glittery deco nails, pedicures, eyelash extensions, eyelash tinting and waxing. They are super professional, very hygienic, and great at what they do. Plus, their prices aren't bad either.

Open: Daily 10am-8pm
Address: 49/1-8 Arak Road. T.Phra Singh

Robin Beauty Bar
The best (and cheapest) waxing service in town- Robin Beauty Bar is popular with western expats, and tourists alike. Kung is the expert waxer who uses a mixture of homemade wax and humor to make the experience less painful and more entertaining. You'll pay 1/3 of what you would at home with 100-baht eye brow waxes and 600-baht Brazilians! It's best to call ahead to make an appointment but you might get lucky with a walk in-the salon near Tha Phae Gate.

Open: Monday-Saturday 10am-6:3pm & Sunday 12pm-6:30pm
Address: Moon Muang Rd Lane 8

New York New York
When you need a root touch up, a good wash, some deep conditioning, or want a total color makeover- this is the place to trust. An Aveda Salon with experienced professionals who have been doing western hair for decades and are constantly studying their craft- it's just like being in the chair at home.

Open: Daily 10am-10pm
Address: Nimmana Haeminda Rd Lane 13, Tambon Su Thep

Fun Thai Fact
Chiang Mai is Thailand's second largest city, after Bangkok.

How to Get Around Chiang Mai

Chiang Mai is relatively small and in theory, you can walk from one corner of the city to the next. But girl, it can get sweaty.

Songthaew
When you see one of these red trucks driving down the road, just wave your arm, run up to their driver-side window to tell them your destination and hop in the back. The standard rate is 20 baht per person, but if you're going from one end of the city to the next, expect a haggle up to 60 baht.

Grab Taxi
Sign up for Grab Taxi and you'll get tons of promotion texts with promo codes. You can literally get rides for free (I did for almost an entire month).

Tuk Tuk
Tuk Tuks are everywhere. It's up to you to haggle your price. You won't usually get lower than 80 baht per ride.

Fun Thai Fact
Elephants in captivity individually chose their human friend. These friends/caretakers are called a Mahouts (pronounced Mah-Hoots).

Chapter 3: Phuket

15 years ago, Phuket was gorgeous. Today, Phuket is one big tourist trap full of crowded beaches and disappointment.

Listen, if you know me or are familiar with my books at all…you know that I'm not a huge fan of Phuket. It's crowded, overpriced, and doesn't represent the tropical paradise you've been dreaming of.

BUT from an island & beaches perspective, there are some upsides.
✓ Phuket's International Airport is an easy hub to fly into.
✓ Flights to the rest of the country are convenient.
✓ The Elephant Sanctuaries are the only ethical ones in the south.
✓ And there's a Hooters. I love fried pickles.

So, no need to spend a week here. Spend a couple days and then escape to a nearby island where you can experience the real Thailand.

While you're here, however, I'll navigate you around the tourist landmines and direct you to the most enjoyable spots on the island while getting the most bang for your buck.

I said I'd never write a Phuket chapter…but here I am. I'm going to give you guys the basics from hotels and transportation to the best beaches – but just enough to spend a day or two. After that, run for your lives.

Getting from the Airport into Town

From Krabi International Airport

Phuket Airport is small for an international airport. It's a quick immigration and baggage claim process before you are out the doors and into Thailand.

The airport is 25 miles from Patong and takes anywhere from 45 minutes to an hour to reach your hotel – depending on how you travel.

Option 1: Fixed Rate Taxi

There are no metered taxis at Phuket Airport- only fixed rate. Prices can vary but the below prices are a good reference.

Where: You will find taxi booths inside the Arrivals Hall
How Much: (give or take 100 baht)
- ❖ Phuket Town – 400 baht
- ❖ Patong – 550 baht
- ❖ Karon – 600 baht
- ❖ Kata – 600 baht

Where: Go out of the arrival doors (you'll still be inside the airport) and you'll see a bright yellow sign with "Taxi Minibus Service" to your left and a less-obnoxiously colored but equally same-service kiosk to your right. There will also be two smaller kiosks outside of the arrival hall – again, offering the same service for the same price.

These stands also offer the Mini Bus option below.

Option 2: Mini Bus

How Much:
- ❖ Phuket Town – 150 baht
- ❖ Patong - 180 baht
- ❖ Karon – 200 baht
- ❖ Kata – 200 baht

When: The Shuttle Bus leaves when they're collected a decent number of passengers. Expect to wait up to 20 minutes for the van to fill up and leave.

Pro Tip

If the minibus stops at a tourist shop and asks you to get out…they're about to try and sell you some tours. You don't have to get out. Just stay put. Once they know that *you know*…they leave you alone. Nothing is forced or scary, just annoying.

Option 3: Pre-Booked Private Transfers

I totally recommend this option

For 100-200 baht extra, you can book a private transfer ahead of time and have a car or minivan waiting to take you to your hotel. The driver will be waiting outside arrivals holding a little sign with your name on it. You can either arrange this with your hotel or go online and find a transfer company like PhuketShuttle.com and PhuketTransfers.com. The price depends on the car you need, but you can expect prices to be similar to these…

How Much:
- ❖ Phuket Town – 700 baht
- ❖ Patong – 680 baht
- ❖ Karon – 750 baht
- ❖ Kata – 800 baht
- ❖ Chalong Pier- 830

Going straight to Krabi from Phuket Airport?

You can either…

1. Arrange a Taxi from Phuket Airport to Krabi
How Long: 2 hours
How Much: $80-$100 USD
The driver picks you up at the airport and drops you directly at your hotel – any time of day or night.

2. Transfer to the pier and take a ferry
How Long: 5 hours total with the ferry, transfer and wait time
How Much: $30 USD / 1000 baht – depending on the company
Head to a taxi kiosk and get a ride to Rassada Pier.

3. Take a Public Bus
How Long: 4.5 hours
How Much: $4.50 USD / 150 baht
Hire a taxi to take you to Phuket Bus Station where you can catch the Krabi Public Bus. The bus leaves every hour. Just know that when you arrive in Krabi, you'll be dropped off at the Krabi Town Bus Station – 7.5 miles away from the beach.

The public bus is fine if you've packed light and have a Thai Sim Card or International Data. You'll need to do some navigating from the Krabi Bus Station to your hotel. OR just download "Krabi Google Maps Offline" and you can show your hotel location to a tuk tuk driver when you arrive.

Area Breakdown

Phuket is the biggest island in Thailand, 40 miles from north to south, and 21 miles from east to west. There are 17 districts – but knowing about each district will do absolutely nothing for planning your trip.

Instead, we're going to break the island up into 4 tourist sections:

The Northwest

Home to Phuket's international airport, Northwest Phuket is perhaps the least chaotic with more upscale resorts and Sririnat National Park. You'll find some of the best beaches up here; beaches that haven't *yet* been spoiled by massive hordes of tourists. Some of the most notable beaches in the north include Bang Thao, Banana Beach, Laem Sing, Mai Khao, Bang Thao, Nai Thon and Nai Yang, and Surin.

Patong and the Southwest

Most tourists that visit Phuket stay in this area. Patong is known as the party capitol of Asia – with tons of western restaurants, shopping everywhere and nightlife that never quits. However, what most people don't know is that you can easily escape this Patong party area and stay at a nearby beach such as Kamala, Karon, Kata, Kata Noi.

Phuket Town

I'm not really sure why anyone stays here to be honest, and so I won't be writing much about it. Phuket Town is just a…town. A typical Thai town with a couple night markets, some malls and cafes. If you're catching a morning ferry, I suppose you could stay in Phuket Town which is home to Rassada Pier – or you can just take a taxi from a more peaceful spot.

Rawai

Rawai encompasses the southeast chunk of Phuket that starts inland and then jets off onto a rocky peninsula called Promthep Cape. Life is a bit quieter down here with some scenic beaches and viewpoints – but not much in terms of socializing or partying.

Fun Thai Fact
There are over 1,445 islands in Thailand.

Accommodation in Phuket

Patong

Bodega Resort $

Head out into the chaos of Phuket and then retreat back to bikini- mode at Bodega's pool where you lounge on a massive pink floating flamingo and sip mojitos. When you come to Bodega, you don't have to worry about making friends – they are built in. The atmosphere is extremely inclusive with Bodega Staff that are essentially sexy camp counselors who are always up to weird antics and rope you into joining. With the most heavenly dorm beds you'll find in Thailand PLUS Bodega's on-site Mexican restaurant, The Cantina – it's is a great place to start or end your trip.

Bodega Tip: Want to be social but have some privacy at the same time? Bodega's private rooms have bathtubs and English TV channels! Be rowdy when you please and then get in some "me" time.

Style: Dorms and Privates
Starts at: $12 USD / 440 THB
Where: 3rd Street – a 5-minute walk to the night markets

Address: 5/5 Sawatdirak Rd, Tambon Patong

Lub D Hostel $

Jaw dropper. There's no other hostel on this planet that has a Muay Thai gym in the lobby and an independent tattoo shop behind reception. This place is massive and packed with every Thai activity that you need to check off your bucket list. Every day, they offer free events like Muay Thai Lessons, cooking classes, Thai language classes, beach excursions…it's seriously incredible. They have a pool, a restaurant and a coworking space all tucked inside this spacious hostel AND it's only a 3-minute walk to the beach.

Style: Dorms and Privates
Starts at: $18 USD / 600 THB
Where: Patong Beach
Address: 5/5 Sawatdirak Rd, Tambon Patong

Pro Tip

If you want to stay in a hostel in Phuket, I suggest splitting half the time between Lub D and Bodega – 2 totally different experiences.

The Charm Resort Phuket $$$

The rooftop infinity pool overlooking the ocean and the sky bar that lights up at night are the main selling points for this lux hotel. The rooms are everything you could want and more. If you plan to hang at your hotel with a few explorations to the beach – this is all you need. Head up: if night markets were on your to-do list, plan on spending $10-$20 round trip getting there – or walking 20 minutes each way. The Charm Resort is located on the north end of Patong Beach.
Starts at: $100 USD / 9500 THB
Where: 5 Minute-Walk from Patong Beach
Address: 212 Thaweewong Road, Kathu

Patong Terrace Boutique Hotel $$

When you want to be alone but not invisible - staying in a small boutique hotel is the way to go. No face goes unnoticed here, but you still have plenty of privacy. The manager, Peter, works with each guest to help you customize the perfect tour of Phuket. See the Big Buddha, go to the best beaches, and even throw a Muay Thai Match in the mix. He'll help you set it all up over breakfast! Afterwards, come home and collapse. The rooms are simple and best for budget travelers - but there are English channels on TV and rain showers with proper water pressure to wash your hair! **Ps.** Try the homemade apple pie with a fresh coffee. To die for.

Style: Privates
Starts at: $30 USD / 1000 THB
Where: 5 Minute-Walk from Patong Beach
Address: 209/12-13 Rat-U-Thit Rd., Patong

Burasari Phuket $$$

Pool or beach? You decide. Burasari Phuket has one of the biggest hotel pools in the city *and* is just a 5-minute walk to the sands of Patong Beach. The hotel is new and the attention to detail is totally Instagram-worthy. From the generous breakfast spread to the enthusiasm of the English-speaking staff, it's hard to find a fault in this ultra-comfortable home away from home.

Starts at: $120 USD / 4000 THB

Where: 5 Minute-Walk from Patong Beach
Address: 18/110 Ruamjai Road, Tambon Patong

Glam Habitat Hotel $$$

The name says it all, queen. Glam Habitat Hotel feels like the set of Sex and The City – with concrete architecture, grassy rooftop gardens, high-tech rooms, a brand-new gym and staff that go the extra mile to make sure you're comfortable. Rooms are stocked with all the papering amenities you need: lush robes, cozy slippers, a lighting makeup mirror…and if you shell out an extra penny, you can slip into the pool from your balcony. The bar here is a must-visit, with handcrafted cocktails (a hard find in this city).

Starts at: $160 USD / 5300 THB
Where: 5 Minute walk to Kamala Beach
Address: 112/39 M.3 Kamala Rd., Kamala, Kathu District

Amari Phuket $$$$

Stay in the Patong area without feeling like you're in Patong. Amari Hotel is uniquely built within the cliffside of Patong, surrounded by jungle with unobstructed views of the ocean. Whether you're in your luxury room or the glittering infinity pool, all you see is beauty. You're just a 15-minute walk to Patong Beach and a 20-minute walk to the night markets and nightlife – or take the daily shuttle into town. Wanna stay in? The clubhouse Happy Hour from 5:30-6:30 offers unlimited drinks and finger food - free of charge. Plus, this is a great way to meet some people! Treat yo'self.

Starts at: $180 USD / 6000 THB
Where: 5-minute walk to Patong Beach
Address: 2 Meun-Ngern Road, Kathu

Karon & Kata Beach

Doolay Beachfront Hostel $

Just a few steps to Karon Beach and a quick 5-minute walk to Kata Beach – Doolay Hostel is the perfect balance between scenic and social. When you're not on the beach, have a lazy day in the common area where there are two big couches and a flat screen. Around sunset, travelers usually have a few beers with the balcony and then head out together in search of a little nightlife. Making friends here is easy.

Starts at: $14 USD / 460 THB

Where: 1-minute walk to Karon Beach
Address: 164 Karon Road Tambon Karon

Allstar Guesthouse $

The perfect place to throw your bags down and go exploring. Allstar Guesthouse is simple, spacious, and clean with friendly hosts who are hands-on in helping you plan your day. They direct you towards the beach, the markets, and give you all the food recommendations. Plus, they'll arrange hotel shuttles, ferry transfers, and around-town taxis – taking so much stress off of you and your plans!

Starts at: $27 USD / 2800 THB
Where: 5-minute walk to Karon Beach
Address: 514/13 Patak Road, 83100 Karon Beach

Sugar Ohana Poshtel $$

Traveling with your laptop and want to get some work done? Or simply want to hang out with some coffee café vibes? This clean and cozy poshtel near Kata Noi beach is a sophisticated oasis with complimentary breakfast, beach bag, and beach towel. The staff are really helpful and will show you where you can catch the local bus into Phuket Town for just 40 baht. Need to arrange an airport or ferry transfer? They do that, too, and for some of the cheapest prices around.

Starts at: $55 USD / 1900 THB
Where: 15-minute walk to both Karon & Kata Beach
Address: 88/5 Kata Road, Karon, Phuket, 83100

The Village Resort & Spa $$$

Who doesn't love a swim-up pool bar? Reasonable beer and cocktail prices plus a 4:00-6:00 pm happy hour is enough to keep you in your swimsuit all day long. Each tropical villa has its own little balcony surrounded by enough greenery to make you feel like you aren't in the city any more. You are 10 minutes to Karon Beach and 10 minutes to Kata Beach – The Village Resort really the best of all worlds when you've got a couple days to spend in Phuket.

Starts at: $100 USD / 3250 THB
Where: 10-minute walk to Karon & Kata Beach
Address: 566/1 Patak Road, Karon Beach

Centara Grand Beach Resort Phuket $$$

Where beachfront actually means beachfront, Centara Grand offers the opportunity to slip out of the pool and step straight onto Karon Beach – but you might not want to leave any of the THREE pools with waterslides, waterfalls, a lazy river and shallow tanning surfaces. There's a gym, a spa, and every room comes with a bathtub. Not to mention, waking up to views of the ocean is definitely #VacationGoals. The only down-side…children may invade your space on occasion. This hotel is family-friendly so just perfect your 'floating away gracefully' skills.

Starts at: $230 USD / 7500 THB
Where: Beachfront on Karon Beach
Address: 683 Patak Road, Muang, 83100 Karon Beach

Rawai

Sea Safari Glamping $$

Glamping on the beach, anyone? Wake up to views of the water in your tent equipped with an electric fan, cozy bed and private bathroom. While the beach isn't great for swimming, the pool is perfect. There's Sea Safari Restaurant next door and a massage place to give you a rub down on the beach. You can rent kayaks for 100 baht a day or play board games with fellow travelers. Outside of that, all there's left to do is nothing. Just unwind and take it easy.

Starts at: $52 USD / 1750 THB
Where: Beachfront on Karon Beach
Address: Moo 5, Wiset Road, Sunrise Beach 1, Phuket, 83150 Rawai Beach

The Northwest

Coriacea Boutique Resort $$

Flying into Phuket for one day and then heading for Krabi? This hotel is my pick for a quick stop over if you plan on taking road transport to Krabi. Coriacea Boutique Resort is a cute little resort situated right across from Mai Khao Beach – one of the best kept beaches in Phuket – and is located at the top of Phuket Island, making an easy public bus ride or private taxi journey to Krabi the next day. Breakfast is plenty, bikes are free, and the staff go above and beyond with true Thai hospitality.

Starts at: $60 USD / 200 THB
Where: Mai Khao Beach
Address: 89/2 Soi Mai Khao 6, Moo 4, T.Maikhao

Naiyang Park Resort $$

Traditional Thailand village vibes with modern amenities next to the most beautiful public beach in Phuket – if you weren't sure what to do with your extra days in Phuket, here is the answer, babe! You'll be tucked into a spacious Thai cottage with wooden floors and a cozy bed. Throw your bags down and kick your feet up on your balcony surrounded by Thai jungle with a wooden walkway that lights up at night, leading you towards the massive pool and quaint restaurant. The beach is a just quick 3-minute walk from the resort and the airport is a 5-minute drive. You're all set.

Starts at: $100 USD / 3500 THB
Where: Nai Yang Beach
Address: 34/5 Tambon Sakoo, Thalang

Andaman White Beach Resort $$$

Situated on a private beach in the middle on the Sririnat National Park, here is where you come to get your zen on. This beach is one of the cleanest, most private and pristine beaches you find in Phuket with soft white sand and crystal-clear water. Best of all…no crowds! Each room gives you a stunning view of the water, as does the pool and restaurant on site. Great pizza, fabulous happy hour, and free afternoon fruit. Just a 10-minute walk into town and 15-mintues from Phuket Airport, this is the perfect place to start or end your Thailand trip.

Starts at: $259 USD / 8560 THB
Where: Between Banana Beach and Nai Thon Beach
Address: 28/4 Moo 4, Tambon Sakoo, Thalang District

Anantara Layan Phuket Resort $$$

Truly, the best resort in Phuket is Anantara Layan located on a private white sand beach at the entrance of Sririnat National Park. This resort is the epitome of luxury, fit for a queen on vacation! Every amenity is top notch and the service is impeccable. Never underestimate attention to detail; the lavender spray for your pillow at night, the beach bags for your trip to the beach, kayaks for exploring and high-quality healthy breakfasts with a mimosa station leaves you feeling pampered and refreshed. This is what you came to Thailand for.

Starts at: $350 USD / 11500 THB
Where: Sririnat National Park
Address: 168 Moo 6, Layan Beach Soi 4, Cherngtala

Smaller Islands Nearby

The Naka Island $$$

A tiny island off the coast of Phuket in Phra Nang Bay, Naka Island IS the postcard destination you've been looking for…the only question is, can you afford it?

This small island has just one resort – and it is fancy! Ranging from $350 - $700 USD per night, The Naka Island submerges you in total luxury with tropical villas and celebrity service. With very few people visiting the island, the island has managed to maintain its colorful corals, pristine beaches, and gorgeous jungle – all for you.

Once you get sick of the 5-star infinity pool resort, don't worry – there's Naka Spa, COMO Beach Club, Z Bar and a couple local shacks to take advantage of. You can also go on snorkeling trips or kayaking adventures.

To get there, you'll head to Ao Po Grand Marina on the Northeast Peninsula of Phuket. The Naka Yai will have arranged a boat for you ahead of time which will be waiting to pick you up.

Starts at: $350 USD / 11500THB
Where: Naka Yai

Where to Eat in Phuket

Phuket is a night market island! The best meals you will have will be at a night market – and you can find the full list in the 'Markets & Shopping' section below.

But if you want to grab a few quick bites, here are the *few* places I recommend...

Cantina
Menu items like "Big Ass Breakfast" and a burger called "Bacon Bacon

Bacon" might give you an idea what La Cantina is all about. When you're so hungry that you're hangry – this is where you come to sort your life out. Decisions are easy, and portions are huge. Plus, there are vegetarian options and authentic Thai food for your picky friends...

Open: 7:00am-9:00pm
Where: Attached to Bodega Resort
Address: 1, 1 Sirirat Rd, Tambon Patong

Surf House Patong Beach & Kata Beach
Surf House is both a fabulous place to grab a juicy western burger or a full on American breakfast AND a place to learn how to surf for around 1000

baht per hour. Surf House has one of those mechanical wave creators that creates a steady wave to surf. If surfing isn't your thing, that's okay – it's just as fun to watch people taking turns surfing and faceplanting.

Open: 9:30am- Midnight
Where: Patong Beach
Address: 151 Thawewong Rd, Tambon Patong
&
Open: 9:30am- Midnight
Where: Kata Beach
Address: 4 Pakbang Road Kata Beach Karon

DooDee

For your first time trying true Asian/Thai food in Thailand, I recommend DooDee for a quick lunch. DooDee 1 serves Thai Food and DooDee 2 serves Cantonese/ Vietnamese soups. They are directly next to each other and are both a must-visit for clean and tasty dishes. Portions are hefty, and prices are cheap. The place is always packed – which is always a good sign!

Open: 6:00 am-3:00am
Where: Patong – 3rd street
Address: 74/1 Phangmuang Sai Kor

Told you I was keepin' this chapter short…

Highlights & Lowlights in Phuket

Phuket Highlights

The Big Buddha

Made mostly of Burmese White Jade Marble, this gorgeous Buddha gracefully sits 45 meters tall at the top of a mountain overlooking Kata Beach. Drive up to pay your respects and then take in the stunning 360-degree views of Phuket. Just remember to bring something to cover your shoulders and knees. I recommend adding this Big Buddha visit into a day of beach hopping....

Beach Hopping

Thought I was going to leave you hanging on that one?

Make the most of your time in Phuket and hire a driver to take you to the beaches of your choosing. Usually, the way it works is like this: you hire a driver for 3/4/5 hours and give him 4-5 destinations you'd like to go. He drops you off and patiently waits for you to do your thang. You don't have to fit all these spots in. If you're having a great time at one beach, stay there!

The most logical way to do this is to cut the island in half, and either do the northern beaches or the southern beaches. You can approach any tourist kiosk and tell them you want a private beach tour. BUT if you are in the Patong area, head over to Patong Terrace Boutique Hotel in the morning and tell them I sent you. You can get a 4-hour tour for 900 baht with drivers who have great track record.

Promthep Cape

The rocky peninsula that jets out of Phuket's Southeast corner is called Promthep Cape. The road leading here is well paved. This is where the majority of tourists stop to take photos or visit the nearby golden elephant lighthouse. Not you, though! Keep going! Throw on a pair of sneakers and take a leisurely hike down the little staircase heading into nature and follow the red dirt path (you'll see it, I promise). This path will lead you to the very tip of the cape. The first section of the path is surrounded by tall jungle and the other half -stunning views of the water and rocky shores below. Once you reach the tip of the cape, you've got a gorgeous 180-degree view of pure island beauty.

Pro Tip

Go in the morning to beat the crowds (they get massive here) or get down to the tip of the cape for sunset!

Muay Thai Boxing Camps

All year round, people come from every corner of the planet to train Muay Thai in Phuket. Girls, guys, celebrities (I've got stories) – every human of every fitness level can come and train. Your goal can be to get in shape or to eventually participate in a real boxing match in a real stadium. Come for a single drop in class for around $10 USD or stay for a few weeks or months – Muay Thai Camps offer accommodation in their longer-term training packages.

Some of the more popular camps to check out:

- Tiger Muay Thai
- Sinbi Muay Thai
- Kinkga Supa Muay Thai

Phuket Elephant Sanctuary & Elephant Park

Phuket Elephant Sanctuary – home to 7 rescued elephants.

When it comes to picking an ethical elephant sanctuary, you've got to be fastidious with your research. There are many "elephant sanctuaries" that hide under the word "sanctuary" while still offering elephant rides and practicing animal abuse at their camp – this happens all around Thailand.

Recently, however, **two** true elephant sanctuaries have opened up in Phuket. They each operate a bit differently. Think of **Phuket Elephant Sanctuary as a private school** with wonderful education for us humans and stimulating playtime facilities for the elephants. Think of **Phuket Elephant Park as a Montessori School** where the elephants are in charge and make their own schedules.

Both sanctuaries are essentially **retirement homes for elephants** that have spent their whole lives doing back-breaking work like tourists rides and logging down here in the south.

At Phuket Elephant Sanctuary, your day will start with a quick educational class on elephant behavior and the plight of Asian elephants in the region. Then you'll change into traditional Karen (Burmese Hill Tribe) clothing and spend the day roaming with and feeding the elephants.

How Much: 2,500 baht for a Half Day
Includes: Lunch & Hotel Pick-up

Also Offered: Full days, overnight stays, and volunteering opportunities.

At Phuket Elephant Park is also a retirement home for elephants, where the elephants roam totally chain-free, wandering their natural habitat freely. At Phuket Elephant Park, plan to spend the day just hanging out with the elephants, walking with the herd, watching them in explore and feeding them when they decide they're hungry.

◆ **How Much:** 3,000 baht for a half day
Includes: Pick up from your Hotel

Good to Know
There are two schools of thought on mud-baths: while the elephants seem to enjoy the mud baths and river, some camps prefer not to keep their elephants on a schedule. Neither of these parks offer elephant bathing.

Not So fun Thai Fact
At the start of the 20th century Thailand had over 100,000 Asian elephants. Today, it's estimated that there are just around 4,000 elephants left, of which just 1,500 live in the wild.
Want to help those numbers increase? Say no to elephant riding establishments. Support elephant sanctuaries.

Soi Dog Foundation
In Thailand, animal rights aren't recognized by locals. This means few dogs are properly cared for, vaccinated, and most definitely, are not neutered. In turn, this has led to Thailand's massive "Soi Dog" or "Street Dog" population. The Soi Dog foundation is a street dog and cat rescue mission, rehabilitation facility and educational awareness center that offers volunteering opportunities to anyone who has a soft spot for these creatures.

You can volunteer by socializing with dogs or cats, to ready them to be fostered or adopted. You can also be a "Flight Volunteer" which means chaperoning a dog or cat back home, on their way to be adopted in the west. While the foundation prefers that volunteers stay for a few weeks at a time, you can pay the foundation a visit (no booking ahead needed) at the times found on their website.

Contact: SoiDog.org
Where: Mi Khao Beach
Address: 167/9 Moo 4, Soi Mai Khao 10, Tambon Mai Khao

Phuket Low Lights

The Phi Phi Island Tour

Every tour office really pushes the Phi Phi Island Tour. What they don't tell you is that you're on a boat for 8 hours. Yep. 4 hours each way inside of a bumpy speed boat. Once you get to Phi Phi, the tour simply lets you lose for a few hours and then you climb back aboard for another 4 hours.

A Better Idea: Go to Phi Phi on your own. Stay 1 or 2 nights, and then come back to Phuket.

Markets & Shopping

Street Shopping

In terms of clothing, everywhere you walk in Patong – you'll find a clothing shop selling bathing suits, dresses, tank tops with cheeky sayings and workout gear that are surprisingly great quality knockoffs of Nike, Under Armour and Adidas. You can also find jewelry, speakers, headphones….knives. Whatever you want.

Phuket Weekend Market / Naka Market

The biggest market in Phuket and one of the biggest markets in all of Thailand – there is so much to buy and taste that it's almost overwhelming! Every food under the sun, plus leather bags, vintage clothes, tradition Thai oils…you name it, they've got it.

Where: Phuket Town near Central Festival
When: Saturday & Sunday 4:00 pm – 9:00 pm

Karon Temple Market

The only market that's worth planning your day around is Karon Market. You'll find the same genre of clothing and food here that you would in other markets (beachwear and funny tank tops) but with more of a variety. Even better news, Karon Market has been dubbed "street food safe" – meaning that the street food here is some of the freshest and so, your odds of getting a sour stomach at few! There's never a guarantee, but this is the closest thing to it.

Where: Karon Beach - 500 meters from the Karon Circle
When: Tuesday and Friday 4:00 pm-10:00 pm

Malin Plaza Patong

Perhaps the best night market in terms of freshness and options, Malin Plaza Patong is a great place to try some local cuisine. You'll find stall after stall of freshly caught fish – all of which are labeled with a clear price (usually 200 baht per), along with crab, oysters and langoustines. Pick what you'd like, and the chefs will grill them up for you on the spot. You'll also find plenty of fruit, fried rice stands, and even a crocodile stand. There are picnic style tables where you can sit down and order a cold beer to go with your piping hot Thai food.

Where: South end of Patong Beach – Near Duangjitt Resort

When: Daily 2:00pm – 12:00am

Phuket Sunday Street Market

If you're okay with crowds, Phuket Sunday Street Market or "Phuket Walking Street" OR "Lard Yai" may suit you. It's more of a chaotic experience to witness rather than a leisurely market excursion – but the location is convenient if you're staying in Phuket town, so why not pop through for a bite to eat?

Where: Phuket Town - Thalang Road
When: Sunday 5:00pm-9pm

Jungceylon Mall

Located on 2nd street in Patong, Jungceylon Mall transports you back home the moment you step inside. They're got every food chain from back home: Starbucks, Burger King, Baskin Robbins, and more. There is also plenty of shopping to be done – including a NYX Makeup store!

Phuket Nightlife

Bodega Pub Crawl

It's a city tour…with booze. You'll start out at Bodega Hostel where everyone is given a Bodega Pub Crawl tank top. Throw it on and you're now all in this together. After a couple pre-party drinking games, a free bucket and shots at the hostel, the whole crew moves out to take over the city. You'll visit three of the best bars in Phuket with free shots at each bar. Weird antics, photo shoots, and cute boys from all over the world, single ladies…this one's for you. **Ps.** You **don't** have to stay at Bodega in order to join the Pub Crawl! Just show up to Bodega Hostel or Bodega Resort around 9pm to sign up.

How Much: $13 USD / 450 baht
Where: Bodega Hostel Phuket
When: Monday, Wednesday, Friday at 10pm

Bangla Road

Stretching from the beach, all the way back near Jungceylon Mall, it's hard to miss Bangla Road on any given night – just follow the music. This street isn't dangerous – it's just a little icky if you're sober. There's clear prostitution and lots of fat old guys with younger Thai girls…but there's also Russian families with their children out for a bite to eat. Bangla Road is Phuket in a nutshell.

The most popular bars are Rock City, Red Hot, Sunset Bar, Shipwreck, and U2 Bar. For dancing and nightclubs, Illusion and White Room offer all night dance vibes that leave you sweaty and broke.

How to Get Around Phuket

Motorbikes
I do not recommend renting a motorbike in Phuket. The #1 way that tourists die in Thailand, specifically, is on a motorbike in Phuket. The roads are extremely steep, and the traffic can be intense. I don't even recommend getting on the back of a local's motorbike.

Songthaew
When you see one of these red trucks driving down the road, just wave your arm, run up to their driver-side window to tell them your destination and hop in the back. The rates range from 40-100 baht depending on where you're going. However, you can always try to haggle…especially if you've been practicing your numbers in Thai.

Tuk Tuk
Tuk Tuks are everywhere, yes. But is haggling a thing? Not really. It's standard to pay 100 or 200 baht to go anywhere. It doesn't matter if its 10-mintues down the road or two. Try haggling if you'd like – but usually the driver sets the price and doesn't budge.

Taxi
Fixed rate taxis are everywhere – schlepping their ridiculously high prices. Stick to what you're willing to pay and don't be afraid to walk away. These men will eventually give in. You can download Grab Taxi and check the estimated prices – and use that to give you an idea of what you should pay. You can try to order a Grab Taxi, but whether or not one will show up depends on the climate of the Taxi Mafia during the time of your visit. #TaxiPolitics

Chapter 4: Krabi

Heaven on earth! Krabi looks like every Thailand Postcard that you've ever seen with crystal blue water, white sand beaches, and coconut cocktails.

You can experience the best of Thailand when you visit Krabi with the opportunity to live it up in fancy resorts or party barefoot with local expats. Most attractive about Krabi, however, are the skyscraper islands that tower over warm blue water and powdery-soft sand beaches.

@aforeigner.abroad

Area Breakdown

Krabi Town: A main hub for transportation and commerce, Krabi Town offers the local side of the region. You'll get more street food for cheaper prices, experience the kindness of locals, and have your pick of affordable guest houses. To get to the beach from here, you'll need to take some form of transportation – Songtheaw are a good option.

Ao Nang Beach: The main tourist area, Ao Nang Beach is highlighted by one very long road in an 'L-Shape' that stretches up the hill and then curves along the beach. The entirety of this massive road is lined with hostels, bars, restaurants, tourist desks and of course, tons of shopping where you can buy swim suits, sun glasses, snorkel gear and more.

Railay: There is a peninsula jetting off from Ao Nang Beach that is absolutely stunning and not to be missed! You'll find four beaches here.
- **Railay Beach-**This is the main beach where most boats dock
- **Phra Nang Cave Beach** – This beach is secluded and insanely beautiful. You can easily walk there through a path on the island that is lined with monkeys!
- **Tonsai Beach-** When the tide is low, you can climb through the rocks where you'll find a large resort on the sand, and a hippie paradise back into the jungle.
- **Railay Easy** – Not really a beach, more of a cove – Railay East is where the party happens at night, home to some stunning hotels, and the location of Railay Pier.

And so easy to get to. You can fly directly into Krabi from Bangkok via a 1-hour flight.

Getting into Krabi Town

Note: Going to Railay Beach or Tonsai Beach? Get to Ao Nang first. There are long tail boats waiting morning to night - willing to take you to the Railay Peninsula for 100 baht per person.

If you're getting in late, stay in Ao Nang Beach – water taxis to Railay Beach are scarce after 8pm.

From Krabi International Airport

Krabi Airport is tiny. This is great for you! It means less time spent inside the airport and zero chance of getting lost.

The airport is 9 miles from the city center, 24 miles from Ao Nang and 14 miles from Had Yao- and there are a couple different ways to reach your destinations.

Expect to take about 45mins – 1 hour to get from the airport to your destination. It sounds like a long ride…but the drive is beautiful!

Option 1: Fixed Rate Taxi

There are no metered taxis at Krabi Airport- only fixed rate. Prices can vary but the below prices are a good reference.

Where: You will find taxi booths inside the Arrivals Hall
How Much: (give or take 100 baht)
- ❖ Krabi Town – 400 baht
- ❖ Ao Nang – 500 baht
- ❖ Had Yao – 800 baht
- ❖ Railay Pier (boat included) – 700 baht

Option 2: Airport Shuttle Bus
Where: You can buy tickets at the same place as the taxi booth inside the Arrivals Hall. Go out of the arrival doors (you'll still be inside the airport) and make a left. You'll see a sign for "Shuttle Bus".

How Much:
- ❖ Krabi Town- 100 baht
- ❖ Ao Nang – 150 baht

116

When: The Shuttle Bus leaves 8-10 times between 8am-8pm (so almost once per hour). Once you get your ticket, you'll go outside of the airport and see a big white bus. Most travelers take this bus, so the staff will wrangle you on board.

Option 3: Pre-Booked Private Transfers

Book ahead of time with YourKrabi.com and have a car or minivan waiting to take you to your hotel.

Hotels in Krabi Town: minivan - 800 Baht
Hotels in the Ao Nang area: minivan - 800 Baht
Hotels in Koh Lanta: minivan - 2500 – 2800 Baht, depending on where on the island you are staying.

Option 4: Songthaews to Krabi Town

Where: Walk about 400 meters to the main road and flag down a public Songthaew.

How Much:
❖ Krabi Town- 30-50 baht
When: 6am-11pm (roughly)

Accommodation in Krabi Province

Krabi Province is quite big and includes Krabi Town, Ao Nang Beach, Railay Beach, and Tonsai. Got all that? Let's break it down…

Krabi Town Accommodation

Closer to the airport than the beach, Krabi Town offers a taste of Thai culture with riverside hotels, night markets, temples, and motorbike adventures.

Staying in Krabi Town is a fun way to spend your last (or first) day or two.

Slumber Party Krabi Town $

Wanna get weird? Here's where you come to do that. Slumber Party never sleeps. You'll meet tons of travelers from all over the world. Together you will go on Pub Crawls, play drinking games, go on beach excursions and boat tours… then bond over how bad your hangover is the morning after. This hostel is located at the very top of the road that leads down to the beach – you can't walk to the beach, but Slumber Party will take care of that with free beach transfers 4x per day. This is a good option for when their beach location is full – which happens often.

Style: Dorms
Starts at: $11 USD/ 370 baht
Address: 376/41 Ao Nang

Snoozz Hotel $

If you've got an early flight, it's always a good idea to stay in town the night before. Get some shut eye at Snoozz Hotel, a quiet place with all-girl dorm rooms. They offer airport transfers for a small charge, have helpful English-speaking staff and a yummy café in the lobby where you can grab a quick bite before you travel.

Style: Dorms and Privates
Starts at: $7.50 USD /250 baht
Address: 52 Maharaj 6 Road, Muang District

Just Fine Krabi $

Not a backpacker's hostel, but not a fancy hotel either – Just Fine Krabi is just fine for the solo traveling girl who wants clean sheets and a central location. Your stay, however, will be more than "just fine" in this nautical themed hotel that is as charming as it is comfortable. The rooms are spacious, there is a social living room to meet other travelers, and the prime location next to the night market and cafes means that you can explore on foot, all without over-spending!

Style: Privates
Starts at: $25 USD / 800 baht
Address: 2/8 Maharach 10, T.Paknam

Family Tree Hotel $$

After a week of living in your bathing suit, sometimes you just want to clean up, wash your hair, and watch the news. Family Tree Hotel is the perfect place to do that before you head to the airport the next day. You can even add a last dose of adventure into your itinerary as this hotel is within walking distance to the night market and a short ride away from Tiger Cave Temple. Alternatively, if you're using Krabi as a jumping off point to Koh Lanta or a nearby destination, this is a convenient spot for smooth transport.

Style: Privates
Starts at: $45 USD/ 1,500 baht
Address: 6 Maharaj Soi.2 Rd., Paknam, Mueang

Ao Nang Beach Accommodation

Ao Nang is the main beach on the mainland. Staying here means that you can shop to your heart's content and go on island hopping tours during the day, then hit up some restaurants and bars with live music at night.

Slumber Party by the Beach $

It'ssss party time. My #1 vote for budget backpackers, social girls, and single ladies in Krabi. Slumber Party is a super social hostel that offers adventures during the day and wild parties at night. Home to Thailand's Biggest Pub Crawl, it's impossible not to make friends here. When your hangover subsides, gather up those new friends for boat trips, kayaking adventures, and beach days with **free** breakfast, nightly cocktail shots, group BBQ & more.

Style: Dorms
Starts at: $13 USD/ 440 baht
Address: Ao Nang Beach

Stay Over Hostel $

Social, clean, and safe with a fabulous location. Stay Over Hostel ticks all the boxes and then some. If you want to be social but your liver needs a break, this is the place for you. The main attraction here is the rooftop with bright green turf with cozy pillows and resort-level views of the Krabi Cliffside. Hang out with fellow travelers for a chill night by the beach.

Style: Dorms
Starts at: $11 USD/ 370 baht
Address: Moo2, Aonang, Meung Krabi

M Boutique & Kitchen $

If you're on a budget and aren't really the "dorm room" type of girl - M Boutique & Kitchen offers a happy medium of privacy and price. Each room has its own little balcony looking down at the main road. Set off on foot about 10-15 minutes and you'll reach the beach. Come back to solitude in our simple, but pleasant room to regroup.

Style: Privates
Starts at: $20 USD/ 670 baht
Address: 43 Moo 2, Tumbol Aonang, Aumphur Meung

PhuPha Aonang Resort $$

Private bungalows and pool nestled amongst a lush tropical garden with friendly service, fabulous breakfast and free shuttles to the beach…this is exactly what you imagined when you pictured coming to Thailand. Tucked away on a side-street off the main drag, you're just a 10-minute walk from the action. Afterwards, you can come back to your little slice of paradise, listen to the crickets and watch the stars.

Style: Privates
Starts at: $38 USD/ 1,300 baht
Address: 395 Moo 2, Soi 13, Muang, Ao Nang

Phra Nang Inn by Vacation Village $$

You came here for the beach, right? Phra Nang Inn puts you 30-seconds from the sand without breaking the bank. Wake up and eat breakfast with views of palm trees and the ocean. When you're ready for an adventure, you're just steps from all the tourist kiosks offering every boat tour imaginable! After your day in the sun, come back and swim in the jungle-esque pool surrounded by lush greenery. Phra Nang Inn offers free cooking classes, handicraft workshops and dancing classes throughout the week – ask the front desk!

Heads Up: You can hear music from nearby bars til about midnight.

Pro Tip

For the best view, ask for room #2469 when you book

Style: Privates
Starts at: $55 USD/ 1,900 baht
Address: 119 Moo 2 Aonang, Muang, Krabi

Railay & Tonsai Beach Accommodation

Both Railay Beach and Tonsai Beach offer access to pristine beaches and islands, as well as rock climbing, kayaking, and a plethora of beach bars and restaurants.

To get to Tonsai, walk to the end of the main beach on Railay. When the tide is low during the day, you can climb through a rock tunnel. When the tide is high, you will have a long-tail boat zip you over.

Chill Out Bar & Bungalow $

No shoes, no bra, no problem. Chill Out Bar is an oasis away from the tourists and away from civilization where you never know what time it is…and it doesn't even matter. Forget your troubles as you take a kayak out for a spin, play a card game with strangers, or learn to rock climb cause YOLO. Minimalistic and simplistic − hit the reset button on life, babe.

Style: Dorms and Bungalows
Starts at: $7 / 200 baht
Address: Tonsai Beach

Blanco Hideout Hostel $

The first and only hostel in Railay, this place is kind of a big deal. Blanco Hideout is a brand-new hostel located on Railay East in the middle of all the action! Check in, throw your bags down, and go exploring on foot! You're 5-minutes from Phra Nang Cave Beach and right next to the best bars and restaurants. The hostel does a pub crawl three times a week (Monday, Wednesday and Friday) with a 2-hour open-bar at Blanco where you can mingle with other travelers. Plus, there's a big pool overlooking the water next to a little lounging deck with amazing views. What more do you need?

Style: Dorms and Privates
Starts at: $9 USD/ 220 baht
Location: Railay East

Tonsai Bay Resort $$

Tonsai Bay Resort is a new-ish resort that has access to the entire bay. There are private villas with balconies or cozy double rooms with all the amenities, just a stone's throw away from the beach. Staying here means enjoying nature as you're tucked into the jungle next to rock climbing and paddle boarding. At night, head inland away from the beach and into the jungle where you'll find a Peter-Pan style neverland of bars and restaurants with barefoot Thai guys and stoner expats who will all be happy to see you.

Style: Privates
Starts at: $28 USD/ 950 baht
Location: Tonsai Beach
How to Get There: Take a longtail boat directly to Tonsai Beach or walk through the rocks from Railay Beach.

Railay Princess Resort and Spa $$$

Fantastic bang for your buck over on Railay East, Princess Resort and Spa would easily cost 3x the price back home...but because it's Thailand, you get two massive pools, a spacious room with a private balcony and the best buffet breakfast in Railay starting at $40 per night. Located directly in the center of Railay East, 20-meters from the pier, you really can't go wrong staying here.

Style: Private
Starts at: $40 USD/ 1,200 baht
Address: Railay East

Railay Bay Resort $$$

Pamper yourself at Railay Bay Resort, located right on the beach! Start your morning with an amazing breakfast buffet on the water where you can watch the longtail boats putter in and out. Then, roll into the only pool on Railay that directly overlooks the ocean. You can get a private room or a secluded villa! The villas are totally private with lounge beds and a mini outdoor pool! Tan naked and fill the little pool up with shower gel for a skinny-dipping bubble bath.

Style: Privates
Starts at: $55 USD/ 1,900 baht
Address: Railay Beach

Avatar Railay $$

A 4-star resort with 2-star prices? Yes, please. Avatar is by far one of my favorite hotels in all of Thailand. The pool-access room is incredible! You get a private balcony with stairs leading into the pool and your own cabana bed. If you don't mind spending a little extra…you can get a villa with a private pool for around $120 – if you book early, that is. Step outside of the hotel and you're on the concrete path that takes you to Railay East nightlife *and* Phra Nang Cave Beach. Ugh, this place is seriously paradise.

Style: Privates
Starts at: $68 USD/ 2,300 baht
Location: East Railay Beach

Off the Beaten Path

Hug Rimtharn

Deep in the jungle, Hug Rimtharn feels more like glamping homestay than staying in a hotel. Your shipping crate bungalow is simple yet cozy with a private balcony where breakfast is brought to you every morning. Spend your days swimming in the natural creek or explore the jungle paths on foot or by ATV.

Style: Privates
Starts at: $70 USD/ 2,400 baht
Address: 172 Moo 6, T.Ao Nang, Krabi,
Location: From Ao Nang, a 25-minute drive northeast into the jungle

124

Where to Eat in Krabi

It's impossible to run out of food options in Krabi. You'll find tons of restaurants and bars up and down the main road leading down to Ao Nang Beach. Everything from authentic Thai food to amazing Indian and everything in-between. You'll find that a lot of restaurants and bars offer similar menus and cocktail prices- but here are a couple favorites to be on the lookout for….

Krabi Town

Chao Fah Night Market

Street food is calling! For 30-60 baht per plate, you can try every Thai dish under the sun alongside southern Muslim curries and Chinese wok dishes. Set in a 1400 sqm. parking lot, there are plenty of tables and chairs mixed in with stall after stall of fresh flavors to taste- there is something here for every palate.

Open: Daily from 5pm – Midnight
Location: Chao Fah Pier – Krabi Town
How to Get There: Jump in a 20 - 40-baht Songthaew

Baitoey Restaurant

Dinner with a view, this Thai restaurant is located across the street from the river where you can watch boats coming in and out underneath the palm trees. The food here is tasty and offers some of the best shellfish and crab in Krabi Town. Paired with the Papaya Salad – you've got a fabulous meal that is light and fresh. A bit more upscale with high-quality ingredients, don't expect street food prices. This place might break the bank at $8 per plate!

Open: Daily 10am-10pm
Location: 79 Khongkha road, Pak Nam, Krabi Town
How to Get There: Walk along the river, 5 minutes south of the night market

Gecko Cabane Restaurant

A casual Thai restaurant with cheap beer and classic dishes, Gecko Cabane is a great place to pop in for lunch or a laid-back dinner. The staff are fabulously hospitable and attentive – they certainly are not on Thai time here! You can expect friendly service along with Thai dishes that represent what Thai people typically eat on any given day in the South of Thailand.

Oh, and don't worry about your food being too spicy- they staff usually ask how spicy you'd like your dish on a 1-10 scale!

Open: Daily 11am-2pm & 5pm-11pm
Location: 1/36-37 Soi Ruamjit, Maharat Road, Krabi Town
How to Get There: Walk 10 minutes west of the night market, into town along Soi Ruamjit

Ao Nang Beach

Krabi Cafe 8.98
When you want a real fresh fruit smoothie or fruit juice that isn't half sugar – this is the place to go. The perfect spot before a day of tours or hikes, give yourself a kick of vitamins and fiber with a yummy Granola Bowl or pack in the protein with a proper eggs bene to go along with your "green + clean" juice.

Open: 7am-11pm
Address: 143/7-8, Ao Nang
How to Get There: 5-minutes up Ao Nang Road on the left

The Last Fisherman Bar
Eat dinner with your toes in the sand right next to the crashing waves! The Last Fisherman Bar is a casual restaurant underneath the trees that brings in freshly-caught seafood every day! Food is extremely well-priced considering the million-dollar ocean front view. Expect dishes to be anywhere from 200 baht – 800 baht made with fresh ingredients. Cocktails start at 180 baht - a small price to pay to watch the sun set in Thailand.

Open: 10am – 11pm
Location: Ao Nang Beachfront
How to Get There: Where the main road first hits Ao Nang beach, go left down the foot path until you cross under a sign that says The Last Fisherman Bar.

Crazy Gringos
Live music. Sports on the flat screen. Easy people watching. Crazy Gringos is the epitome of a "vacation bar" filled with expats and vacationers looking for a taste of home. Famous for their chicken wings and cocktails, you could easily spend all evening at this bar without breaking the bank. With lots of solo travelers passing through, Crazy Gringo's is an easy place to start up a conversation with a stranger!

Open: 3pm-1am
Address: 459/2 4203, Tambon Ao Nang
How to Get There: Located inside the small shopping alley at the curve of the L-shaped Ao Nang Road.

Lotus Court Restaurant

Oysters, lobster tails, salmon steak, Wagyu beef burgers and nitrogen ice cream made at the table- treat yo self, girl. Lotus Court is on the upscale-side of dining but for Thai prices. Order a bottle of wine, melt into the tunes of live piano music, and leave without having spent a fortune.

Open: Daily 11:30 - Midnight
Address: 396-396/1 Moo 2 | Centara Grand Beach Resort & Villas Krabi
How to Get There: Walk to Centara Grand Beach Resort

Railay Beach

One Stop Take Away Shop

Vegans and Vegetarians will fall in love with One Stop, aka Govinda's at the Beach. When you've had a long day and you're craving some clean eating, this place has Veggie Pizza, Hummus, Soy Meat Burritos, Cheese Empanadas...you name it. They've also got a huge menu of sweet treats like Oreo milkshakes and fruit smoothies to cool you down!

Open: Breakfast-Dinner
Location: East side of Railay Beach

Railay Family Restaurant

Eating grilled shrimp and fried rice out of a pineapple underneath a straw-thatched roof hut- it doesn't get more Thailand than this! Unsurprisingly, this place gets pretty popular around dinner time and will be the only restaurant with a line- but trust me, it's worth the wait.

Open: Daily Lunch til Close
Location: Between Railay Beach and East Railay Beach
Address: 354 Moo 2, Railay Beach

Railay Rapala Rock Wood Resort

Nachos. Pizza. Indian. Vegetarian. Vegan. When you're craving something other than Thai food on Railay Beach, this is the place to go. Nestled in the jungle, Rapala is a tranquil experience with yummy food where you can eat in peace with a good book and a cold beer or Iced Coffee.

Open: 10am-10pm
Location: Railay East

Coffee Station

Remember Owl from Winnie the Pooh? As owls do, he lived comfortably in a little wooden nook where his friends gathered for tea and a chat. The same goes for Coffee Station, except in place of tea, you have freshly ground Italian Coffee prepared right before your eyes. The coffee is strong, there is a book swap station, and the Thai staff who sleeps upstairs are some of the friendliest guys you'll meet.

Open: Morning til night
Location: Railay – next to Jamaica Bar

A couple more mentions...

Friendship Restaurant – Yummy breakfast and coffee
Local- The best deep friend Papaya Salad ever!
Last Bar – Great Thai food at local prices
Joy Beach Bar – Wood fire pizza

Things to Do around Krabi

The Krabi Province, including Ao Nang Beach, Railay Beach and Tonsai Beach, is quite compact. Any tour that you want to go on can be reached from any of the above locations. It doesn't matter where you stay- there is a long-tail boat waiting to take you to that destination. So, let's get into it…

Krabi Sunset Cruise

The best day you'll have in Krabi – this 5-island Sunset Cruise is your one-stop-shop to make new friends, snorkel with colorful fish, jump off the rooftop of a pirate ship, kayak or paddle board while the sunsets, and swim with glow-in-the-dark bioluminescent plankton in pitch black water. Or…don't do any of that. You can just chill on the rooftop tanning and drinking beers all day, too. Do as little or as much as you like. The tour includes pick up from Ao Nang or Railay AND a really yummy Thai dinner – suitable for both carnivores and vegetarians. This is a day you'll never forget.

Pro Tip

Not a confident swimmer? This is the best tour for you, girl. Michael, the cute Aussie Boat Captain, will drag your ass around using an inflatable tube that you can hold onto while you snorkel safely. He's a freakishly strong swimmer and there is also a crew of Thai guys who can help you in and out of the water.

When: Everyday 1pm-8pm
How Much: $80 USD / 2,600 Baht - Includes dinner, pickup, drop off, snorkel mask, flippers, kayaks, paddle boards, snacks, drinks, and dinner.

The 4-Islands Tour

Everywhere you look, you'll see the "4 Islands Tour" being offered. This tour takes you to the most desirable Krabi beaches and islands with unspoiled white sand islands where you can hop off and snorkel with spectacular sea life. The tours are led by Thai people, so there's not social element or informational angle – rather an opportunity to visit some gorgeous sights and take photos that will make all of your friends jealous.

Price: Starting at $30 USD /1000 baht

Mangrove & Cave Kayaking Tour

Explore a maze of mangroves, caves, and jungle via kayak! The laziest way to get into nature and sightsee, these guided tours feel super relaxed as you glide over still water channels with barely any current at all- just a little paddle navigation required. If ever there was a time to try kayaking for the first time- this is it, sister! The mangrove tours are half-day tours that include hotel transfers, snacks, and some swimming! If you're in the mood for a crazier adventure, there are full-day tours over slightly more challenging routes, as well. Check out Sea-Kayak Krabi or Krabi Cavemen for options!

Price: Tours from $30 USD / 1000 baht

Tiger Cave Temple

What does 1,237 steps up a Thai mountain get you? A 360 -degree panoramic view of Krabi Town along with a gorgeous Buddhist Temple that glistens in the sun! This Buddhist Temple dates back to 1975, founded by monk looking to meditate in peace....who instead found a cave full of tigers. This spot became sacred for the monks, who adorned the mountain with golden Buddhist statues and shrines. Plan to spend 1-hour hiking and 30 minutes wandering...and 5 minutes to buy some bananas and feed the monkeys.

Pro Tip

Dress respectfully by covering your shoulders and knees.

Open: All day
Location: About 2 miles from Krabi Town

To Get There: Rent a motorbike for ~$5 and follow the signs OR hire a tuk tuk driver to take you up.

Ya's Thai Cookery School Class

While you'll find tons of fabulous cooking schools in Krabi – this is the cooking class that I took and loved. You'll start your day at the market shopping for fresh ingredients to whip up 6 Thai dishes. The chef, Ya, speaks English and has a great sense of humor – so don't worry about being a master chef! Just have fun.

After every course is cooked, you'll sit down to eat! When the class is over, you'll go home with a recipe book and perhaps the best souvenir ever: the skills to cook Thai food at home. Going alone or with a friend? This is a great way to meet new people as each class is an intimate group of 4-6 people.

How Much: $60 USD / 2000 baht

The Emerald Pool

The Emerald Pool is this gorgeous blue, almost glowing, natural spring in the middle of the jungle! The water is cool and crystal clear with little streams and mini pools surrounding it– perfect for swimming! To reach the Emerald Pool, you'll stroll along a jungle path leading to smaller pools and the Blue Pool (closed May-October) scattered along the way. Stop and swim wherever you please.

The trick to enjoying the Emerald Pool is to go in the morning before the crowd! Drive yourself on a motorbike or hire a tuk tuk driver to take you so that you can avoid the organized van tour times that make the Emerald Pool feel like a public pool.

Entrance Fee: 30 baht
Open: 8:00am – 5:00pm

Krabi Hot Springs

Riiiiight nearby The Emerald Pool you can find these natural hot springs that reach up to 95-107 F (35-42 C). Just like the Emerald Pool, the hot springs are surrounded by forest with hot little pools and waterfalls where you can climb, swim, and soak. There is also a cool river at the base of the hot springs where you can take a refreshing dip at the end of your natural spa day!

To get there on your own, literally just plug "Krabi Hot Springs" into the GPS and you're all set. Once you reach the parking lot, you go through a gate and pay a small entrance fee. Follow the grey brick path where you'll pass the first hot spring – but this one looks more like a sparkly swimming pool with concrete bottom.

Go Rock Climbing on Tonsai Beach

The natural cliff edge on Tonsai is a rock climbers dream. In fact, rock climbers travel near and far just to scale the cliff with gorgeous views of the sand and water below. The rock climbing crew has up-to-date gear and offers lessons for beginners and advanced climbers.

Where: Tonsai Beach
Price: Starting at $24 USD / 800 baht with Basecamp Tonsai

Explore Phra Nang Cave Beach

Staying on Railay? You can access one of the most beautiful beaches you've ever seen via an easy, concrete-paved path. Located on the East Side of Railay, just follow the signs or ask a local to point you in the right direction. As you follow the path, you walk underneath some trees – look up! This is where the monkeys live. There is a penis-shrine temple (yes, you read that right) tucked in a cave and a steep hike/rock climb you can take (before the penises on the path, you'll see a long rope and red clay where people climb) that offers gorgeous views of the area. Bring snacks and a beach towel and hang out here all-day long.

Tab Kak Hang Nak Hill Nature Trail

Half scooter and half feet – this is a bucket list adventure for my girls who like to get sweaty. Tab Kak Hang Nak Hill Nature Trail is a true hike through the jungle on a moderately steep 2.5-mile path. The paths are clearly marked to keep you on track as you make your way over little bridges, under the tall jungle canopy and on top of pure earth, rocks, and roots at your feet. During the two to three-hour trek, you will come across stunning vistas and viewpoints of rolling mountains and crystal blue shores. Along the way, you'll find small natural waterfalls and swimming holes. Then at the very top, you'll reach the 360-degree viewpoint – called Hang Na Cape - that makes the whole butt-burning hike worth it.

To Get There: Drive an hour out of Krabi Town to Khao Ngon Nak National Park. At the entrance of the park, you'll find a little parking lot next to the trail entrance with a big map of the trail, the paths, and the viewpoints!

Pro Tip

Start in the morning and check the weather! You don't want to hike in a downpour

Nightlife in Krabi

Ao Nang

You'll find tons of laid back beach bars all along the Ao Nang strip, some clubs in Ao Nang Center Point, and if you want to do some epic people watching, visit Soi RCA where men go to find "intimate company" for the night. All areas are well-lit and busy with tourists from all walks of life. Also! There is a Krabi Pub Crawl that tours around every Monday, Wednesday and Friday with Slumber Party Hostel for 450 Baht.

Railay Beach

Let's be real, your cocktail hour will probably begin at 3pm. If that's the case, start at Bamboo Bar for a cold beer, then hop over to Jamaica Bar or Black Pearl for live music in the evening, and then walk over to Railay East for Why Not Bar and Last Bar at night where there is Muay Thai and Fire Dancing. You can also join the Railay Pub Crawl which is pretty small in terms of bars but throws you into an instant social situation for the night!

Tonsai Beach

The party scene here is definitely happening…but with more of a trippy 60's "hippie" influence, if you catch my drift. There is fire dancing, reggae music, dance parties- all of it. If you plan to partake in hippie activities, stay the night at a guest house on Tonsai.

Which brings me to my next point which I cannot stress enough!
At night, only party on Tonsai Beach if your accommodation is on Tonsai Beach. Once the sun starts to set and the tide comes up, it is extremely difficult to get back to Railay in the dark, especially if you are a bit buzzed or have been partaking in party activities.

How to Get Around Krabi Town

Walk
Krabi Town, Ao Nang, and Railay/Tonsai are all walkable! You could go your whole trip and not take any public transportation if you bring the right pair of shoes and some sunscreen.

Songthaews
Just like in the rest of Thailand, you can flag down a Songthaew, tell them where you're going, and jump in the back. Press the little buzzer button if you want to hop off early. Most Songthaew rides in Krabi town will cost 20 baht.

Longtail Boats
These classic Thai Longtail boats are waiting at practically every beach to take you on a day tour, to the islands, back to the mainland, etc. Consider them private water taxis.

From Ao Nang to Railay (and vice versa), tickets are 100 baht per person. In Ao Nang, there is a bright yellow kiosk at the bottom of the hill next to the beach where you can buy your ticket. The boats wait for 8 people to buy a ticket before they set sail – sometimes you can wait 5 minutes and sometimes 20 minutes. Want to rent the whole boat and get going? 800 baht will do it.

To head back from Railay to Ao Nang: Head to Railay East where you can buy a 100-baht longtail boat ticket for a Tourist Kiosk or hang at the entrance to the pier where you can directly pay one of the boat drivers.

To head back to the Airport from Ao Nang: Every Tourist Kiosk offers a 150 Baht Airport Shuttle. You can book same-day!

How to Get to Krabi Town from Phuket

Flying into Phuket first. Heading to Krabi second.
It's an easy route and you've got options.

Option 1: Ferry Boat

There are multiple ferry companies leaving at multiple times throughout the day. Check out the boat time tables at the back of this book.

How Much: $30 USD / 1000 Baht
How Long: 4 hours one the boat + transfers from the pier & your hotel

Option 2: Private Taxi

A private taxi can pick you up anywhere – any time and get you to Krabi on your schedule.

How Much: $70 - $100 USD
How Long: 2.5 hours
For Booking: KiwiTaxi.com or 12Go.Asia

Option 3: Minibus

Go to any tour agency in Phuket and tell them you want a minibus to Krabi. They'll set you up right away with a minivan that goes from hotel to hotel picking up passengers. Sometimes you will wait 30-minutes and sometimes an hour. I suggest booking this a couple hours or even a day ahead of time.

Don't be alarmed if the minivan takes you to a bus station where you switch vans – they are just optimizing their trip to get a full van.

Good to Know

The minivans drive pretty crazy and have you holding onto the "oh shit" handle. Crashes are rare, getting car sick is not.

How Long: 3-4 hours
How Much: $13 USD / 450 baht

Option 4: Public Bus

How Long: 4.5 hours
How Much: $4.50 USD / 150 baht

Hire a taxi to take you to Phuket Bus Station where you can catch the Krabi Public Bus. The bus leaves every hour. Just know that when you arrive in Krabi, you'll be dropped off at the Krabi Town Bus Station – 7.5 miles away from the beach.

The public bus is fine if you've packed light and have a Thai Sim Card or International Data. You'll need to do some navigating from the Krabi Bus Station to your hotel. OR just download "Krabi Google Maps Offline" and you can show your hotel location to a tuk tuk driver when you arrive.

Super Pro Tip

If you're on a really tight schedule but want to see Koh Phi Phi or Koh Yao – you can take a ferry from Phuket to either of those islands first.

Koh Yao – you can stay the night and take a morning ferry to Krabi.
Koh Phi Phi- You can stay the night and take a morning ferry, OR you can do a quick 4-hour stop over to explore Koh Phi Phi and head on your merry way.

Just arrange your ticket to Krabi before you go exploring

Chapter 5: Thai Islands

Spending a week or two on the Thai Islands feels like being transported to another universe where your only problems are deciding whether to have two Mojitos or three.

Each island is different. While all the islands have insanely gorgeous beaches, yummy restaurants, and have the ability to fit every budget- they each have their own personality.

Koh Samui is the island with the most 'Western' amenities.
Koh Tao and Koh Lanta are famous diving islands.
Koh Phangan and Koh Phi Phi are big party destinations.
You get the picture.

But...

Please please please get travel insurance before visiting the islands.

Motorbike crashes are common amongst tourists, cutting your foot on coral is a real possibility, and letting your inhibitions down sometimes leads to a little hospital visit.

Your life isn't in danger, but your bank account might be if you don't opt for a basic Travel Plan first.

My go-to travel insurance is from WorldNomads.com. They are cheap and thorough.

Enough of that. Island time.

Chapter 6: Koh Phi Phi

Southeast of Phuket is Koh Phi Phi, an island known for 2 things: pristine beaches and wild parties.

You get the best of both worlds here. Spend the day snorkeling with schools of colorful fish and the nights with booze on the beach.

This bucket-list worthy spot in Southern Thailand became popular after the release of the movie The Beach in 2000. Since then, travelers have been visiting Koh Phi Phi to admire the towering rock formations, hidden beaches, fine white sand, and emerald-green waters. A total walking island, the cobblestone streets are lined with both western and Thai restaurants alongside clothing stalls, party bars, and tattoo shops.

Accommodation on Koh Phi Phi

I'm going to give it to you straight. Here's the deal with Koh Phi Phi accommodation: Almost every hotel and hostel offers a slice of paradise…but on a party island. Don't expect super tranquil evenings with the sound of trickling water to lull you to sleep. Phi Phi is for boat trips during the day and cocktails at night. Once you accept these party vibes, you can truly enjoy your hotels for being a place to rest your head in-between some epic adventures!

Freedom Hostels@PhiPhi $

Guaranteed to give you a great night's sleep, Freedom Hostel is known for its super comfy beds, pitch black rooms, and all the air conditioning you can imagine. This is a newly renovated hostel with a lush garden on site and an inviting lobby area to meet other travelers. The shared bathrooms leave much to be desired, but for an island hostel- that's to be expected, my queen! What their bathrooms lack, their central location totally makes up for- just a short wander away from the center.

Style: Dorms
Starts at: $9 USD/ 300 baht
Where: 10 Minutes from Tonsai Pier

Blanco Beach Bar $

100% guaranteed to meet people, make friends, and have a great time when you stay at this party hostel right on the beach! Join the crazy Blanco Boat Party's to Maya Bay every day and return for beach parties and events every night. Bring your bathing suit, party dresses… and maybe some ear plugs if you plan to go to bed early. This place is so much fun!

Style: Dorms
Starts at: $12 USD/ 160 baht
Where: 10 Minutes from Tonsai Pier - Loh Dalam Bay

Uphill Cottage $

Get your cardio on, girl! The hike to Uphill Cottage will burn your glutes…but only for 5 minutes or so. Up here, you get gorgeous views of the island and something very rare on Phi Phi… total peace and quiet! Rooms are breezy with natural lighting. And every cottage has a sunny balcony where you can melt into your island vacation. Just be sure to keep an eye on the bikini you've laid out to dry…there are lots of curious monkeys up here.

Style: Privates
Starts at: $24 USD/ 800 baht
Where: Ton Sai Bay – 5-minute walk to the center

U Rip Resort $$

Breakfast overlooking the ocean, anyone? Step straight off the restaurant steps into the sand at U Rip Resort. A brand-new resort in Phi Phi, U Rip offers comfortable hotel amenities to transport you into vacation mode on arrival. You've got a spacious pool with lounge beds, lush green jungle trees all around, a restaurant on site, gorgeous views of the island, and a tour desk to help you arrange a day of island hopping. Nestled into the hills and just a 10-minute walk to the center – you get the best of both worlds at U Rip.

Style: Privates
Starts at: $50 USD/ 1665 baht
Where: Tonsai Bay
Address: 65 moo.7 T. Ao-nang

Viking Nature Resort $

Because a king-size bed isn't always enough, the good folks at Viking Nature resort also decided to give guests their own private hammocks on each balcony. The view from the hammock is even better. Located on a beautiful private beach, and within walking distance to two more off-the-beaten path beaches, this is the perfect place for some alone time.

Style: Privates
Starts at: $52/1709 baht
Where: 5-minute walk to Long Beach

The Cobble Beach $$

Pick your poison. There's an infinity pool overlooking the sea and the beautiful beach with warm ocean water only a 2-minute walk from your bed. If you plan on being in your bikini all day, The Cobble Beach offers you the perfect opportunity. Breakfast is included, and staff will help you book any tour you want. Everything you need is right here.
Style: Privates
Starts at: $73 USD/ 2330 baht
Where: Main Beach

Phi Phi Relax Beach Resort $$

Located right on the water, the Phi Phi Relax Beach Resort doesn't overcomplicate its natural beauty with enhancements. Instead, it features the stunning natural beauty as a part of the experience, offering snorkeling adventures and kayaks to its guests, welcoming you to take in all there is to see and do on the popular island. Traditional fisherman boats take guests out on the water to explore neighboring islands for a day adventure, before returning for a freshly prepared meal in the on-site restaurant. It's luxury living with a rustic twist, perfect for a short stay or long holiday.

Style: Privates
Starts at: $79 USD/ 2,614 baht
Where: 1 mile from Loh Lana Bay

P.P. Blue Sky Resort $$$

Location, location, location. P.P. Blue Sky Resort is tucked into the trees on long beach, just steps from the sand. Eat breakfast by the beach with an undisturbed view of the waves crashing on the shore. P.P. Blue Sky Resort is the peaceful getaway that you needed. Take some 'me time' in your private bungalow or grab a snorkel and get in touch with your inner mermaid.

Style: Privates
Starts at: $90 USD/ 3000 baht
Where: Long Beach
Address: Longbeach, Koh Phi Phi, 138/2, Moo 7

PP Charlie Beach Resort $$$

Party girls…you're going to want to check out PP Charlie Beach Resort. Nicer than a hostel but not as button-up as a resort - here is your happy medium where you can finally meet travelers outside of the budget backpacker scene. Daily pool parties with live DJs offer the perfect opportunity to mingle with cute boys and fellow travel girls.
Heads up: if you're looking for peace a quiet – it's only found after the clubs die down! Sleep when you're dead, babe.

Style: Privates
Starts at: $115 USD/ 3777 baht
Where: Central

Where to Eat on Koh Phi Phi

Everything is within walking distance on Koh Phi Phi. Just start wandering around and you'll get familiar with the cobble stone streets and establishments in no time.

Only Noodles Pad Thai

This island restaurant makes one dish and one dish only- and damn, do they make it well. Choose your style of noodles and your protein and you'll have fresh Pad Thai made to order for less than 100 baht.

Dubliners Irish Pub

Burgers, Bangers, and Banana Pancakes- when you need flavor from home, Dubliner's has got you covered. You can expect tasty western food at western prices that come in massive portions to hit the spot.

Tuk's BBQ

Head over to Reggae Bar and keep your eye out for the street vendor grilling up smokey sticks of meat and veggies starting at 30 baht each. This is true to the Thai Street Food tradition that every traveler should experience.

Papaya

Eat where the locals eat…and where the tourists eat! Everyone eats at Papaya and for good reason- their Thai food and Indian dishes are incredible! Made with Muslim influence, you've got your choice of classic garlic prawns or get eastern with some freshly made naan and curry. As this place is a Muslim establishment, BYOB.

….oh, and **McDonalds.** Yep. That's here now.

Things to Do on Koh Phi Phi

Go Scuba Diving

You can either party or Scuba – but you can't do both.

If you want to get your Open Water Dive Certificate, Koh Phi Phi is a pretty gorgeous places to do so. But you must commit to 4 days of PADI Dive Classes with no boozing it up at night.

Get to bed early and you'll be rewarded with some of the most beautiful dive sites in the world. There are ship wrecks to see, manta rays to swim with and even small sharks to help you cross a big ticket off your bucket list. The course usually lasts 3-4 days and often, comes with a discount on accommodation so pick your dive center first, and hotel second.

Ps. Plan a week in Phi Phi and you **can** party after the course.

How Much: Open Water courses typically start at $103 USD / 3,500 baht

Phi Phi Pirate Boat Booze Cruise

What would a pirate boat be without drunken sailors? While most boat tours frown upon drinking alcohol on board, the Phi Phi Pirate Boat brings the liquor for you! You'll spend the day partying AND sightseeing along with a DJ, insane views, and amazing captains to lead the adventure.

The tour stops at the most popular destinations, including Monkey Beach, Viking Cave, Pilleh Lagoon, Loh Samah Bay and Sunset Point. You'll have the option of snorkeling, kayaking, or just relaxing on board with a beer. Take off is at 12:30 every afternoon with the tour ending at sunset. All you need is a swim suit and a ticket, and one of those is optional.

Pro Tip

If you've come to Phi Phi alone and want to make friends fast – this is the way to do it.

Starts at: $39/ 1300
Where: Phi Phi Pier

Koh Phi Phi Viewpoint

If you swipe through Tinder in Thailand, you'll come across the same scenic photo where a dude is standing on top of a mountain and below is a narrow strip of land between two beaches. That's this place. The hike offers 3 viewpoints that reach up to 186 m above sea level. The walk is only about 15-25 minutes but get ready to sweat- it's steep!

How Much: $1 USD/ 30 baht (for the first 2 viewpoints) and $1.75 USD /50 baht (for the 3rd)

Monkey Beach

Most island-hopping tours on offer make a stop at Monkey Beach, a gorgeous stretch of sand inhabited by the curios macaques. There's tons of them ready to take selfies with you…but they are also ready to take your shit. If it is not securely attached to your body, these little thieves will run with it – hats, water bottles, even earrings are a risky move. The monkeys however are mostly harmless, but they do have an ego, so don't tease them.

So, while you can visit Monkey Beach with a tour – the beach is more enjoyable before the crowds get there. I suggest venturing over to Monkey Beach on foot, with a kayak or if you're hiring a longtail boat for a private tour, go to Monkey Beach first.

Ibiza Pool Party

The biggest pool party on Koh Phi Phi! Pack a cute suit - you're not going to want to miss this! Every Tuesday, Thursday and Sunday from 1pm – 9pm, Ibiza throws a giant pool party where travelers gather to drink, swim and socialize alongside live DJ spinning some island-worthy tunes. With drink specials, beer pong, and a diverse mix of international travelers – Ibiza Pool Party kind of feels like a pool party that you'd find in Vegas…. but way cheaper and no entry fee. This is the perfect opportunity for you solo girls to make some friends- the vibes here are always super welcoming.

How Much: $8 USD / 200 baht admission that includes one free drink

Nightlife on Koh Phi Phi

So, listen. Koh Phi Phi is one of the best party islands in Southeast Asia. In fact, partying is the main activity for travelers who stay on Koh Phi Phi. Don't fight it.

Banana Bar

Beer pong, flip cup, movie nights, live streaming of sport matches and all around fun vibes- Banana Bar is possibly the most famous party spot on Phi Phi. Not to mention, they've got some of the best western food to help you soak up that alcohol.

Where: Central Tonsai– you'll walk past it everyday

Phi Phi Reggae Bar

Muay Thai and Mojitos are the perfect combination for a rowdy night on this island paradise. Fights kick off at 9pm for an organized slice of chaos. Lots of opportunity to mingle with strangers and have a fun time. In the same vicinity of Jordan's Irish Pub in Tonsai Village, it's inevitable that you'll eventually gravitate here.

The Main Beach / Loh Dalum Beach

Follow the flock and wander down to the main beach lined with a collection of bars whose patrons melt together to create one big party. Some bars paint everyone with florescent face paint, others have bean bags on the beach positioned to watch the fire show, and most offer massive fishbowl buckets of booze to get tipsy.

The most popular bars you'll find are **Slinky Bar** where they light rope on fire and drunk people try to jump rope (fun to watch but a stupid idea), **Ibiza** with the pool parties mentioned earlier, and **Carlito's** which stays open officially until 2am.

Pro Tip

Skip the buckets. The booze they use might be homemade and give you a terrible hangover. Beer is a safer bet.

Classy Girl Tip

OR just buy your own bottle of Whiskey from 7-Eleven, keep it in your purse, order soda and mix it under the table. You think I'm kidding? I'm not.

Full Moon Party

For adventure-seekers and partygoers visiting Thailand, it's almost a sin not to attend one of the monthly Full Moon Parties – at least once in your life! So epic, that backpackers and travellers from all over the world flock to Thailand just to experience this wild event.

While the Full Moon Part is most famously help on Koh Phangan – Koh Phi Phi also throws a pretty epic Full Moon Party, too. It's slightly smaller than Koh Phangan's Full Moon Party but less overwhelming if you're not a hardcore party girl.

How do you buy tickets? You don't need to pre-buy tickets, just show up and pay 100 baht – which partially goes towards a beach clean- up post-event. Once you're in, you buy drinks like normal – bucket drinks are usually $10 / 300 baht.

Where is it? On Koh Phi Phi, the Full Moon Party is help on the main beach aka Loh Dalum Beach.

How to Get Around Koh Phi Phi

Walk

Phi Phi is a walking island with paved roads and trodden dirt paths. No need to rent a bike or a tuk tuk.

That was easy.

Chapter 7: Koh Lanta

Calling all mermaids, Koh Lanta is where you come to become one with the ocean and all of its creatures! Approximately 4 miles wide and 19 miles long, Koh Lanta is the perfect size for exploring and relaxing. Less popular than other tourist destinations, you can expect more unspoiled beaches, less tourists and insanely colorful underwater marine life.

The majority of the action happens along the sandy west coast collection of beaches.

- **Klong Dao** is Koh Lanta's busiest beach attracting tourists with its warm shallow waters and budget accommodation.
- **Long Beach, or Phra Ae Beach** in Thai, is another one of Lanta's most popular beaches with some of the best swimming conditions and a range of accommodation nearby.
- **Klong Khong** is where the parties are at! You'll find tons of little beach bars and music humming every night. The beach however, is quite rocky so don't expect to frolic in the water.

Rough Location: Off the southwest coast of Thailand near Krabi.

How to Get There: There are ferry boats that leave every from the following locations…
- Krabi Town
- Koh Phi Phi
- Phuket

Accommodation on Koh Lanta

Slacklines Hostel $

Photo Credit: Slacklines Hostel

You might plan on staying one night, but odds are that you're going to fall in love with Slacklines' welcoming energy, sense of community amongst travelers, and its playground property. There is a big pool with a slackline to goof off on during the day and party cabana where travelers gather in the night. Oh, and you're just a quick walk to the beach!

Style: Dorms & Private Villas
Starts at: $10 USD/ 300 baht
Where: Phra Ae Beach
Address: 482 Moo 3 Long Beach, Koh Lanta

Hub of Joys Hostel $$

The staff at Hub of Joys Hostel seem to have taken the name a bit literal, because they always seem to be smiling, happy to help you with everything. Unlike the classic corn flakes and sliced white bread hostels are known to serve for breakfast, you'll be treated to fresh muffins when staying here. This isn't the place for supreme privacy, as dorm rooms are the only option, but you're sure to make friends and adventure buddies in the well-designed common areas.

Style: Dorms
Starts at: $19 USD/ 626 baht
Where: 2 miles from Saladan Pier
Address: 341/6, Moo.3, Saladan, Lanta

Sincere Hostel Bar and Bistro $

Right next to the pier and walking street, Sincere Hostel is such a convenient location especially if you're leaving the island early or coming in late. The lounging deck is a pier itself where you can dangle your feet over the water and clear your mind. It's a great start and end to any Lanta holiday.

Style: Private Rooms
Starts at: $24 USD/ 800 baht
Where: Sala Dan Pier
Address: 150 Moo 1, Saladan, Koh Lanta

SER-EN-DIP-I-TY $$

The friendly Thai owner of Serendipity is an ever-present figure at his beloved hostel where he personally welcomes his guests, gives them great tips for navigating the island and provides warm Thai hospitality that you won't find at big hotels. You're a 2-minute walk from restaurants and markets in one direction, and a 2-minute walk from Long Beach in the other. What's not to love?

Style: Private Villas
Starts at: $50 USD/ 1700 baht
Where: Phra Ae Beach
Address: 482 Moo 3 Long Beach, Koh Lanta

Coco Lanta Eco Resort $$

Whether you're seeking a quiet vacation to become one with nature, or you want to remind yourself how fabulous you are, Coco Lanta Resort has what you need. The bungalows located directly on the beach are actually the cheapest option. Can you say major budget win? If you spring for the air-conditioned rooms, you won't regret it. The bathrooms are like a bonus room, perfect for pampering.

Style: Privates
Starts at: $69/ 2,273 baht

Where: Near Lanta Secret Beach
Address: Sala Dan, Ko Lanta District

Alama Sea Village Resort $$$

If it's luxury you're looking for, here it is. Alama Sea Village Resort has everything an island princess needs: hardwood floor villas, cushioned hammocks, an amazing restaurant and an infinity pool with an insane view of the ocean. Being so high up in the trees, you can also expect lots of monkey sightings!

Style: Private Villas
Starts at: $80 USD/ 3800 baht
Where: Bakantiang Beach
Address: 333 Moo 5, Ko Lanta Yai

Siri Lanta Resort $$$

Every room at Siri Lanta Resort opens up to a small garden, which is such a great way to start every morning. Only a short walk from the main road, or the beach, it is centrally located for exploration and relaxation. If you really want to get to know Koh Lanta, you can rent a motorbike from the front desk for reasonable rates and no hassle. When you're done with your wild adventure, come back to Siri Lanta and slip into the pool. What a perfect day!

Style: Privates
Starts at: $80 USD/ 3,800 baht
Where: 2.5 miles to Saladan Pier
Address: 631 Tambon Sala Dan, Amphoe Ko Lanta

Eco Lanta Hideaway Resort $$$

Get away from the hustle and bustle of the real world with a relaxing stay in a traditional, yet comfortable beachside bungalow. Each bungalow has its own porch, hammock, and wicker walls for an ultra-Thai feel. Surrounded by sky-high palm trees and just steps to the beach- this place is paradise.

Style: Private Bungalows
Starts at: $147 USD/ 4,900 baht
Where: Phra Ae Beach
Address: 535 Moo 3, Tambol, Saladan, Lanta Ya

Where to Eat on Koh Lanta

L. Maladee Restaurant

Thai cuisine with a tropical spin- L. Maladee is a must-try spot on Koh Lanta, especially if you love seafood. They've got fresh crab and lobsters still swimming around just waiting to be ordered; shrimp paired with sweet and savory sauces for serious foodies, and the chefs can make just about any dish with fresh squid. Everything here is to die for.

Open: Daily 5pm-10pm
Where: Between Sala Dan and Klong Dao Beach
Address: 535 Moo 3, Tambol,Saladan, Lanta Yai

Kunda Vegan Vegetarian Café

You don't have to live a vegan or vegetarian lifestyle to fall in love with this café. At Kunda, every dish is made from scratch with fresh ingredients full of nutrition, flavor, and love! And after a week or two of salty Thai food, your body certainly needs a clean reboot full of fruits, veggies, and maybe even a healthy dose of chocolate.

Open: Daily 9am-5pm
Where: Klong Khong Beach
Address: 91/16 Klong Khong | Koh Lanta Yai

Fruit Tree Lodge & Coffee Shop

The Fruit Tree Lodge & Coffee Shop is the perfect escape when you're hungry or hangry. Think nature, trees, yoga and homecooked breakfasts. Come for the fresh Columbian coffee, chai latte, pancakes, eggs benedict, energy balls and granola. It's all healthy, fresh, and the perfect boost of vitamins that you need during your Pad Thai Tour of Thailand.

Open: Wednesday to Monday, 7:30am-5pm
Address: 557 Moo 2, Saladan, Koh Lanta

Phad Thai Rock n Roll

The cheapest and most sought-after Thai food on Koh Lanta can be found at this quirky street side stand. Phad Thai Rock n Roll offers six simple choices: pad thai, fried rice and spicy curry. Nothing too complicated. Just extremely fresh and made the way the food gods intended. Fresh tropical smoothies and exotic shakes complete the experience. The place is owned by a funky musician named Jeab. As it is quite popular, come early to get ahead of the crowds.

Open: Daily, 11am-4pm, 6pm-9pm
Address: 208 Moo 5, Kantiang Bay, Koh Lantayai

Lazy Days Restaurant

I'm sure that when you imagined vacationing on a tropical island, you pictured eating Pad Thai by the beach with a cool beer in your hand as you watch the waves crash on the shore. Well, your dreams have officially come true at Lazy Days Restaurant.

Open: Saturday-Friday 7:30am-9:30pm
Where: Phra Ae Beach
Address: 775 Moo 2, Saladan Sub District, Ko Lanta

Greek Taverna

Switch things up a bit with some Mediterranean flavors. This Greek-run beach bar serves all the classics from Kebabs with lamb and Tzatziki sauce to homestyle Mousaka. Portions are huge which makes for great value for money- especially on a traveler's budget!

Open: Daily 10am-10pm
Where: Khlong Dao Beach
Address: Moo 3, House 231, Ko Lanta

Things to Do on Koh Lanta

Kayaking

Fun Fact: Koh Lanta's mangroves are nearly as big as the island itself. Set out on the still waters for a day of leisurely paddling as you search for wild monkeys and monitor lizards while listening to exotic birds singing in the trees.

Best of all, the channel is so calm that kayaking here feels like you're gliding over a lake. However, if fighting ocean currents sounds fun to you, check out Talaben Sea Kayaking for more advanced adventures.

Starts at: $36/1200 baht
Where: Hotel Pick Up

Go Scuba Diving

Unlike many other islands whose coral reefs have been destroyed by an influx of tourism, Koh Lanta's sea life remains relatively intact. The crystal-clear water offers insane visibility to get up close with rays, sharks, and countless communities of colorful fish.

While the quality of other dive sites in Thailand vary depending on the season, Koh Lanta's waters are warm and clear nearly year-round. This makes the underwater conditions ideal for the caves, pinnacles and drop offs in this spectacular diving region.

How Much: Open Water Courses average around $382 USD/ 13,000 baht

4 Island Tour to Emerald Cave

Rise and shine! A car will be at your hotel at 8am, ready to whisk you away to the pier. You'll spend the day snorkeling, swimming, and beach hopping while admiring the gorgeous limestone rock formations the jet out of the water forming these other-worldly islands.

1st Stop: Koh Chuak where you'll snorkel with colorful school of fish living in the island's thriving coral reef system.

2nd Stop: Koh Mook, home of the spectacular hidden lagoon called Emerald Cave. When the tide is low, you will actually swim through the cave entrance until you reach the hidden white sand beach enclosed by massive cliff walls.

Mini Break: Return to the boat for a Thai buffet lunch on deck.

3rd Stop: Near Koh Kradan – you won't dock on the island, rather you'll hop off the boat into the clear water where you can swim and snorkel.

The Final Stop: Koh Ngai, a tiny mountainous island with rocky headlands, white sand beaches, and thick forests – practically desolate except for a few guest houses. Chill out on the beach and walk along the shoreline before you head back to Koh Lanta.

Starts at: $47/1544 baht
Where: Hotel Pick Up
Available: November to April

Khao Mai Kaew Caves

Trek 30 minutes into the jungle and climb 20 minutes through a dark cave with bats and spiders. How does that sound? Still reading? Cool.

Located in the center of the island, you'll climb, crawl and duck your way through the Khao Mai Kaew Caves along with your guide. Head lamps will be provided but just know, this is no walk in the park – you're going to break a sweat, girl.

How much: Tours start around $20USD / 600 baht
Entrance Fee: $10 USD / 300 baht if you show up on your own

Rent a Scooter

You won't get lost! There's only one big road to navigate the island and this big road has no traffic! Koh Lanta is the perfect place to learn how to drive a scooter and you drive around looking for beaches to play on.

How to Get Around Koh Lanta

Motorbikes

The #1 best way to get around is with a motorbike. Similar to motorbike rentals all across the country, expect to spend around to $9 USD / 300 baht per day to rent a scooter. If you are staying a long time, try your luck negotiating the rates for multiple rental days.

Koh Lanta is a great place to learn how to ride a scooter. And if you're going to be a traveler, this is a skill you need! Just wear a helmet and please get travel insurance!

Tuk Tuk

Translates as "three wheels" in Thai, tuk tuks are convenient if you intend to sightsee or just need to get from one beach to another.

Fun Thai Fact

World-famous golfer Tiger Woods is the son of an American father and a Thai mother.

Chapter 8: Koh Samui

The most popular and well-developed island in Thailand, Koh Samui is a one-stop-shop for the solo girl who is working with a tight schedule but still

wants to experience a tropical island!

Koh Samui is relatively easy to get to and once you're there- you can stay put while soaking up Thai culture, beaches, and activities. As one circular island with a road wrapping all the way around, you can beach hop all day long.

- **Chaweng Beach** is the most western area and home to the best nightlife on Koh Samui. Bars, restaurants, hotels, shopping – it's all here.

- **Lamai Beach** Lamai is the 2nd most popular vacation beach, situated just below Chaweng. The sand is soft, the water is great for swimming, and the energy is a bit toned down compared to Chaweng, while still offering options in terms of hotels and nightlife.

- **Bophut Beach**, also known as Fisherman's Village, has a boutique feel to it where everything just feels personal! As for the 2km beach, I call it "Body Scrub Beach," in that the sand is grainy but soft. The water is perfect for a shallow dip and a DIY scrub.

- **MaeNam** is meant for the girl who came to Samui for the beaches! The sand is powdery and white. The water is turquoise and warm. Staying in Mae Nam is perfect for luxury resorts and quiet guesthouses!

- **Lipa Noi** has a more "beach town" feel with a collection of bars and restaurants with chilled out vibes, yet plenty of options when it comes to food and budget. Plus, sunset here is amazing!

Rough Location: Off the southeast coast of Thailand in the Surat Thani Province

How to Get There:
- **By Boat-** Take a 45-minute Ferry Boat from Surat Thani Pier or one of the nearby islands.
- **By Plane-** Fly into Koh Samui International Airport

Accommodation on Koh Samui

Lub d Hostel and Beachfront Resort $

Lub d Koh Samui is the newest edition to the glamourous Lub d hostel network. Feeling more like a social resort than a hostel, you'll find that everything here is just a little bit…extra. From the beachfront catamaran hammocks to the Floating DJ booth, swim up bar and infinity pool… there's no reason to stay anywhere else if tropical vibes are what you're after. Lub d Samui offers accommodation to suit all styles, from the thriftiest of backpackers to the fanciest Flashpackers (backpackers with a bigger budget)! Pack your cutest suits. Vacation starts here.

Ps. Lub d translates to "sleep well" in Thai, and here on Koh Samui - it's no different. Sleep safe, sleep well, and if you're going to miss sleep, they'll give you a party worth missing sleep for.
Style: Dorms & Privates
Starts at: $15 - $80 USD / 500 − 2,650 baht
Where: Chaweng Beach
Address: 159/88 Moo 2, Bophut Koh Samui

Tiki Tiki Beach Hostel $

Spend money like a backpacker, vacation like a trust-fund baby. Inside, your dorm room is basic with beds that are just fine and shared bathrooms. Put on your sexiest swimsuit and step out into the beach front pool and bar that will make you feel like you're actually paying 4x the price. With tree swings hanging from shady branches and white sand between your toes – this place is the definition of a steal. Plus, the hostel is quite intimate which makes meeting people and making friends a breeze!

Style: Dorms
Starts at: $10 USD/ 300 baht
Where: Lamai Beach
Address: 441/14 Tambon Maret Main road, Ampheu Koh Samui

Treehouse Silent Beach Resort

One of Mae Nam's best kept secrets, Treehouse Silent Beach Resort is pure zen. Silent Beach has white sand and clean water for swimming. The bungalows range from backpacker-budget huts to mid-range sea view villas with air-conditioning. The restaurant is my favorite on the island – known for healthy food made with clean ingredients. Try the Mojitos – they come in every flavor. The bar lights up with tiki torches at night. Have a drink here and then walk down to the swanky W Hotel and pretend to be fancy in their beachfront palace bar. **Heads Up:** Intimate and exclusive, sometimes you can only book through their website - tree-house.org

Style: Privates
Starts at: $10 - $45 USD / 300 – 1500 baht
Where: Bophut Beach
Address: 12/2 Moo 1 Soi Rainbow Maenam

Riviera Hotel

Get the sea view room. I guarantee that you won't make it 24 hours without looking out and saying "Oh my god" at least once. This tiny 3-story guest house makes you feel like you are waking up IN the ocean. The beds are huge, there are English channels on TV and the balcony is everything!!! To get your tan on, go downstairs and drag a bean bag to the sand. Flop down and people watch until you're ready to go explore Fisherman's Village.

Style: Privates
Starts at: $50 USD / 1700 baht
Where: Bophut Beach
Address: 6/1 M.1, Bophut, Fisherman's Village

Sensimar Resort and Spa – Adults Only 16+

My #1 pick for a luxury resort on Koh Samui – Sensimar Resort and Spa will throw you into full-on vacation mode the second you arrive. Suites overlook the glittering pool and ocean with pillow-soft beds and private balconies, but girl, the private pool rooms are a game changer. Stay in a private pool villa where you can turn the music up and tan topless with a pool that is big enough to do laps. When you're ready to put your top back on, head to the pool.

The eccentric infinity pool is truly an art piece. There are over 20 sunbeds with poolside service and the same goes for the beachfront sunbeds – the staff will bring that margarita to you! When you're not sunning, mingle with other guests at the swim up pool bar – happy hour starts at 4pm with 2 for 1 cocktails. The beach is only a few steps away with powdery soft sand and free kayaks to get your heart pumping.

Speaking of, Sensimar offers daily workout classes for guests including sunrise yoga and private training sessions in the gym – free of charge.

The restaurant is full service with steak and pasta cooked to perfection and a wine list that is perfect for pairing. Try the Caprese Salad… I couldn't get enough. Truly an experience worth every penny. Treat yourself, babe.

Style: Privates

Starts at: $110 USD / 3700 baht
Where: Maenam Beach
Address: 44/134 Moo 1, Maenam Beach

The Waterfront Boutique Hotel

The best and most affordable resort in Fisherman's Village! The Waterfront is located at the very end of walking street – which means no noise but instant access to all the best shopping and restaurants. It's also located at the very end of Bophut Beach – which means peace, privacy, and the cleanest water. Flop on a lounge chair in the sand and run into the sea when you get too hot. Back in the bungalows, you've got a fabulous rain shower and one of the comfiest beds I've ever slept in. Breakfast in the morning is cooked to order and the British owner, Robin, is around to give you local tips…or just shoot the shit.

Style: Privates
Starts at: $60 USD/ 2000 baht
Where: Bo Phut Beach
Address: 71/2 M. 1, Bo Phut, Koh Samui

Montien House $$

Instead of staying at the coveted beach club, Ark Bar, stay right next door. You can remain within walking distance to the action but get some actual sleep without techno music blaring in your dreams. Montien House is sandwiched between the best of Chaweng with the best shopping and restaurants on one end, and the beach on the other. The pool villas here are amazing and affordable – by the way! They are spacious, clean, and a fun place to bring a boy (just sayin').

Style: Privates
Starts at: $50 USD / 1700 baht
Where: Chaweng Beach
Address: 5 Moo 2, Bophut, Koh Samui

The Library $$$$

When a resort has a "pillow menu," you know it's going to be fancy. Famous for its bright red infinity pool overlooking the water and futuristic architecture, The Library is a splurge that's worth it just for the photos alone! Rooms range from "Smart Studios" with 42-inch plasma TVs with all the good channels to "Secret Pool Villas" that are just over the top. You must try The Drink Gallery and The Tapas Bar where they're just as creative with cocktails and dishes.

Style: Privates
Starts at: $342 USD / 11,300 baht
Where: Chaweng Beach
Address: 14/1 Moo.2 Chaweng Beach, Bo Phut, Koh Samui

Where to Eat on Koh Samui

So many night markets!!!
If you're planning dinner, check the night market schedule at first.

The Black Pearl
It's always a good sign when you see both Thai and Western people eating in a restaurant! I was introduced to this secret spot by a local Thai girl. Sitting at the very end of Lamai Beach, the sand is powdery soft and the rock formations in the water make for a great view while you eat. Order the whole grilled fish (Nam Pla) and Green Papaya Sala (Som Tam) – just let them know how spicy you like it. They've got lots of fresh squid, shrimp and veggie plates, too – and for super reasonable prices.

Open: Daily 8:00 am – 10:30 pm
Where: Lamai
Address: 127/64 Moo 3, Maret

The Jungle Club
The views are insane at the Jungle Club. This should be one of the first restaurants or pitstops on your trip in Samui. The Jungle Club really sets the tone for the rest of your trip. Melt into a bean bag chair and order off one of the best Thai and western tapas menus on the island. Drinks can be a bit pricey but consider it a premium for the view!

Where: Bophut
Address: Soi Panyadee, Bophut, Ko Samui

Silent Beach Resort
The most popular dish on the menu is one you've got to try: Khao Soi. This northern noodle soup is served with juicy chicken in a fragrant coconut milk broth and topped with crispy wonton noodles. It's a staple in Thai culture, but a dish that isn't very well-known in the west. Now is your chance to try something you may never find at Thai restaurants back home.

Aside from Khao Soi, Silent Beach Resort is known for their healthy, yet totally yummy menu options like hummus, falafel wraps, Indian dahl and all things vegetarian. Plus, every day there is a 4pm to 7pm Mojito Happy Hour with 99-baht tropical mojitos of every kind!

Ps. This is a super local & expat spot – not too many tourists know about this place. I find that kind of fun...
Where: Mae Nam

Address: 12/2 Moo 1 Soi Rainbow Maenam
Open: Lunch to 10pm

Green Bird – Thai Food

It's safe to say that Green Bird is the most famous Thai Food restaurant in Chaweng. Their colorful menu includes all of the Thai staples you love, and also introduces you to a variety of classic Thai dishes that you certainly wouldn't find at home. Order the Razor Clams with Basil, the mussels with spicy Thai dipping sauce, or the Pad Thai wrapped in Omelette. Finish it all off with Mango Sticky Rice and now, you've officially conquered true Thai food!

Open: Daily 11:00 am – 10:00 pm
Where: Chaweng
Address: 157/17 Moo 2 Chaweng Beach Road

RockPool Samui Restaurant

Uninterrupted jaw-dropping views of the ocean, Rockpool Restaurant is a hidden gem that you must visit while you're here! Bring your appetite and your flip flops to this waterfront restaurant with a little sandy beach below. I love this place for tapas like calamari and oysters on the half shell. They've also got fantastic wood fired pizza! Come for lunch and a dip in the beach below, or venture over for Happy Hour, every day from 5-7pm for two-for-one drinks.

Open: Daily 7am-10pm
Where: Bophut
Address: 80/32 Moo 5, Kanda Residences Samui

The Shack

The place to go for steak and wine! The Shack imports all of their juicy cuts of meat from lamb shanks and ribs to the juiciest steaks – even compared to the steaks you've been eating back home! And since you're on vacation in Thailand, treat yourself to a true Surf and Turf with local lobster and Tiger prawns.

Pro Tip

When you sit down, tell your server that "The Waterfront Resort" sent you and you *should* get 20% off your bill.

Where: Bo Phut
Address: 88/3 Moo 1 Fisherman's Village, Bophut
Open: Daily 5:30pm – 10:30pm

Night Markets

Monday: Mini Fisherman's Village Walking Street
Thursday: Mae Nam Night Market
Friday: Fisherman's Village Walking Street
Sunday: Lamai Night Market
Daily: Chaweng Night Market, Chaweng Walking Street, Lamai Night Plaza

(Use Blank Spaces to Take Notes!)

168

Things to Do on Koh Samui

Ride a Motorbike Around the Island

If – and only if - you are comfortable on a motorbike ...continue reading. The roads on Koh Samui can be chaotic in Chasweng, but once you're out of that madness - the loop road around Koh Samui is pretty fun to drive. Use your GPS, and wear one headphones with one earphone to listen to directions and leave one ear free to listen to traffic. GPS has mapped everything from waterfalls, restaurants, beaches and temples. The west coast of the island is much less chaotic than driving on the east coast, by the way.

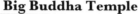

Big Buddha Temple

Wat Phra Yai is the most popular Buddhist Temple on Koh Samui and for good reason, starting with its impressive size. 12-meters high and covered in reflective gold paint, Wat Phra Yai shimmers under the sun which you can see from the bottom of the 45-step staircase leading up to the giant statue. Sitting in the classic mediation pose known as "Buddha defying Mara" – or resisting temptation to reach enlightenment.

Before you head up the stairs, visit the monk sitting to the left under the shade. You can give a donation of 20 baht, and then kneel with your hands in prayer and head down, as he blesses you with incense and holy water.

Where: Bophut
Address: Route 4171, Bophut, Ko Samui

Wat Plai Laem

In my opinion, this is the most impressive temple grounds on Koh Samui, but half as many tourists visit here! What makes this temple so special is that it combines Buddhism and Hinduism. There are countless statutes and temples that pay tribute to the gods, spirits, and ancestors – you can easily spend 30 minutes walking around in awe.

But the most awe-inspiring of all is Wat Plai Laem, the 18-arm statue of Guanyin, the Goddess of Mercy and Compassion. Colorful, unique, and #FemaleEmpowerment, Guanyin is believed to be a source of unconditional love, a protector of all beings and a fertility goddess. She is the Goddess to whom local women come to pray for a child, and healthy family.

Where: Bo Phut – 1.9 miles east of Wat Phra Yai
Address: Wat Plai Laem, Road 4171

Ang Thong Marine Park Day Tour

Ang Thong Marine Park is one of the most stunning underwater habitats in the Gulf of Thailand. There are 42 islands total, all with preserved corals and protected marine life. And you can see them up close with this incredible tour. Wake up bright and early - a car will be at your hotel waiting to pick you up at 7:30 am. Next stop, the pier! You'll board a speed boat with about 30 other tourists from all over the world. You'll put on life jackets and be given a quick brief on the day. Then you'll be handed your snorkel and the fun begins.

- ✓ Island Viewpoints to see the whole Marine Park
- ✓ Small deserted white sand beaches and islands
- ✓ Snorkeling with colorful schools of fish, eels, and urchins
- ✓ Local Thai food lunch and cold bottles of water.

The whole day is a whirlwind of tropical paradise!

How Much: Average $54 USD / 1800 baht

Grandma and Grandpa Rock

Can you spot Grandma and Grandpa? In Lamai, there is a gorgeous rocky peninsula that jets into the water giving you gorgeous views of Lamai beach and the bay. There's more to do here than just enjoy the view, however. There are two rocks that represent Grandma and Grandpa. Grandpa is pretty easy to find, Grandma take a bit of effort, don't be afraid to ask someone where to find her. Once you see them, congratulations, you officially understand Thai humor in a nutshell. Oh, and there are some cute boutiques and a little street market on the way down to the rocks!

Where: Lamai
Address: 92 84310 126/92 Moo 3 Ko Samui District

Watch a Muay Thai Fight

When you're walking down the streets of Chaweng, you'll see and hear trucks driving through the center blasting advertising for 'big Muay Thai fight tonight!' There's always a fight going on at Chaweng Boxing Stadium, often featuring western fighters which is a pretty thrilling sight to see.

Pro Tip

Free Muay Thai Match in Lamai on Saturday Nights from evening to 10pm. You're expected to buy a drink when you're in there – but they won't force you if you say, "Later later".

Where: Chaweng Boxing Stadium
Cost: Around 1500 baht

*Want to try your hands at a Muay Thai Boxing Class? Try Jackie Muay Thai – 1st lesson is usually 400 baht

Nightlife on Koh Samui

Ark Bar

Sitting on 150 meters of beach front property, Ark Bar has made the loud and clear statement that they are party central on Chaweng Beach! During the day, join the pool party with a swim up bar. At night, party goers are lured in with live DJs and fire spinners. The vibes here stay pretty mellow with tropical cocktails and beachfront lounge chairs- but the fun doesn't stop until at least 2am.

Where: Chaweng Beach
Open: Daily 7am-2am

Chaweng Center

Bar hopping is the thing to do in Chaweng. Like a school of fish, people seem to flow together or follow the live music. There are hole in the wall bars, music venues with amazing cover bands and a couple sleazy bars where you can catch a glimpse of the old man – Thai girl relationships. The most popular bars to visit on any given night:

- The Palm
- Green Mango
- Hendrix

- Stadium
- Henry Afrika

Hush Bar Samui

In the mood to dance and mingle? Throw yourself onto the dance floor at Hush Bar – where every night there is a different DJ spinning everything from Hip Hop & RnB to UK Garage, Commercial House, Dubstep and Drum n Bass. They've got super cheap buckets until 9pm, just remember to watch your drink and take it easy! Hush Bar's reputation is just fine – just keep your wits about you, my love. **Heads Up:** After Hush Bar, the crowd usually flows to the next dance/clubbing spot – Stadium which is open til 7am.

Where: Soi Green Mango, Chaweng Beach
Open: Daily 7pm-2:30am

On Street Bar

Not the house-music clubbing type of gal? No problem. On Street Bar is a quirky little watering hole next to KC Beach Club- so tiny that you might miss it if you're not paying attention. Built with upcycled tin walls and decorated with a collection of colorful light fixtures and random figurines- consider this the speak easy of Koh Samui. Live music, cheap beer, good people.
Where: Chaweng Road next to KC Beach Club
Open: Daily 7pm-2am+

Starz Cabaret

No matter how hard us girls try, we will never be as feminine or glamourous as a lady boy – and this show proves it. At a glance, you'd never know these glamourous stage performers covered in feathers and pearls were born as boys. They are so sensual and feminine as they glide across the stage, performing choreographed dance numbers and over-the-top lip-syncing Britney Spears bits. Each show is 45 minutes long and your entrance includes one drink.

How much: $7 USD / 220 baht
When: 3 shows daily – 8:30pm, 9:30pm & 10:30pm
Where: Chaweng - 1st floor at Khun Chaweng Resort
Address: 200/11 Moo 2, Chaweng Beach Road

CocoTam's

A must-visit, no matter where you're staying on the island. Get you cute butt up to CocoTam's for cocktails on the beach. This sprawling beachfront bar feels like an adult playground: There are bar-side swings for chairs, catamaran style net beds, bean bags in the sand, movies every night, two pool tables, and a beer pong table. YET, they keep things real classy and vibes stay super chill. Try a margarita or a Mango Mojito. You can trust that the alcohol is western quality – so go for it, babe.

Ps. Sitting on those swings all night is an easy way to get chatting to some new people!

Open: 1:00pm – 1:00am
Where: Bophut Fisherman's Village
Address: 62/1 moo 1 Bophut

How to Get Around Koh Samui

Grab Taxi
The Uber of Thailand. Grab Taxi is convenient because you can hook it up to your ATM card. If you run out of cash or don't want to keep track of your cash, you've got a guaranteed way to get home.

Navigo
Just like Grab Taxi and Uber, Navigo is Koh Samui's on-call driving service. I often find Navigo to be cheaper than Grab Taxi, but sometimes Grab Taxi is more convenient. It's nice to have options.

Motorbike
You can rent a motorbike on Koh Samui…but I only recommend riding during the day and avoiding driving through the busy streets of Chaweng. There is a street that loops around the whole island – it gets pretty calm on the west coast.

Fun Thai Fact
When we go to the cinema in Thailand, we all stand for the King's Anthem before the film begins.

Chapter 9: Koh Phangan

Pronounced "Ko Pan-Yang" - Koh Phangan is synonymous with parties! There's the Full Moon Party, Jungle Party, Waterfall Party and random parties every damn day of the week. While partying is certainly the main attraction on this small tropical island…there is more to Koh Phangan than just partying!

Being the fifth largest island in Thailand, Koh Phangan offers plenty of relaxing beaches and natural wonders to explore. There are day waterfalls, sand bars, viewpoints and…parties. Okay, it's a party island.

If you're coming to party, you could stay for a week and have a great time socializing and bar hopping. If you're a mild partier, 3 days on Koh Phangan is more than enough to see all there is to see!

While Koh Phangan is a relatively small island, you've still got your choice of beaches.
- **Haad Rin** is where the full moon, half moon, and other wild parties go down. This is Koh Phangan's busiest beach and beach neighborhood- always alive with energy.
- **Bottle Beach** is one of my Top 10 Beaches in Thailand - Bottle Beach is stunning, unspoiled and a must-visit when on Koh Phangan. Tiny and pristine, there are only a few bungalows and restaurants tucked into the jungle, overlooking the beach.
- **Haad Yao Beach** is a gorgeous stretch of white sand within walking distance to restaurants, bars, and guest houses, staying at Haad Yao is a fabulous idea.
- **Leela Beach is** situated opposite of Haad Rin Beach with the bluest waters and the softest white sand. A few resorts are available here with every budget in mind.
- **Chaloklum Bay** is a tranquil beach perfect for travelers looking for complete relaxation. Activities you can engage in at Chaloklum Bay include windsurfing, kiting, surfing, wakeboarding, and diving.
- **Ban Tai Beach,** where the party never ends. Once the sun starts to set, Ban Tai transforms into party heaven. Restaurants and bars come alive with live music, drink specials and bucket drinks. Still around, it only gets wilder.
- **Thongsala** is my favorite area to stay in Koh Phangan, with coffee shops, craft beer, night markets and peaceful

accommodation – all within walking distance to Thongsala Ferry Pier.

On Koh Phangan, backpackers tend rent motorbikes without knowing how to drive them…and they crash…often into other motorbikes. Always wear a helmet and pay attention to the doofus driving beside you AND be on the lookout for street dogs lying in the road.

Rough Location: North of Koh Samui & South of Koh Tao, off the east coast of Thailand.

How to Get There:
- **By Boat-** Take a 4-5-hour Ferry Boat from Surat Thani Pier
  These ferries leave at all times of the day with over
  5 companies. Or take a Speed Boat or Ferry from Koh   Samui
or Koh Tao leaving multiple times per day

Accommodation on Koh Phangan

Goodtime Backpackers $

Like to be social but also like to have your space? Goodtime Backpackers is the perfect place to mingle and relax. Start the morning off in your air-conditioned room, then migrate to the party pool or play a game of beach volleyball with the naturally social crew of travelers that migrate here. The pool is open 24/7 and so is the bar! If you're here during any big party, be it Waterfall, Jungle, or Full Moon, Goodtime Backpackers has a preparty and guests transport to the party together – creating an instant friend group. But…if humans aren't your thing, you can always just hang out with Kevin Bacon…the resident pet pig.

Style: Privates and Dorms
Starts at: $11/360 baht
Where: Less than a mile from the Centre
Address: 101/2 Moo 1 Baan Tai Road

Phangan Arena Hostel $

Imagine an adult summer camp, that's what Phangan Arena Hostel is. There's a soccer (footy) field, massive pool with bean bags all around for tanning, beer pong table, internet café, free gym, movie room, and non-stop bucket drinks- it's hard to pass this place up…especially for 100-baht dorm beds. The crowd is usually a mix of travelers in their 20's, very social, and carry on socializing well into the night. If you want to make a few friends, then get your cute butt over here.

Style: Dorms and Privates
Starting at: $15 USD / 500 baht
Where: Ban Tai
Address: 111 Moo 1 Bantai Koh Phangan

Angkana Hotel Bungalows $$

Recharge your spiritual battery under the palm trees at Angkana's private beach resort. With only a handful of bungalows on this beachfront property, you can expect total peace and quiet. The entire resort is white sand, from reception to the shore – the sand is constantly being combed by the staff, creating this dreamlike world.
Wade out into the still waters of the shallow bay and just sit in silence. Watch the occasional fisherman putter in with his day's catch and watch the sky change from bright blue to red and then orange.

Head back to your bungalow and sway the night away in your private hammock. Walk 15-minutes to Thong Sala Night Market or Thong Sala Town – an area with some of the best cafes and bistros on the island.

Starting at: $60 USD / 2000 baht
Where: Thong Sala
Address: Moo 2 Thongsala, Koh Phangan

Sarikantang Resort and Spa $$

On one hand, you're classy and like to spend the day sunbathing with a mojito by your side and a flower in your hair. On the other hand, you want to go to the Full Moon Party and dance your face off until the sun comes up. I feel you, girl. Sarikantang is the place to be both sophisticated and spastic. You've got this superb beachfront resort isolated on the white sands of Seekantang Beach – sunset and privacy included – which is only a 10-minute walk or free hotel tuk tuk ride to Haad Rin Center where all the partying goes down. Go have a wild night and walk home to your sanctuary when you're ready.

Starting at: $54 USD / 1780 baht
Where: Seekantang Beach, 10-minute walk to Haad Rin
Address: 129/3 Moo.6, Haad Rin

The Coast Resort – Adults Only $$$

The Coast is my #1 pick for a luxury resort that still has social vibes and party opportunities!

Charge up your camera, iPhone, mental camera, whatever...because this place is Instagram-worthy by definition! The Coast sits beachfront on the quiet end of Haad Rin under palm trees with sunset views! The bright red and orange bean bag chairs and pool umbrellas create a trendy "beach club" vibe – and the swim-up pool only adds to it.

When it comes to food, the pizza and house wine are to die for...and reasonably priced! When you want to party, just walk to the left on the beach. You'll come across a treehouse bar called "Escobar" and just a bit further than that are beach clubs, pool parties and the Full Moon Party beach.

Starting at: $115 USD / 3770 baht
Where: Rin Nai Beach, 10-minute walk to Haad Rin
Address: 117/21 Rin Nai Beach

Where to Eat on Koh Phangan

Soho

Draft beer and craft beer – oh, how I've missed you. For beer snobs, drinking Chang all week can get pretty old. At Soho, they feature local microbrews from the region – particularly from Cambodia. They've got all your favorites on tap, too, like Carlberg and Tiger. If you're into sports, they've always got a match of some sort on the TVs and incredible Mexican food and western tapas to go along with the mood.

Open: 9:30am- 1:00pm
Where: Thong Sala
Address: 44/56 Moo1 Thong Sala

Amsterdam Bar & Restaurant

Over and over on the island, I heard "we're going to Amsterdam Bar" so I had to see what the fuss was about. So, imagine a beach club that isn't actually on the beach, but rather, in the jungle with insane views of the water and beach below. That's Amsterdam Bar. It's a viewpoint bar full of travelers lounging on mats on the floor with small tables and big portions of western food. There's a pool that no one really gets in, but it sets the mood – along with the live DJ. If you're looking to mingle – this is the place to do it. Be here for sunset – it's stunning from up here.

Open: Daily 12.00 PM - 1.00 AM
Where: Koh Pha Ngan
Address: Wok Tum, Koh Pha Ngan 84280, Thailand

Café 2401 and Guesthouse

As if fabulous food weren't enough, this café sits atop a cliff overlooking the sea with views of Koh Samui in the distance. Order the most delicious bowl of Tom Yum Soup or go western with a Full English Breakfast – the ingredients are fresh, and food is made to order. Not to mention, the staff are delightful! Go go go!

Open: Daily 10am-3pm & 6pm-10pm
Where: Ban Thai
Address: 32/4 Moo 4

House People

Under a large, farm-style thatched roof with warm, dim lighting and plenty of space between tables, this is the place to come with that cute boy you met on the ferry. Ambiance is key, and the food certainly helps. Happy hour has some great drink specials to go along with your authentic Thai food cooked with just the amount of spice that you prefer.

Open: Sunday-Friday 3:30pm-11pm
Where: Had Yao/Secret Beach
Address: Haad Yao, Ko Pha Ngan 84280, Thailand

Rasta Baby

A sub sect of Thai culture seems to overlap with old school Jamaican culture. You'll find sprinkles of places like Rasta Baby with Bob Marley music, eclectic bartenders, beers with mellow prices, and Thai food that was made with lots of love for flavor. So, when you climb the stairs to reach Rasta Baby, plan on staying for a while.

Open: Daily 10am-2am
Where: Near Haad Rin
Address: Thong Nai Pan Noi Beach

Things to Do on Koh Phangan

Slip N Fly

The best daytime party on the island, Slip N Fly proved that you're never too old to enjoy a waterslide…especially when it's 131 feet long. There's a massive pool with floaties and tanning spaces, plus drinks and a bar and boys and fun. Slip N Fly offers daily passes and Full Moon Party promotions so check out their website when you get to the island!

Starting at: $20 USD / 650 bath
Where: The middle of the island!
Address: 98/5 Moo 3 Madeuwan

Explore the National Marine Park

Over 40 tropical islands await you at Ang Thong National Marine Park. If you missed the opportunity to explore while you were on Koh Samui, it's no problem. You can take the speedboat tour from Koh Phangan and explore the entire park! See the hidden lagoons, the Emerald Green Lagoon Lake, coral gardens, white sand beaches, and even bizarre rock formations

See the Sunset from the Secret Mountain

Get your blood pumping with a hike straight up Secret Mountain where you'll get a panoramic view of the entire island. Sunset is amazing from here! And there are tuk tuks at the top, waiting to drive you back down after your hike.

Literally any tour desk or even your hostel/hotel will offer this tour ranging anywhere from $30 - $50 per person.

Go Snorkeling

Just like Samui, you can build your own snorkel adventure or join a tour.

Option 1: By Beach

Rent a mask for the day and beach hop by motorbike. You're after the beaches with the most preserved coral and thus, the best underwater marine life.

- ✓ Mae Haad
- ✓ Chao Phao
- ✓ Haad Khom
- ✓ Koh Ma

Option 2: By Boat

Go into any tour office and ask about a snorkel boat trip! Just like Samui, you can join a bigger island-hopping tour like the Angthong Marine Park Day Tour that includes snorkeling but isn't all about snorkeling. Or pop into a dive center – their trips will be smaller and come with cute boys.

Thong Sala Night Market – Koh Phangan

Thanon khon dern. Road person walk. That is exactly what you do as Thong Sala Night Market comes to life in the evenings, particularly on Saturdays.

The long and narrow road is packed with food stalls selling everything from Thai donuts to quail eggs. And in proper Thai fashion, you'll find every kind of meat on a stick, as well. In the center of this walking street, there will be vendors on the ground who have laid out second hand t-shirt and toys, as well as, vendors selling leather purses, sparkly fanny packs and jewelry galore.

Open: 4pm-11pm
Where: Thong Sala

The Best Tour

Mingalaba Island Tour

You'll drive almost the entire perimeter of the island in one day, stopping off at the best beaches, climbing up one of the most gorgeous waterfalls, and exploring a natural sand bar where you can snorkel! The last stop is Three Sixty Bar for instance views of the island and a drink. On the way back, the driver will keep his eye out for monkeys and stop if he's sees them. Hop out for a quick photoshoot.

All of this is done in an intimate group of 7 or 8 people in the back of a songthaew, making it easy to make some friends.

Responsible Traveler Tip

When you make your booking, emphasize that you DO NOT want to stop at the Elephant Riding Camp – and make the company confirm your demand. Visiting the camp is "optional" in the tour, so if people in your car ask to go there, the driver might oblige in order to receive a hefty commission from the camp.

The only way to end Elephant Riding practices is to refuse to participate.

How Much: Starts at $15 USD / 500 baht
When: 10am-3pm (roughly)
Where: Hotel Pickup

Nightlife on Koh Phangan

Infinity Beach Club

At any and every moment, you can walk outside your front door and find a party raging on Koh Phangan. Prime example: Infinity Beach Club. With 3 bars, 2 restaurants, and 1 big ass pool occupying 1,000sqm of prime beach front property- this place is alive at all hours of the day. Bring your suit and get ready to mingle. Happy hour is between 5-6pm for discounts on food and drink.

Open: 10am– 2am
Where: On Baan Tai Beach, 1 mile south east of Baan Tai Pier

Fubar

Traveling solo, right? Stop by Fubar any time of day or night and make some friends. The booze is always flowing, tunes are always going, and the bartenders are always up for a decent convo. They throw live DJ parties, partake in green activities and there's always a crowd ready to go bar hopping. You don't have to be a guest to join in on the fun.

Open: 24/7…yep.
Where: Right on Haad Rin Beach East

Ku Club

A legit nightclub on Koh Phangan, Ku Club is where you come to dance your face off past midnight. It's always packed thanks to seriously talented DJs, drink specials, and an inviting open-air venue.

Open: Daily 6pm-1am
Where: Baan Tai Beach
Address: The Beach Village

Full Moon Party

The famous Full Moon Party kicks off once or twice a month on Haad Rin Beach. It's such an epic party that backpackers and vacationers alike plan their entire Thailand vacation around this event. Expect tons of booze, dress in fluorescent colors, and I dare you to try and make it out of there without someone painting your face.

Solo Girl Tips for the Full Moon Party

✓ Book a hotel in Haad Rin so that you can easily get back to your hotel without relying on other people or transportation.

✓ Know that MANY hotels will require a minimum booking of anywhere from 2-5 days during the week of the Full Moon party.

✓ Expect hotel prices to be more expensive during the Full Moon party- it's annoying but consider it an investment in fun memories!

✓ Partygoers like to pop some fun pills here and smoke all sorts of weird stuff. Before you partake, make sure you are with a group of people who you trust and will stick with the rest of the night.

✓ Bring an over-the-shoulder purse and don't take it off. It's so easy to lose your bag at the Full Moon Party with all the chaos- so keep your belongings close.

✓ Watch your pockets as pick pockets prey on drunk people who have their guard down.

✓ Drink lots and lots of water. Write the word 'water' on your hand before you go out- especially if you plan to party hard. Water will keep you from blacking out and will keep you hydrated and healthy.

Ps. You'll also hear of **"Waterfall Party"** and **"Jungle Party"**. Similar concepts to the Full Moon Party but on a smaller scale and in the jungle! Check with Goodtime Backpackers for the scoop.

How to Get Around Koh Phangan

Not a Motorbike

I strongly do not recommend riding a motorbike on Koh Phangan. The roads are incredibly steep, windy and narrow with sandy patches that people wipe out on all the time.

Pair that with traffic and a collection of overconfident and sometimes, drunk travelers driving motorbikes and you've got tons of accidents.

Walk

If you're staying in the Haad Rin Area, everything you need is within walking distance! In fact, most beaches have a handful of restaurants and mom & pop shops within walking distance.

Songtheaw

Flag a Songtheaw down on the side of the road or have your hotel call one for you. On Koh Phangan, you're going to pay anywhere from 100 – 300 baht for a one-way ride.

Chapter 10: Koh Tao

The scuba diving island! Koh Tao is one of the cheapest (and most beautiful) places on Earth to get your PADI or SSI Diving Certification. When you're not diving, melt into the sand with a mojito in your hand while you watch unobstructed sunsets like you've never seen before.

The smallest of the 3 islands, Koh Tao has a lot of diversity to offer in terms of beaches…

- **Sairee Beach-** The biggest beach on Koh Tao, Sairee stretches just over 1 mile and serves as the center of all the action! You'll find tons of dive shops, beachside bars, guest houses, and shopping opportunities here- but it's not the best spot for swimming. What it is great for is watching the sunset at a candlelit table in the sand…however, don't party here at night.
- **Chalok Bay –** Centrally located, just head down the main street and you'll find Chalok Bay lined with restaurants, shops, and home to a turtle conservation center!
- **Tanote Bay-** Surrounded by green rolling hills, this small private beach is ideal for snorkeling with sea turtles and preserved coral reefs.

Rough Location: North of Koh Phangan, off the east coast of Thailand.

How to Get There:
By Boat- Take an 8-hour overnight boat from Surat Thani Pier, a speed boat from Koh Phangan, or a ferry from Koh Samui.

189

Accommodation on Koh Tao

Black Wood Hostel $

Located right next to the main pier and a 30-minute walk from the popular Sairee Beach, Black Wood Hostel is the perfect location to finish your trip before you jump back on the ferry. Every night, Black Wood Hostel offers a free cooking class (just have to pay for ingredients) where you can meet other tourists and learn a bit about Thai culture. Rustic, communal, and comfortable – staying here is an experience you'll remember.
Style: Dorms and Privates
Starts at: $7 USD / 250 THB
Where: Mae Haad Bay

White Jail at Koh Tao Hostel $

Weird name, super cool space -White Jail is the perfect balance between hostel and hotel with clean rooms *and* opportunities to meet other travelers. Get a chic private room or a tidy dorm room that offers you a decent amount of privacy. When you're ready to be social, go next door to the Jamaican Themed bar called "Rasta Baby" for music, dancing, and free BBQ every Friday night. The music does go til late so don't plan on going to sleep early.
Style: Dorms and Privates
Starts at: $10 USD / 300 THB
Where: Mae Haad Bay

In Touch Resort $

Direct beach access and a 2-minute walk from the best bars and shops- what else could you ask for? The main selling point of In Touch Resort is the beachfront deck where you can lounge on a floor mat under the trees while you watch the waves crash along the shore. Once you're all rested, the staff will help you arrange all of your boat tours and island adventures! Or you can simply wander across the street to SUP Tao Paddle Boarding and sort yourself out!
Style: Privates
Starts at: $67 USD
Where: Sairee Beach

Tanote Villa Hill

Tucked between jungle and palm trees overlooking the ocean, Tanote Villa Hill is breathtaking! Every single room has its own private balcony, and when you're located along a private beach, there is no bad view. The pools (yes, plural) mean that you never have to bump elbows with other vacationers or fight for a poolside lounge chair. After a full day of sunbathing, cool off at the bar or dig into a traditional Thai meal at the onsite restaurant. And if you're missing home, don't worry, they have a full western menu, too.

Style: Privates

Starts at: $97 USD/ 3,195 baht

Where: Tanote Bay

Sai Daeng Resort $$$

Wake up to views of the ocean from your private balcony, head down to breakfast with fresh tropical fruit, and then take a dip in the warm water. To get to this isolated resort with private beach, you can expect a free shuttle that picks you up at the pier (which you can arrange beforehand with the resort). Snorkel gear is free to rent, and the restaurant has plenty of amazing dishes to keep your palate entertained. This place is perfect for a little self-reflection where you can forget the world.

Style: Privates

Starts at: $118 USD / 4,000 baht

Where: Sai Daeng

Koh Tao Cabana $$$

Your accommodation options at Koh Tao Cabana are breathtaking. Cottage Treetop Villa. Whitesand Cabana. 260 Degree Cottage Villa. Koi Pool Villa. You get the picture? Every room is your Pinterest board come to life with stunning tropical views in the most exotic location on the island. This is a 'treat yo'self' hotel that is worth every penny.

Style: Privates

Starts at: $154 USD / 5,000 baht

Where: Sairee Beach

Jamahkiri Resort

A perfect place to get away from the hustle and bustle of the center of the island, Jamahkiri Resort is located far enough to give you peace and quiet, but close enough for a bike adventure into town. If you don't want to spend the extra money renting a bike, just hop on their free shuttle when you want to go in town. Honestly, there's really no reason to ever leave the resort. Even the cheapest room comes with a sea view, and its prime real estate boasts a private beach perfect for snorkeling.

Style: Privates

Starts at: $173 USD/ 5,700 baht

Where: Shark Bay

Address: 21/2 Moo3 Koh Tao, Ao Thian Og

Where to Eat on Koh Tao

Koh Tao is a "walk and see" kind of eating scene. With tons of little sit-down Thai spots, picking random places to eat is part of the fun while staying on a small island.

But if you're looking to make lunch or dinner into an event, here are the must-try spots.

Barracuda Restaurant & Bar

Photo Credit: Barracuda Bar

Another popular seafood spot - Barracuda is where you can eat family style with massive platters full of shrimp, mussels, calamari, and fish that have been seasoned to perfection and served with homemade sauces that are to die for. So fresh. So worth it.

Where: Sairee Beach
Address: 9/9 Moo 1

Seafood by Pawn

When you've got a Thai grandmother in the kitchen, you know that this Thai food is the real deal! Seafood by Pawn has got all the classics like whole grilled fish, som tam salad, and every curry dish under the sun. They also serve Beer Lao here- definitely a must if you're a beer drinker.
Where: Mae Haad Village

VegetaBowl

After a week of stir-fried Thai food, your body will start to crave clean ingredients. VegetaBowl is fresh fresh fresh with salads, smoothies, and grilled veggies to replenish all the healthy nutrients your system craves. You can go full on vegan, vegetarian and dairy-free with every type of cuisine from Mediterranean with hummus or Japanese with handrolls! Pair with a fresh coconut and your body will thank you.

Where: Sairee, Near Ban's Diving
Ban Ko Tao
Open: Daily 11:30am-8:00pm

Thaita Italian Restaurant

Take advantage of the abundance of fresh seafood with some killer ceviche at Thaita Italian Restaurant! Of course, you can find all of the Italian classics – handmade by Italians, might I add- such as gnocchi, Bolognese, and tiramisu. Every bite is next level!

Where: Sairee Beach – Next to Suksamarin Villas
Open: Daily 7pm-10:30 pm

Things to Do on Koh Tao

Go Scuba Diving
Koh Tao is one of the cheapest places in the world to get your Scuba certifications – and that is primarily what travelers come here to do.

This well-preserved island is a mecca for Scuba Divers- both brand new and experienced. Divers come from all over the world to swim with whale sharks, sea turtles, eels, and National Geographic-style schools of fish. You've got lots of options when it comes to dive shops- compare prices!

I got my certification with **Phoenix Divers**, who took me through a 4-day Dive Course with classroom training, pool practice, and the real deal – underwater dives. Another popular dive school is **Big Blue Dive School.**

Go Snorkeling
Koh Tao has some of the best snorkeling!
I won't bore you with filler here, I'll just tell you the best snorkel spots to go after when you're choosing a boat trip.

- Shark Bay
- Hin Wong Bay
- Mango Bay
- Aow Leuk

John Suwan View Point
John Suwan Viewpoint is located on the southern tip of Koh Tao, with stunning panoramic views of Chalok Baan Kao Bay, Shark Bay, and Thian Og Bay. It's a sea of crystal clear waters, green hills and palm trees!

From the base of the viewpoint, it's just a 15-minute hike to reach the top – with a 50 Baht entrance fee. Alternatively, you can hike up the 500-metre hill, accessible via Freedom Beach. Also, a 50 baht entrance fee. Neither hikes are too strenuous, but you will need to wear a pair of tennies.

How Much: 50 Baht
Best Time to Visit: Between 6:00 am for amazing sunrise views and less tourists.
Time Needed: Around one hour.

Visit Koh Nangyuan Island

Hop in a longtail boat on the west side of Koh Toa where you'll take a blissful 10-minute boat ride to the gorgeous shores of Koh Nangyuan. This beautifully peculiar strip of white sand beach connects three islands where you can climb, swim, and tan. Make sure to bring a camera- totally Instagram worthy. You can hire boats straight from the beach or have your hotel arrange a tour for you.

Ps. They close at 5pm.

Nightlife on Koh Tao

Be Aware: Sairee Beach has a sinister reputation. Full Disclosure: there have been murders, rape, and drugs in girls' drinks over the years, the most recent incident of drug and rape happening to a British girl in August 2018.

This behavior is extremely rare for Thailand, but a pattern on Sairee Beach – particularly at Leo Bar. **Do not go to Leo Bar.**

So, how do you stay safe and go out on Koh Tao?
> Rule #1: No Bucket Drinks. Beers only.
> Rule #2: Do not let your drink out of your sight!
> Rule #3: Do not let a man buy you a drink.
> Rule #4: Never *ever* walk on the beach past midnight, not even with a tall strong man who you think can protect you.
> Rule #5: Be home by midnight.

Now that you're terrified (sorry 'bout that, sugar) – here's what you can do.

- Have some cocktails on the beach during the day and around dinner time.
- Watch the fire spinners on the beach and hang out with a big group of travelers
- Drink some beers and head back to your hotel by midnight

The predators on the island are Thai men looking for that solo backpacker girl who is in party mode and can be easily drugged.

The police aren't much help if something does go wrong, either. It's best to play it safe on Koh Tao.

Koh Tao Pub Crawl

The best way to meet other travelers and a few cute boys! The Koh Tao Pub Crawl hops from the best bars to the Ladyboy Cabaret to the beach for a fire show, collecting a free drink at each spot. The whole gang wears Koh Tao Pub Crawl tank tops (it's a unity thing, just go with it), and by the end of the night, you'll have made some new friends, gotten a decent buzz, and have gotten a lay of the land.

When: Every Monday, Wednesday, and Friday at 6pm
Where: Meet at Choppers Bar on Sairee Beach

How Much: $14 USD /450 baht

CoCo Bar

Sairee Beach's go-to party spot, CoCo Bar is a must-visit. This place is like a magnet for social creatures. Show up alone and you'll make friends within no time. Amazing cocktails and music that you actually want to listen to. Plus…there's always lots of cute boys here.

Where: Sairee Beach

Lotus Beach Bar

Grab a seat near the water's edge. Lotus has comfy floor tables and bean bags where you can sip cocktails with your toes in the sand while you watch Thai fire spinners perform some questionable, yet entertaining, stunts. Come for sunset and don't be surprised if you spend your whole night here.

Where: Sairee Beach

Avoid Fish Bowl Bar and Leo Bar

Yes, it's the most popular party spot on the island…but this is where the majority of crime takes place. Don't let other travelers hype you up that this is a good idea, either. It's so easy to get swept up in the mood but you can find an even better mood elsewhere on the island. I pinkie promise.

Did I freak you out? Need some reassurance?
Feel free to reach out to me on Instagram **@SoloGirlsTravelGuide**

How to Get Around Koh Tao

Motorbike
By now, you know that I don't recommend using a motorbike on Koh Tao or Koh Phangan. This is also not the place to learn how to drive a scooter with an island consisting of steep and risky hills. If you rent a bike here, use extreme caution. Rental shops require you to leave a passport or a very high deposit – because crashes are so common. Rentals start at 200 THB to 300.

Walk
The island is relatively small so almost everything worth visiting is within walking distance, via Koh Tao's cobblestone roads.

Taxi
Not really taxis, but pick-up trucks, rather. The trucks transfer you from piers to hotels and can also be hired to take you to viewpoints or other beaches on the island. However, they are expensive at 300 baht for a quick ride.

Itineraries for Thailand

The biggest mistake I see girls making when planning a trip to Thailand is trying to see it ALL!

Thailand is huge and traveling between islands *can* take time. While trying to cover so many places and visit so many beaches in such short amounts of time, you end up rushing the most beautiful experiences.

Everyone you talk to about Thailand is going to have an opinion of where you HAVE to go and what you HAVE to see. Yeah yeah yeah, we get it.

Everyone cherishes their experiences, and naturally wants to share them with you. But then you just get overloaded with this massive checklist and now your vacation is a chore.

In order for you to have the best possible experience, you've got to be realistic with your time.

You've also got to choose the routes that are easiest to travel with regards to how many days you have in Thailand. After all, you don't want to spend half your trip in a bus.

So, here are some realistic itineraries to help you plan an unforgettable trip with just the right amount of activity to relaxation.

1 Week: City, Jungle & Elephants

Day 1: Bangkok
- Fly into Bangkok
- Explore one of the Train Markets with food, drinks, shopping, and live music.

Day 2: Bangkok
- Go sightseeing around the Khao San Road area where you'll find Bangkok's most impressive temples and The Grand Palace.
- Do some shopping on Khao San Road where you can have dinner and a couple of beers with the best people watching ever.

Day 3: Bangkok
- Wake up early for a half-day tour at the Floating Market.
- In the evening, go to a Muay Thai Fight or visit the Ladyboy Cabaret.
- Have a cocktail at one of Bangkok's glittering Sky Bars.

Day 4: Chiang Mai
- Fly or take a night train (day 3) to Chiang Mai.
- Visit one of the many temples such as Doi Kham or Doi Su Thep- consider hiking through the jungle to get there!
- Visit a Night Market or the Night Bazaar.

Day 5: Chiang Mai
- Wake up early for a day spent at an elephant sanctuary (or consider spending the night)
- Wander 'Old Town' and see how many ancient temples you can find before the sun goes down.
- Visit Chiang Mai's best Thai restaurant, Lert Ros.

Day 6: Chiang Mai
- Wake up early again for a cooking class.
- Get a Thai Massage.
- Hit the Chiang Mai Nightlife Scene starting at Zoe in Yellow or go to a mellow bar by the moat.

Day 7: Bangkok
- Fly to Bangkok from Chiang Mai to make your connecting flight or take a night train down (day 6).

- Do some last-minute souvenir shopping at Chatuchak Weekend Market or MBK Center if you have time.

1 Week: Active Adventure Babe

Day 1: Krabi
- Fly into Krabi Town.
- Stay at a villa near Ao Nang Beach.
- Have lunch at Krabi Cafe 8.98
- After a long flight, relax with your first Thai massage!
- Head over to Krabi Town Night Market for some people watching, beer drinking, and street food eating.

Day 2: Ao Nang Beach
- Sign up for a morning Kayak Tour through the mangroves
- Come back and have a pool day
- Go to The Last Fisherman's Bar for sunset dinner and cocktails.
- Wander Ao Nang's boardwalk with Thai street shopping and hole in the wall bars

Day 3: Ao Nang Beach
- Rent a motorbike and drive to Tiger Cave Temple for a morning hike to the top
- Drive to the Emerald Pool and Hot Springs
- Come back to your hotel and collapse
- Eat local street food

Day 4: Railay
- Take a quick long-tail boat over to Railay Beach.
- Check into your new accommodation
- Head over to Tonsai for a 2pm- 6pm Rock Climbing course
- Have dinner at Family Restaurant

Day 5: Railay
- Spend the morning at the beautiful Phra Nang Cave Beach
- Hop on Krabi Sunset Cruise – leaving at 1pm!
- Dinner onboard the boat!
- Freshen up at your hotel
- Then head over to Railay East, where the Krabi Sunset Cruise crew will be partying and watching Muay Thai

201

Day 6: Koh Lanta
- Jump on a boat to Koh Lanta
- Rent a motorbike and have a relaxed day of beach hopping

Day 7: Koh Lanta
- Up early for the 4 Island Tour to Emerald Cave
- Have dinner at Surya Restaurant & Bar, watch the sunset while you eat

Day 8: Koh Lanta & Back
- Go on a morning tour to Khao Mai Kaew Caves
- Head on an afternoon ferry to Phuket/Krabi for your flight home!
-

2 Weeks: Island Hopping Mermaid

Mermaids, you'll be in your bathing suit every day!

Day 1: Koh Samui
- Fly into Koh Samui and stay on Chaweng Beach
- Put on your suit and head straight to the beach for a swim
- Do a little street shopping, then have dinner at Green Bird
- Head to Ark Bar for sunset and fire spinners
- Get to bed at a decent time!

Day 2: Koh Samui
- Up early for Ang Thong Marine Park Day Tour
- Snorkel and explore some of the last virgin islands on earth
- Head for a Thai Massage after your boat tour
- Experience Starz Cabaret in the evening

Day 3: Koh Samui
- Visit Lamai Beach in the morning – sightsee at Grandmother & Grandfather Rocks.
- Put your suit on for Ark Bar pool party in the afternoon
- Have a quick bite to eat at The Islander
- Go to a Muay Thai Fight in the evening

Day 4: Koh Samui
- Move hotels – up to Sensimar Resort
- Have an infinity pool day and socialize at the pool bar
- Zen out on the gorgeous Mae Nam Beach

- Check to see which night markets are near you or head to Silent Beach for happy hour.

Day 5: Koh Phangan
- Take a ferry over to Koh Phangan
- Check into your hostel or resort
- Explore the beach nearest to you!
- Head to Jungle Bar or Amsterdam Bar for sunset

Day 6: Koh Phangan
- Up early for the 10:00am Mingalaba Island Tour
- Explore Haad Rin's party area at night!

Day 8-12: Koh Tao
- Jump on a ferry to Koh Tao
- Head to Phoenix Divers for a 4-day Open Water Scuba Diving Course

Day 13: Koh Tao
- You've earned a day off – lounge on Sairee Beach all day or explore Tanote Bay
- Order a coconut and tan
- Go to Dinner at Barracuda!

Day 14: Back Home
- Jump on a boat to Surat Thani or Koh Samui and fly home!

10 Days: City, Jungle & Beaches

Day 1: Bangkok
- Fly into Bangkok.
- Check into your hotel and explore the neighborhood!
- Visit one of the nighttime Train Markets with food, drinks, shopping, and live music.

Day 2: Bangkok
- Go sightseeing around the Khao San Road area where you'll find Bangkok's most impressive temples and The Grand Palace.
- Do some shopping on Khao San Road where you can have dinner and a couple of beers.

Day 3: Bangkok
- Wake up early for a half-day tour at the Floating Market.
- Go to a Muay Thai Fight or visit the Ladyboy Cabaret.
- Have a cocktail at one of Bangkok's glittering Sky Bars.

Day 4: Chiang Mai
- Fly or take a night train (day 3) to Chiang Mai.
- Visit one of the many temples such as Doi Kham or Doi Su Thep- consider hiking!
- Feast a local night market or the Night Bazaar.

Day 5: Chiang Mai
- Wake up early for a day at an elephant sanctuary (or consider spending the night).
- Visit Chiang Mai's most amazing Thai restaurant, Lert Ros.

Day 6: Chiang Mai
- Wake up early again for a Thai cooking class.
- Get a Thai Massage.
- Hit the Chiang Mai Nightlife Scene starting at Zoe in Yellow or have a chilled-out beer by the moat.

Day 7: Fly down to Krabi Town
- Stay in a cute villa near Ao Nang Beach.
- Hire a long-tail boat and go island hopping, snorkeling, and swimming.
- Spend the evening Ao Nang Beach where you can eat dinner with ocean views and socialize at some beach bars.

Day 8: Ao Nang Beach
- Sign up for a day of kayaking through the mangroves!
- Come back and have a pool day.
- Head over to Chao Fah Night Market for some people watching, beer drinking, and street food eating.

Day 9: Ao Nang / Railay
- Take a day trip over to Railay via a quick long-tail boat.
- Go Paddle Boarding, kayaking, rock climbing, or just explore the winding island paths.
- Have a massive seafood dinner at Lotus Court Restaurant before heading back to Ao Nang.

Day 10: Head Back Home
- Do some last-minute shopping, eating and swimming.
- Get a tuk tuk or taxi to the airport

If you have more than 10 days- then you're a lucky girl. Mix and match these itineraries!

Thai Food Guide

There's more to life than just Pad Thai...

Tom Yum - A spicy and sour lemongrass soup, often served with shrimp

Tom Kha Gai- Hot and sour soup with coconut & kaffir lime leaf base served with chili, mushrooms, and chicken

Massaman Curry- A southern Thai curry with a peanut and potato broth served with steamed rice

Penang Curry- My #1 recommended curry dish that is sweet and fragrant with lime kaffir lime leaves, basil and coconut

Gang Kiew Wan Gai- Green curry with chicken served with steamed rice

Khao Man Gai– Hainanese chicken and rice served with a simple chicken broth

Pad Ga Prow Moo (kai dow)- Chili basil stir-fried pork (with a fried egg on top)

Pad See Ew- Wide rice noodles stir-fried in soy sauce with broccoli and protein (chicken, seafood, pork)

Som Tam- Green Papaya Salad with dried shrimp

Pla Kapong Neung Manao- A whole steamed bass with lemon and chili in a shallow broth, often served at the table over fire

Khao Ka Moo
Stewed, fall-off-the-bone pork leg topped with rice and rich pork broth

Kow Neuw- Sticky rice

Khao Soi- A Burmese/Laos inspired soup made with coconut milk, red curry paste, yellow egg noodles and topped with crispy wonton strips

Kanom Krok- Little fried pancakes with a crispy shell

Kow Neuw Mamuang (Mango Sticky Rice)- Sweet and salty coconut sticky rice served with fresh mango

Kanom Tuay- Layered sweet and salty coconut dessert pre-set in tiny bowls

Safety in Thailand

A quick briefing...

❖ Violent crime against tourists is rare.
❖ Crime here typically comes in the form of scams rather than actual danger.
❖ Assaults typically happen between two travelers, rather than a traveler and a local.
❖ It is safer to walk in Bangkok at night than it is to walk in Seattle at night.
❖ Use street smarts like you would back home and you'll be fine.
❖ Koh Tao is an exception to all of the above! Check out the Koh Tao Nightlife Section for details.

Wear a Cross Shoulder Bag
Although theft is not a huge issue over here, it's always better to play it safe. No one would be dumb enough to try and pull a cross-shoulder bag off of you. At least, not in Thailand.

Look Both Ways Before You Cross the Street
Duh, but really- traffic here is different than back home. Pedestrians don't have the right of way here- even on a green light. When crossing the street, don't just look for cars- look for motorbikes that whiz between the cars, too!

Walking at Night
Make smart choices. Stay on lit roads, don't walk down a dark beach late at night, walk with a friend when possible, and don't get super drunk and wander off by yourself. Follow those commonsense rules and you'll be fine.

Use ATMs inside Convenience Stores
As a universal travel rule, ATMs inside supermarkets, convenient stores, and banks are your biggest insurance policies against becoming a victim of using a fraudulent ATM or having a wad of cash ripped out of your hand - although, I've never heard of either of these things happening in Thailand).

Bucket Drinks + "Fake" Alcohol = Wicked Hangover
It's a common scam: Thai vendors will concoct homemade alcohol and pour it into name brand bottles; usually the white stuff like gin and vodka.

Bucket drinks are staple island parties and you'll be offered buckets everywhere you go. While you're not likely to experience liver failure after

208

one of these drinks, you are certainly going to experience an intense hangover. Stick to beer – unless you're drinking at a reputable hotel or hostel. Bodega Hostels, LUB D and pretty much any accommodation in this guide is safe on the alcohol & buckets front.

Beware of Sneaky Bartenders

When paying bartenders, make sure you say out loud "Here's 1000 baht" or "500 baht" to make sure they can't claim that you paid a lesser amount – which they've been known to do in party areas in hopes that you're too drunk to notice.

Let's Talk about Sexual Assault

Foreign women (that's us) are statistically more likely to be sexually assaulted by a foreign man (other travelers) on holiday than they are to be sexually assaulted by a Thai man. Think about it; in hostels, hotels and bars- we are more likely to be hanging around foreign men, quite possibly with alcohol in our systems, and therefore exposed to that risk. Just like you would at home, monitor your sobriety levels and be aware of your surroundings.

Gem & Jewelry Store Scams

In Thailand, the most common scam is one where a tuk tuk or taxi driver takes you to a jewelry store where they get commission if you buy. It's annoying and a waste of time, but not dangerous.

Here's how they get you…

- ❖ "Closed today" Declarations: If you want to go to a temple and the tuk tuk driver tells you that the temple is closed or opening late today due to a "Buddhist Holiday" …they're lying and are trying to get you to a jewelry store.

- ❖ 20 Baht Rides: If a taxi driver offers you a suspiciously low rate for a day of sightseeing, expect to pass all the tourist destinations and be taken straight to a jewelry store.

Other Tuk Tuk Scams

Rule of Thumb: If a tuk tuk driver takes you to ANY place other than the place you have requested – they are scamming you.

- ❖ Government Travel Agencies aren't a thing and they won't give you a better deal – don't let a driver tell you otherwise.
- ❖ "Stopping for lunch" means "I'm taking you to my friend's shitty restaurant, so I can make some extra cash"

- ✦ In conclusion! As foreign women, we can expect to feel safe in Thailand as long as we use common sense and don't get too wasted. It's really as simple as that.

Tourist Visas for Thailand

Three Options for Tourist Visas for Thailand

1. Visa on Arrival via Air

Fly into Thailand and get a 30-day stamp in your passport- no need to prepare a single document.

2. Visa on Arrival via Land

Cross into Thailand by land and get a 30- day stamp in your passport- no need to prepare a single document.

***Occasionally,** instead of a 30-day visa, Thai immigration will change this tourist allowance to a 15-day visa when crossing over via land. It doesn't happen often, but has happened in the past. Double-check with your Thai embassy's website if you plan to enter Thailand by bus or taxi.

3. 60-Day Tourist Visa

Before you come to Thailand, you can go to the nearest Thai Embassy and apply for a 60-Day tourist visa. You can do this in any country where there is a Thai Embassy- it doesn't have to be your own country.

It costs about $60 USD & you'll need to have proof of an exit flight. Don't have an exit flight? Check out BestOnwardTicket.com for a temporary exit flight.

Bonus: The 60-day Tourist Visa can be extended an extra 30-days (equaling 90-days total)! You can extend this visa while in Thailand, starting 7 days before your visa expires.

Example: My 60 days expires on June 7th. So I can go to immigration on June 1st (or any day in-between) to renew. To do this, go to the nearest Thai immigration office and pay an extra $60 USD/$2,000 baht along with proof of an exit flight.

These rules apply for tourists coming from western countries such as Canada, The UK, South Africa, The USA, Australia, and Ireland.

If you live elsewhere, the rules may be different for you so check your local Thai embassy website.

Quick Thai Lesson

Girls end every phrase with: Kah
Boys end every phrase with: Kap

Greetings

Hello - Sa-wa-dee-kah
How are you? - Sa-bai-dee
What's your name? - Kun chêu a-rai?
My name is… - Rao chêu …
Nice to meet you - yin dee têe dâi róo jà
Where's the toilet? - hông náam yòo năi?
Bye – Bye

Day to Day

No Problem – Mai pen rai
Whatever (doesn't matter) – A rai ga dai
I don't know- Mai ru
I don't understand – Mai kow jai
Please say that again - pôot èek tee dâai măi
Please speak more slowly - pôot cháa long nòi
How do you say ____ in Thai? - pasa tai … poot waa yàng-rai

Shopping

How much? – Tao rai?
I need ____ - Chan tong tan _____
I want ____ - Ow ____
I **don't want a bag** – Mai ow tung
Big – Yai
Small – Lek
I like it – Chan chok man

Food

Delicious – aròi
Chicken - Gai
Pork - Moo
Beef- Neau
Fish/Shrimp- Plah/Goon
Vegetarian – mang-sà-wí-rát
Rice – Khao
Coconut – Maprao
Spicy- Pet
I'm hungry – Chan hew
I'm full – Chan im

Emergency Phrases

Leave me alone! - Yā yung kap chan!
Help! – Chuay Duay!
Fire! – Fai mâi!
Stop! – Yut!
Call the police - rîak dtam-rùat maa!

The best way you can prepare for Thailand is to learn basic Thai with correct pronunciation! Take a **Survival Thai Course** with me via Skype, where you'll learn to haggle in a market, order dinner, and make friends.

Check out **TheSoloGirlsTravelGuide.com** for info!

Thai Festivals and Holidays

February

✦ Chinese New Year

When: February 5th, 2019

Year of the Dragon will be celebrated in Bangkok's neighborhood of Yarowat (or Chinatown, duh) and in Phuket, namely the "Four Old Streets" of Thalang Road, Krabi Road, Dibuk Road and Phang Nga Road.

While the firecrackers and parades are fun...I have to warn you!!! Thailand is a massive vacation destination for the Chinese right now. With a full week off in China, you can expect an influx of tourists to Thailand. Particularly to Phuket and Koh Samui.

My Suggestion: Head for the smaller islands on February 5th and stay a few days.

Most Popular Celebration Spots:
- Phuket's "Four Old Streets"
- Bangkok's Chinatown

✦ Makha Bucha (Magha Puja)

When: February 19th, 2019

Marking Buddha's enlightenment, this is a very special holiday around South East Asia. Thai monks and locals will visit temples to give offerings, pray, and chant. You are welcome to visit any temple and join in. PS. Bars will not be open on this day.

Most Popular Celebration Spots:
- Wat Saket Bangkok / Golden Mountain - Bangkok
- Wat Benjamabopit / The Marble Temple – Bangkok

April

When: April 13th-April 15th, 2019

Thailand's water festival is one of the biggest holidays of the year for both Thais and tourists. The water fight madness represents cleansing for the New Year in hopes for a bountiful harvest. For 4 days- you can't leave your hotel without getting soaked by water guns or strangers dumping water over your head. It's wild.

Most Popular Celebration Spots:
- The entire city of Chiang Mai
- Silom, Bangkok
-

October

✦ **Passing of King Bhumibol**

When: October 13th

Thailand lost their beloved King Bhumibol in 2016. He was loved and respected deeply. On October 13th, Thai People will wear black in commemoration and there will be a moment silence held across the country at 3.52pm. It's not always for sure, but there's a strong chance that alcohol will not be sold on this day.

Most Popular Celebration Spots:

- Bangkok – The Grand Palace

November

✦ Loi Krathong - The Lantern Festival

When: November 13th, 2019

Loi Krathong is a once in a lifetime festival where thousands of lanterns are released into the sky. This Buddhist holiday represents the birth, enlightenment, and death of Buddha- and is celebrated nationwide.

Most Popular Celebration Spots:
- Chiang Mai- Ping River or Nawarat bridge
- Bangkok – Bejakitti Park

Fun Thai Fact
It's relatively easy to get a Student Visa that grants you a 1-year stay in Thailand while you study Thai and take Thai Language Classes.

How to Travel Around Thailand from Bangkok

Pro Tip
There are 2 airports in Bangkok- Suvarnabhumi Airport (BKK/SVB) and Don Mueang Airport (DMK). Both have international and domestic flights! Check your ticket!

Chiang Mai

Chiang Mai has mountains, elephants, and laid-back vibes and serves as digital nomad central! You can also use Chiang Mai as a jumping off point to Pai or Mae Hong Son.

➢ By Sleeper Train
A must-have experience if you've got time! The Sleeper Train is comfortable, affordable, and saves you one night's accommodation. Buy your tickets at least 2 days in advance! You can do this via a travel agency or by going directly to the station.

Pro Tip
Go with the 2nd class fan option. 1st class is just the same but blasts the air conditioning so high that it's a miserably cold ride.

Pro Tip 2
Try to get a bottom bunk! They are more comfortable, and you don't have to climb a ladder to go to the bathroom in the middle of the night!

Pro Tip 3
If you're visiting during Thai holidays, buy your train tickets as early as you can. You can book 1 month in advance!

Point of Departure: Hua Lamphong Station
When: 8:30am, 1:45pm, 6:10pm, 7:30pm, 10pm
Duration: 13-14 hours (of sleep time, reading time, and seeing the countryside time)
Cost: Starting at $18 USD / 590 baht

> ➤ **By Plane**
Point of Departure: BKK/SVB or DMK
Duration: 1 hour & 10 minutes
Cost: Starting at $60 USD / 2,000 baht

> ➤ **By Bus**
Point of Departure: Mo Chit Bus Terminal (Northern Bus Terminal)
When: Every hour between 5:30am and 10pm
Duration: Roughly 10 hours
Cost: Starting at $16 USD / 530 baht

Phuket

Southwest of Bangkok, Phuket is a popular beach destination for scuba diving and snorkeling. Just a little expensive…

> ➤ **By Bus**
Point of Departure: Bangkok's Southern Bus Terminal & Khao San Road
Duration: 14 hours
Cost: Starting at $21 USD / 700 baht

> ➤ **By Plane**
Point of Departure: BKK/SVB or DMK
Duration: 1 hour & 25 minutes
Cost: Starting at $75 USD / $2,500 baht

Krabi

Krabi is a dream come true with a selection of gorgeous beaches such as Railay or Tonsai, access to day trip islands, and nearby to the popular **Koh Phi Phi.**

> ➤ **By Plane**
Point of Departure: BKK/SVB airport or DMK airport
When: All day every day
Duration: 1 hour & 20 mins
Cost: Starting at $60 USD / 2,000 baht

> **By Bus**

Point of Departure: Bangkok's Southern Bus Terminal or Khao San Road
When: Typically, overnight busses leaving in the evenings
Duration: 10-13 hours
Cost: Starting at $30 USD / 1,000 baht

Surat Thani & the Islands

To get to Koh Tao, Koh Phangan, and Koh Samui from Bangkok – you've got options, girl! You can travel via Boat, Train, Bus or Plane.

> **Bus to Surat Thani Town**

If you're on a tight budget, you can bus/minivan down to Surat Thani Town and then transport yourself to the pier. This can save you around $10-$15.

Point of Departure: Southern Bus Terminal- also known as Sai Tai Mai
When: 2 buses at 7am & 6 buses between 6:30pm-11pm
Duration: 12 hours
Cost: Starting at $15 USD / 500 baht

> **Minivan**

Point of Departure: Khao San Road
When: Mornings and evenings- check with a local travel agency
Duration: 10 hours
Cost: Starting at $25 USD / 800 baht

> **Bus + Ferry Combo via Chumpon**

To have everything organized for you, get a combo ticket from Bangkok!

Point of Departure: Khao San Road or Hua Lamphong Train Station
Time of Departure: Most buses leave Bangkok around 6 or 7pm
Duration: Around 13 hours total
Cost: ~$36 USD / 1200 baht

Pro Tips:

✓ You will find plenty of tour companies and hostels selling an island transportation package on Khao San Road.

✓ If you're in the Sukhumvit Area, go to Bodega Hostel where they sell the combo for cheap – you can buy the day before you go!

✓ A long bus might sound like a nightmare…but it's the best way to meet other travelers on the way to the islands.

> ### ➤ By Plane + Ferry Combo Via Surat Thani

Point of Departure: BKK/SVB Airport or DMK Airport
When: All day every day
Duration: Around 5 hours total
Cost: Starting at $30 USD / 1,000 baht

You'll fly to Surat Thani town. At the airport, there will be a tour desk offering tickets for the shuttle bus + ferry boat to the islands.

Ferry operations are all throughout the day from 9am-5:30pm.
The price of the ferry starts at 600 baht, depending on the company and your destination.

> ### ➤ By Train
You can get a daytime train or the overnight sleeper train- depending on when you're catching the ferry. Arrive in Surat Thani and then head to the local pier.

Point of Departure: Hua Lamphong Railway Station
When: There's one train at 8am, and 14 trains from 13:00-19:30
Duration: 9-12 hours
Cost: Starting at $25 USD / 850 baht

Saigon/Ho Chi Minh, Vietnam

Explore up and down the coast of Vietnam where you can have dresses made, eat oysters fresh from the sea, and put your toes in the sand.

➢ **By Plane**
Point of Departure: BKK/SVB Airport or DMK Airport
When: 15 flights per day!
Duration: 1 hour & 35 minutes
Cost: Starting at $90 USD / 3,000 baht

Phnom Penh, Cambodia

Phnom Penh feels like the old west with crazy traffic and old markets.

Tip for all of Cambodia: Have US cash ($25-30) for the border fee. If you don't have US cash, you can get pay in baht but it will be a bit more expensive.

➢ **By Plane**
Point of Departure: BKK/SVB Airport or DMK Airport
When: 11 flights per day
Duration: 1.5 hours
Cost: Starting at $75 USD / 2,500 baht

➢ **By Bus**
Point of Departure: Mo Chit Bus Terminal (Northern Bus Terminal)
When: 5am
Duration: 11 hours
Cost: Starting at $30 USD / 1,000 baht

Siem Reap, Cambodia

Home to Angkor Wat

➢ **By Plane**
Point of Departure: BKK/SVB Airport or DMK Airport
When: 11 flights per day
Duration: 1.5 hours
Cost: Starting at $45 USD/ 1,500 baht

> ➢ **By Bus**

This long trip does include bathroom breaks and food stops, don't worry.

Point of Departure: Mo Chit Bus Terminal (Northern Bus Terminal) & Ekkamai (Eastern) Terminal
When: 8am & 9am (at Mo Chit) / hourly from 7am to 4pm
Duration: 8-11 hours (depending on weather)
Cost: Starting at $20 USD / 800 baht

> ➢ **By Mini Van**

Point of Departure: Ekkamai (Eastern) Terminal
When: Every 2 hours from 7am to 4pm
Duration: 7 hours
Cost: Starting at $23 USD / 750 baht

Pro Tips

- Book with a company called 'Giant Ibis' for the most comfortable and reliable journey. This bus journey is pretty comfortable considering its long duration, the staff are professional, AND they hand out snacks and water during the trip.

- When you get to the border, you can leave your bags on the bus. You'll cross immigration and the bus will meet you on the other side. Check out the Visa and Immigration section for more info on how this process works!

> ➢ **By Train**

To ride in a 3rd class train with locals is such an amazing experience. You'll be crammed in a decently comfy seat with chickens and children sitting next to you. Reach out the window during stops to grab snacks from railway vendors. Take photos of rural life and soak up the beauty.

Point of Departure: Hua Lamphong Railway Station
When: Every day at 5:55am (there are more trains, but they won't get you across the border in 1 day)
Duration: 6 hour train – but a 12 hour journey (see below)
Cost: $2 (amazing, right?)

Important Note: The train's destination is to the border town of Aranyaprathet, which is a 10-minute Tuk Tuk ride to Cambodia's border, costing around 100 baht. The driver might try to take you to a

"Visa Agency" – tell him you have an e-visa (even if you don't) and he'll take you to the border where you will walk out of Thailand and into Cambodia.

From the Border in Aranyaprathet:

After immigration, hop on the free 10-minute bus to Popiet Tourist Passenger International Terminal. The bus will be waiting for you, don't worry. At the terminal, your transport options to Siem Reap are as follows

- Bus or Minivan - $10
- Private Taxi - $50

Pro Tip

- Don't let taxi drivers pressure you into their services by saying "the bus is full" or "the bus is leaving soon". In fact, the bus waits for passengers to fill up...which can take an hour.
- If you have the cash, take a taxi. Pay him half up front and half when you arrive at your hotel.

Sihanoukville, Cambodia

You'll transit through the town of Trat, then cross over via Koh Kong. From Koh Kong, you'll travel by bus or taxi to Sihanoukville. You can spend a few days in this quirky beach town or island hop to Koh Rong & Koh Rong Samleom.

> **By Bus**

Point of Departure: Mo Chit Bus Terminal (Northern Bus Terminal) or Ekkamai (Eastern) Terminal
When: 6am
Duration: 5 hours to Trat

In Trat, take a 120 baht taxi to the border of Koh Kong.

In Koh Kong, you have two options:

1: Take a taxi to the bus station ($4) and then a bus to Sihanoukville ($15) with another 6-hour journey
2: Hire a taxi at the border ($50) who will take you to your hotel in Sihanoukville with a 5-hour journey

Check out the Sihanoukville Chapter to get more information!

Thailand Directory

Tourist Police – English Speaking
Phone: 1155 (free call from any phone) or 678-6800
Address: TPI Tower, 25/26 Liab Khong Rd., Chong Nonsi Junction, New Chan Rd.

British Embassy
Emergency Line: 02 305 8333
Address: 14 Wireless Road   Lumpini   Pathumwan

American Embassy
Emergency Line: 02-205-4000
Address: 95 Wireless Rd Khwaeng Lumphini Pathumwan

Canadian Embassy
Emergency Line: 02646-4300
Address: 15th Floor, Abdulrahim Place 990 Rama IV Road Bangrak

South African Embassy
Emergency Line: 02659-2900
Address: 12th A Floor, M Thai Tower, All Seasons Place, 87 Wireless Road, Lumphini Pathumwa

Australian Embassy
Emergency Line: 02 344 6300
Address: 37 South Sathorn Road
Tungmahamek, Sathorn

Gynecology Services & Female Stuff

Women's Center (OB/GYN) | Bumrungrad Hospital Bangkok
All of the services including birth control, ultrasounds, STD testing, etc.
Open: Monday through Friday 7am to 8pm/ Saturday 7am to 7pm/ Sunday 8am to 8pm
How to Get There: BTS Nana
Address: 33 Soi Sukhumvit 3

Birth Control
You can buy birth control pills and contraception over the counter in Thailand
Where: All pharmacies and Boots Drug Stores

Morning After Pill
Where: Every pharmacy carries it under "Postinor" or "Madona" (I know, right?) for 40-60 baht

Unwanted Pregnancy - Klong Tun Medical Center
Open: 24/7
How to Get There: BTS Phra Khanong- Next to Cabbages and Condoms Restaurant on Sukhumvit 12
Address: 3284 New Petchburi Road Bangkapi Khet Huai Khwang
Phone: 02 319 2101

For more information, check out gynopedia.org/Bangkok

And please, just visit WorldNomads.com to check out Travel Insurance. It's better to have it and not need it; than to need it and not have it.

The Thailand Bucketlist

- ✓ Ride in a Tuk Tuk
- ✓ Get a Thai Massage
- ✓ Eat a 7/11 Toastie
- ✓ Selfie with an Elephant
- ✓ Drink a Coconut on the Beach
- ✓ Eat a Bug or a Scorpion
- ✓ Visit a Night Market
- ✓ Ride in a Longtail-boat
- ✓ Drink Thai Tea
- ✓ Snorkel with Colorful Schools of Fish
- ✓ Learn How to Say 3 Words in Thai
- ✓ Visit a Thai Temple
- ✓ Take a Cooking Class
- ✓ Drink a Beer on Khao San Road
- ✓ Make a Thai Friend
- ✓ Get Lost

Send me photos of you checking off your Thai Bucket List!!! @ SoloGirlsTravelGuide

TIMETABLE
Transfer service

SEATRAN DISCOVERY
HIGH SPEED FERRIES

✉ INFO@SEATRANDISCOVERY.COM
🖥 WWW.SEATRANDISCOVERY.COM

from Koh Tao — Mae Haad pier

To	Dep.	Arr.
Koh Phangan	06:30 / 09:00 / 15:00	08:00 / 10:00 / 16:00
Koh Samui	06:30 / 09:00 / 15:00	08:30 / 11:00 / 16:30
Donsak	06:30 / 09:00 / 15:00	17:00-17:30
Khaosok	06:30 / 09:00	10:30-11:00 / 13:00-13:30
Surat Thani City	06:30 / 09:00	12:00 / 15:00
Surat Thani Airport	06:30 / 09:00	12:30 / 15:30
Nakhon Si Thammarat (Town)	06:30 / 09:00	12:00 / 15:00
Nakhon Si Thammarat (Airport)	06:30 / 09:00	12:30 / 15:30
Surat Thani Train Station	09:00	17:40
Krabi Town	06:30 / 09:00	14:00 / 17:00
Aonang (Krabi)	06:30 / 09:00	14:30 / 17:30
Railay Beach (Krabi)	06:30 / 09:00	14:30 / 17:30
Koh Lanta	06:30 / 09:00	17:00 / 20:00
Koh Phi Phi (Tonsai Pier)	06:30 / 09:00	16:30 / 20:00
Phuket (Rassada Pier)	06:30	17:30
Hat Yai	06:30	16:00

from Koh Phangan — Thong Sala pier

To	Dep.	Arr.
Koh Tao	08:30 / 13:30 / 17:00	10:00-10:30 / 15:00-15:30 / 18:30-19:00
Koh Samui	08:00 / 10:30 / 16:30	08:30 / 11:00 / 17:00
Donsak	08:00 / 10:30	10:30-11:00 / 13:30-13:30
Khaosok	08:00	15:00
Surat Thani City	08:00 / 10:30	12:00 / 15:00
Surat Thani Airport	08:00 / 10:30	12:30 / 15:30
Nakhon Si Thammarat (Town)	08:00 / 10:30	12:00 / 15:00
Nakhon Si Thammarat (Airport)	08:00 / 10:30	12:30 / 15:30
Surat Thani Train Station	10:30	17:40
Krabi Town	08:00 / 10:30	14:00 / 17:00
Aonang (Krabi)	08:00 / 10:30	14:30 / 17:30
Railay Beach (Krabi)	08:00 / 10:30	14:30 / 17:30
Koh Lanta	08:00 / 10:30	17:00 / 20:00
Koh Phi Phi (Tonsai Pier)	08:00	16:30
Phuket (Rassada Pier)	08:00	17:30
Hat Yai	08:00	16:00

from Koh Samui — Bangrak pier

To	Dep.	Arr.
Koh Phangan	08:00 / 13:00 / 16:30	08:30 / 13:30 / 17:00
Koh Tao	08:00 / 13:00 / 16:30	10:00-10:30 / 15:00-15:30 / 18:30-19:00
Donsak	09:00 / 11:30	10:30-11:00 / 13:00-13:30
Khaosok	09:00	15:00
Surat Thani City	09:00 / 11:30	12:00 / 15:00
Surat Thani Airport	09:00 / 11:30	12:30 / 15:30
Nakhon Si Thammarat (Town)	09:00 / 11:30	12:00 / 15:00
Nakhon Si Thammarat (Airport)	09:00 / 11:30	12:30 / 15:30
Surat Thani Train Station	11:30	17:40
Krabi Town	09:00 / 11:30	14:00 / 17:00
Aonang (Krabi)	09:00 / 11:30	14:30 / 17:30
Railay Beach (Krabi)	09:00 / 11:30	14:30 / 17:30
Koh Lanta	09:00 / 11:30	17:00 / 20:00
Koh Phi Phi (Tonsai Pier)	09:00	16:30
Phuket (Rassada Pier)	09:00	17:30
Hat Yai	09:00	16:00

from Krabi

To	Dep.	Arr.
Koh Tao	08:00 / 11:00	15:00-15:30 / 18:30-19:00
Koh Phangan	08:00 / 11:00	13:30 / 17:00
Koh Lanta	08:00	17:00
Koh Phi Phi	08:00	12:30
Koh Samui	08:00 / 11:00	16:00

from Phuket — Rassada pier

To	Dep.	Arr.
Koh Tao	08:30	18:30-19:00
Koh Phangan	08:30	17:00
Koh Samui	08:30	16:00

from Koh PhiPhi — Tonsai pier

To	Dep.	Arr.
Koh Tao	09:00	18:30-19:00
Koh Phangan	09:00	17:00
Koh Samui	09:00	16:00

Dep = Departure time, Arr = Arrival time

Cambodia

Pssst.

Cambodia is relatively new to the tourism industry- that's what makes it such an exciting destination!

However, this also means that some destinations are still a bit choppy in terms of traveling from Point A to Point B.

For the destinations that have their shit together (Phnom Penh, Siem Reap, Battambang, etc.), getting there is as easy as asking your hotel to book a bus or a minivan – and your transportation will pick you up directly from your hotel.

When it comes to islands, border crossings and off the beaten path destinations, however, you'll need a little extra help. For these destinations, I've added some extra insider advice to get you there safely, quickly, and without spending all your cash!

Throughout this Cambodia Guide, you'll occasionally come across the extra "How to Get There" section at the end of various chapters. These are the cheat codes and travel hacks to make your journey smoother.

Let's go!

Intro to Cambodia

Cambodia is a land of contrasts.

You've got mystical ancient temples in the north, one of the fastest growing cities in the world nestled in the center and a breathtaking collection of virgin beaches in the south. All of which are packed into one tiny country the size as Washington State.

Most tourists come to Cambodia with the sole intention of visiting Angkor Wat - a mystifying temple complex spanning over 400 square kilometers with Tomb Raider style architecture in the middle of the jungle. But this stunning site is only the tip of the iceberg when it comes to experience the beauty of Cambodia.

Get ready for a well-rounded vacation in this underrated Southeast Asian country.

Witness the harrowing recent history of the country at Phnom Penh's Killing Fields and S21 prison. A visit not for the faint of heart, but an important piece of this country's puzzle.

Sip sunset cocktails by the river in Kampot or rent a scooter and drive up the mountain to abandoned French mansions on Bokor Mountain.

Party till dawn with fellow solo travelers and experienced expats on the beaches of Sihanoukville where you can have a complete night out for under $10.

If a digital detox is what you're looking for - check out the island of Koh Ta Kiev, there's no electricity so you can kick back and relax offline for a few days.

And while everyone on Earth knows about Thailand's islands, filling them to the brim with tourists – Cambodia's islands remain relatively unspoiled with white sand and turquoise waters. The tourism clock is ticking…now is your chance to visit Koh Rong and Koh Rong Samleom before mass tourism takes over in just a few years' time.

Whether you've got a few days, a week or even a month – Cambodia is going to make its way into your heart one way or another.

Fun Cambo Fact
Cambodia is a cash country…that uses US dollars! Use the ATM to withdraw your cash – you'll barely use your card after that.

Weather in Cambodia

The Good News: Weather patterns are easily predictable with 2 whole seasons per year.
The Bad News: It's humid and sticky no matter what.

When planning your epic Cambodian adventure, keep these two seasons in mind as they can be the make or break for a lot of activities...

Dry Season runs from late **October to April.** This is the season with the least rain. Come November – January, and you'll experience the pleasant temperatures in the high 60s. However, after January, the temperatures start to heat up. April is usually boiling with temps that reach over 100 °.

Wet Season lasts from **May to October** with monsoons bringing lots of rainfall. The beginning of Wet Season **(May to July)** is relatively cool with temps ranging from 75° to 80° and rain falling only a couple hours per day.

The second half of rainy season **(August-October),** however, is no stranger to full days of non-stop rain. With Cambodia's underdeveloped roads and limited septic systems, expect travel delays with flooded roads and flooded septic tanks. It's not exactly barefoot beach weather, ya know.

These weather patterns correspond to **the tourist industry's High Season and Low Season.** Each season has it's perks and pitfalls.

The Low Season (May-September) sees a lower volume of tourists due to the rain. While you won't get an amazing tan during this time period, you will get discounted hotel prices and flights! You'll also experience lush green jungles and unobstructed photo ops at Angkor Wat.

The High Season (November to February) has the most gorgeous weather that is best for beach days and flip flops! Weather will not be getting in your way, but the larger flocks of tourists might. Expect social beaches and full-priced flights. If you're a people person or a bargain hunter, you might enjoy this challenge.

So to sum all of that up…

Hottest Months: May-June 95 ° F / 35 ° C and hotter
Coolest Months: November-December 75 ° F /24 ° C with a breeze
Most Humid Months: March-April
Most Ideal Time to Visit Cambodia: November- February or "High Season"

Top 10 Cambodia Experiences

1- Bicycle Tour through Angkor Wat, Siem Reap

2- The Killing Fields, Phnom Penh

3- Tuol Sleng Genocide Museum, Phnom Penh

4- Elephant Valley Project, Senmonorom

5- The Beaches of Koh Rong Samloem

6- Adventure Adam Boat Tour, Koh Rong

7- Motorbike up Bokor Mountain, Kampot

8- Phare Circus, Siem Reap

9- Swim with Plankton, Koh Rong Samloem

10- Taco Tuesday, Karma Traders Kampot

Cambodia Culture Norms

101

Kindness and manners are free.

Do's & Don'ts in Cambo

Here's a quick list of cultural and local norms to make you feel more comfortable from the start.

Do...

Haggle
Aside from restaurants and food stalls, you can pretty much haggle any price in Cambodia. Tuk Tuk drivers, taxi drivers, street market vendors, clothing stalls...every price is negotiable especially when you're buying more than one dress or are traveling with more than one person in a tuk tuk. Worst case, they don't budge.

Cover your Shoulders & Knees in Temples
Modesty is required inside spiritual spaces. Wear a long skirt, or buy a beautiful shawl to wrap around your waist and/or shoulders when you visit the temples.

Tip Your Salon Lady
Massages, pedicures, haircuts- these kinds of services definitely deserve a tip. 15-20% should do it.

Conceal your Cell Phone

Instead of leaving your cell phone sitting on your table or casually texting in public, keep it protected or hidden. Too often, Khmers will snatch it out of your hand.

Get a Walking Beer

When in Rome! There are no 'open carry' laws here so feel free to crack open a cold one as you peruse the night markets or walk along the beach.

Refer to Cambodians as Khmers

You'll hear this word a lot. Khmer (Ka-Mair) people speak Khmer (Ka-My) language. The same spelling but a different pronunciation. Now you know!

Don't...

Wear Bikinis in Public

I know you're on vacation, but Khmers are not. Save your banging bod for the beach or the pool and cover up while you walk around town.

Tip Taxis or Servers

I mean, you can if you want to. But typically, Khmers don't tip. In some situations, tipping is actually quite awkward.

Touch a Monk

No one- not me, not you, not the Pope- can touch a monk. No handshakes, no selfies, and no hugs.

Walk Alone at Night

In the recent years, Cambodia has seen a spike in petty theft. In Phnom Penh, be aware of Cambodians on motorbikes that wait to follow you and grab your purse. It's best not to carry a purse at all.

Activities to Avoid in Cambodia

You don't know what you don't know. Here's some quick insight into responsible tourism in The Bode.

Volunteering at an Orphanage

A rule of thumb for Cambodia: If an organization allows strangers to come and play with their children, then this organization does not have the children's best intentions at heart.

The "volun-tourism" industry in Cambodia is booming. Kind-hearted tourists and travelers visit Cambodia with good intentions set on helping disadvantaged children, women, and youth.

Knowing that there is essentially a market for kind hearts, dark and twisted "charities" and "orphanages" have been popping up all over the third and developing world. These organizations pose as orphanages, filling their beds with children who have literally been rented from their families, but are nothing more than money-making schemes. In fact, the standard estimate is that 70% of these children have at least 1 parent who is alive and capable of care. These children are not orphans, they are rented props living in Child Zoos.

So, while you believe that you are teaching English, helping the orphanage build a well, or spending time with abandoned babies…what is actually happening is that you are feeding an industry that exploits children for profit.

You must be very very careful when choosing where to volunteer. As a rule of thumb, avoid ANY organization that offers you the change to "play with the kids."

If you still want to volunteer, there is a respected and transparent organization called **CHOICE** which provides resources to Cambodia's poorest communities. When you volunteer with CHOICE, you'll join in on a village trip where you'll collect water and food and then deliver these resources to villages in need.

There will not be any Facebook photos or opportunities to play with the kids. Instead, you'll contribute in a sustainable and impactful way with $15 donation to the organization and leave with an insight into the true status of poverty in South East Asia and what the world can do to help.

For more volunteer opportunities, check out the Volunteer Section for some fabulous volunteer opportunities around Cambodia!

Getting Tattoos of Buddha

Buddha is sacred in these parts. So much so, that in nearby Myanmar, a backpacker was once jailed for having a tattoo of Buddha. That is quite unlikely to happen to you in Cambodia, but it goes to show how disrespectful it is.

Riding Elephants

What may seem like a 'Bucket List' activity is actually an industry bred out of animal cruelty and torture. Instead of riding elephants, find an elephant sanctuary that allows you to feed, trek and bathe in the river with elephants rescued from the circus, work camps and elephant riding tourist centers around Cambodia. Check out the elephant sanctuary, EVP, in Mondulkiri or visit nearby Thailand which has plenty of amazing Elephant Sanctuaries throughout the country. Check out the Thailand section of this book for more info.

Visiting Tiger Temples

Those cute baby tigers that you're about to take a photo with…do you ever wonder where they come from? Tigers are essentially farmed, taken from their mothers at 2 weeks old, and given to tourists to bottle feed. And that's only the beginning…

Fun Cambo Fact
The local language is called "Khmer" – pronounced "Ka-My."

Some Tips Before You Go!

Bring US Dollars

Cambodia uses two currencies: the US Dollar and the Cambodian Riel. You can use them interchangeably.

Learn to Count Riel

...because while you may but a beer with a $10 US bill, it's likely that you'll get your change in Riel. Think of it as the paper version of coins.

Carry Small Bills

Tuk Tuk drivers can't (or will pretend like they can't) break a $10 or $20. Always have $5s and $1s on you.

Have a Shawl Within Reach

For cold bus rides and modest temples, you'll find yourself grabbing your shawl or scarf often. Don't have one? You can buy a gorgeous scarf in Cambodia for cheap. Just get one sooner rather than later.

Get a SIM Card

While internet around Cambodia isn't too reliable, mobile data plans are! With service available on remote islands, 4G is a lifesaver. I use two companies: 'Smart' and 'Metfone'- they've got the most comprehensive coverage around the country. SIM Cards are available starting at $5 USD. You can find a kiosk outside any airport...or literally everywhere in town.

Wear Bug Spray on the Beach

Sand flies are all too common. They love to nibble your ankles when you walk- any time of day.

Ok! You're all set for an epic adventure! Shall we?

Chapter 11: Phnom Penh

To understand Phnom Penh, you must first understand its history. Not long ago, in the 1970s, Cambodia suffered extreme genocide by the hands of a vicious regime called the Khmer Rouge. A regime based in Phnom Penh.

The Khmer Rouge sought to eradicate the population of anyone who was intelligent, educated, international, or could be considered "free thinkers." You see, if they killed all the men wearing glasses and all the teenagers who spoke English, it would be easier to indoctrinate the leftover population with their beliefs.

So, for 4 years, the Khmer Rouge terrorized a nation, took over a capitol city, and a committed genocide on a population. In 1979, when the Khmer Rouge fell, over 2 million people had been killed. This was only 40 years ago. This is a country and city that is still rebuilding, a population that is still recovering and a nation that is rebuilding their national identity.

When you visit Phnom Penh, understand that part of the package is learning about this brutal history. There are museums and landmarks that will truly change your world perspective.

But don't worry, your visit to Phnom Penh won't be heavy the whole time; there are fun things to do here, too. This is the city of rooftop pools. Nearly every standard hotel has one, guaranteeing you to leave with a tan. There are also markets, shops, and an amazing mix of international food. I recommend spending 2 or 3 days in Phnom Penh. That is enough time to soak up the history and have a few great meals before moving on.

From the Airport into Town

Okay- let's get you into Phnom Penh!

For an international airport, Phnom Penh Airport is quite small and easy to navigate. There's one arrival hall, one immigration check point and one main exit. Easy peasy.

Option 1: Hire a Car to Pick you Up

My favorite option! Have a car waiting for you at the airport with your cute lil' name on a sign.

Where: They'll be waiting for you right when you exit the airport.
How Much: $15 or less

You can use Skype Credit or get a SIM card to call one of my taxi guys (I've spent countless hours driving with these professional dudes).

Mr. La
Phone Number: 0885464432 / 098 63 58 71
Area & Route: Sihanoukville to Phnom Penh (and within these cities)

Mr. Dara
Phone Number: 0777 77 20 21 / 017 89 19 81
Area & Route: Kampot to Phnom Penh (and within these cities)

OR visit the Facebook **Page 'Taxi Share Cambodia'** to wrangle an English-speaking taxi driver in no time OR share a taxi with another traveler (especially if you want to go straight from Phnom Penh to another city).

Option 2: Grab Taxi

All you need to do is buy a SIM card outside the airport ($5), fire it up and order your car. Grab Taxi is just like Uber and will be life savers during your trip in Phnom Penh.

Where: At the arrivals gate, right when you exit the airport.
How Much: Typically $15 or less

Option 3: Jump in a Tuk Tuk

Start your trip off with some excitement as your Tuk Tuk weaves around traffic and bounces over potholes. This is a fun option for someone who is traveling with a backpack that is easy to hold along the way.

Where: Walk through the parking lot and exit the airport. There will be Tuk Tuks lined around the perimeter, having just dropped off other guests.
How Much: $5-$8

~Airport Pro Tips~

❖ I wouldn't recommend hiring a Taxi or Tuk Tuk from the tourist stands inside the airport- their prices tend to be higher.
❖ There will be taxi drivers that approach you the second you step outside of the airport. They'll be offering you rides. Rides that start at pretty expensive prices. If you can haggle them down to the prices that you've read about here today, there's no harm in driving with these guys.
❖ A public bus does exist but girl, it's slow and old and just not worth it.

Areas to Explore in PP

BKK

Spas. Western food. Nightlife. Expats. Tourists. Hostels. Get the picture? Split into 3 sections: BKK1, BKK2, and BKK3 – BKK is the most modern district in Phnom Penh. You'll find all the comforts of home here but with an international twist. BKK encompasses what it's like to live abroad in Phnom Penh's melting pot district with a community of expats from around the world. With this comes Salsa nights, Trivia nights, live DJ dance parties, and an abundance of eclectic bars. Stay in this area to be close to all the action.

Riverside

Phnom Penh's Sisowath Quay Boardwalk lights up at night while vendors stroll along selling beers and snacks. Have a seat on a park bench and watch the boats come in while you drink and eat. Kids will come along to collect your cans. Locals will bring picnics and a straw mat where they'll feast on local dishes. Right across the road, the main street is lined with international bars and restaurants and nearby are some of Phnom Penh's main attractions such as the Royal Palace and National Museum.

Russian Market

Also known as Toul Tom Poung in Khmer, the Russian Market District is worth a visit. While the epicenter of this area is obviously a large market selling mostly fabrics - the area surrounding the market offers a beautiful blend between old and new. The market is surrounded by food! Eat grilled meat from a roadside BBQ cart or pop into KFC to experience Cambodia's love for the colonel. Stop by a family-run shop for some instant coffee or kick your feet up at a trendy café. This is a fun area to aimlessly explore.

Prek Leap

Outside the international hustle and bustle is Prek Leap- a district where you'll find more locals, lots of Khmer food and karaoke for days! Silk Island is close by, as is the ferry terminal for any Mekong trips. You can find lots of cheap guest houses and even cheaper food around this old school district.

244

Accommodation in Phnom Penh

Mad Monkey Hostel $

Mad Monkey has their shit together. Need to book a bus? Reception will do it for you. Need to extend your visa? Let them handle it Want to go on an ATV tour through Khmer villages? Of course, they do that, too. Mad Monkey makes every part of your stay so smooth- including making friends. Join the Sunset BBQ on Thursdays, Keg Parties on Sundays, Pub Crawls on Fridays and happy hour every night.

Style: Dorms & Privates
Starts at: $30 USD
Where: BKK
Address: No. 3, Off Street 310

Sla Boutique Hostel $

When you're in a social mood...but not a party mood, Sla Boutique Hostel is the best place to meet other travelers with whom you can enjoy yummy food and good conversation. Venture out with you new pals to explore the area. The Royal Palace, riverside boardwalk, and a plethora of massage parlors are only 900 meters away. And there's nothing like coming back to a quiet dorm with crisp clean sheets after a hot day of sight-seeing.

Style: Dorms & Privates
Starts at: $15 USD
Where: Riverside
Address: No. 15, Street 174, Daun Penh

VS Sweet Home $

A one stop shop for happiness and hospitality. This homestay tucked away on the perimeter of Phnom Penh will give you the warm and fuzzies. Spend your days riding around town with the owner who will give you a personal city tour for half the price of a hired taxi. Then come home to chill out on the rooftop with a few cold beers. And just like mom and dad, your hosts will drive you to the airport or bus station to see you off.

Style: Privates
Starts at: $25 USD
Where: North of the Russian Market
Address: 245 Lumstreet, khlang Sang, Russey Keo

The Pavilion $$

For $100 a night, you can get a gorgeous room with…A PRIVATE POOL. Go skinny dipping. No tan lines here! Or if you want to save a couple bucks, the opulent hotel pool lined with overhanging palm trees and full bar service doesn't suck either. This French Colonial property offers a papered oasis away from the hustle and bustle of city life. The cherry on top of your quiet ice cream Sunday? No children allowed.

Style: Privates
Starts at: $76
Where: Riverside
Address: St 19, No. 227, Daun Penh

Diamond Palace Resort & Skybar $$

My go-to hotel every time I visit Phnom Penh, Diamond Palace is offers clean & modern rooms with fabulous room service, a secure safe for your valuables, a generous buffet breakfast…and best of all, a full-service rooftop pool. Everything a girl could want! When you want to venture out, you're just a 3-minute walk to Bassac Lane (308 Street) which is a trendy little alley lined with hole-in-the-wall bars and restaurants offering fare from around the world. **Ps.** Don't confuse Diamond Palace Resort with Diamond Hotel. Two totally different spots.

Style: Privates
Starts at: $30 USD

Where: BKK
Address: No. 3, Off Street 310

Aquarius Hotel and Urban Resort $$

What the rooms lack in flair, the infinity pool overlooking the city certainly makes up for in brilliance. Aquarius has the best pool in the entire city with cushions for sun tanning, big umbrellas for reading, poolside service for being lazy and a see-through pool wall for America's Next Top Model – style photos. To round out the perfect hotel stay, expect gourmet food, professional staff and super comfortable beds.

Style: Privates
Starts at: $55 USD
Where: Riverside
Address: #5A Street 240, Daun Penh

The Bale Phnom Penh Resort $$$

Fab-U-Lous. This resort would easily cost $700 bucks a night back in the good ol' USA. But because…Cambodia…you can stay in the lap of luxury for a fraction of the price. With only 18 rooms in the entire resort, prepare to be doted on like a queen. Spend your days at the pristine pool lined with palm trees overlooking the Mekong River, have a soak in your Jacuzzi tub, and wander the property adorned with stunning Buddha statues everywhere you look. This place is zen as fuck. **Ps.** For a balance of lavish life and local experience, take a day trip across the river to Koh Dach.

Style: Chic Privates
Starts at: $200 USD
Where: 13km North of the City Center – Riverside across from Koh Dach
Address: National Road 6A, Bridge No. 8 Sangkat Bak Khaeng

Where to Eat in Phnom Penh

ST. 63 Bassac Restaurant

White table cloth venue with upscale Khmer dishes & chilled bottles of wine in a breezy outdoor setting amongst tropical plants with top-notch service...and I haven't even told you the best part yet. This place is street-food level cheap! I don't know how this family-run restaurant gets away with charging $3 for Pumpkin Curry but I'm not complaining.

Open: Monday-Saturday 11am-11pm
How to Get There: Drop you off at St. 308 and go straight down the alley until you see a residential style property on your right.
Address: 308 St. | Just 4 doors north of 294 St.

Daughters of Cambodia

The sex trade in Cambodia is still very active. For the lucky women and children who escape, rehabilitation is Step 1 to creating a new life. Helping these women liberate themselves, Daughters of Cambodia Restaurant offers jobs and training to former sex trafficking victims. When you eat here, you can Ffeel good in your heart and in your tummy. Have a fresh salad, some crisp fish and chips, and take some pastries to go. The food is definitely on point here.

Open: Monday-Saturday 9am – 5:30pm
Where: The Riverside
Address: 321 Sisowath Quay

David's Noodle Restaurant

The freshest noodles you've ever had. They are literally made right in front of your eyes! Enjoy artisan dumplings and noodles from scratch when you dine at David's Restaurant in Phnom Penh. Try the Dumpling Soup. One bite and you'll understand why locals and visitors alike end up eating here 3-4 times per week.

Open: Everyday 10am-10pm
Where: Near the Royal Palace
Address: No. 213, 13 Preah Ang Eng St. (13)

Katy Peri's Peri Peri Chicken and Pizza

What a name. What a concept. A wood-fire pizza oven built into a Tuk Tuk that travels around Phnom Penh serving pizza to the masses. Pizza so good that this oven on wheels is legendary in Phnom Penh and has amassed a loyal following. Starting at $2.50 for a Margherita pizza, it's easy to fall in love and lust with these sexy pies.

Open Hours: 9:30 - Late
How to Get There: Take a Pass App!
Address: Daily on Street 51, Corner 172 / Monday + Thursday at Showbox Bar

The Sushi Bar 1 BKK

Sushi? In Phnom Penh? I used to be skeptical, too but I love this place. Every time I go in, it's filled with Japanese patrons sipping on Miso Soup and scarfing down large sushi platters with nigiri and generous rolls. Prices are cheap and portions are enough to fill you up. While the sushi isn't out of this world amazing- it certainly hits the spot. Also, expect a 10% service charge. It's stupid but if you know beforehand, you're less likely to be annoyed when you get your bill.

Open: Everyday 11am-10pm
Where: BKK 1 – up the road from Mad Monkey
Address: 2D, Street 302 (Use Mad Monkey as your starting point)

D2 Smokehouse

What do you get when you give a country boy from South Carolina full access to amazing cuts of locally sourced pork, chicken wings, market fresh produce, and an offset barrel smoker? Answer: some mighty fine, melt in your mouth comfort food with all the fixins.

Open: Tuesday-Sunday 11am-8:30pm
Where: The Food Village
Address: Phum Dong St 160

Second Location: Crossfit YiQi
Open: Mon-Sat 11am - 8:30pm
Where: 16 Street 352, Between St 51 and St 57

Phnom Penh India

If you've never had true Indian Curry, now is your chance- in Cambodia, of all places. Praise the curry gods for the Indian community in Phnom Penh that has given us Phnom Penh India, a cute little restaurant with views of the river. Order the Butter Chicken with Garlic Nan for a massive life changer. Best of all, you can order an all 3-course meal for two people and walk away spending around $20. So worth it.

Open: Everyday 9am-11pm
Where: Riverside
Address: 335 Sisowath | Phnom Peng

Sights & History in Phnom Penh

Pro Tip
To see these sights, hire a Tuk Tuk for the day

Remember to dress appropriately for Buddhist temples and royal palaces. Women must cover their knees and shoulders. Men should wear shirts with sleeves and shorts that aren't too short.

The Killing Fields
The Killing Fields are emotional and for some, downright gut wrenching- but to truly understand Cambodia's history, you need to witness the Khmer Rouge's heinous acts with your own eyes.

While there are many killing fields all over the country, this particular killing field in Phnom Penh is one of the most significant. This is where hundreds of thousands of men, women, and children were murdered by the hands of Khmer Rouge soldiers. Their limp bodies were then thrown in massive graves, dubbed The Killing Fields, where their bones still remain today.

During your visit to The Killing Fields, you'll wear a headset that will guide you through a paved walkway with numbered markers. The headset will narrate the history of this site at each marker, including personal stories from survivors. Walk silently and respectfully as you take it all in.

The Tuol Sleng Genocide Museum - S21 Prison
When the Khmer Rouge took power in Phnom Penh, they converted a local high school into a torture prison. During their 4 years of terror, 14,000 civilians entered Tuol Sleng and only 7 walked out alive.

Today, you can visit the prison which has been converted into a museum. You'll walk through the prison, past photo exhibitions and preserved torture chambers, giving you an intense understanding of the crimes committed here.

The Silver Pagoda
The glittering <u>golden</u> roof of the Silver Pagoda might have you confused by its name. Get a little bit closer and you'll discover that the floor is covered in 5,000 glossy silver tiles. Keep exploring up the grand staircase to find the Temple of the Emerald Buddha, covered in 2086 glittering diamonds, sitting next to an 80kg bronze Buddha, a silver-gold Buddha and a totally pure gold Buddha - each with a fascinating tale to tell.

You can easily visit these next two places on your own

251

The National Museum

This 1920's – inspired Khmer building glitters in the sun with a golden roof and intricate detail. Head inside for a deep dive into Khmer culture with ancient artifacts from the 1600s, accolades of Cambodian warriors, photo exhibitions of modern day farming and more.

How Much: $5-$10, depending on whether you opt for the audio guide to take you through the museum.
Open: Everyday 8am – 5pm
Where: Riverside
Address: Preah Ang Eng St. (13)

The Royal Palace

Since the 1860s, this riverside property has served as the royal residence in Phnom Penh (minus the brief period of abandonment during the reign of the Khmer Rouge). Opulent and awe-inspiring, come have a stroll through the gardens and learn about Cambodia's royal family throughout history.

How Much: $6.50 solo - $10 with a guide
Open: Everyday 8am – 10:30am / 2pm – 5pm
Where: Riverside
Address: Samdach Sothearos Blvd (3)

Off the Beaten Path- Elephant Adventure

There is just one ethical elephant park in Cambodia! While it is nowhere near Phnom Penh...a 6-hour bust via Phnom Penh is the best way to get to Mondulkiri, Cambodia.

Take a 2-day, 3-day, or 1-week detour from the typical Cambodia tourist path and volunteer at the Elephant Valley Project in Senmonorom. Home to 10 elephants on 1,500 hectares of forest, rivers, grassland, and bamboo groves – Elephant Valley Project is the largest elephant sanctuary in Asia! Here, the elephants roam freely in their natural habitat, playing in mud, bathing in the river and roaming the grounds.

When you visit, trek through the forest while shadowing two elephant families and learning about their incredible and saddening stories – and then you'll dine on a traditional Khmer lunch buffet.

Not only does your visit and contribution help protect the animals, but it also goes towards empowering the community. EVP pays for over 300 children to go to school and takes care of literally thousands of local people's health care while also providing jobs. It's a community effort to support and protect these animals, something that you have the opportunity to be part of, as well.

Check out their website and you'll see all the different kinds of visits they offer: day trips, overnight trips, and volunteer opportunities for 1 week or more.

Starting at: $95 USD
How to Get There: 6-hour Bus. When you book, EVP will guide you through the process of how to make it from Phnom Penh to Mondulkiri.

Fun Fact: Mondulkiri is home to the tallest waterfall in Asia and there is a Zip Line that goes over this waterfall! Head to EVP before the waterfall to grab a 15% off zipline voucher!

Fun Cambo Fact
5 hours north of Phnom Penh, you can find dolphins swimming in the Mekong Rive. Visit the town of Kratie for a closer look.

Shopping in Phnom Penh

The Old Market
Set your alarm! Vendors start the day's trade at 5am! The Old Market (aka Phsar Chas) is a traditional Cambodian market popular for its produce. In other words, here is where you try all the exotic fruit you've never heard of like jackfruit and mangosteen.

The Russian Market
As you walk around Phnom Penh, tuk tuk drivers will shout at you while offering a ride to the Russian Market. It's just that popular. While it's called "The Russian Market," you won't find many Russians or Russian-culture here. While this area was popular with Russian expats back in the 1980s, today you can expect to find Cambodian souvenirs like silk scarves, chess boards, exotic oils, and more.

Central Market
Knock-off NBA jerseys, cute clothes for your niece and nephew, wooden statues of the most random shit…it's all here. To fuel your hour-long search through the Central Market, there is row after row of a variety of food stalls hawking soups, fried bugs, fresh fruit and meat on a stick. This experience is truly Khmer.

The Olympic Market
Three floor levels of colorful fabrics, soft silk and gorgeous lace! The Olympic Market is a fabulous place to have curtain, bed sheets, or table cloths made. These tailors know what they're doing and can give you advice while you're trying to pick a fabric for your project.

When it comes to clothing, however, remember that these people are tailors, not designers. While they make custom men's suits that fit like a glove and are 1/4 of the price compared to back home…women's clothes are not their forte. Don't even try to get a simple dress made. Pants, maybe. Everything else, nah.

Phnom Penh Night Market
After a long day of exploring the city, you'll be ready to eat! Just like any fabulous night market, you'll find all the Cambodian staples: hot soups, deep-fried seafood, dried fruit, grilled meat on sticks, fruit shakes and noodles in every form. The market has a little section with plastic tables and chairs where you can lay out all of your dishes and feast.

Phnom Penh Night Life

Pub Street

As with any pub street around the world, weekends tend to be crazier than weekdays. On Pub Street, you get a collection of local expats and travelers who crowd into popular bars like Top Banana where draft beer is $1 and appetizers are $3. This small stretch of street is enough to keep any traveler entertained for a long evening out.

Bassac Lane (Street 308)

Bassac Lane is a picturesque little street lined with upscale bars, dive restaurants, and gourmet eateries. Jetting off from Bassac Lane, you'll find a winding little alley with a collection of hole-in-the-wall bars that cater to both a Khmer and Western clientele. Hop from one spot to another on foot until the night is through.

Street 51

Heart of Darkness, Shanghai, White Cobra, Black Cat…with names like these, you can probably guess that these bars aren't playing around. They take cocktails and atmosphere to the next level with quirky décor and gorgeous drinks. Once your buzz kicks in, wander Street 51 where you'll find night clubs, Billiard bars, and the widely popular Walkabout Hotel Bar and Restaurant which is open 24/7. This is a fun street for people watching, partying, and drunk eating.

Showbox

This expat-friendly pub is serves as a laid back venue for live music, trivia nights, Bingo, and a general drinking spot all week long. Open mic night is on Wednesday, live music performances on Friday and Sunday, and Katy Peri's Pizza draws in crowds on Monday and Thursday. Show up, have a seat at the bar, join in on the festivities and you're sure to make a couple friends by the end of the night!

How to Get Around Phnom Penh

PassApp

PassApp is Phnom Penh's version of Uber and it's the safest way to travel in the city. Taking away the headache of navigation and haggling a price, just type in your destination and go. Pay in cash. Most trips are less than $1 on PassApp. Oh and there's a fun part! Instead of a car, you'll be picked up in a cute little Indian-style rickshaw!

Pro Tip: You'll need an international phone number or a Cambodian Sim card to work with this app. Make sure you pick one up ASAP.

Tuk Tuks

Tuk Tuk drivers are everywhere! Flag one down and for $2-$5, they'll take you where you need to go. Find one that speaks a decent amount of English? Take his number down for future trips! You can also hire a Tuk Tuk driver for an entire day or half day to take you sightseeing around the city (for usually $20). Just be sure to keep your bags and phones close or concealed in the tuk tuk- otherwise it might get snatched in traffic.

Walk

During the day, you're safe to walk around the markets, along the riverside, and down the main roads of BKK. At night, however, refrain from walking at all costs (other than the riverside area – just hold your purse tight). Take a Tuk Tuk or a PassApp, instead.

Private Taxi

Long distance or full-day tours can be way more comfortable in an air-conditioned Lexus SUV, rather than a bumpy bus. Check out the driver directory at the end of the Cambodia section.

Crime & Safety in Phnom Penh

Petty Theft is Widespread

Stealing phones and purses- that the specialty of thieves in Phnom Penh. But don't let this whole theft thing freak you out BECAUSE thieves look for travelers who have their guard down. They look for the easiest targets possible because even thieves are lazy. You're already reading this which means that you've lowered the chances that you'll become a victim.

<u>Watch out for these Thievery Tactics</u>

Tactic: Motorbikes following you at night
What to Do: Make eye contact, give them a bitch face and tell them to go away. Talk to them, let them know that you see them. Many times the thieves are kids. Confrontation is enough to fend them off.

Tactic: Swooping a phone out of a texter's hands
What to Do: Text on your phone like your sexting at the dinner table. Hide it so that it is difficult to see.

Tactic: Reaching inside of the Tuk Tuk and driving off with your bag
What to Do: Keep your purse behind your body in the Tuk Tuk and physically clip your larger bags to the Tuk Tuk.

Chapter 12: Siem Reap

Angkor Wat is the ultimate Bucketlist destination, and it's located right here in Siem Reap! A pillar of Cambodian culture and history, Angkor Wat is the world's largest religious monument, covering an area of 162.6 hectares, just waiting to be explore.

Outside of the mystifying Angkor Wat temple tours, this ancient city is teeming with culture, food, and outdoor adventures. Learn how to use local ingredients in a Khmer cooking class, take a walk through history with war museums, go on a bicycle ride through rural villages, and when your brain has had enough stimulation, wander pub street and mingle with other travelers.

You can see how easy it is to spend a full week in Siem Reap and never run out of things to do. Furthermore, the selection of modern hotels and hostels is fabulous. Some of the best hotels in Southeast Asia can be found in Siem Reap and the same goes for the food. Keep reading and you'll see what I mean…

From the Airport in Siem Reap

The Siem Reap airport is quite tiny! And surprisingly well organized for an operation of its size. This means that you can get usually in and out of the airport at lightening speed and can start the short 7km journey into town sooner rather than later.

Now, what to do once you're out of arrivals….

Option 1: Taxi on Arrival

Where: When you exit the airport, you'll see a taxi stand where you can arrange your ride.
 ❖ There are regular 4-person taxis and 6+ person taxi vans available.

How Much: $9 for a Van Taxi and $10 for a Regular Taxi (they run on price per meter + the car's size).

Option 2: Tuk Tuk on Arrival

Siem Reap is full of Tuk Tuk drivers that go to and from the airport all day long. They do not work for the airport so you're able to get a cheaper rate.

Where: Walk outside of the airport and pass the taxi stand (ignoring anyone trying to sell you a taxi ride). Continue walking through the parking lot until you exit. There will be plenty of public tuk tuks waiting to give you a ride.

 ❖ Tuk Tuks can fit up to 4 people – as long as you don't have an obscene amount of luggage.
How Much: You can haggle your price between $4-6.

Pro Tip: Any tuk tuk driver directly outside of the airport works for the airport. Their price will be higher and they have a reputation of always trying to sell you Angkor Wat Tours at an inflated price. They're fine for a 1-way journey. Just don't make further plans with them.

Option 3: Motorbike on Arrival

For just one person carrying a backpack, this is a cheap & fun option.

Where: The same spot where you'll find the tuk tuk drivers. Walk outside of the airport and pass the taxi stand (ignoring anyone trying to sell you a taxi ride). Continue walking through the parking lot until you exit. These guys are plainly dressed. Nothing to be alarmed by.
How Much: You can haggle your price between $2-$4

Pro Tip: Don't wear your purse or handbag loosely as you ride- it can be snatched. Instead, wear it on the front of your body, across your chest.

Option 4: Arrange Pick-Up Before

Save yourself the hassle of explaining where you're going or haggling prices. Have transportation waiting for you at the airport.

How: Ask your hotel about pick-up services or arrange pick-up with a local Tuk Tuk driver 1-2 days before.

How Much: Hotels will usually charge around $7 or $8 while private Tuk Tuks charge $5 or $6

Areas to Explore in Siem Reap

Old Market

Old Market refers to both the actual market (Psar Chaa) and the busy area that surrounds it. Most people stay in the Old Market area when they visit Siem Reap because it's convenient and where all the action is. This area is full of hotels, within walking distance to a variety of markets and has all of the western amenities that you need!

Pub Street

Imagine a walking street lines with neon lights, clubs, food trucks, bucket drinks and massage parlors – and now you've got Pub Street. Well-lit and filled with people from every walk of life, Pub Street is a fun place to hang out when the sun goes down. Eat, drink, get massaged, and do some shopping in the mini market filled with scarves and souvenirs.

Pub Street is not only an entertaining place to hang out, it's also used as the main point of reference in Siem Reap. Your hotel might be "North of Pub Street" or the restaurant "2 steets down from Pub Street," so it's useful to be familiar with this area!

Alley West

Just to the west of the Old Market is this artsy little street lined with cute cafes and charitable handicraft stores. This area is more modern with refurbished buildings and European accents. It's a great place for shopping and eating…but also for some stunning photography.

Wat Bo Road and Surrounding Area

Just across the river is Wat Bo Road – an area with trendy restaurants, classy bars, yummy cafes, upscale Khmer food, and local shops. Tucked away from the party vibes of Pub Street, sleeping on this side of the river ensures a bit more peace and quiet. You'll find nice hotels over where catering to an older crowd.

Accommodation in Siem Reap

Onederz Hostel $

Pool party time! Everyone at Onederz Hostel is there for the same 2 reasons: to visit Angkor Wat and to socialize with people from around the world. If you're traveling solo, don't hesitate to throw yourself in the mix. The hostel is brand new with 1 ground level pool and 1 rooftop pool with sunset views. The beds are comfy, lockers are secure, and staff are super helpful when you need to book a tour or transportation.

Style: Dorms & Privates
Starting at: $8.50 USD
Where: Right next to Angkor Night Market
Address: Corner of Taphul Road & Angkor Night Market Street

Boutique Dormitory Kochi-ke $

Take a trip to Japan for the night. I accidently booked this Japanese hostel for 1 night and it was the best mistake ever! Almost all of the customers are Japanese and if you know anything about the Japanese, they are ultra polite and extra considerate. Listen to them quietly chatter in Japanese and watch them respectfully bow when they walk past you. And at night, the dorm rooms are silent so you can drift to sleep in your cozy little pod-style bed.
Bonus: Kochi-ke has all-female dorm rooms!

Style: Pod Dorms & Privates
Starting at: $3 USD
Where: Just east of Pub Street- central location

Address: Between Sok San Road and Artisan'd Angkor

Indochine D'Angkor $

Luxury on a budget, here's is a hotel where you can pamper yourself in a cabana by the pool surrounded by lush green trees and tall bamboo walls. Bright red, orange, and gold everywhere you look, the hotel is decorated in traditional Khmer style! Every room has a balcony to breathe in the morning air and each bathroom has a rain shower nozzle for the most soul-cleansing experience! Just 15 minutes from pub street, Indochine D'Angkor is the perfect balance of city and sanctuary.

Style: Privates
Starting at: $20 USD
Where: 15 minutes east of Pub Street- Tuk Tuks can transport you for $2
Address: Street 27, Wat Bo Village

S Hotel Siem Reap $$

Free fish spa and a free 60 minute massage! Are you really going to pass that up? What are they compensating for, you may wonder? Surprisingly…nothing. The pool is surrounded by a lush green garden with pool boys who bring you fresh towels and drinks, the rooms are big and bright with a complimentary basket of fresh fruit, and the location is fabulous. Go go go.
Style: Privates
Starting at: $30 USD
Where: 5 minute walk to Pub Street & Angkor Night Market
Address: Artisan D' Angkor road, Phum Steung Thmey

Cambana d'Angkor Suites $$

After a day of sightseeing in the heat, come back to your own personal oasis at this intimate boutique hotel. A wonderland of elephant carvings, vibrant historical paintings and tall green jungle foliage really makes you feel like you're in Cambodia, while the modern amenities immediately transfer you into vacation mode. Swim in the pool, have a cappuccino in the café and enjoy the smiles and care of the super attentive, English-speaking Khmer staff.

Style: Privates
Starting at: $60 USD
Where: Next to Khmer Pub Lane
Address: Road No. 6, Salakanseng Village

FCC Angkor $$$

Treat yo self, girl. FCC is one classy joint. You'll be treated like royalty the moment you check in. Take a dip in the glamorous pool and have a soak in the spacious bath tub. Enjoy room service eaten on your private terrace or hit the restaurant for some of the best eats in Siem Reap. And while this place may be fancy, beer on tap is still around $2 per pint. Heads up, this place isn't walking distance to the market or Pub Street, BUT they've got a Tuk Tuk on staff to drop you off wherever you need to go.

Style: Privates
Starting at: $120 USD
Where: Next to the River & Royal Gardens – 7 minute Tuk Tuk to Pub Street
Address: Pokambor Ave

Where to Eat in Siem Reap

Fresh Fruit Factory

Make a **breakfast reservation** online (a few days in advance) to take a bite out of this colorful café. Passion Fruit Pancakes, Mango French Toast, Smoothie Bowls and the famous Ice Mountain topped with whichever fresh fruit speaks to your taste buds. Here, you can eat super clean! Clean, fresh fruit from Cambodia, clean kitchen, and clean water give you peace of mind for your tummy's first few days abroad.

Open: Tuesday-Sunday 11am – 8pm
Where: Next to the Angkor National Museum
Address: #155 Taphul Road

The Missing Socks Laundry Café

I love this place for breakfast, brunch & lunch. It's all about the waffles. Order classic waffles with bacon and eggs or step outside the bun with a waffle burger. Every plate is perfection. Don't worry if you slop on yourself, this place is also a laundry mat. Get your clothes cleaned while you sip on an artisan coffee. You'll leave a clean and caffeinated woman!

Open: Daily 7am-7pm
Where: East of Pub Street by S Hotel and Kochi-ke hostel.
Address: #55 Steung Tmey Village

Mahob Khmer Cuisine

Cambodian Food at it's finest! Here, the Khmer chef and restaurateur utilizes quintessential Asian ingredients to elevate classic Khmer dishes to modern works of culinary art. Local clams with tamarind sauce, slow braised ox tail, deep fried frog legs- you'll never truly understand Khmer cuisine until you dine at Mahob. The entire experience is set in a traditional wooden Khmer house on stilts with lush greenery all around you. So sublime.

Open: Daily 11:30am -10:30pm
Where: North of the Night Market
Address: River Rd, Krong

Love U Restaurant

If you've ever wanted to know what it feels like to eat a home-cooked meal in a Khmer kitchen, Love U Restaurant will give you a pretty good idea. This genuine Khmer dining experience represent how locals eat and cook at home- but with a little extra attention to presentation. Popular dishes to order are Khmer Chicken Curry, Chicken Amok and Beef Lok Lak. Prices are cheap and hospitality is unlimited.
Open: Daily 10am-10pm
Where: Across the river, opposite of La Niche d'Angkor Boutique
Address: Street 27, Wat Bo Road

Marum

When in Siem Reap…eat ants. At Marum, the most popular dish is Red Tree Ants with Beef, Kaffir Lime & Chili Stir Fry. Each plate is big enough for 1-2 to share in the experience. Besides having an awesome menu, Marum is also an NGO with an awesome cause: to give free hospitality and culinary training to students. You'll walk away from this meal feeling satisfied in more ways than one.

Open: Daily 11am-11pm
Where: Next to the Angkor National Museum
Address: #8A,B Phum Slor Kram

Street Food

South East Asia is all about the street food! Where vendors load their ingredients into carts to feed the working class, this is one of the most authentic ways to experience local cuisine. Visit the Old Market for some spring rolls or try some ice cream made on the spot with cold-plate food carts outside of Pub Street.

Pro Tip

Street Food in Cambodia can be sketchier than in Thailand or Malaysia. Outside of the two street food areas above, eat with caution. If you want to go on a super yummy street food tour with vendors that have been vetted for clean eats, go on the Street Food Tour with a company called **River Garden's Tour** for $25 per person.

Fun Cambo Fact

Angkor Wat means "Temple City" or "City of Temples" in Khmer.

Sights & History in Siem Reap

Cambodia Landmine Museum

Remnants of the Vietnam War are still affecting Cambodian people in the worst way possible. Hidden in the fields of Cambodia, it is estimated that 6 million landmines still remain. Hundreds, if not thousands, of Cambodians have lost limbs and lives while farming and trekking on their own land. To educate the public and help eradicate the problem, The Cambodia Landmine Museum gives tours and runs programs to help those effected while also leading initiatives to safely remove landmines today.

Open: Daily 7:30am - 5:30pm.
Where: Angkor National Park – 4 miles south of Banteay Srey Temple
How Much: $5

Angkor Centre for Conservation of Biodiversity

Animal lovers, come hither! The Angkor Centre for Conservation of Biodiversity is your chance to get up close and personal with animal species native to the region, while also supporting a great cause. The ACCB focuses on habitat preservation and species protection via breeding, rehabilitation, community education, conservation and research.

The center offers two tours during the day: one a 9am and one at 1pm. On these tours, the knowledgeable and passionate guides will explain how they rehabilitate otters, porcupines, birds and other animals so that they can be reintroduced into the wild.

Open: Monday-Saturday 8:30am – 3:30pm.
Where: Phnom Kulen National Park
How Much: $3

Visit the Temples of Angkor Wat

Don't even think about visiting Cambodia and not making it a priority to see Angkor Wat. Mesmerizing, historical, and spiritual – this is a bucket list destination that you sincerely, will never forget.

What you know as "Angkor Wat" is actually a collection of 12ᵗʰ century temples, each one built to serve a different purpose. Initially, the temples were created as a funereal temple for King Suryavarman II, each structure representing phases of life, death, and beyond. Spanning over 500 acres of land, these temples eventually morphed into an ancient city. So while you explore the temples, ducking under stone archways and climbing up weathered stone stairs, you'll actually be stepping into chambers of a civilization long forgotten.

Pro Tip #1

Hire an Angkor Wat Tour Guide! Either hire a singular guide to lead you through this stone maze while telling stories of a world that once was, or join an Angkor Wat Bicycle Tour or ATV Tour that helps you get off the beaten path. There are so many of these tours that are equally fantastic but vary in price and paths. The best way to choose which tour is right for you? Trip Advisor. Siem Reap tours run on Trip Advisor.

Pro Tip #2

The most popular time to visit Angkor Wat is at sunrise. To watch the sun creep up behind the temple is absolutely gorgeous…if the crowds aren't too big. During high season, this crowd is too much for me, personally.

I'd much rather brave the heat at noon, right when everyone is starting to go home. This way, you can explore the temple grounds with half the crowd! That's just my two cents…

Open: Daily, 5am - 6pm
Location: Angkor Archaeological Park
How much: One day $37, three days $62, five days $72.

Do's and Don'ts of Angkor Wat

Do...

Do Dress Appropriately: Angkor Wat is a religious site so cover your shoulders and knees if you want to be respectful.

Do Explore Respectfully: Believe it or not, in just the past few years, tourists have been punished for smashing ancient statues, writing on temple walls, and even having nude photo shoots. Come on, people!

Do Wear Comfortable Shoes: There is lots of walking to be done! Uneven terrain is not conducive with wedge shoes or stiff sandals. Sneakers or tennis shoes are ideal for climbing stairs and wandering for hours at a time, however, comfortable sandals or flip-flops will do the trick.

Don't...

Don't Take Souvenirs: You'd think this would be common sense, but apparently it isn't. Not only is it illegal to steal artifacts from Angkor Wat, but it is also extremely disrespectful to the spirits that locals believe still reside in this city.

Don't Explore Hung-over: This is a once in a lifetime experience! Plan accordingly. Get some good sleep the night before so that you can absorb all the history and handle all the walking.

Fun Things to Do in Siem Reap

Take a Cooking Class

Spend the morning in **Lily's Secret Garden,** a traditional Khmer kitchen where you'll use local organic ingredients to cook up a 3-course Khmer meal. For an hour and a half, you'll learn how to make authentic Khmer dishes by an English-speaking cook and teacher. At the end, you'll sit down and taste! This is a great way to meet other travelers! Plus, exotic culinary skills are possibly the best souvenirs to take home, don't ya think?

Contact: LilySecretGarden.com
Starting at: $24

Cycle Tour

With rural roads, farming villages, and the paths of Angkor Wat, you're better off exploring on two wheels. **Butterfly Tours Asia** offers several guided bicycle tours with modern gear and snacks! One of the most popular tours is the "Off the Beaten Track" tour. On this tour, you'll cycle nearly 13-miles through rural areas, giving you a glimpse into the day-to-day life of rural Cambodia. The tour lasts around 4 hours with an English-speaking guide!

Pro Tip: Bring stickers = make friends with local kids

Contact: ButterflyTours.asia
Starting at: $27

Pro Tip

It's best to visit the trails during dry season, otherwise you'll be pedaling though mud in the rainy season!

Phare: The Cambodian Circus

A mesmerizing circus with a humanitarian cause, Phare puts on a thrilling show with fire, acrobatics, and entrancing music that is worth every penny. The passionate performers are former street kids or low-income artists who receive free circus and art education by Phare. Memorable, inspirational, and charitable, this one is a MUST when visiting Siem Reap!

How Much: $38 USD
When: Daily at 7pm
Where: Phare Circus Ring Road, south of the intersection with Sok San Road
Visit **pharecircus.org** for tickets

Shopping in Siem Reap

The Old Market

"Psar Chaa" or "The Old Market" was built in the 1920's as a local market selling produce and small trinkets, and the tradition is still the same today. The Old Market is a fabulous place to try exotic Asian fruit, freshly made sausages, and dried shrimp. You'll walk past vendors sitting on straw mats, with their goods laid out around them. While most locals come here to buy in bulk, it's just as easy to buy small samples of whatever strikes your fancy.

Open: Daily 7am-10pm
Where: Two Blocks South of Pub Street

Angkor Night Market

Just a 2-minute walk from Pub Street, Angkor Night Market is a great place to do some drunk shopping! This night market has all of the quintessential Khmer handicrafts and artwork to take home like silk scarves, rings, wooden elephants- you know the drill. You'll also find lots of cute dresses, trek-worthy tank tops, and those cozy elephant pants (embrace them)!

Open: 5pm-12am
Where: North East of Pub Street

AHA's Fair Trade Village

At the AHA's Fair Trade Village, the money you spend goes directly towards the artists who sew, paint and carve all of the handicrafts sold. This non-profit market supports the local community by promoting a sustainable industry. Take home temple paintings, woven handbags, silk scarves, or delicate jewelry- rather than the mass-produced trinkets like you can find in the other markets.

Open: Monday - Friday 10am - 7pm
Where: On the road to the Temples ticket offic

Spas & Salons in Siem Reap

Lemongrass Garden

Come for the total spa treatment but leave without spending your entire travel budget! Lemongrass Garden is a professional spa that will pamper you with massages, body scrubs, facials, pedicures and waxing. Only a couple dollars more than the common street massage parlors, the services at Lemongrass Garden are worth it!

Open: Daily 11am-11pm
Where: Near Pub Street
Address: 202, Sivatha Blvd, Krong Siem Reap

Street Foot Massage

For just a quick massage after a trek or before a long bus ride, just walk down Pub Street where massage chairs line the street, waiting for you to flop down. Get a foot massage with prices ranging from $1 for 15 minutes to $5 for an hour. These spots also offer oil massages and Khmer massages on the spot and are open late.

Open: Evening - Late
Where: Pub Street

Fish Foot Spa

Stick your feet into the clear tanks filled with hungry fish that absolutely love the taste of dry skin. Instantly, they being to nibble away at those calluses, cuticles and dry soles that you've acquired while traveling. Don't worry, it doesn't hurt but it really tickles. To find these fish spas, stroll down Walking Street and you'll see dozens of fish spas offering 20 minute sessions for around $3.
Open: Evening – Late
Where: Pub Street

Siem Reap Nightlife

Pub Street

Where the magic happens! Pub Street is the main attraction in Siem Reap once the sun goes down. With bright lights and music spilling out of bars and clubs until 4am, the road itself is worth a stroll. Lined with food trucks, clothing vendors, and beer specials, this is where travelers come to let their hair down and fill up on international cuisine. You can have a low-key night here or get really wild depending on where you choose to drink. There are always Tuk Tuks waiting at the end of the road to take you home.

Temple Club

Sports fans! Come mingle with your brethren at this flat-screen lined sports bar on Pub Street. If there is a big match on, it will likely be playing. If you want to catch a specific game from home, connect with Temple Bar on Facebook and ask them to stream your team. When the game is over, you can head to the second floor to watch traditional Khmer dancers or head to the rooftop where you can melt into a bean bag chair to celebrate or mourn your team's success.

Open: Daily 10am-4am
Where: Pub Street

X Bar

Live music, fluorescent face paint, pool tables, a projector screen for the footy matches…oh and a half-pipe skate ramp on the roof: X Bar represents what is so fun about backpacking Asia. Back home, this place would never be up to code. Here, you can do whatever the hell you want. Buckets are cheap and so is the beer. Its impossible to not make a new friend here. (I can't bring myself to delete that rhyme).

Open: Daily 3pm-6am (Sunday closes at midnight)
Where: East End of Pub Street

Khmer Pub Lane

You'll most likely see "Khmer Pub Lane" on Google Maps and get curious so I might as well give you the run down now. This street is full of Karaoke Bars…aka prostitute bars. Guys come here to buy Khmer girls drinks, play pool, and take a girl home or into one of the "love hotels". If you are curious and want to peek into this world, then come take a walk or have an overpriced beer for the experience.

How to Get Around Siem Reap

Walk

Put on some comfy shoes and go explore! This relatively small city is easy to navigate and difficult to get lost.

Note: In the rainy season, roads are muddy. Don't wear anything too cute!

Tuk Tuk

Tuk Tuks are everywhere in Siem Reap! Expect to spend $1-5 to get anywhere in the city (depending on your haggling skills).

Pro Tip

As you walk around the city, Tuk Tuk drivers will be offering you tours or rides all day long. Hear one that has great English? Or see one with a genuine smile? Stop what you're doing and get their phone number. These guys are hard to find!

You don't need to make plans in the moment- but having a go-to Tuk Tuk driver will make your trip so much easier. These hard workers are just one call away when you need a ride.

Motorbike

For quick rides across the city or a ride home from the bars, you can hop on the back of a motorbike for 50 ¢ (2k Riel). You'll find these plainly-clothed dudes next to their motorbikes, usually hanging outside popular hotels and markets- waiting to give rides to tourists.

Pro Tip: While sketchy motorbike drivers are not usually a problem in Siem Reap, be cautious at night and choose to ride a Tuk Tuk driver rather than a lone man.

Rent a Bicycle

For around $2 a day, you can rent a bicycle and create your own city tour. Ride along the river, discover local restaurants down winding alleyways or take a map and go temple hunting.

Keep an eye out for guest houses that offer bikes for rent or visit **thewhitebicycles.org** for a list of places that rent bicycles with profits going to clean drinking water.

For Day Tours: Tuk Tuks & Taxis

Ready to explore Angkor Wat? Want to go on a tour of local villages? You can arrange your transportation right on the street with a Tuk Tuk driver. Want a Taxi instead? Ask a Tuk Tuk driver to connect you with a Taxi Friend (they always have a friend!). Day tours in a Tuk Tuk usually cost around $18-$20 per day. Day tours in a Taxi can run anywhere from $25-$40.

Chapter 13: Kampot

What once served as Cambodia's capitol city under French rule is now a sleepy riverside jungle town with innovative restaurants and creative hotel concepts. When you're not sipping on a cold coconut shake while swinging in a palm tree hammock, you can expect your days to be filled with adventure.

Take a kayak out on the lazy river where you can watch and listen for wildlife, drive a motorbike over red dirt paths or up to the top of the famous Bokor Mountain, or challenge yourself with rock climbing or paddle boarding. Kampot is the perfect balance of lazy days and Indiana Jones-style adventures.

All in all, Kampot is unlike any other Cambodian city you'll find. If you like natural scenery, historical discoveries and a vibrant expat community, don't skip over this hidden gem of a city.

Areas to Explore

There's more than meets the eye when it comes to exploring the tiny town of Kampot.

Kampot Town

Bus stations, pharmacies, hostels, clothing shops, motorbike rentals, western & Khmer restaurants...it's all condensed into a small city center with bustling traffic. You'll often hear people give directions using "The Durian" round about as a point of reference.

The Other Side of the River

...as the locals call it. There are a couple bridges (one for cars and one for motorbikes) that stretch over to the more jungley side of Kampot. Over here, you'll find lots of lazy riverside guesthouses, a few yummy restaurants, and Bokor Mountain.

Arcadia Backpackers

Accommodation in Kampot

Kampot is still pretty off the grid. That being said, addresses aren't really a thing over here. When you arrive in Kampot, you can tell your driver or Tuk Tuk driver the name of the place where you're staying and they'll get you there one way or another.

Karma Traders $

Confession: Karma Traders is my second home in Cambodia. The epicenter of a warm and friendly expat social circle, you are always welcome to pull up a stool at the bar and join in on the positive vibes and weird conversation. This place has never known a stranger.

There is a brand new social swimming pool on site, rooftop bar with serene sunset views over Bokor Mountain, cozy guest rooms and dorms for rest, and a collection of furry animals to be cuddled. How can you pass this up?

Try to schedule your visit to fall on Taco Tuesday where amazing musicians from around the world play as you feast on some seriously impressive tacos. Not around on Tuesdays? No worries. Enjoy happy hour everyday from 5-7pm.
Ps. Show the bartenders your copy of this book and get 1 free Joss Shot on Alexa's tab!

Style: Dorms & Privates
Starts at: $5 USD
Where: Kampot Town

The Plantation $

Not to be confused with "La Plantation", THE Plantation is a gorgeous escape into the lush jungle of Cambodia. Choose between brand new dorm rooms and private Khmer style villas where total peace, quiet, and darkness make you feel as if you're a million miles away from civilization...despite the close proximity to town. You're just a 10 minute walk to The Old Market and a 5 minute scooter ride to the other side of the river. The best of both worlds.

Also! Be on the lookout for The Plantation's brand new music venue opening soon- inviting international and locals bands to grace the stage with their presence.

Style: Dorms & Privates
Starts at: $4
Where: Kampot Town

Meraki $

Where Instagram dreams come to life- Meraki is a gorgeous riverside garden paradise with tropical flowers and plants surrounding simple, thatched-roof bungalows. Lounge in a hammock while you watch small-engine boats tug by on the water or play a game of pool with a draft beer in hand. Here is where problems melt away. Ps. These guys are super 420 friendly.

Style: Privates
Starts at: $18
Where: The Other Side of the River

Arcadia Backpackers Guesthouse $

A waterpark paradise & social guesthouse- Arcadia is legendary in Kampot. On sunny days, you'll find heaps of travelers and backpackers playing on waterslides and tanning on a floating raft on the river. On the cloudy days, there's a ping pong table, gaming system, and massive bar to keep everyone entertained. Once the sun goes down, the party really begins with beer pong, drinking games, and fun antics. They've got themed nights all week long with BBQ nights and pontoon parties- making it easy for shy people to come out of their shell and mingle!

Style: Dorms & Privates
Starts at: $7 USD
Where: The Other Side of the River

Greenhouse Bungalows

Get a taste of village life and a peek into nature when you stay at Greenhouse Bungalows, a gorgeous riverside property located a bit off the beaten path in the "Snam Prampi" village in Kampot. Choose between a riverfront bungalow where you can roll out of bed and jump in the water, or a garden bungalow where the sounds of the jungle lull you to sleep. Rent a bicycle and explore hidden waterfalls, have a picnic at the Teuk Chhou rapids, or take one of their kayaks out for a sunset spin.

Style: Private Bungalows
Starts at: $25 USD
Where: Between Kampot Town and the Jungle

Hotel Five.S

Right in the center WITH a pool. You get the whole goose when you stay at Hotel Five.S. Each room has it own tropical garden, a unique open-air bathroom, a heavenly bed, and a fully stocked bathroom with lovely smelling soaps and shampoos. Up your budget just a bit for a private balcony overlooking the city. Perfect for a bottle of wine to finish off a relaxing Kampot vacation.

Style: Privates
Starts at: $70
Where: Kampot Town

Fun Cambo Fact

The current monarch is King Norodom Sihamon, an ex-ballet dancer and unmarried 51-year-old with rather progressive views.

Where to Eat in Kampot

Karma Trader's Kampot

Schedule your Kampot trip to fall on a Tuesday for the tastiest Taco Tuesday ever. Every week, Karma Traders serves up the best tacos in town- almost always selling out by the end of the night. Choose between Spiced Pumpkin, 7hr Slow-cooked Coca-Cola Pulled Pork, and Paprika Shredded Chicken fillings served with fresh pico de gallo, crunchy coleslaw, spicy pineapple salsa, Tapatio mayo and lime. $2 each or $5 for 3. Pair with a tasty cocktail or ice cold beer from the tap. Pure bliss.

Open: Every day from 8am to late
Where: Kampot Town

Epic Arts Café

This NGO-run café and art gallery is one of the yummiest places to eat in Kampot. In fact, I've never had a meal here that didn't blow me away, especially for breakfast! They've got eggs benedict, pancakes, and fantastic coffee. But the best part about eating at Epic Arts Café? You are nourishing your stomach and your heart by contributing to an amazing cause.

Epic Arts Café gives work opportunities to disabled people in Kampot while using profits to grow local art programs. In fact, some of the staff at Epic Arts Cafe are deaf, so you'll order either by marking the boxes on your menu or using the Cambodian Sign Language guide to try and communicate with your waiter. Don't worry, they've got a good sense of humor if you totally fail.

Open: Everyday 7:30 am - 5:00 pm
Address: #67 Oosaupia Muoy
Where: Kampot Town near the Old Market

Twenty Three

Never trust a massive menu. Rather, you want to look for the charming restaurants with small menus, where each dish is executed with complete and utter perfection. And that's exactly what you'll find here at Twenty Three, the gourmet gastro pub in Kampot. Serving Charcuterie Boards, braised pork belly, lamb shanks, fresh tuna - if it wasn't for the $10 price tags, you'd have thought you were dining in a Michelin star restaurant…

Open: Wednesday-Monday 5:30am-9:30pm (closed on Tuesday)
Address: 23 East Street
Where: Kampot Town near the river

Tertúlia

Seeking seafood Portuguese style? The culinary geniuses at Tertúlia have taken advantage of the fish, snails, squid and shellfish in the region to create gorgeous dishes right here in Kampot. Try the Tuna Tartare or the Tiger Prawns with Kampot Peppers – and treat yourself to a glass of red wine. Don't worry, with dishes averaging around $7, you can definitely afford it.

Open: Tuesday to Friday 5pm – 11pm & Saturday 12 pm - 11pm
Address: Tuek Chhu Road
Where: Just over the New Bridge

Kampot Coffee & Cocktails

Besides the obvious, KCC is the most popular place in town to get fresh oysters! I am talking…straight from the oyster farm to the table fresh. Come on Wednesdays where you get 6 oysters on the half shell for $3. Ice cold beer is on tap to help you wash em' down.
Open: Tuesday to Friday 5pm – 11pm & Saturday 12 pm - 11pm
Address: Shop 8 on Street 722
Where: Kampot Town

The Looking Glass

Hidden amongst the tarnished bricks of Kampot's Old Market, there's a new foodie wonderland to be discovered. Step through the magical mirror in Mathilda's tattoo shop and into this secret little nook in Kampot. 'The Looking Glass' is a Bar/Cafe serving gourmet toasted sandwiches (toasties), homemade iced teas and all you favorite bar snacks. Take a break from your day of exploring and shopping to recharge and refresh in this centrally located gem.

Open: Everyday 12pm-12am
Address: Behind Mathilda's Tattoo Shop
Where: Inside the Old Marke

Fun Cambo Fact

Tourism is fast becoming Cambodia's second largest industry, just behind garment manufacturing

Things to Do in Kampot

Hang Out in your Bathing Suit

Have a pool day at Karma Traders, lounge in an inner tube on the river at Naga House or slide until your bum is bruised at Arcadia Water Park & Guest House. You don't have to be a guest- just a patron who buys drinks and/or food. **PS.** Kampot's guest houses are very 420 friendly, if you're into that sort of thing.

Drive to Bokor National Park

Bokor National Park is home to colorful birds, lush tropical flowers, trickling rivers, and a collection of abandoned French Colonial mansions. You'll experience all of this on your drive up, and then at the top of the mountain, you'll be met with a towering statue of Buddha overlooking insanely beautiful views of winding valleys and farmland. If you're not comfortable driving a motorbike, you can easily hire a car or a tuk tuk to take you on a Bokor Mountain adventure.

Drive to Kep

15.5 miles east from Kampot is Kep, a quaint beachside town that is a foodie heaven. Rent a motorbike and take the easy scenic drive down the highway. The ride to Kep is a comfortable journey, even for beginner drivers.

When you reach Kep, you'll find gazebos filled with hammocks. Lay down and wait for the crab vendors to come to you. Yes, crab! Kampot Pepper Crab, to be exact. Pair with a cold drink and you could spend hours just swinging and eating. Afterwards, cross the street and walk over the small beachside seaside market where vendors grill dried squid and fresh fish. Order your fill and eat on the spot.

Kayak on the River

You've got 18.6 miles waiting for you to explore on the Kampot River! You can sign up for a kayak tour on your own or rent a kayak from a local guest for as little as $2 an hour.

To rent on your own, visit **Samon Village Kampot or Greenhouse Guest House**. They'll provide rentals and some route suggestions to help you find mangroves and wildlife.

Get a Tattoo

It's a rite of passage to get a tattoo from Mathilda, the mother of tattoos here in the south of Cambodia. A French expat who showed up on Koh Rong 5 years ago, barely speaking English, she is now a staple in the community. Become a part of the Cambodia family with an ultra-feminine, spiritual, or minimalistic tattoo that will forever remind you of your journey in South East Asia. Don't be surprised if you bump into other people in the world with Mathilda tattoos – we're everywhere!

Where: Find her tattoo shop on Old Market Street AND Mathilda has a tattoo station set up at Karma Traders!
Open: 9am-midnight
Contact: Facebook- Mathilda Tattoos in Kampot

Organize a Date with Nature
✓ Watch the sunset on the river with Lazy Day River Tours
✓ From the riverside, watch the fishing boats head out to sea at sunset
✓ Spectacular bird watching in the evenings from the balcony at Paris Guesthouse 1 - next to Mr. Chims

Shopping in Kampot

Kampot Night Market
Located near "The Big Durian" roundabout, you'll find Kampot Night Market! They've got everything: clothing, trinkets, spices, shoes, and bags. This is a great place to practice your haggling skills! Never accept the first price! After you've shopped all your energy away, nourish yourself with noodle soup, fruit shakes and of course, meat on a stick.

Open: Everyday 8am-10pm
Where: Kampot Town
Address: Near the Durian Roundabout

Touche Hombre
Looking for flowy hippie tunics and vintage denim shorts? Touche Hombre is filled with vibrant colors and whacky prints for decent prices. Run by the most fashionable Aussie man in town, Touche Hombre offers tops, T's, bathing suits and everything cute & quirky for a fashionista vacation.

Where: Kampot Town
Open: Monday-Saturday 10am-5pm
Address: 50m from Epic Arts café – the street that runs parallel

Fun Cambo Fact
Another one about the king! He lived in France for 20 years, starting in the early 1980s.

289

Spas & Salons

Banteay Srey

Welcome to Banteay Srey, a women-only spa in that helps "women connect with women". The girls who work here come from abusive or neglectful backgrounds. This salon trains them in spa services, giving them a chance at an independent life. Here, you can feel extra good about treating yourself to a traditional Khmer massage or an indulgent facial.

Open: Daily 11am-7pm
Where: Tuek Chhu Rd

Jolie Jolie Beauty Salon

Facials with fresh oranges and yogurt, waxing with organic products, pedicures with high-quality paint – pamper yourself, darling! This little boutique sells more than just handicrafts and handmade clothing. They also sell pure relaxation.

Treatments last from 1 to 1.5 hours with prices starting at $15. Try getting that at home! Check out the manicure + facial spa packages or the mani/pedi sets which you can actually afford.

Open: Daily 10am-8pm
Where: Near the Old Market, Kampot 07000, Cambodia

Kampot Nightlife

This sleepy town doesn't have a huge party scene, rather, you'll find a handful of guest houses that throw live music nights, themed parties or a steady flow low-key boozing.

- ❖ **Monday:**
  - ✓ Open Mic Night at Magic Sponge – 7pm

- ❖ **Tuesday**
  - ✓ Taco Tuesday & Live Music at Karma Traders – 6:30 pm

- ❖ **Thursday:**
  - ✓ Live Music and Open Mic Night at The Plantation
  - ✓ Rhymes on the River: Sunset boat cruise down Kampot river from 5pm-9pm with live music & delicious grub cooked on board (runs only during high season)

- ❖ **Friday:**
  - ✓ Live Music and DJs at Banyan Tree

- ❖ **Saturday**
  - ✓ Live DJs and drink specials at Naga House

- ❖ **Sunday:**
  - ✓ Pool Parties that bleed into tipsy BBQ night at Arcadia
  - ✓ Free Trivia at Karma Traders starting at 6:30pm with 'Build your own Bokor Burgers' for $5 each

How to Get Around Kampot

PassApp
The Uber-esque Rikshaws are now in Kampot! Download the app and order your ride to come pick you up!

Rent a Motorbike
If and only if you're comfortable on a motorbike, go ahead a rent one. Traffic in the center of Kampot can be a little hectic but once you're in the mountains and the "other side of the river", motorbikes are the best way to really soak up everything Kampot has to offer.

Rent a Bicycle
Many guesthouses have bicycles for rent or know where you can find one. Bicycles are great for exploring the flat city, just keep in mind that traffic is fast-paced so try to keep to the shoulder and give yourself plenty of time when crossing busy intersections. Drivers won't slow down for you.

Tuk Tuk
When you need to get from your guesthouse to a bar or restaurant, have reception ring you a Tuk Tuk. Prices are usually $1-5 per person depending on where you're going and how many people you've got.

Walk
Staying in Kampot Town? It's easy to get around on your own two feet. Walk along the riverside or explore the side streets full of small business and shops.

Crime & Safety in Kampot

Crime

Only recently has petty crime made an appearance in the town of Kampot. It's the same old story: motorbike drivers might try to snatch your purse as you ride or walk alongside them. Sketchy hostels might magically swallow up belongings left unattended in bathrooms, dorm rooms, or left out on bar counters. Keep your valuables close and stay at trusted hostels and guesthouses.

Safety

Motorbike accidents are common in Cambodia with both travelers and locals. Always wear a helmet and close-toed shoes (no flip flops) and be extra cautious while riding at night.

Fun Cambo Fact

The Cambodian flag is the only flag in the world that features a building (Angkor Wat, of course).

How to Get to Kampot

From Phnom Penh

➢ By Private Taxi
Point of Departure: Pick up at your hotel
When: Whenever you want
Duration: 3 hours
Cost: $40
Book: Check out the 'Driver Directory' to find a driver.

➢ By Train
Point of Departure: Phnom Penh Railway Station
When: Friday at 3pm, Saturday at 7am, Sunday at 7 am, Monday at 4pm
Duration: 4-5 hours
Cost: $6

➢ By Bus
Point of Departure: Giant Ibis Bus Terminal
When: Daily at 8am and 2:45pm
Duration: 2.5 hours
Cost: $15
Book: www.12go.asia/en

From Sihanoukville

➢ By Private Taxi
Point of Departure: Pick up at your hotel
When: Whenever you want
Duration: 2 hours
Cost: $30+
Book: Check out our section called 'Driver Directory' for more info.

➢ By Minibus
Point of Departure: Minivan pick up at your hotel
When: Multiple times per day
Duration: 2
Cost: $6-10

Chapter 14: Sihanoukville

Pronounced Si-han-uk-ville, this eclectic beachside town is the jumping off point for some of the most gorgeous islands in South East Asia....but Sihanoukville itself doesn't have too much to offer lately.

You see, the town has recently been bought by the Chinese who have converted it from a charming beach destination into China's #1 gambling destination. This means that the idyllic guesthouses and beach shacks were torn down and replaced with tall Chinese hotels and casinos. Mainland tour groups come collectively by the dozens, trashing the beach, running small Cambodian businesses out of operation and repelling would-be vacationers. Central Sihanoukville is dead.

HOWEVER, if you venture out of central Sihanoukville towards the east end of the coast, you'll find two stretches of beach that aren't yet ruined. These areas are called Otres 1 and Otres 2.

You'll find fire spinning hippies on Otres 1 and quiet boutique guesthouses on Otres 2.

Still, both of these beaches are only enough to keep you entertained for a day or two. Do a little roadside shopping, get drunk on the beach for cheap, and relax with massage spas that charge $13 per hour.

My no-bullshit recommendation is this: Either skip Sihanoukville all together or stay exclusively at a hotel which I've recommended so that, ideally, you an escape from the chaos.

From the Airport in Sihanoukville

When you land at the tiny airport in Sihanoukville, there will be Tuk Tuks and taxis who are ready to take you to your hotel. OR you can arrange a taxi ahead of time to pick you up.

How Much: Taxis are around $17 and Tuk Tuks are
How Long: The drive into town is about 20 minutes

From the Bus Station in Sihanoukville

The bus station is not within walking distance to town. You'll need to take a Tuk Tuk to your hotel or the Koh Rong pier.

How Much: The Tuk Tuk drivers will tell you $5 per person BUT if three of more people…don't pay more than $15 – this is the max rate you should pay.
How Long: 10 minutes

Not so Fun Fact
The average wage is less than $3 per day in Cambodia. The Khmers working at expat-owned bars and businesses, however, tend to be paid higher **and** work in more-enjoyable atmospheres.

Areas to Explore

Serendipity Beach (Ochhuerteal Beach)

Nestled right next to the main boat pier, you'll find Serendipity Beach lined with a cement boardwalk/path. All along the boardwalk, there are beachfront restaurants and shady umbrella stands to match. This boardwalk is getting busier and busier but the beach shacks aren't able to accommodate the influx of travelers. So if you decide to come here for the day, come for the people watching and experience, rather than the "toes in the sand" vacation vibes.

…I'm really selling it, aren't I?

Otres 1

More aimed towards backpackers, this beach offers tons of budget options with cheap rooms and dorms.

Otres 2

Otres 2 offer the posh life with upscale resorts, swimming pools with a view, and fantastic service.

Sihanoukville City

Wild, busy and full of chaos! But…there is a KFC.

Accommodation in Sihanoukville

Onederz Sihanoukville $

Onederz Hostel has three very appealing traits that other dorms in Sihanoukville just don't offer: social pool, fast internet & sparkling clean rooms with brand new beds. On top of that, the location is fabulous! You're just a 10-minute walk to the beach and a 3-minute walk to all the best restaurants and bars. As a fairly new brand, the staff are freshly trained and enthusiastic to help you plan your trip! Female dorms available!

Style: Dorms
Starting at: $9
Where: At the top of Serendipity Road
Address: Golden Lion Traffic Circle

Stray Cats Guest House $

Low maintenance girls with musical talents and hippie tendencies will fit right in at Stray Cats, a laidback guest house run by a welcoming collection of western expats just 10 minutes from the beach. With musical jam nights on Tuesdays and Fridays and Otres market just a quick walk down the road, there's always something to do here. Bonus points for vegetarians and vegans! Stray Cat's kitchen makes some V-friendly menu items that even a carnivore can appreciate. Rooms are basic but trust me, the atmosphere is beyond fabulous.

Style: Privates
Starting at: $10
Where: Otres Village- a 10-minute walk to Otres Market & a 10-minute walk to the beach
Address: Otres Village Songkat 4

Mama Clares $

Escape it all! Located at the very end of Otres Two, you'll find these wooden bungalows with fascinating grass-thatched roofs that sit quietly on the river which stretched back into the mainland. Take a kayak out for a spin on the calm river channel and look for wildlife in this unspoiled area or take a bicycle out on jungle paths. When you want to explore in town, the staff will call you a tuk tuk or a taxi, and even help you set up bus tickets.

Style: Privates
Starting at: $18
Where: Otres Village
Address: Otres Village Songkat 4

Monkey Maya Ream National Park $

Through the jungle, next to the National Park on an isolated private beach is this gem- Monkey Maya. 18 kilometers from Sihanoukville, adventure to a spot that many tourists don't even know exists. Be one with the monkeys, take morning strolls through the forest, and sip coffee on the beach. No wifi, no social media, and no thoughts of the outside world. This is a pure escape.

Style: Luxury Bungalows
Starting at: $35
Where: Ream National Park, Phsar Ream

Tamu Cambodia Hotel $$$

Luxury. It's not a word you hear often in Cambodia, but it's what Tamu offers. Situated right on the beach, you can eat breakfast barefoot while overlooking the ocean, take a dip in their full-sun pool, and enjoy cloud-soft beds. Housekeeping comes every day to maintain your dreamland oasis and restock the minibar! Tamu's restaurant features specials every night and makes some amazing pasta. Oh, and the Tamu Sour is a must-try cocktail. With private lounge chairs on the beach, soak up some rays and get a massage for $5 by one of the lady hawkers on the beach. No shoes needed.
Style: Privates
Starting at: $90
Where: The end of Otres 2- Marina Road

White Boutique Hotel and Residences$$

The most pristine stretch of beach that you'll find in Sihanoukville, take advantage of the prime location! Step out of your room into a tropical wonderland full of tall palm treed and vibrant flowers. Before you even get to the shore, your toes are in the sand. The grounds of White Boutique Hotel are covered in white sand that is maintained all day long! It's so easy to lounge here, with day beds everywhere and even swings overlooking the ocean. The rooms, while simple, are the most comfortable you will find in Sihanoukville. You've got all the amenities: Wifi, a flat screen TV, a safe for your valuables, clean towels - the essentials that some other hotels are likely missing. Even better, the staff are superb, the restaurant is top-notch, and the cocktails are exotic. This is the place you've been looking for.
Style: Privates
Starting at: $120
Where: The end of Otres 2- Marina Road
Address: Otres 2

Where to Eat in Sihanoukville

Green Pepper

Just one street back from Otres 2 beach, Green Pepper is an authentic Italian restaurant run by a collection of Europeans and an Italian pizza chef. Settle in to their open-air dining room that catches the warm Cambodian breeze beautifully. Watch the talented chefs hand toss the dough for your fresh pizza made with local and imported ingredients. Risen to perfection in a classic wood-fired pizza oven, it doesn't get much better than this. For a divine palate cleanser, try the Limoncello.

Open: Daily from 10am – 10pm
Location: Behind Otres 2
How to Get There: Otres Beach "Far O", 2nd road next to the Mangrove River Resort.

Shin Sushi Bar

Sushi isn't a splurge over here. Maki Rolls are $3, a Spicy Tuna Roll is $4.50, and sushi sets are $10. The service is also fantastic. The staff bring you a jasmine scented cleansing towel when you sit down and then dote on you like you're the ambassador of wherever the hell you're from. Beer is cheap. Daily specials are also.

Open: Daily from 11:30am – 10pm (last order at 9:30pm)
Location: Serendipity
Address: Serendipity Road across from ANA Travel

Olive Olive

Mediterranean tapas, pastas, and dessert; Olive and Olive never disappoints, especially when they drop a complimentary basket of bread or come by with a free Tiramisu at the end of your meal. The portions are huge so expect to leave with leftovers (i.e. Second Dinner).

Open: Daily from 11:30am – 10pm (last order at 9:30pm)
Location: Serendipity
Address: Right before the Golden Lion roundabout.

Khmer Food on the Beach

Serendipity Beach is lined with fresh seafood displays chilling on ice and menus filled with classic Khmer dishes. Cooked to order, you eat with your toes in your sand, a cold beer in your hand, and some fantastic people watching (sorry that didn't rhyme with sand or hand).

Shopping in Sihanoukville

Otres Market

Featured on an episode of 'Vice', Otres Market has been referred to as a "Neverland of food and booze." They're not wrong there. With western & vegan food stalls, hippy hula hoopers, a diverse international crowd and eclectic trinkets and clothing from around the world- this neon lit market is a trippy experience. Come on Saturdays around 6 to enjoy some live music while you shop.

Where: Otres Lake

Phsar Leu Market

This massive flea market in Sihanoukville is such a cultural experience, and not that "historical" kind of culture. I'm talking about the real and raw day-to-day life of Cambodian locals just doing their thang. Come with your people-watching eyes open!

To get here, you'll make your want into the center of Sihanoukville town. Here you'll find a massive plaza buzzing with nearly 100 vendors. Inside, the vendors are selling everything from gold watches to children's clothing. Outside, you can find every kind of vegetable, fruit and meat; including tanks of life fish and frogs! Want to try some food on the spot? There are nuts, fried dough and fresh mango everywhere you turn.

Where: Sihanoukville Town

Shops along Serendipity Road

Wander the main road that leads down to Serendipity Beach. There are a few remaining clothing stores selling beachy cover-ups and flowy dresses at around $12 a pop. You can also buy electronics, DVDs, iPods with music loaded to go, purses made from recycled materials, sunglasses, post cards and my favorite…snacks to stuff in your purse for later.
Where: Serendipity Road

Things to Do in Sihanoukville

Go on an Island-Hopping Tour
Don't have time to stay on all the islands? Visit them all in one day with Otres Island Hopper Tours. For $20, you get an incredible ocean adventure where you'll snorkel in crystal clear water with colorful fish and stop off at some of the most gorgeous beaches that you've ever seen! Your tour includes lunch, snorkeling gear, water and beer!

Pro Tip

During high season, it is possible to ask the tour boat to drop you off at Koh Ta Kiev for 1 or 2 nights. You'll hop back on their boat when they visit next. 2 birds with 1 stone!

Check it out: Pop into any tour office or ask you hotel. The same few tours are offered everywhere!

Party Cycle Tours
Who knew drinking and driving could be so fun? The concept is simple: sit, cycle & drink. The most unique way to see the city, you'll sit at a round table mounted on wheels with 13 other travelers as you leisurely pedal through Tuk Tuk traffic- all with a cold beer or mixed drink in your hand. $15 gets you unlimited drinks for the whole hour- $25 for 2 hours. Solo girls, there's no better way to make friends in Sihanoukville than this! Just show up, park yourself in a seat, and get to laughing.

Check it out: PartyCycleToursAsia.com

Take a Cooking Class
The most reputable cooking school in Sihanoukville is called **Tastes of Cambodia.** Here, in a clean kitchen with fresh ingredients and an English-speaking teacher, you will learn to make authentic Khmer dishes like green papaya salad, fish amok, and the famous ginger dumplings. After all your hard work, you'll sit down and enjoy the fruits of your labor.

Check it out: Facebook.com/TastesofCambodia

Sihanoukville Nightlife

Serendipity Beach

At night, the boardwalk comes alive with loud music, flashing lights, and a younger crowd of both travelers and Cambodians who love to party. Walking around the main road, you'll be approached by barefoot bartenders passing out free drink coupons for JJs or other beach front clubs. This is how they fill that place up night after night during high season!

Pro Tip: Be sure to watch your purse and pockets! The cute little beggar kids roaming around the beach are quite skilled with the elusive bag snatch.

Not in the mood for a beach party? Check these out!

- ❖ **Wednesday**
  - ✓ Quiz Night at Divers Inc Hotel

- ❖ **Thursday**
  - ✓ Movie Night at BOHO in Otres Village – 8pm

- ❖ **Friday:**
  - ✓ The Big Easy Pub Crawl
  - ✓ Open Jam Night at Stray Cat's

- ❖ **Saturday**
  - ✓ Live music at Otres Market

- ❖ **Sunday**
  - ✓ Otres Market

Crime & Safety in Sihanoukville

Little Thieves on Serendipity Beach
While you are getting all carefree with your cocktails on the beach, little beggar kids are getting to work. While you're distracted, they'll snatch your purse, wallet, or phone in a second. I would know…it happened to me.

Walking at Night
Stay on Serendipity Road near all the businesses and you'll be fine. Just steer clear of back roads and residential streets.

Responsible Drinking and Drug(ging?)
Whatever it is that you like to partake in, be it alcohol, ganja or something a bit stronger- do so with caution. Parties tend to get wild in Sihanoukville. The expats that live here are used to partying every night and make hardcore partying seem like a piece of cake. Don't try to keep up. Watch your pace. Keep your wits about you.

Police and Drugs
Right now, we have a friend sitting in the Sihanoukville jail/prison. She's doing some serious time after getting caught manufacturing drugs to resell. While I'm sure you aren't coming here to become a drug lord…just know that the police here are aware of foreigners' love for pills and weed. Don't carry it on your body or in your bag. Getting caught can be expensive…or worse.

Pro Tip: While it sounds like a stupid tip and an irresponsible tip- trust me when I say…if you're renting a motorbike and drive up on a police check point (usually near the Golden Lion round-about), don't stop. Don't make eye contact and just drive right by them or choose a different route. They won't chase you. They just want to stop you and shake you down for whatever cash you've got on you.

How to Get Around Sihanoukville

Walk
Each little area of Sihanoukville is walkable. By that I mean, whether you're staying in Otres 1 or on Serendipity Beach, there will be restaurants, bars, and tourism offices within walking distance from your hotel.

PassApp
Making life so easy, order a PassApp to go to the beach or the market! Great for little distance rides!

Tuk Tuk
This is a Tuk Tuk city! Getting around is made easy with $1 Tuk Tuk rides in Sihanoukville town and $5 Tuk Tuk rides between Serendipity and Otres.

Fun Cambo Fact
With a growth rate of 6% in the last ten years, Cambodia has one of the fastest-growing economies in Asia

How to Get to Sihanoukville From Thailand

You can always fly! It's the fastest and easiest way...but also the most expensive way.

However, if you're on a budget and plan on doing a land-crossing, you'll need some advice before you go. Here are the insider tips to make it easier.

Start in Bangkok.

> ➤ **You'll Travel by Bus**

This trip can be completed in 3 back-to-back legs that take around 15 hours in total. It sounds really complicated, but the journey is well-traveled and runs smoothly with transport staff and Tuk Tuk drivers there to guide you.

1st Leg of the Trip: Bangkok to Trat

Point of Departure: Bangkok - Mo Chit Bus Terminal (Northern Bus Terminal) or Ekamai (Eastern Bus Terminal)
When: Daily 6am
Duration: 5-6 Hours
Cost: Around $8 USD

2nd Leg of the Trip: Trat to Hat Lek Border Crossing (Koh Kong)

Point of Departure: Trat Bus Terminal
When: Upon arrival
Duration: 1 Hour
Cost: $4-5 USD

3nd Leg of the Trip: Koh Kong to Sihanoukville

You'll take a $3 Tuk Tuk from Koh Kong border to the bus terminal – about 15km- then you'll hop on a bus. You're almost finished!
Point of Departure: Small Bus Terminal in Koh Kong
When: Daily at 1pm
Duration: 4 Hours
Cost: Around $7.50 USD

Pro Tip

To speed things up, you can hire a Taxi from the border or from the bus terminal to take you straight to Sihanoukville and skip all this bouncing around! Ask a few other travelers around you if they want to split the $50 fare for a much less stressful ride.

Heads Up

✓ At the border, there will be a desk with a big sign that says "quarantine" and some plainly clothed men sitting behind it. It's so obviously a scam that it's laughable. They'll tell you that you are required to get a "health check" which is just them taking your temperature...and guess what! It will cost you $1. However, there is absolutely no law that states you need a health check. Seasoned expats have learned to ignore them and keep walking with a stern 'No' and a bit of confidence. Worse case...you don't feel comfortable saying no and you pay $1 to the corruption fund.

✓ For all other immigration tips, check out the Visa Section at the beginning of this chapter.

Sobering Cambo Fact

As a result of the Khmer Rouge massacre, around half of Cambodia's population is younger than 15 years old

Chapter 15: Koh Rong Island

What was once a tiny fishing beach for tired fishermen to camp overnight, Koh Rong is now Cambodia's #1 travel destination.

How does 27 miles of white sand beaches lined with coconut trees overlooking crystal clear water sound? Spend your days tanning on the beach, ziplining through the jungle, or going on a boat trip around the island. Then, have a walk along the beach and you'll find an international collection of expats turned locals who have opened hostels, restaurants, and bars. It's a travelers playground over here.

Fun Cambo Fact
4k Beach is so pristine that it was used one of the campsites for a recent season of Survivor.

Areas to Explore on Koh Rong

Koh Rong might be the size of Hong Kong, but it is relatively underdeveloped. No Tuk Tuk transportation here. Just white sand beaches and longtail boats.

Koh Toch Village
Right when you step off the ferry pier (and carrying on to the left of the pier), is Koh Toch Village. This is where locals live, children play, and chickens wander. Koh Toch is a bit quieter with family run guesthouses and dorms. You can get $1 smoothies and $1 bowls of soup all day long.

White Beach
To the right of the main pier you'll find western-style bars, guesthouses and bungalows known for their tasty food and eccentric parties. Drinking starts bright and early so get your party pants on.

Long Beach
On the other side of the mountain from Koh Toch Beach lies 7km of white sand paradise that is certainly worth the hike. Take a dip in the bathwater warm water or grab a fresh fruit shake. As the day nears the end, groups of travelers gather on the shore to watch the gorgeous sunset. Once the sun is down, hike back or hop in a long tail boat waiting to take you back to the main beach.

Police Beach
Begin the morning on Police Beach when its quiet. Plan to spend the day on sunning in your bathing suit, playing in the water or joining in on a volleyball match. As the day carries on, the beach attracts a friendly crowd and now, the party has come to you.

To get here, no boats needed; just follow the well-trodden path past Green Ocean Guest House into the jungle and you'll come out on the other side at Police Beach.

Longset / 4k Beach
Walk all the way to the end White Beach and you'll see a little jungle path. Follow it. You'll walk down a foot-trodden dirt path under tall jungle, pass the Tree House Bungalows and walk over a few improvised bridges until you reach Long Set Beach / 4k Beach. Spend your day in the soft sand, drinking at Nest Bar, or sipping on a coconut from one of the few beach vendors here.

Accommodation on Koh Rong

Chai Family Guest House $

Run by my favorite Khmer family on the island, this guesthouse sits on the smaller pier just left of the main pier. The rooms are literally above the water (and for $1, their chicken soup is insane). The sounds of the waves will lull you to sleep if your beer doesn't do the trick. The catch: the toilet is a squatty potty located at the bottom of a ladder (a challenge that I always find kind of fun).

Style: Privates
Starting at: $5
Where: The Pier Right next to the Main Pier (you'll see it immediately)

Nest Beach Club $

Brand new western-style air-conditioned dorms are a god-send when all you want to do is escape the heat. Nest is one the best kept secrets on Koh Rong. Here, you get the best of both worlds: modern facilities steps from the white sandy beach and local budget prices. This getaway is where many of the expats come to enjoy the 6-9pm Happy Hour and gather for live music nights and parties. Oh, and the beach is insane. In…sane.

Style: Dorms
Starting at: $15
Where: Walk to the end of White Beach, through the jungle path past Tree House Bungalows and you'll come out on Longset Beach, the home of Nest.

Coconut Beach Bungalows $

Like staying at your best friend's place if that place was on a pristine beach in paradise. Your hosts, Pia and Robbie go out of their way to put a smile on your face and memories in your noggin. Choose between a futon tent or sea view bungalows. The beach is yours with hammocks and swings, crystal clear water, and photo ops for days. The beach is isolated, but Robbie will help you book a quick $5 transfer from the main pier. The journey is worth it.

Style: Private Tent or Bungalow
Starting at: $15
Where: Coconut Beach

Tree House Bungalows $

A private beach in the jungle? How can you say no? As the name suggests, you'll find a collection of sturdy tree houses lining this tiny beach with balconies that offer unspoiled views of the ocean and unpolluted darkness at night for the most amazing star gazing. If the tree house is out of your budget, there are quiet bungalows tucked amidst the trees. On site is a bar and restaurant, as well as lounge chairs in the sand where you can get that nice vacay glow.

Style: Private Bungalows & Tree Houses
Starting at: $27
Where: At the end of White Beach through the jungle

Angkor Chom Bungalows $

Like a scene out of a movie, each private beach bungalow is nestled right in the sand just a few steps away from the water. Fall asleep to the sound of the waves crashing on the shore- but not before you splash with glowing plankton in the water at night. To get away from the boats and chickens, just take a short walk down the beach for pure isolation.

Style: Private Beach Bungalows
Starting at: $35
Where: The end of Long Beach

Where to Eat on Koh Rong

Sigi N' Thai Food

Pad Thai in Cambodia? Hell yes. Meet the Thai food King on Koh Rong-Sigi. Originally from Thailand, Sigi wandered over to Koh Rong several years ago and eventually, built a wooden Thai food stall with his own two hands. Have a seat under the thatched roof and grab a menu. All your favorites are there. Order whatever you want - a pad thai, a curry, some stir fried veggies - and he'll cook up massive portions of Thai dishes right in front of you.

Open: Everyday from 5pm
Where: Koh Toch Village behind Dream Catch Inn

Chai Family Guest House

Right next to the main pier, you'll see a smaller pier with some picnic tables and a crowd. That is Chai Family's mom and pop hot soup stall. This local family is a pillar of their community – partly thanks to their soup and partly thanks to their friendly vibes. Using fresh ingredients and fresh local chicken, you're only paying around $1-2 per bowl. Make use of the jars of spicy chili sauce. It is life.

Open: Every day 9am-8pm
Where: On the Pier next to the Main Pier

Da Matti? Italian Restaurant & Reggae Bar

Located next to Chai Family is a rasta-style Italian restaurant with authentic dishes, refreshing cocktails and views of the moon. Gnocci is my go-to here but they also make some killer pizza! Add in a bottle of wine, and you've got quite the serene candlelit dining experience right on the pier.

Open: All day Err day (…everyday)
Where: On the Pier next to the Main Pier

Fresh Smoothies

There are several fresh smoothie stands lining all along the beach! Particularly in Koh Toch Village. Manos, bananas, dragon fruit…oreos! They've got it all and for around $1 or $2 per smoothie. Support local families and small business while starting your day with a boost of clean eating.

Things to Do on Koh Rong

Rent a Motorbike

Roads are brand new to Koh Rong…and when I say roads, I actually mean red dirt jungle paths. You can now rent motorbikes on Koh Rong and zoom around the island, exploring isolated beaches and remote villages. Consider this an extreme adventure rather than a mode of transport!

How Much: $10 -$15 per day
Where: Head over to 4k Beach where you'll find bikes for rent

Zipline through the Jungle

Here's something to cross off your bucket list! **High Point Zip Line** is the most thrilling ropes course in Cambodia with 25 platforms, 3 zip lines and 400 meters of pure adrenaline. Plus, you get a free T-shirt and bandana to flaunt how badass you are. The team of Russians behind this adventure are professional, fun, and internationally recognized in the Zip Lining World!

When: 5 sessions per day from 9:30am-4pm
How Much: $30 USD
Where: Koh Toch Village, up the hill & past the school

Boat Trip around the Island

Throw your suit on, grab a beer, and hop in a long tail boat that's ready to zip you around the island. In between the best snorkel spots and whitest sand beaches, you can also visit local villages and contribute to their small economy by buying homemade snacks and cold drinks. The tour also includes a big Cambodian BBQ lunch, snorkel gear, life jackets, beers, and whiskey to make for the best day ever on Koh Rong.

When: Monday, Wednesday & Saturday at 9am
How Much: $25 USD
Where: Koh Toch Village

Go Kayaking

You don't have to be a kayak pro to manage in these waters as their pretty calm *and* you won't need to head too far out to sea in order to find adventure. To get a kayak, wander down to Koh Toch village and ask a local selling adventure tours, or walk over to Long Set Beach where you'll find kayaks for rent at Sky and Sand Bar.

How Much: Just under $5 for a half day

Where: All along White Beach

Join in on a Beach Clean Up

Solo girls! The beach clean-up is an amazing way to meet some locals, make traveler friends & hang out with some cool kids all the while giving back to the island! **KREA** (Koh Rong Ecological Alliance) is run by a mix of local Cambodians and some island expats who are dedicated to keeping the island clean, the animals safe, and educating the local kids about how they can be environmental ambassadors in the future.

When: Saturday at 2pm
Where: Meet at the Friends of Koh Rong office in Koh Toch Village

Swim with the Plankton

You've seen the movie "The Beach," right? Do you remember the scene where Leonardo DiCaprio goes swimming in the glittering water at night? The same thing happens here! At night, you'll need to find compete darkness in the water. Either you can walk and find a spot on the beach with no light pollution OR take a boat trip that includes night swimming. Hop in the water. With every movement, the plankton are disturbed and light up in the water just like stars in the sky.

Koh Rong Nightlife

Richie Rich Pub Crawl

Coming to Koh Rong solo? Want to make some friends, get introduced to the best island drinking holes, and get a nice buzz going all at once? Join the one and only **Richie Rich Pub Crawl.** The pub crawl…crawls to 8 of the best bars on the island while completing challenges, drinking dranks, and of course, taking shots. And while the drinking part is fun, the whole "bonding with strangers on a beach in Cambodia" is so surreal and wonderful that friendships happen naturally. Get into it.

When: Every Tuesday and Friday from 8pm to 2am
Where: Starts at Monkey Island
How Much: $7 per person (includes your drinks)

Police Beach Parties

Wednesday through Saturday (during high season), Police Beach is where the party's at. This small beach surrounded by jungle fills up by DJ's, fire spinners, food stands, drinks stalls, and travelers from all over the world. Located through a path at the end of Koh Toch Beach, make sure you bring a flashlight and a cold beer for the jungle stroll.

Ps. Police Beach is also home to Koh Rong's Full Moon Party!

When: Wednesday-Saturday during High Season
Where: Through a path after Koh Toch Village (you'll see signs)

Fun Cambo Fact
Cambodia has changed its name 4 times in the past 50 years.
#IdentityCrisis

How to Get Around Koh Rong

Walk
Look down. You see those two cute little feet on the ground? That's your transportation. There are no beach roads here. It's all walkable.

Long Tail Boat
If you want to get to another beach or make a day trip to Koh Rong Samloem, there is always a longtail boat for hire or a speed ferry that you can jump on! Inquire at Ankounamatata or your guesthouse.

Motorbike
You can also rent motorbikes to explore the island and access isolated villages!

Crime & Safety on Koh Rong

The biggest danger on the island is never leaving...because you'll love it that much. It happened to me. It can happen to you! Besides falling miserably in love with this place, you don't have toooooo much to worry about.

Violent crime isn't a big deal here. You'll have the occasional fight between drunk western guys but that's usually it. Be aware of petty theft, keep your room locked when you leave, and don't hike the trails at night alone- just like you wouldn't do at home.

Some Tips Before You Go!

✓ **Bring Cash**
There are no ATMs on Koh Rong and Debit Cards are not typically accepted by bars or guesthouses. Bring cash. If you run out of cash, Island Boys can work out a loan for you.

✓ **Take care of your Cuts**
When you're barefoot 24/7, you're bound to get a scratch here and a bump there. And with the ocean mixed with sand and humidity- little cuts can turn into infected situations real quick. It's important to keep your cuts clean. Almost every bar has a medical kit with cleaning solution and band aids that they'd be happy to let you use.

✓ **Don't Scratch your Bug Bites**
Those will get infected, too.

✓ **You Might get Island Belly**
It won't hurt. You'll just be pooping 3x a day. Embrace it. At least it keeps you from feeling bloated...right? Once you get back on the mainland, everything goes right back to normal, I promise.

How to Get to Koh Rong Island

First, get your cute butt to Sihanoukville and book a ferry when you arrive. During high season, boats can fill up pretty quickly, so I recommend booking at least a day in advance so that you have more options in terms of what time you leave and arrive.

There are multiple speed boat companies that make getting to the island a breeze. While they are all reliable, I've always used a company called **Speed Ferry Cambodia** where you can book at ticket at the Koh Rong Dive Shop opposite The Big Easy in Sihanoukville.

When: Daily 9 am, 11:30 am, 3 pm
Where: The main pier at the end of bottom of the hill (you'll know what I'm talking about once you get to Sihanoukville).
How Much: $20 round-trip
How Long: 40-60 minutes (depending if they make a stop at Koh Rong Samloem).

Pro Tip

- ✓ You want to go to Koh Rong, the big island. Not Koh Rong Samloem (not yet, anyways). Sit tight. You're the last stop on the Speed Boat journey.
- ✓ To book your return, simply go into the Dive Shop the day before (just to be safe) and let them know that you want to leave the next day. If you forget to do this, they'll let you hop on the boat as long as they have room.
- ✓ A visit to Koh Rong is not a day trip – plan to spend at least 1 night on the island. You'll love it.

Chapter 16: Koh Rong Samloem

Were you looking for that white sand paradise? Now you've found it.

Silky smooth sand, bath-warm water, and stunning ocean views for days, Koh Rong Samloem is Asia's best kept secret.

Areas to Explore on Koh Rong Samloem

M'Pai Bay

Right across from big Koh Rong is M'Pai Bay- which only started collecting expat-run guesthouses a few years ago. Island life for Khmers is still very much in tact here. M'Pai Bay is a Cambodian community first and a tourist destination second with guesthouse owners very invested in creating a harmonious balance between the two. You can just as easily join a group of backpackers for a beer as you could join some Khmers drinking at a local minimart.

Saracen Bay

Get ready to make all of your friends jealous with an Instagram feed looking like you're vacationing with the Olsen Twins (or how I assume Billionaires vacation). Because holy moly, Saracen Bay will take your breath away. Powdery white sand beaches with bright turquoise water that remains shallow for a few meters out allowing you to bathe in the sun. This is one of my favorite places on Earth.

Sunset Beach

The name says it all! A chilled out slice of sand with only a couple guest houses, you don't have to battle crowds to get a piece of the pie. Consider staying on this corner of the island for solitude and silence.

Massive Pro Tip

There are no ATMs on Koh Rong and Debit Cards are not typically accepted. Bring cash. If you run out of cash, Bong's can work out a loan for you.

Fun Cambo Fact

Since the 19th century, there have been inconsistencies on whether 'Samloem' or 'Sanloem' is the correct spelling for this island. You'll see it spelled both ways.

320

Accommodation in Koh Rong Samloem

❖ Saracen Bay offers more upscale accommodation- many with hot water showers, air-conditioning and solace.
❖ M'Pai Bay has that laidback backpacker vibe going on with cold showers, fan rooms and local watering holes where it's easy to chat with other travelers.

Mad Monkey $

No hostel on earth can compare to Mad Monkey, located in its own private bay on Koh Rong Samloem. This place is a utopia and real-life adult playground. There are hammocks and swings IN the water, fire shows, water parties, and swimming with the glowing plankton at night. Almost like an adult summer camp, there is no WIFI here which means that you are totally unplugged from the outside world – and totally plugged into this social experiment on an island with likeminded travelers from around the world. You can choose to stay in a rustic dorm or a private cottage overlooking the water with your own balcony and hammock. Ps. There are no ATMs here, cash only babe.

Starts at: $7
Style: Dorms and Private Bungalows
How to Get There: Inquire at any Mad Monkey or visit the Speed Ferry Booking Office near the Golden Lions Roundabout in Sihanoukville.

Longvek Guest House $

Stay at Andrew's home. I met this vibrant Aussie expat one morning after I had suffered a crazy injury to my foot. He took a pen, a water bottle and a bottle of iodine and worked miracles to heal me- without even knowing my name. He's the kind of guy that gets excited to show you his favorite place for squid fishing, introduce all of his chickens by name, and share a homecooked dinner with everyone staying at his place. It's a social, family-feel that you won't forget.

Starts at: $5
Style: Privates
Where: M'Pai Bay

Easy Tiger $

I remember the days when Easy Tiger was the only guest house on the beach. The pioneers of M'Pai Bay, Easy Tiger has all of the answers when it comes to hiking, waterfalls, swimming – because no one knows this side of the island quite like them. If you're planning an adventure-filled island stay, plan to stay here.

Style: Dorms & Privates
Where: M'Pai Bay
Starts at: $6

The Sleeping Buffalo $

The Sleeping Buffalo has it all: live music events, snorkeling trips, and best of all, the Buffalo Bar with ice cold beer overlooking M'Pai Bay. Best of all, the hospitality over at the Sleeping Buffalo makes you feel right at home with Dave, the owner, welcoming each of his guest with a warm smile and conversation. **Warning**: you may plan to come for 1-2 days, but this place has a magnetic pull that magically extends your trip to 3-4 days.

Style: Private Beach Bungalows
Where: Sunset Beach
Starts at: $25

Bongs $

Live music, burgers, and great company. Bongs has been a Koh Rong staple for years. Come for the mouth-watering breakfasts and stay for the laid-back vibes that roll into a island party atmosphere in the night.

Pro Tip

The private rooms at Bongs are possibly the nicest budget rooms in the bay with brand new everything!

Style: Privates
Where: M'Pai Bay
Starts at: $20

Sweet Dreams Samloem $$

Want to stay on the most gorgeous beach in the country without blowing your whole travel fund? Sweet Dreams Samloem has fan bungalows just steps from the beach at $50 a night AND beachfront bungalows for $100 a night. Both gets you fab service via the Ukrainian family that runs this place. They'll welcome you at the pier and lug your bags to your room with a smile.

Style: Private Beach Bungalows
Where: Saracen Bay Beachfront
Starts at: $50

The One Resort $$$

If you're chasing that idyllic postcard dream, look no further! The dream is alive at The One. High-end bungalows situated on pure white sand beaches that feel like walking on powder next to turquoise water that is as warm as it is clear, here's the ultimate get away. Jump from the ocean into the resort pool lined with cabanas with poolside food and drink service. I wish I could live here.

Style: Private Beach Bungalows
Where: Saracen Bay Beachfront
Starts at: $110+

BOUNTY Boutique $$$

On such an isolated island, luxurious amenities can be hard to come by- but not at Bounty. Enjoy 24-hour electricity, air conditioning, wifi, and hot water showers- all in these super futuristic pods on the beach with unobstructed views of white sand and turquoise waters right from your bed the instant you wake up. With only 7 pods on site, you get 5 star-service. This is ultra-comfort. I'm jealous of you already.

Style: Private Beach Pods
Where: Saracen Bay Beachfront
Starts at: $150+

Huba Huba $

Remember all those other resorts that I said were paradise? Just forget all about them. This place really is heaven on earth. Let your worries wash away in a hammock on the beach, a cocktail in your hand and turquoise water as far as you can see. Fall asleep listening to the jungle coming alive and wake up to the sounds of waves crashing on the shore.

Enjoy your sleep in picturesque bungalows tucked away in the trees or little cabanas on the beach. Better yet, you'll get to know fellow guests and bartenders here very quickly. The vibes are communal, and the property is isolated. Your solo trip has no become a group vacation!

To Get There: Ready for an island adventure? Take the speed boat to Saracen Bay (Specify the Orchid Pier – it's more convenient). Then find the path located at The Dive Shop. You'll take an easy trek through the jungle for 30-40 minutes before arriving at Huba Huba. Pack light!

Pro Tip

Huba Huba has a supply boat that goes straight from their beach to Sihanoukville every day at 9am ($10 per person). So, if you plan to stay here and only here, make sure you explain to the Speed Ferry Ticket Office that you only need to purchase a one-way ticket from them. Or not. You can always jump on the speed ferry at a later time in the day. Up to you.

Style: Private Beach Bungalows
Where: Sunset Beach
Starts at: $25

Where to Eat on Koh Rong Samloem

The Fishing Hook

Hello, island ambiance. Take a seat on the floor amidst quirky maritime stylings of driftwood and nautical rope. Located right on the main pier, you get a nice cool breeze from the water with the sounds of waves in the background. Choose between classic Khmer dishes and comfort food from home. Prices are reasonable and service is friendly. This is the most professional establishment in M'Pai Bay!

Where: M'Pai Bay, Oon the main pier
Open: Every day from 12pm (noon) – 3pm & 6pm – 10:30pm

Bongs

Bongs always have the best breakfast with breaky sausages, baked beans, bacon, baguettes…the works. Try the Fat Boy Breakfast to soak up all of the booze from the morning before. This is a place that will not pass judgment if you want to have a beer for breakfast. If that's too heavy for you, try the Espresso Martini or Bloody Mary.

Where: M'Pai Bay, Directly at the end of the pier
Open: Breakfast to late

Erin's Kitchen

Homecooked meals with a beach front view. What more could you ask for? The cheerful Khmer staff at Erin's Kitchen are just getting used to the influx of tourists who seem to love what they're cooking up. Imagine making Amok Curry, Beef Lok Lak, and fruit pancakes your whole life, only to discover that these weird, tall gangly people from far away lands love it, too.

Where: M'Pai Bay on the very right side of the beach
Open: Morning to night

Things to Do on Samloem

Watch the Sunrise at M'Pai Bay Pier
It's tradition- for me at least. Right before dawn, I walk down to the pier and wake up with the sun. Bring your journal or a coffee and take the time to check back in with yourself while your feet dangle over the water, feeling like your sitting at the edge of the Earth. When the sun is up, dive in for a soul-cleansing swim. Quiet, peaceful and relaxing.

Go Kayaking
Saracen Bay guesthouses have kayaks for rent! It's typically $25 for 4 hours which gives you plenty of time to visit the mangroves, isolated beaches, fishing villages and nearby Rocky Island. Remember to wear sunscreen and bring a couple waters!

Take a Boat Trip around the Island
The best way to see all that the island has to offer is with a boat tour around the island. A Khmer boat captain will take you to fishing villages, isolated beaches, the lighthouse, and other must-see spots. You can snorkel or go fishing. You can even go for dark to splash around with the glowing plankton. Pop into Easy Tiger where they've got the best trips mapped out for you.

Snuba
No, it's not a typo. Snorkel + Scuba = Snuba. Attached to a long air tube, this hybrid experience allows you to dive down below the surface to get up close with colorful fish and intricate corals. Visit the dive center for more info!

Mountain Bike Tour
You've got 3 Mountain Bike Tour options: The Lazy Beach Tour, The Waterfall Tour, or the Lighthouse Tour- all run by **The Beach Island Resort on Saracen Bay**. This is an exciting way to explore off the beaten path while seeing some of the islands coolest attractions. All levels are welcome! Tours start at $15 per person.

Take a Jungle Hike
Ask your guest house to point out some of the jungle paths that wind through the tall green trees and rolling hills. You can hike to the waterfall, go bird watching (cooler than it sounds) or venture to another beach. Just watch the clock- sun sets around 6.

Samloem Nightlife

Full Moon Parties

..and Half Moon Parties and Black Moon Parties and 'Just Because' parties. **Good Vibz Camp** is a hippie haven located deep (ish) in the jungle between Saracen Bay and M'Pai Bay. It's a god damn jungle party with live DJs, fire dancers, fluorescent paint, and travelers who have flocked from all corners of the country just to trade some amazing karma and have a good time! Don't miss this one. Check out their Facebook page to see dates and info!

Bonus: There's a free camping area and sleeping area so you don't have to worry about trekking back to your hotel after you've been partaking in party activities.

Bar Hop

There are 2 types of people on an isolated island with minimal wifi and no roads: those who day drink and those who should day drink. Start from one end to of the beach and have a beer or cocktail at each guesthouse and local Khmer shop- collecting new friends and snacks along the way. Day bleeds into night and now you're night drinking like a responsible human. I knew you could do it.

Live Music Nights at Bongs

It's not every night or even every other night that there is live music at Bong's. But during High Season, the crew will throw a party with impressive musicians from around the globe. If you want to be that impressive musician and entertain the beach, shoot them a message. Live music guests get free drinks all night long.

How to Get to Koh Rong Samloem

There are 2 ways to get to Koh Rong Samloem…

Option 1: Start off in Sihanoukville

And take a ferry (see the 'How to Get to Koh Rong' Section). Instead of buying a ticket to Koh Rong, buy yours to Koh Rong Samleom and specify which beach you want to go to: Saracen or M'Pai.

Option 2: Start off on Koh Rong

And take a boat to Samloem from there.

Here are your options for boating over…

✓ Hire a private long tail boat from Koh Rong to Koh Rong Samloem for $25
✓ Take a $7 **Speed Ferry to M'Pai Bay:** Every day at 8am, 12pm, 1pm and 4pm
✓ Take a $7 **Speed Ferry to Saracen Bay:** The times change all the time with the addition of new boats. But don't worry, there are multiple boats per day! Inquire on Koh Rong and you can schedule your ride over.
✓ Jump on the $7 Long Tail Shuttle Boat leaving from Koh Toch every day at 12pm and 5pm – You can get tickets at the little stall in front of Rising Sun, called Bun Rong

And don't forget, you can make Koh Rong Samloem a quick day trip when you stay on big Koh Rong.

Itineraries for Cambodia

Don't try to see it all in one week. It ain't possible, babe. Instead, pick a few places and really dive deep.

If you've got the budget to fly and a couple weeks to burn…it's possible to hop around the entire country. But if you're working with a week and plan to bus it- don't try to be a hero and see it all. Instead, consider squeezing as much as you can get out of a couple destinations, rather than skimming the surface of every location.

No matter your situation, I've got you covered.

Here are some realistic itineraries to help you plan an unforgettable trip with just the right amount of activity to relaxation.

The One Resort - Samloem

329

1 Week: History & Culture

Day 1: Phnom Penh
- Fly into Phnom Penh
- Go shopping at the Russian Market and the Olympic Market
- Eat a modern Khmer dinner at ST 63 on Bassac Lane

Day 2: Phnom Penh
- Wake up around 8am for breakfast
- Hire a Tuk Tuk at 9am – Visit the Killing Fields and S21 Prison
- After an emotional day, take time to process on a rooftop pool
- Explore Pub Street and have some reasonably priced cocktails

Day 3: Battambang
- Hire a private taxi to Battambang
- Rent a motorbike or hire a Tuk Tuk – Visit Kampong Pil Pagoda & the Banan Temple
- Eat dinner Smokin' Pot
- Spend the evening at the Phare Circus

Day 4: Battambang
- Hire a Kayak and explore along village riversides and the countryside
- Unwind at the Prasat Phnom Banon Winery

Day 5: Siem Reap
- Take the morning bus to Siem Reap
- Go shopping in Alley West – sit down for a nice cup of coffee
- Explore the Night Market & Pub Street
- Straight to bed!

Day 6: Siem Reap
- Wake up at 5am to catch sunrise at Angkor Wat
- Spend the morning visiting temples and ask your Tuk Tuk driver to stop for a coconut on the way back.
- Unwind at the pool for a couple of hours
- Head out for a nice Khmer dinner at Mahob Khmer Cuisine

Day 7: Siem Reap
- Have breakfast at the Missing Socks Laundry Cafe

- Take a Bicycle Tour with Butterfly Tours Asia – ride through farm land and rice paddies to see rural Siem Reap
- Treat yourself to a massage at Lemon Grass Garden
- Fly Home! (You can route back through Phnom Penh with a quick 1-hour flight)

1 Week: Beaches

Day 1: Phnom Penh
- Fly into Phnom Penh
- Waste no time - Hire a Tuk Tuk to visit the Killing Fields and S21 Prison (it's about a 3-hour tour)
- After an emotional day, take time to process on a rooftop pool
- Visit Bassac Lane for reasonably prices cocktails and a Khmer dinner at ST 63

Day 2: Sihanoukville
- Travel down to Sihanoukville
- Go chasing waterfalls at Kbal Chhay Waterfall or take an afternoon cooking class
- Unwind on Otres Beach – visit Otres Market
- Go have an evening massage before dinner

Day 3: Koh Rong Island
- Take the morning ferry to Koh Rong
- Monkey around at High Point Ropes Course or hike to Long Beach
- Eat dinner at Sigi N' Thai Food
- Join the Richie Rich Pub Crawl or climb up to SkyBar

Day 4: Koh Rong Island
- Go on an all-day boat tour around the island
- Have a surreal dinner at Da Matti? Italian Restaurant & Reggae Bar
- Before bed, splash around in the water with the glowing plankton

Day 5: Koh Rong Samloem
- Take a ferry over to Saracen Bay
- Go kayaking around the mangroves and villages
- Spend the rest of the day relaxing on the most gorgeous beach you've ever seen!
- Have dinner while watching the sunset

Day 6: Koh Rong Samloem
- Go on a leisurely mountain bike tour through the jungle or hike to the waterfall
- Enjoy a swim at the beach
- Take the afternoon ferry back to Sihanoukville
- One last night out on Serendipity Beach
- Sleep in Sihanoukville or take a night bus to Phnom Penh

Day 7: Phnom Penh
- Visit the Russian Market to pick up some souvenirs in the morning
- Enjoy a rooftop pool day
- Before the sun sets, tour the Royal Palace
- Go across the street for a riverside stroll & dinner
- Have a safe flight home!

2 Weeks: North to South

Day 1: Fly into Siem Reap
- Go shopping in Alley West – sit down for a nice cup of coffee
- Explore the Night Market & grab dinner on Pub Street
- Get a foot massage on Pub Street with the best people watching!
- Straight to bed!

Day 2: Siem Reap
- Wake up at 5am to catch sunrise at Angkor Wat
- Spend the morning visiting temples and ask your Tuk Tuk driver to stop for a coconut on the way back.
- Unwind at the pool for a couple of hours or get a massage at Lemongrass Spa
- Head out for a nice Khmer dinner at Mahob Khmer Cuisine

Day 3: Battambang
- Travel 3 hours to Battambang
- Rent a motorbike or hire a Tuk Tuk – tour Kampong Pil Pagoda & the Banan Temple
- Unwind at the Prasat Phnom Banon Winery
- Spend the evening at the Phare Circus

Day 4: Battambang
- Up early for a morning hike to the Killing Cave
- Rent a motorbike and explore local neighborhoods

- Eat dinner at Smokin' Pot!
-

Day 5: Phnom Penh
- Travel to Phnom Penh
- Have a Pool Day!
- Visit the Russian market in the late afternoon
- Head to Bassac Lane for reasonably prices cocktails and a Khmer dinner at ST 63

Day 6 & 7: Elephant Valley Park
- Spend 2 days and one night at EVP in Mondulkiri.

Day 8: Back to Phnom Penh
- Up early for a full day of sightseeing!
- Hire a Tuk Tuk to visit the Killing Fields and S21 Prison (it's about a 3-hour tour)
- If you've got more energy, visit the Silver Pagoda
- Back to your hotel to unwind
- Before sunset, tour the Royal Palace
- Then go across the street for a riverside stroll & dinner

Day 9: Kampot
- Take the morning train to Kampot
- Check into your riverside accommodation
- Go Kayaking through the mangroves or rent a motorbike and drive up to Bokor Mountain
- Go for dinner and enjoy fresh, local ingredients at Teritula.

Day 10: Kampot
- Have a lazy river day in Kampot
- Kayak or float in the river
- Read a book and take a breather – something that's so easy to do here.

Day 11: Koh Rong
- Take a morning bus to Sihanoukville
- Hop on an early afternoon ferry to Koh Rong
- Wander Koh Toch Village then walk to 4k Beach
- Chill out at Nest Beach Club
- Eat dinner at Sigi N' Thai Food
- Join the Richie Rich Pub Crawl

Day 12: Koh Rong Island
- Go on an all-day boat tour around the island and fishing villages
- Have a fabulous dinner on the pier at Da Matti? Italian Restaurant & Reggae Bar
- Before bed, splash around in the water with the glowing plankton

Day 13: Koh Rong
- Up early for Monkey around at High Point Ropes Course
- Carry on and hike to Long Beach for the afternoon and sunset
- Take a boat back to Koh Toch and pass out

Day 14: Koh Rong Samloem
- Take a ferry over to Saracen Bay
- Spend the day kayaking around the mangroves and fishing villages
- Have dinner while watching the sunset

Day 15: Sihanoukville
- Take the ferry back to Sihanoukville
- Treat yourself to one last massage or body scrub
- Save travels home!

Want me to plan your trip on your budget?
Visit **TheSoloGirlsTravelGuide.com** for info

Volunteering in Cambodia

As I've mentioned once before, you must take extreme caution when deciding to volunteer in Cambodia – particularly with children. "Volun-tourism" is a massive industry that is both misleading to the well-intentioned travelers who want to do a good deed and exploitive to impoverished families here in Cambodia who are all too often taken advantage of.

An easy key to decipher whether an organization is moral is this: if any organization allows you to spend 1 day, 1 week, 2 weeks, 3 weeks, a month with their school children/orphanage/rescued sex workers/street children…they are exploiting those people for your money, donation, or "room and board fee".

Before volunteering with children or formerly abused people in Cambodia, ask yourself these questions….

- How is my involvement contributing to this organization?
- Has this organization just let you (a stranger) walk straight into an environment with vulnerable at-risk children and adults?
- If you pay for your experience – how much of that cash actually benefits the children or people involved?

Fact: Hundreds of organizations around Cambodia exists solely to profit from volun-tourism. The children and women rarely see or feel a penny.

To truly leave a positive mark on Cambodia, here is a list of fabulous organizations around the country that offer beautiful opportunities for outsiders to immerse themselves in the local culture, make a sustainable difference, and support a well-deserving cause.

Marine Conservation Center in Kep

Nature lovers can get in on sustainable conservation projects that directly impact sustainable environmental practices here in the south of Cambodia. From marine research on seahorse populations to actually joining patrol teams that survey the waters watching for illegal fishing and poaching- this organization is ready for you to come help. MCC also offers academic internships for students of conservation, marine science and related areas!

Contact: MarineConservationCambodia.org

Phare Circus in Siem Reap

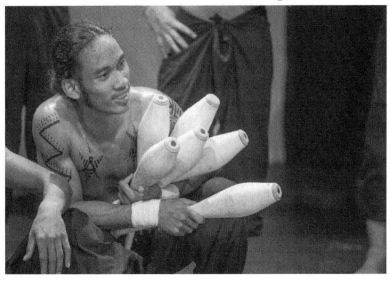

Helping young Khmer artists realize their dreams of performing, the fabulous Phare Circus needs techy and social media savvy volunteers! This is a great role for Digital Nomads who can commit to long term projects for 3 - 6 months. In return, Phare provides a living stipend of 100 USD per month and covers your visa extension fee during the whole period of contract. Plus…admission to the Phare circus family.

Contact: PhareCircus.org

Elephant Valley Project

Wouldn't it be a dream come true to wake up every morning with elephant friends?! When you volunteer at Elephant Valley Project, you are truly making a difference in the elephant's lives, the organizations success and the local community's well-being.

While it's a general rule of thumb that you should never pay to volunteer, EVP is the one exception. Your volunteer donation covers your basic needs (food and housing) and the rest allows EVP to rehabilitate and shelter abused elephants, protect the jungle, provide sustainable jobs for locals and cover vet costs. In other words, you get to stay at the elephant park for a longer amount of time for a fraction of the price – while bonding with and supporting Cambodia's elephants.

Volunteers usually stay two to four weeks.

336

Contact: ElephantValleyProject.ort

Friends of Koh Rong

The heart and soul of the Koh Toch village on Koh Rong- this Community Based Organization focuses on education and community development for an island full of children, families and businesses. This amazing organization was founded by a group of traveler girls who saw a need and went with it. They run the school, beach clean ups, environmental education and more. FOKR volunteers must dedicate a minimum of 2 months to their position. There are only a few positions open at a time! Apply for a volunteer position online.

Contact: FriendsOfKohRong.org

Bartend Anywhere!

5 years ago, I landed on the shores of Koh Rong without any travel (or bartending) experience under my belt. I planned to stay on the island for 2 days…I ended up staying a month. That's because within an hour of arriving on Koh Rong, I somehow landed a bartending job at Island Boys (RIP). With that bartending job came a built-in family of travelers that inspired me and empowered me to live this life of traveling the world. My life was literally never the same.

That first month eventually turned into 5 years of on and off Cambodia living, hence why I am writing this book. But that's a story for another time….

There's always a bar hiring in Siem Reap, Phnom Penh, Kampot, Sihanoukville, Koh Rong and beyond that typically require a 3 week+ commitment. You get a free room, food, and drinks. Do it.

Where to Next - How to Get to Other Countries from Cambodia

To Thailand

Bangkok is going to be your landing point in Thailand! Spend a few fun days there and then jet off towards elephants in the jungle up north or monkeys on the beach down south.

Check out my Thailand guides on Amazon to plan the best adventure ever filled with pro tips and money saving secrets.

Pro Tip: Always choose Giant Ibis for the safest and most comfortable long-distance journeys.

➢ **By Minivan from Phnom Penh**
Where: It depends on the companies! Ask your booking agent.
When: Daily at 5am
How Long: 11.5 hours
How Much: $26

➢ **By Bus from Phnom Penh**
Where: Giant Ibis Bus Terminal
When: Daily at 8 pm, 9 pm, 9:30 pm
How Long: 11 hours
How Much: $23

➢ **By Bus from Sihanoukville**
Where: Sihanoukville Bus Station
When: Daily at 8:30pm
How Long: 10 hours
How Much: $25

➢ **By Bus from Siem Reap**
Where: Giant Ibis Bus Terminal
When: Daily at 7:45am
How Long: 8.5 hours
How Much: $32

➢ **By Plane from any International Airport in Cambodia**
When: Multiple flights per day
How Long: About 1 hour
How Much: Anywhere from $50-100

To Laos

➢ **By Bus from Phnom Penh**
There are multiple minivans and buses that travel to Ho Chi Minh every day. For safety and comfort, you know which company I'm recommending…Giant Ibis (duh).

Where: Giant Ibis Bus Terminal
When: Daily at 8 am and 12:30 pm
How Long: 6.5-7 hours
How Much: $18

➢ **By Plane**
The routes you can take are:
Siem Reap > Pakse (Stopover)
Siem Reap > Luang Prabang (Direct)
Phnom Penh > Vientiane (Direct)

When: Multiple flights per day
How Long: All flights are under 2 hours
How Much: Anywhere from $70-400

To Vietnam

Pro Tip: Be sure to apply for a Vietnamese Visa a few days in advance! You can do this at any tourist agency in Cambo or online.

By ground, you will travel to Ho Chi Minh, formerly known as Saigon, in the south of Vietnam. **By air**, you can fly to any city with an international airport.

➢ **By Bus from Phnom Penh**
There are multiple minivans and buses that travel to Ho Chi Minh every day. For safety and comfort, you know which company I'm recommending...Giant Ibis (duh).

Where: Giant Ibis Bus Terminal
When: Daily at 8 am and 12:30 pm
How Long: 6.5-7 hours
How Much: $18

Note: You can take buses from Sihanoukville, Kampot, and Siem Reap – but they will all pass through Phnom Penh.

➢ **By Plane**
When: Multiple flights per day
How Long: 45 minutes - 1 hour
How Much: Anywhere from $60-100

Fun Cambo Fact
In Cambodia, there are **1.3 million motorbikes** for a population of just over 1.5 million people.

Transportation Tips for Cambodia

Avoid Olympic Express Limousine Bus Company – Ride with the reputable company called Giant Ibis.

Remember, Cambodia is a 3rd world country. There are 0 safety regulations enforced upon public transport. Busses breakdown, staff can be sketchy, drivers are overworked and often fall asleep at the wheel or take amphetamines to stay awake.

Giant Ibis is the only company that has self-imposed safety standards and professional training for their staff. For long distance rides, Giant Ibis hires 2 drivers who switch positions when the other gets sleepy. Plus, they are air conditioned, provide water and snacks, and have electric sockets onboard. I promote Giant Ibis as often as I can. I don't work for them or get any commission. I just trust them with my life.

When Hiring a Long-Distance Taxi Driver...

The faster they drive, the more money they can squeeze into a day. Makes sense. BUT these fast driving taxis are not invincible to road accidents. I **always** offer my drivers an extra $5 to drive slower. "How long does the trip take? 3 hours. Ok, I'll pay you and extra $5 if you make it 3.5 hours."

When the trip is $40 for a 4 hour ride, that extra $5 is a fair incentive to slow down. And <u>then</u> you can feel justified if you feel compelled to ask the driver to slow down along your journey.

Want to Share a Taxi?

Taxi rides can be more comfortable than minivan rides and faster than bus rides. Sharing taxis is a common thing here in Cambodia! It's convenient and also, a great way to meet new people. Before you travel in-between cities...

- Check out the Facebook group **Taxi Share Cambodia.** There may be someone offering a Taxi share or you can suggest one.
- Or ask the reception at your hotel or hostel if you can post a Taxi Sign Up Sheet with your trip details.

Crime & Safety in Cambodia

Your life is not in danger, but your wallet certainly may be.

Crime in Cambodia typically comes in the form of **scams and theft.** Each city varies in terms of what scams are run and which methods are used by thieves use to target foreigners. Let's get into it....

Milk Scams

Female beggars will approach you, usually with a baby, and ask you to buy powdered milk to feed their baby. You'll go with them to a shop and buy the milk – thinking that you've done a low risk good deed since no cash was exchanged. Not so fast. Sadly, the mothers are working with the shop keepers. The shop keepers take back the milk and a cut of the money, while the mothers keep the rest of the cash.

Where: These scams are most popular in Siem Reap.
What to do: Beggars lose interest easily when they see that you're not interested. Say 'no' once and then don't make eye contact. It's a sucky feeling…but you can solve the entire problem in one night.

Thieves on Motorbikes

Motorbikes will drive by and snatch your purse or jewelry right off of your body. They will also take your phone right from your hands. Tuk Tuks are not a safe zone either. Thieves will reach into a Tuk Tuk and grab your bags that are lying on the floor. Theives are ruthless and are not afraid to cause injury.

Where: This crime is prominent in Phnom Penh and Sihanoukville. Incidents in Kampot are also on the rise.
What to do: Avoid walking at night. If you must walk…don't carry a purse or bag at all. Spend the extra $3 to take a Tuk Tuk back to your hotel and if you're in Phnom Penh, use the driving service called PassApp (kind of like Uber but with a Rickshaw).

An anecdotal story for you...

One night, in Phnom Penh, I was walking home from a bar with 2 friends: 1 small girl and 1 very tall guy. We noticed two motorbikes following us, passing us and then turning back around. Circling us. They were waiting for the right opportunity to drive up next to us and grab our purses. Our guy friend confronted them with a "Hey, we see what you're trying to do" attitude and they eventually gave up. **Lesson:** always be on guard no matter how many people are in your group. Don't be afraid to speak up.

Motorbikes and Car Crashes

Man oh man. There are far too many traffic accidents in Cambodia. You have monster 16-wheel trucks next to tiny motorbikes passing each other on dirt roads. You have cows in the road. You have drunk drivers galore.

Where: Everywhere
What to do: Always wear your seatbelt in a car and always secure your helmet tightly when riding a motorbike. Don't ride or drive with someone you have an uneasy feeling about. Practice riding your motorbike in rural areas before driving in the city or on main roads.

Landmines

It is estimated that there are 4-6 million unexploded landmines in Cambodia which are left over from the Vietnam war.

Where: With it's unexplored jungles and protected Angkor Wat empire, there is a lot of land left untouched in the north of Cambodia.
What to do: Don't stray from the paths around Angkor Wat, in the jungle or in rural areas and farmland.

Safety Tips for Cambodia

Wear a Cross Shoulder Bag
This certainly makes it more difficult for thieves to remove your bag from your body. Also make sure the straps of the bag are relatively thick and aren't easy to cut.

Use ATMs inside Convenience Stores
As a universal travel rule, ATMs inside supermarkets, convenient stores, and banks are your biggest insurance policies against you becoming a victim of fraud or having a wad of cash ripped out of your hand.

Look Both Ways Before you Cross the Street
Duh, but really- traffic here is different than back home. Pedestrians don't have the right of way here- even on a green light. When crossing the street, don't just look for cars- look for motorbikes that whiz between the cars, too!

Let's Talk about Sexual Assault
Foreign women (that's us) are statistically more likely to be sexually assaulted by a foreign man (other travelers) on vacation than they are to be sexually assaulted by a Khmer man. Think about it; in hostels, hotels and bars- we are more likely to be hanging around foreign men, quite possibly with alcohol in our systems, and therefore exposed to that risk. Just like you would at home, monitor your sobriety levels and be aware of your surroundings.

Hide your Phone
While on the street, text on your phone like you would when you're not supposed to be texting in class. Don't hold your phone out in front of you while texting or ordering a PassApp. Also, don't leave your phone sitting on the table at a restaurant. It may disappear.

Put your Bags Behind your Body in a Tuk Tuk
Conceal your bags and make them difficult to grab. Thieves like convenience.

Be So Careful Walking at Night
Make smart choices. Stay on lit roads, walk with a friend, and don't get super drunk and wander off by yourself. All of the about will make you a target very quickly.

Areas that are <u>Relatively</u> Safe to Walk at Night:

- ✓ **The Riverside in Phnom Penh:** I've only had lovely experiences here – but I am aware that little thieves are waiting for someone to set their purse down. Just keep an eye out while you stroll along the river in the evening (before 9 or 10pm).
- ✓ **Serendipity Road and Beach in Sihanoukville:** I personally know women who have been victims of motorbike thieves in Sihanoukville, but not directly on Serendipity Road. You **do** need to watch your purse very carefully on the beach, however. My purse was stolen while I had it sitting next to me in a beach chair - I didn't even notice.
- ✓ **The Night Market in Siem Reap:** This area doesn't see too much crime.
- ✓ **All of Koh Rong:** The islands never sleep so you don't get a "seedy" time of night. That being said, don't get too carefree with your belongings on a night out. Keep your bag on your body. If you set it down, someone else will pick it up.

Check out a company called **World Nomads** which offers full-coverage theft plans for extremely reasonable prices.

Tourist Visa for Cambodia

Yay for passport stamps. Or in this case, full page passport stickers.

Here's the deal: tourists are allowed to enter and explore Cambodia for 30 days on arrival.

There are 2 ways to obtain your Tourist Visa.

1. Visa on Arrival
No steps or paperwork to file before you come to Cambodia. You can get your visa when you enter the country either by air or by land.

What you need:
- ✓ 1 Passport Photo
- ✓ $30 US Cash
- ✓ 1 Full Blank Page in your Passport
- ✓ Application Form (that you receive and fill out at immigration)

There are many visa options on the Application Form. You want to check the T Visa.
*If there is a chance that you'll want to extend your visa and stay in the country for longer than 30 days, apply for the Business Visa (Visa E for $35).

2. The Online e-Visa
Hallelujah! The Cambodia has recently launched the e-Visa. This process allows you to apply online for your visa- before you come to Cambodia. This will save you time in lines (at least, hypothetically). Print out your form and bring it with you to immigration.

Here's how to do it:

Step 1: Go to the e-Visa webpage: **www.evisa.gov.kh**
Step 2: Fill in the application
Step 3: Pay the fee or $30 USD plus $6 for the service fee
Step 4: Wait for visa approval. You'll get an email with your visa within 3 business days.
Step 5: Print your visa and present it at immigration in Cambodia.

Important Note: The e-Visa is only accepted at Siem Reap and Phnom Penh airports, Koh Kong & Poipet Border Crossing (from Thailand), and Bavet Border Crossing (from Vietnam).

346

What to Expect at Immigration

Airport Immigration is smooth. You get off the plane, walk up to the immigration desk, hand them all your documents with your passport and wait about 10-30 minutes for your visa to be put in your passport. Then you go through the official immigration line and viola! – Welcome to Cambodia!

At least, that's airport immigration….

Border Immigration, however, can be overwhelming. When leaving Thailand, Laos, or Vietnam – there are two checkpoints for you to cross. First, you will officially exit the country by visiting that country's immigration checkpoint where you'll receive your exit stamp. Then, you'll then walk through a strange 'no man's land' between the two countries. Just follow the people. You can't mess this up. You will then arrive at Cambodia's border, collect an application form, fill it out and then stand in line to receive your visa.

Ps. At land border crossings, you might be approached by porters who speak incredible English, offer to carry your bag and help you with the visa process. For a $5 fee, of course. When the lines are super long with lots of travelers, I see no harm in slipping a dude some cash to skip the line for you.

Not So Fun Fact #2
The female life expectancy in Cambodia is only 61.5 years.

Not So Fun Fact #1
The male life expectancy in Cambodia is 60.3 years.

Cambodian Festivals and Holidays

A little festival incentive to help you plan your big trip!

January

✦ **December 31st – January 1st : Western New Year**
Cities and islands that have been dusted with international influence put on
big New Years parties and celebrations just like back home. On a bigger
scale, bars and clubs will go all out with DJs, drink specials, and festive
decor. On a smaller scale, you might find Khmer kids in the streets with
illegal fireworks! Bring something sparkly and plan to stay up until
midnight.

Best Place to Celebrate
- Koh Rong Island – All of it!
- Phnom Penh Western Hotels like Sofitel or Sokha
- Phnom Penh Clubs like Vito or Heart of Darkness

✦ **January 7th – Victory over Genocide Day**
The Khmer Rouge fell on January 7th, 1979. While this is a celebratory day
for most Khmer people, it can be a contentious day for Khmers who found
themselves fighting alongside the regime. Regardless, it's a monumental day
for the country's history- particularly in Phnom Penh where you can attend
a gathering and parade where military and civilians gather to listen to
speeches and presentations. You might not understand every word, but
you'll certainly feel the sentiments and emotion.

Best Place to Commemorate
- Koh Pich in Phnom Penh

✦ **End of January (depending on the moon)- Meak Bochea**
On this full-moon day, Buddhists repent from their mistakes and sins by
visiting temples for special ceremonies and gathering for massive parades in
the streets. To honor Buddha and his teachings, you'll witness traditions and
rituals with chanting, incense and candles on a fascinating large scale.

Best Spot to Celebrate

- Tuol Sleng Genocide Museum (Phnom Penh) to witness repenting
- Preah Reachtroap Mount in Ponhea Leu District for a parade

- Both big and small Buddhist Temples around Cambodia

February

✦ February 15th, 2019 - Chinese New Year

While there are plenty of Chinese-Khmer citizens in Cambodia, there isn't a central China Town for celebrations. Rather, those celebrating Chinese New Year celebrate in a small family setting.

Pro Tip: If you can, avoid visiting during Chinese New Year. Cambodia is the new hot spot destination for Chinese Tour Groups. With direct flights from China, you can expect the beaches to be crowded, hotels to be over-booked, ferry boats to fill up in advance, and airports to be an absolute shit show.

March

✦ March 8th – International Women's Day

Cambodian women are a force to be reckoned with! Most countries that have been struck by unimaginable tragedy remain broken. But not Cambodia. Thanks largely to the women of this country who got to work quickly, repairing business, healing families, and inspiring cultural growth and change. Womens day celebrates women of all ages! It's a beautiful day to be in Cambodia.

Most Popular Celebration Spots
- Koh Rong Island – The local organization 'Friends of Koh Rong' throws an annual celebration of women and girls on the island. Gather in the village to witness and join in on the empowerment of local ladies.

April

✦ **April 14th-16ᵗʰ - Khmer New Year (Chol Chnam Thmey)**
Get ready for 3 days of beer, whiskey, and baby powder. Yes, baby powder. Khmers cover each other in this stuff and carry on drinking while looking like ghosts. Night time feasts are common and music lasts well into mid-morning until the beer lulls everyone to sleep.
- Day 1: Maha Sangkran- a day to pay homage to Buddha by visiting temples
- Day 2: Vireak Vanabat- the day of charity and donations
- Day 3: Vearak Loeng Sak- A day to wash away sins by washing Buddhist statues and pouring clean water on the elderly

Most Popular Celebration Spots
- Wat Phnom in Phnom Penh for traditional ceremonies
- Visit small villages or small corner stores where locals will be drinking (and would love for you to join)
- My Personal Recommendation: Koh Rong Samleom Village. From the pier, go left in the sand and keep walking until you go over a tiny bridge. You'll enter the village where you can join in on a day of drinking and dancing with the locals!

October

✦ **Octover 8-10ᵗʰ - Pchum Ben (Ancestor's Day)**
It is believed that on this day, spirits and ancestors come down from the heavens to visit family members and friends. The living visit pagodas, offering food, incense and money to help ease spirits' burdens and connect with their loved ones who have passed. Business and government offices shut down while temples fill up.

Most Popular Celebration Spots:
- Angkor Wat
- Temples and pagodas of all sizes

✦ **October 29ᵗʰ - Coronation Day**
Not exactly like Elsa's party in Frozen, but still well worth a trip to the palace- Coronation Day marks the anniversary of when King Norodom Sihamoni took the throne. The Royal Palace is lit up and decorated with extra special touches!

Most Popular Celebration Spots:
- Phnom Penh's Royal Palace

November

✦ November 9th - Independence Day

Ceremonies in the morning and fireworks in the evening- Cambodia's Independence Day is done right. Commemorating Cambodia's independence from France and paying tribute to King Sihanok who is credited for reaching independence, this is a fantastic opportunity to soak up some history.

Most Popular Celebration Spots:
- Phnom Penh's Independence Monument in the morning
- Phnom Penh's Riverfront in the evening

✦ November 10th- 12th 2019 - Bon Om Touk Water Festival

Dragon Boat Races! To celebrate the end of the rainy season and to say 'thank you' to the rivers that give life to this country- millions of Khmers gather in the capitol! For 3 days, there are boat races, concerts, parades and a special rice treat called Ak Ambok that is specially made.

Most Popular Celebration Spots:
- Tonle Sap River that runs in front of the Royal Palace

Cambodian Directory

Tourist Police – English Speaking
- ✓ **Phnom Penh**
  Phone: 012 942 484
  Address: St. 598, 12107, Phnom Penh

- ✓ **Siem Reap**
  Phone: 012 402 424
  Address: Mondul 3 Village, Sangkat Slor Kram

American Embassy
Emergency Line: 023 728 000
Address: 1 Christopher Howes (96), Phnom Penh, Cambodia

Australian Embassy
Emergency Line: 023 213 470
Address: National Assembly Street, Phnom Penh, Cambodia

British Embassy
Emergency Line: 023 427 124
Address: Preah Botum Soriyavong St. (75), Phnom Penh, Cambodia

Canadian Embassy
Emergency Line: 023 213 470
Address: Street 254 (Senei Vinnavat Oum), House #9

Thai Embassy
Emergency Line: 023 726 306
Address: 196 Preah Norodom Blvd (41), Phnom Penh, Cambodia

Royal Phnom Penh Hospital – For Serious Injury
Western standards- more expensive than other Cambodian hospitals but cheaper than American hospitals!
Phone: 023 991 000
Address: 888 Russian Confederation Blvd, Toeuk Thla, Phnom Penh

Travellers Medical Clinic – $40 per Visit
Phone: 023 306 802
Address: 88 Street 108 (Wat Phnom Quarter), Phnom Penh

Driver Directory for Cambodia

Mr. Lem
Transportation: Tuk Tuk
Area: Siem Reap
Phone Number/WhatsApp: +855885473246
Facebook: Lem Live

Capacity: 1-4 people

Mr. Samith
Transportation: Tuk Tuk
Area: Siem Reap
Phone Number: +85569221250
Capacity: 1-4 people

Mr. La
Transportation: Lexus RS
Area & Route: Sihanoukville to Phnom Penh (or within these cities)
Phone Number: 0885464432 / 098 63 58 71
Capacity: 4 People

Mr. Dara
Transportation: Lexus RS
Area & Route: Kampot to Phnom Penh (or within these cities)
Phone Number: 0777 77 20 21 / 017 89 19 81
Capacity: 4 People

When these drivers are booked up, they will often send one of their Taxi driver friends in their place. It's a country full of wonderful hustlers and hard workers!

For more drivers or to schedule a ride share with other travelers, check out the Facebook group called '**Taxi Share Cambodia**'.

Pro Tip: When calling from outside of Cambodia with an international number (anything other than Cambodian), add the country code (+855) and make sure you've dropped the first 0. When calling with a Cambodian number, drop the country code and add a 0.

For example: +855 23 427 124 = 023 427 124
Same number. Different input.

Gynecology Services & Female Stuff

Women's Center (OB/GYN) | Khema Clinic and Maternity All of the services including birth control, ultrasounds, STD testing, Pap smears, etc.
Open: Daily 24/7
Phone: 023 880 949
Address: 18 Street 528, Toul Kork, Phnom Penh

Birth Control Pills
You can buy birth control pills over the counter in Cambodia. Look for tested brands called FMP, OK, Anna or Microgynon ED.
Where: All pharmacies

Other Birth Control Methods
The patch, IUDS, Shots and more can be found at many English-speaking clinics around the country- and usually for a cheaper price than back home.
Where: Reproductive Health Association of Cambodia (RHAC), Khema Clinic and Maternity, & Marie Stopes International are recommended by female expats.

Morning After Pill
Where: Most pharmacies carry these pills under "Pregnon" (I know, right?) or "Anlitin" for around $5

Unwanted Pregnancy
Where: Marie Stopes International
Legal up to 12 weeks but not widely available.
Locations in Phnom Penh, Siem Reap and Battambang
Contact: hotline@mariestopes.org.kh

Medical Abortion Pill – Metabon
Where: Pharmacies carry this pill which is effective for up to 9 weeks after pregnancy. I recommend calling or consulting a clinic before you take the pill.

For more information, check out gynopedia.org/Cambodia

The Cambodia Bucket List

- ✓ Eat Bugs
- ✓ Take a Joss Shot
- ✓ Visit Angkor Wat
- ✓ Ride in a Tuk Tuk
- ✓ Go on a Boat Tour
- ✓ Befriend a Beach Dog
- ✓ Make a Khmer Friend
- ✓ Visit a Buddhist Temple
- ✓ Drink Angkor Draft Beer
- ✓ Take a photo of a Water Buffalo
- ✓ Swim with the Plankton at night
- ✓ Sunbathe on any White Sand Beach
- ✓ Learn How to Say 3 Words in Khmer
- ✓ Get Lost

Send me photos of your Bucket List accomplishments on
Instagram @ SoloGirlsTravelGuide

Vietnam

"If I'm an advocate for anything, it's to move. As far as you can, as much as you can. Across the ocean, or simple across the river. The extent to which you can walk in someone else's shoes or at least eat their food, it's a plus for everybody. Open your mind, get off the couch, move."

-Anthony Bourdain – a lover of Vietnam, it's people, and it's food.

Introduction: Vietnam 101

Most people come to Vietnam with images of rice fields, straw hats, and remnants of war in their minds. And those people aren't wrong. But Vietnam is more than just farming and historical tragedy.

In the North, every mountain pass and collection of rolling hills looks like it came straight out of a Disney movie. Unspoiled nature, ancient traditions in weaving, and tons of Vietnamese dishes you've never even heard of are all hiding in the north.

Make your way down through the center of the country and the scene changes. Limestone cliffs stand tall up in the distance, reaching towards the sky like some futuristic city. There are caves to be explored, underground rivers to swim in, and the most colorful towns to be explored.

Suddenly, you're in the South sipping on cocktails while relaxing on pristine, seemingly untouched beaches. The cosmopolitan life calls out to you while the old traditions of Vietnam are scattered in-between.

To put things simply, Vietnam feels like 50 different worlds pushed together into one country; every city with its own galaxy.

However, no matter where you are in Vietnam, a few themes never change…

Learn about the country's war history, discovering the lasting impacts of chemical warfare. Find out just what prisoners of war went through, and how resilient the people of Vietnam are.

Taste your way through every city and discover that each region has its own specialties. There's not a corner without street vendors galore.

Party until you drop, whether you're looking for the big city pub crawls or late nights at beach bars.

Take in the natural scenery, trekking through jungles, canyons, and mountain passes for those Insta-worthy views.

Try your hand on a motorbike, seeing what it feels like to speed through changing landscapes with the wind in your hair and a smile on your face.

And of course, leave with the overwhelming desire to come back as soon as possible.

Vietnam Weather

Unlike its South East Asian neighbors, Vietnam's weather cannot be summed up with one simple weather pattern. Spanning over 3,000 kilometers from North to South, every region offers a different environment from dry deserts to icy mountain passages.

The Far North

Most backpackers would consider the 'Far North' anything beyond Hanoi. This region includes mountainous destinations like Sapa and Ha Giang. Up here, you'll experience colder temperatures and more rain. Just assume that you'll be bundled up and wet to some degree- and go with the flow.

Sometimes you'll need a rain jacket and boots that are prepared for wet and muddy hikes; and sometimes a heavy coat and sneakers will do the trick.

Hottest Months: June - August (21° C / 70° F) with heavy, sporadic rain fall to cool you down.
Coldest Months: December - January (10-12° C /50-54° F) with dry but frosty conditions.

Wettest Months: June - July with heavy mist and hours of rain
Official Monsoon Season: April - September
Most Ideal Time to Visit: February - April (to avoid the coldest, wettest months).

The North

North Vietnam is home to some of the country's most popular backpacking destinations like Hanoi, Halong Bay, and Ninh Binh. While you'll be drier and warmer here than up in the mountains, but you're not in tropical territory yet!

Hanoi weather has two seasons: one of which feels like Seattle or London with gray skies, rainy days, and cold ass temperatures. The other season feels like Florida with hot and sweaty weather.

Hottest Months: July - September (28-29° C / 82-84° F) and wet
Coldest Months: January - March (17-22° C / 63-72° F) and dry

Wettest Months: July - September
Official Monsoon Season: May - October
Most Ideal Time to Visit: August - October for a mix of warm and dry weather

The Center

As far as weather is concerned, Central Vietnam is a dream come true. Hoi An, Hue, and Nha Trang experience the most temperate climate with dry conditions and pleasant tank-top weather...practically year-round.

Hottest Months: June - August (34-35° C / 93-95° F) and dry
Coldest Months: December - February (25-26° C / 77-79° F) and dry

Wettest Months: October - November with heavy, short showers
Official Monsoon Season: September - December
Most Ideal Time to Visit: December – May for moderate temperatures and dry weather

The South

Unlike its relatives to the North, Southern Vietnam enjoys relatively stable weather. As a result, you don't have to prepare for anything other than the occasional storm. That makes this region a perfect start or end to any trip across Vietnam. The south includes destinations like Ho Chi Minh City, Mui Ne, the Mekong Delta, and Phu Quoc Island.

Hottest Months: March - May (29-30° C / 84-86° F) and dry
Coldest Months: October - December (27° C / 81° F) with occasional showers

Wettest Months: June - August with short, heavy afternoon showers
Official Monsoon Season: May - November
Most Ideal Time to Visit: December - March for smaller crowds and dry weather

So, here's a quick tip for how to plan your Vietnam itinerary...

❖ If you're visiting during Spring/Summer, travel South to North

❖ If you're visiting during Autumn/Winter, travel North to South

Top 10 Veitnam Experiences

1- Trek through the mountainous region of Sapa

2- Halong Bay Boat Cruise, Halong Bay

3- The War Remnants Museum, Saigon

4- Hoi An Old City, Hoi An

5- The Caves of Phong Nha, Phong Ngh

6- Mua Caves and Dragon Mountain, Ninh Binh

7- Tam Coc Boat Ride, Ninh Binh

8- Waterfall Rappelling, Dalat

9- Nguyen Shack, Ninh Binh

10- Cu Chi Tunnels, Saigon

Vietnam Culture Norms 101

One of the most progressive countries in Southeast Asia, common sense will get you far.

Here's just a couple of tips to navigate the tough stuff.

Do's and Don'ts for Vietnam

Just real quick, some things to keep in mind to make your journey safer and more convenient.

Do...

❖ Have a Currency Cheat Sheet

Don't get ripped off. Know how much your spending with a currency cheat sheet. On a piece of paper, write down each Vietnamese note and its **rough** equivalent in your currency.

For example:

20k = $1
100k = $4.50
And so on. Just round up to make life easier.

Then, take a picture of said paper and set it as your home screen on your phone. No more whipping out the calculator and no more getting ripped off. A quick glance at your phone and you can convert in an instant!

❖ Carry Small Notes

Most places can't break a 500k bill. It's best to break these in a restaurant or convenient store ASAP.

❖ Carry a Shawl

You'll need to cover your shoulders anytime you enter a pagoda or a Buddhist Temple. Also, those bus rides get cold! You can use your shawl as a blanket.

❖ Carry Toilet Paper

Most toilets don't have toilet paper. BUT at nearly every shop, you can find little rectangular packets of tissue that will fit in your purse. You'll need these as most toilets just have a 'bum gun' used like a bidet.

❖ Dress like You're on Vacation with your Parents

Keep your beach wear on the beach and be tasteful when it comes to short shorts and low-cut tops. Boobies and butt cheeks should be tucked in, you know what I mean.

Oh, and don't bicycle around town in a bikini top. Police have actually started fining tourists for this in some towns.

❖ Remember to Drink Lots of Water

It's easy to forget! The heat (and beer) will dehydrate you so quickly in Vietnam. Don't neglect that refreshing H2O.

❖ Have Travel Insurance

Motorbike crashes are common here, crossing the road is sketchy, and all outdoor activities come with risk. Luckily, Vietnam has a fabulous international health care system. You'd be a silly girl not to travel with travel insurance.

My go-to for travel insurance is **WorldNomads.com**. They'll cover everything from doctor visits for a tummy ache and medivacs in case your fall off a mountain (that shit happens).

Don't...

❖ Show Off

You want to look like you have no money and nothing to steal. Keep your phone, iPad, and laptop low key.

❖ Volunteer Short-Term

Any volunteer program that involves an orphanage or a 1-4-week stint teaching English to children is a scam and exploits Vietnamese youth. If you want to volunteer, be ready to commit to at least 3 months. Check out the 'Volunteer in Vietnam' section for some respected programs.

❖ Cause Vietnamese People to "Lose Face"

Vietnamese people do not take embarrassment or confrontation lightly. Causing a fuss, losing your temper or disrespecting a local can put you in some serious danger. Smile through even the bitchiest interactions and you're more likely to get your way.

❖ Eat the "Free" Donuts

In the big cities, women walk around carrying baskets of fried bread. They'll entice you to try one "for free", but once you take a bite, they will not leave you alone until you buy. They might follow you or physically grab you until you buy. And watch for the 'swapping your 500k note for a 50k note' trick. These ladies are masters at getting the most out of naive tourists.

❖ Take Pictures or Videos without Permission

Uniformed police officers eating an ice cream cone, Vietnamese women wearing traditional dresses, and especially children in villages – always ask permission before you take someone's picture.

❖ Talk about the Vietnam War

If an older local engages you in wartime conversation, the safest bet is just not to get into it. However, these conversations can be more open-minded and insightful with college-aged Vietnamese. This young generation of Vietnamese are incredibly insightful.

Quick Vietnam Travel Tips

- **Get a SIM Card Immediately.**

Internet access will be your lifeline…and only for $9.

In Vietnam especially, you'll find that you heavily rely on a SIM card for necessary internet shenanigans like…

- ✓ Grab Taxi
- ✓ Google Maps
- ✓ Getting un-lost
- ✓ Tinder (yea…why not?)
- ✓ Life in General

When you **land at the airport**, after you pass through customs and enter the arrival hall, you'll see plenty of kiosks selling SIM Cards.

Look for the carrier Mobifone or Viettel.

A 4G plan with UNLIMITED Data for 1 month is around $9 USD/ 200k VND.

You'll have package options that include phone calls, which I've found useful. But it's not a must.

The customer service dude will set everything up for you. Just check that your mobile data is working before you leave the kiosk.

If you **enter Vietnam by land** or forget to buy a Sim at the airport, find one of these stores in town for the most comprehensive data packages and staff that will set everything up for you.
- Viettel Store
- Mobifone Store
- TheGioidiDong

Buying SIM cards from local shops or mini marts is a confusing process.

A SIM will keep you safe and give you that reassurance to travel and explore solo.

- Consider the 'Hop On / Hop Off Bus Ticket that will tour you around Vietnam on your schedule.

- Use the website 12go.Asia or Baolau.com to check travel routes between cities and to book your transport (especially trains). You can print out your tickets at your hotel or present your e-ticket at the counter.

- Beware of all taxis. Even while traveling with Vietnamese people, the meters magically multiply the fare. If you must flag down a taxi in Vietnam, use Mai Linh Taxi or Vinasun. Look for white and green taxis.

Chapter 17: Ho Chi Minh City

If there was ever a tale of two cities, Ho Chi Minh fits the bill. It's traditional and modern. Hectic and organized. Tied to the past and reaching for the future.

Formerly known as Saigon, this city has seen more than its fair share of dramatic history. In the late 1800s, Saigon was the center of the French trade in Indochina. By the 1950s, it was the capitol of independent South with dreams of capitalism and hopes to conquer the communist North. Pairing up with American forces, Saigon served as the base for American military operations during this time.

In the end, its fall to the communistic North would bring an end to twenty years of war and an official name change of the city from Saigon to Ho Chi Minh (the name of the leader of the North).

Today, Ho Chi Minh City is still lovingly referred to as Saigon by locals and expats alike. Eight million people (and three million motorbikes) call this bustling place home.

From budget deals on accommodation to upscale rooftop bars, there's an adventure here for everyone. Immerse yourself in the city's center, enjoying the backpacker nightlife of Bui Vien. Venture out into China Town, Little

Japan, and Little Korea to take advantage of the close cuisine proximity. Soak up some history and perspective at the War Remnants Museum.

Whatever you do, just make sure to leave with a bowl of Pho in your stomach and a cold beer in your hand. The rest will stick with you for years to come.

Fun Vietnam Fact
The Bin Chao Hot Springs, three hours east of HCMC, are hot enough to boil eggs.

From the Airport into HCMC

Almost every traveler starts their Vietnam adventure in HCMC. With super cheap flights from Bangkok and Phnom Penh, odds are that you'll fly in, too.

Once you're out of the airport, here's what you'll do next!

Option 1: Grab Taxi

Once you're outside the airport, order a grab. They'll take you anywhere you need to go and help you with your bags.

How Much: Around $9 USD / 200k VND
Duration: 30-40 minutes

Option 2: The Bus

Outside of the arrival hall, you can hop on a very cheap bus to the District 1 (where most hostels and hotels are).

Look for bus Number 152.
You'll pay 5,000 dong for yourself and 5,000 dong for your bag.

You board, tell the driver "District 1", and he'll tell you when to get off. You'll likely see other backpackers doing the same- so if all else fails, you can just follow their lead.

The bus drops you off near Ben Thanh Market, not far from Boi Vien Street.

How Much: $0.23 USD / 5k VND
Duration: 55 minutes depending on traffic
Where: Right outside the terminal
When: Every day, every 15 minutes.
*This bus stops running around 6pm.

Huge Pro Tip

If for some reason you need to take a public taxi, ONLY ride with Mai Linh or Vinasun Taxi.

Areas to Explore in Ho Chi Minh City

Unlike other cities in Southeast Asia, Ho Chi Minh is broken up into manageable, bite-sized pieces. Each of its twenty-four districts has a unique vibe and stands out among the crowd. Some are known for their nightlife and others for the best food in the city.

Let's highlight the most popular districts in Saigon, shall we?

District 1

If you're a backpacker, odds are that you'll be staying in District 1. It's Ho Chi Minh's hotspot for hostels, bars, and restaurants. This is the epitome of backpacker life + close proximity to tours and sightseeing.

Start your day off with the district's many museums and architectural landmarks. There are parks, monuments, and the must-see War Remnants Museum within walking distance.

Afterwards, treat yourself to cheap food sold by street vendors on every corner. Next, plan to shop til you drop with markets galore selling knock-off handbags and handmade trinkets. Be prepared to haggle to your heart's desire.

When night hits, things get crazy around here! Locals and backpackers hit the streets for street food, bars, club hopping, or just sitting in plastic chairs with a beer and the best people watching you could ever imagine.

District 2

As Vietnam's largest city, Ho Chi Minh attracts endless expats. The vast majority of these foreigners choose to live in District 2, giving it a uniquely Western feel in a city that is undoubtedly Asian. For a taste of what living abroad may look like (and for some of the comforts of home) checking out District 2 is a great idea for an afternoon adventure.

It's best to come here with an empty stomach, a cute outfit, and your camera ready for some Instagram action. You'll be spending the next few hours diving in and out of small hipster cafés and shops. With a little wander about, you'll find that street murals are aplenty. Leaving without a few selfies is a cardinal sin!

While you're here, check out Saigon Outcast, a popular bar that manages to mix beach energy with urban life. Aside from the great drinks, the graffiti-covered walls and industrial decor make for one of the coolest spots around.

District 3

Get local in District 3. With fewer tourists and tourist attractions, you get the chance to mix in with resident Vietnamese who are simply going about their daily routines amongst beautiful French-style architecture and Buddhist traditions. In fact, District 3 is home to the vast majority of the city's Buddhist pagodas.

And for any foodies reading, District 3 is definitely the place to be in terms of local food! While Bahn Mi and Pho are delicious, you'll have ample opportunity to taste Vietnamese delicacies and dishes that are not so well known in the west.

You Can't Miss: Women's Museum, Ky Dong Church, Archbishop's Palace, Xai Lot Pagoda, Vinh Nghiem Pagoda, and the Jade Emperor Pagoda

Where to Eat: Nguyen Thien Thuat Street, Ky Dong Street, Vuon Chuoi Market, and the Phu Nhuan District.

Pro Tip: If you plan to visit Buddhist pagodas in District 3, dress for the occasion if with an outfit that covers your knees and shoulders.

District 5 (Cho Lon)

I know, I know. If you wanted to experience China, you'd probably be there instead of Vietnam. However, you're so close to China that this is the next best thing! Why not experience the Chinese-Vietnamese fusion known as Cho Lon. This district boasts the largest market in all of Vietnam, Chinese temples...and of course, Chinese food.

Cho Lon literally translates to "big market". You'll understand why the simple name is so fitting after a visit to Binh Tay. It's a great spot to spend a few hours, eating your way through a variety of dishes and shopping for little trinkets to take home.

What makes District 5 so unique—despite every city in the world having a China Town—is its specific history. Throughout the 1970s, the government launched anti-Chinese campaigns in Ho Chi Minh City. They sought to remove the Chinese influence on Vietnam, and in turn worked to dismantle China Town. Luckily, those efforts simply resulted in a neighborhood that is a unique mix of the two cultures, showing the resiliency of the people who live there.

You Can't Miss: Binh Tay Market, Nghia An Hoi Quan Pagoda, Tam Son Hoi Quan Pagoda, and Thien Hau Pagoda.

District 7 (Phu My Hung)

Sick of the smog, traffic, and crowds? District 7 may be the oasis you've been searching for! While still providing access to everything you love about Ho Chi Minh City, this district feels world's away from the city center and is worth a visit just for a few breaths of fresh air!

District 7 is Ho Chi Minh's second most popular expat neighborhood with all the modern amenities – resulting in a very diverse community. Here you'll find Little Japan and Little Korea nestled amongst with countless western spots.

You Can't Miss: Little Japan and Little Korea! Even if you're looking to stick to the city center's backpacker prices and vibes, it's interesting to see the stark contrast between the alleys of downtown and the broad, pristine streets of District 7. It's a picture-perfect example of the duality Ho Chi Minh City is known for.

Accommodation in HCMC

Pro Tip

Compared to hotels in Ho Chi Minh City, AirBnb offers some incredible properties for a fraction of the price. That being said, the hotels that made it on this list score above and beyond the rest in terms of value for money, location, AND experience - that will match every traveler's budget.

Ps. Accommodation prices fluctuate depending on the season. Throughout this book, you can take these prices as an average to get an idea if they fit your budget!

Saigon Backpackers Hostel $

More commonly known as Vietnam Backpackers Hostel, there's a reason why VHB is the most famous hostel group in Vietnam. They throw epic parties, put on fun and informational tours, are a hub for motorbike tourists, and will help you sort out any visas for Vietnam and beyond! You'll find their hostels all up and down Vietnam- starting here in Saigon. Start your trip by making some friends who you might link up with and travel the country together- it happens all the time!

Style: Dorms & Privates
Starts at: $5 & $20 USD / 114k & 455k VND
Where: District 1
Address: 200 Le Lai, Pham Ngu Lao

The Hideout Hostel $

The perfect hostel for solo girls to meet other travelers! The Hideout Hostel has been voted "The Most Popular Hostel in Ho Chi Minh City" 2 years running... although I've rated them #1 for at least 5. They're well-known on the backpacking circuit for social events like the Saigon Pub Crawl, Trivia Night, and free-beer hour for guests. They also have a movie room where you can chill out while you wait for your bus or flight to the next destination.

Style: Dorm Beds
Starts at: $7 USD/ 160k VND
Where: District 1
Address: 281 Phạm Ngũ Lão, Phường Phạm Ngũ Lão, Quận 1

Here I am #406 – AirBnb $

Treat yourself to a swanky Vietnamese style loft with a cozy couch, kitchen, and pitch-black sleeping space with extra quiet surroundings. You're just a 5-minute walk to the popular Bui Vien Street, the Saigon Night Market, and all of the street shopping you could ever dream of. Wake up at 6am and walk to Da An Park just 10 minutes away- the park is alive with Zumba classes, badminton, and old men having coffee. This place is a gem.

Style: Private Loft
Starts at: $29 USD / 640k VND
Where: District 1
Address: 22 Nguyen Trai, Ben Thanh, District 1

Alagon Saigon Hotel & Spa $$

Time to be a queen, queen. The rooms are chicly decorated, there is a bathtub to soak, you can eat breakfast in the garden, the pool has plenty of lounge beds, there's a god damn jacuzzi, the views from the rooftop are perfect for an evening beer...I could go on. But girl, this is what $60 gets you in Vietnam. You can even upgrade to have your stay include 'High Tea' like a proper lady. Take advantage.
Style: Private
Starts at: $60 USD / 1,370,000 VND
Where: District 1

Address: 301-303 Ly Tu Trong, Ben Thanh

A&EM Signature Hotel $$

Damn, this place is sexy. Marble everywhere, snuggly Tinder-approved rooftop couches, an amazing cocktail menu at the rooftop bar, and a spa on site. This is one of the most lavish hotels in Saigon AND it won't break your bank. Score! The location is perfect for evening adventures and the staff go out of their way to make your visit as comfortable as possible.

Style: Private
Starts at: $75 USD / 1,712,000 VND
Where: District 1
Address: 52 Thu Khoa Huan Street, Ben Thanh Ward

Where to Eat in HCMC

Saigon Cafes

Milkbar
Milkbar is only a fifteen-minute walk from the War Remnants Museum and nearby to many popular markets, making it a great start to a morning of exploring District 3 where you can get your coffee, then hit up a market for breakfast, and then dive into sightseeing. Milkbar is ultra popular for their gourmet iced lattes and their classic milkshakes. And also popular for their resident cats and kittens!

Open: 7am-10pm
Where: District 3
Address: 100 Tran Quoc Toan Street

The Workshop
Out of all the cafes on this list, The Workshop will definitely be the busiest—and for good reason! This industrial-themed spot is a hit with young Vietnamese students and professionals. While it isn't the spot for a cozy morning read, it's a great option to get a few hours of laptop work or journaling. Its social atmosphere paired with Australia-grade coffee make it a must-do for any digital nomad.

Open: 8am-9am
Where: District 1
Address: 27 Ngo Duc Ke Street

Vietcetera Cafe & Shoppe
Vietcetera has snacks, meals, books, gifts, coffees, etcetera. Hence the name! This is the perfect spot to come if you're just not sure what you're looking for (or want to be transported to the Vietnamese version of hipsterville). You can sip on a cold drink or eat a toasted sandwich while exploring their small shop of local handcrafts. It's a great place to pick up souvenirs while recharging after a morning of adventure.

Open: 8:00 - 21:00
Where: District 3
Address: 290 Nguyen Thi Minh Khai Street

The Note Coffee

This cafe truly lives up to its name! Note Coffee has taken an unconventional approach to decorating their walls, allowing patrons to cover them in post-it notes full of affirmations, quotes and memories. It's a unique approach at spreading positivity, which mirrors their equally unique and fun menu. Trek up to their second floor, take in the morning sun, and enjoy a coconut iced coffee!

Open: 8am-Midnight
Where: District 1
Address: 183 Bui Vien Street

Goc Ha Noi

Nestled at the end of a narrow alley, Goc Ha Noi is the definition of a hole in the wall coffee shop. They're well known among both locals and tourists as one of the best spots in Saigon to grab an egg coffee. Their cozy decorations—including black and white historical photographs—make the perfect setting for cuddling up with a book. I recommend heading to their upstairs seating area to enjoy a nice breeze with some fabulous people watching.

Open: 8am-10pm
Where: District 1
Address: 165/3 Bui Vien Stree

Brunch in HCMC

Ho Chi Minh City's weather makes it the perfect brunch destination. You can certainly plop down in a plastic stool and enjoy a bowl of pho with the locals. Just look on any street corner or alley between the hours of 7am-11am and you'll find some pho to rock your world.

But when you're in the mood for a more international brunch or a brunch with some pizazz, here you go…

Q.Itchen Factory

The best things in life never come easy. Q.Itchen Factory is a bit off the beaten path but totally worth the journey. Better yet, it gives you an excuse to explore a new district! The restaurant has one of the coolest vibes around as its housed within an old factory in an industrial area. The food is a mix of western and eastern and all locally sourced.

Ps. This spot is a bit on the pricey end – but as a big brunch, it will cover breakfast AND lunch and therefore, is totally justifiable.

Open: 11am – 2pm, 6pm – 10:30pm
Where: District 7
Address: Lot 9, Road 7

The Hungry Pig

This little hole in the wall has managed to bring a bit of England to southern Vietnam- seamlessly. You'll see what I mean with the Full English Breakfast that comes complete with all the fixins'. Just remember to come hungry because the portion sizes are more Western than they are Asian.

Open: 7am-9pm
Where: Pham Ngu Lao Ward
Address: 144 Cong Quynh Street

Propaganda Bistro Restaurant

The murals that decorate Propaganda Bistro are all inspired by traditional Vietnamese propaganda posters. It's a journey back in time that also offers some tasty breakfast options- both Vietnamese and western. This place is so popular for their decor; however, I'm surprised they haven't stopped selling food and switched to just charging visitors for selfies. Enjoy the controversial vintage vibes and local cuisine before heading for a post-brunch stroll in the park across the street.

Open: 7:30am – 11pm
Where: District 1
Address: 21 Han Thuyen

The Vintage Emporium
Brunch is all about easing into your day. But when you're surrounded by countless motorbikes and car horns, that can be hard to do. Luckily, the Vintage Emporium serves as an oasis, with some of the most calming vibes in all of Saigon. They offer traditional brunch dishes that are affordable and delicious. I recommend trying a chocolate banana smoothie…or mimosas (because vacation)!

Open: 7am-9pm
Where: Near the Vietnam History Museum
Address: 95B Nguyen Van Thu Street

Lunch in HCMC

If you're anything like me, your days are saved for adventuring. You may start the morning off trekking through Saigon, exploring its hidden alleyways and markets. Afterwards, you'll have a massive afternoon filled with plans for museum visits and taking in the sites. Hitting up some of the town's best bars may even be in order to celebrate a day well done! But somewhere in between, you'll need to recharge and regroup. Where better than the perfect lunch spot?

Journeys Sandwich Bistro
If you've been looking for the best sandwich in Saigon—that isn't a Bahn Mi—you can find it here at Journeys. You'll find huge-portioned sandwiches inspired by America, Europe, Latin America, Asia, and even Africa. Some sandwiches are creative, and some are classic- let your stomach do the choosing. And to go with your massive meal, they've got a list of sides like coleslaw, mac & cheese, and fries (of course).

Open: 7:30am – 10pm
Where: Ben Thanh Ward
Address: 30-36 Phan Boi Chau

Poke Saigon

As you may have picked up by now, Saigon is the place where worlds clash—old and new, Western culture and Eastern culture, and so on. And when it comes to Poke Saigon, that remains true. This lunch spot offers a fascinating blend of Japanese and Hawaiian flavors in a Vietnamese setting. Plus, it's a good idea to get your fill of veggies and vitamins in between all the bread, noodles, and pork you'll be consuming during your galavant around the country.

Open: 10am- 9pm
Where: District 1 (near the river)
Address: 42/25 Nguyen Hue Street

Den Long - Home Cooked Vietnamese Restaurant

Backpackers are always looking for the "authentic" travel experience. Most want to veer off the beaten path, finding new dives that offer meals the way the locals like them. And while Den Long is becoming popular with tourists, its homemade Vietnamese food is based on generations of traditional recipes. Better yet, the staff are always available to answer your questions about how the food is made and the cultural significance of each dish. It's a lesson and a meal in one!

Open: 11:00 - 22:00
Where: District 1
Address: 130 Nguyen Trai

Dinner in HCMC

Dinner time in Saigon always feels like a mini celebration; a time to reflect on your long day full of walking for hours in sticky weather. Replenish and enjoy – you've earned it.

The Chopsticks Saigon Restaurant

Just finding The Chopsticks Saigon Restaurant is an adventure. Located at the end of an obscure alley and quite easy to miss...you probably won't notice where to go until an usher calls you in, directing you to your table (they're used to it). The menu is full of elevated Vietnamese dishes, made by professional chefs in a clean kitchen with gourmet ingredients. For a unique take on a Vietnamese staple, try their coconut rice!

Open: 11:30am - 10:30pm
Where: District 3
Address: 216/4 Dien Bien Phu Street

Pizza 4P's (Ben Thanh)

Somehow, the best pizza outside of Italy is in Vietnam! With locations in Ho Chi Minh City, Da Nang, and Hanoi, don't be surprised when I suggest this place over and over again- it's just that good!

The pizza is mind-blowing with the highest quality ingredients around. Their specialty? Pizzas served with a fist-sized ball of mozzarella that is opened up like a blooming flower at the table, giving each bite of pizza the freshest touch.

Pro Tip

On the weekend, you'll likely need a reservation. Call ahead and request a seat near the oven so you can watch the magic happen.

Open: 10am - 10:30pm
Where: District 1
Address: 8/15 Lê Thánh Tô

The Garlik De Tham Restaurant

Have a hot Tinder date? This is the place to suggest. The Garlik De Tham is modern and chic, but still playful and affordable- breaking that first date tension. With a menu full of Asian Fusion, every dish is an adventure to be shared with flavor blends and texture combinations that have never even crossed your mind.

Open: 11:30am- 10:30pm
Where: Pham Ngu Lao Ward
Address: 216 De Tham Street

While these restaurants are to die for…most of the dinner magic in Saigon happens at the night markets. Keep reading…

Street Food & Night Markets in HCMC

Pick any street, alley, neighborhood, or living room and you're sure to find someone cooking! Saigon is basically one giant kitchen. Whether you're on a tipsy night out or simply on your own street food tour, this is where some of the tastiest action is at.

Van Kiep Street

Van Kiep Street is, by far, one of the best spots in all of Saigon to sample all the Vietnamese food your heart desires. Rain or shine, the street is bustling with food vendors. It's a super long street littered with neon signs advertising everything from Pho to more bizarre treats like crickets and larva. Better yet, it's situated directly between Phu Nhuan and Bin Thang Districts—two of the most lively nightlife spots in town. Just keep in mind that you'll have around 100 vendors to choose from, so don't settle on the first stall you see!

Open: Evening to Late
Where: Phu Nhuan District / Bin Thanh District

Tran Khac Chan Street

If Vietnamese street food is meant to do anything, it's to overwhelm your senses! And if you want Saigon's best sensory overload, Tran Khac Chan Street is the place to be. Motorbikes, car, foreigners, locals, street vendors, and restaurants stretch as far as the eye can see. It's madness. Despite being no longer than two-hundred meters, over 50 street vendors pack themselves into every available space. Just follow your nose and eyes and eat spontaneously.

Open: Evening to Late
Where: District 3

Vinh Khanh Street

Vinh Khanh is unique. It's extremely popular with young Vietnamese locals and is rumored to be popular with mafia members (don't worry, this strangely keeps the streets safer in terms of pick pockets). What makes this night market so unique is the representation of South Korea and Japan's hottest shopping trends AND the plethora of University students that descend on the abundance of cheap eats. Pull up a plastic stool, crack open some crab legs, and enjoy a cold beer amongst the madness.

Open: Evening to Late
Where: Binh Thanh District

Minh Phung / Cay Go Night Market

Minh Phung Night Market is known to many locals and expats as Cay Go Night Market. While many of Saigon's night markets occupy entire streets, Minh Phung weaves in and out of alleyways. It can feel like a maze after a while, which adds to the excitement of bartering and finding the best deals you can! Expect vendors selling everything from cheap t-shirts to hair ties and bracelets. A few vendors will have food, but this night market is definitely a shopping experience more than it is a culinary adventure.

Open: 2pm-Midnight
Where: District 6

Bars & Nightlife in Ho Chi Minh City

Pasteur Street Brewing Company
American craft brewing meets local Vietnamese ingredients to make the best craft beer in the country. From IPAs to seasonal batches, you can find all the flavors of high-quality craft beer right here in Vietnam. Head to their most popular tap room and mingle with expats, tourists and locals. You'll also find Pasteur Street beers sold in restaurants all over Vietnam- so, if you don't get a chance to make it here, keep an eye out as you dine up and down the country.

Open: Daily 11am - 11pm
Where: District 1
Address: 144 Pasteur | In the Alley Next to the Rex Hotel

Mary Jane's The Bar
Rooftop real estate with basement prices! Mary Jane's offers 360 sweeping views of Saigon, plus one of the best seats in the city to witness the gorgeous sunset. All seating is outdoors where you catch a cool breeze while sipping on cold beer and fresh mojitos. To add a little mystery to the magic, Mary Jane's is a hidden spot with no signs. Enter a tall bank building and take the elevator to the roof. This is as local as it gets. Just show up to the address below and you'll figure it out.

Open: Daily 9am - 11:30pm
Happy Hour: 10am – 12pm = 60k Mojitos
Where: District 3
Address: 85 Nguyen Huu Cau, Tan Dinh, District 1

Ellui Club
This is the place to go if your group can't ever agree on a playlist. Ellui blasts a great mix of hip hop, pop, and house music. There's something for every taste, and always a great beat to dance to! Like most of Saigon's best clubs, Ellui is in the main backpacker district of Bui Vien. That means it has a younger crowd and that prices will be geared towards backpackers. The drinks here are strong, so you can trust that you'll get the bang for your buck!

Open: 9pm – 3am
Where: District 1
Address: 107 Pasteur Street

My House Bar and Café

If you're looking for a more intimate experience, My House is the place to be. Living up to its name, this bar truly makes you feel like you're at home. The bartenders are among the most talented in all of Saigon, making cocktails that certainly stand out in a crowd. Some of the most charming customers even enjoy drinks invented specifically for them! Stop by in the early evening for a post-dinner cocktail and snack. It's a great spot to grab drinks before heading out for a night on the town.

Open: 11am- 1am
Where: District 1
Address: 28 Cao Ba Quat Street

TNR Saigon

Dive bar, anyone? TNR Saigon is the Saigon's best hole in the wall! option for anyone craving a unique bar experience. The atmosphere is lighthearted and fun, yet underground and urban. It serves as the perfect escape from the backpacker bars and clubs, featuring old school hip hop in place of pop and house. Better yet, the drinks are cheap!! If authenticity is what you're after, you've found it.

Open: 6pm-5am
Where: District 1
Address: 57 Do Quang Dau Street

Republic Club

The Republic Club somehow manages to be equal parts relaxing and insane! Located in the main backpacker district, you're in for a great night as soon as you step in the doors. It's comparable to European clubs but with mostly Vietnamese party-goers...meaning you can expect decent drink prices and youthful music. Republic is truly one of the only spots in Saigon that lives up to the hype as you dance the night away!

Open: 9pm – 2am
Where: District 1
Address: 19 Do Quang Dau

History & Culture in Ho Chi Minh City

Ho Chi Minh City is known for its endless war museums and sites. In fact, it's a shame to visit Saigon and not spend at least a day immersing yourself in the war that defined so much of the country's history. Join us in taking a break from urban exploring and day drinking to learn more about where Vietnam has been and where it's going!

Cu Chi Tunnels

Entry to the Cu Chi Tunnels – Get the same picture taken!

The Cu Chi Tunnels are one of the most powerful Vietnam War sites you can visit while in Saigon. They're a true testament to how creative and determined Vietnamese troops were when it came to winning the war. You'll crawl through dark, winding tunnels to reach hidden rooms and storage space. You'll see the terrifying traps the Vietnamese relied on to fend off opposing troops. You'll even get the chance to try the wartime staples Vietnamese troops relied on to survive. And the few meters you explore will leave you wondering what life was like full-time in the tunnel network that spans over one-hundred kilometers.

Cost: 110k Admissions (+90k if you opt for a tour)
Open: 7am – 5pm
Where: 30km North of Ho Chi Minh City (Cu Chi District)

War Remnants Museum

Come prepared with some tissue, patience, and an open mind. This isn't going to be easy- particularly for Americans. When it comes to war, it's easy to imagine that it's all over when the shooting stops. However, the effects of the Vietnam War are still visible in Vietnam today. Even new generations—born decades after the war's end—are still facing the consequences. The War Remnants Museum highlights important details and events during the war in addition to its aftermath. Several exhibits are centered around photographing, highlighting everything from the terror of napalm bombs to the crippling effects of agent orange. It's an intense, sobering experience, but one that everyone in Saigon should have.

How much: $.60 USD/ 15k VND
Open: 7:30 - 18:00

Reunification Palace

If you thought this name would be self-explanatory, you were right! The Reunification Palace is the site of the end of the Vietnam War. Here, the North Vietnamese Army officially captured Saigon and reunited the country under communist rule. Today, you can stroll through the peaceful gardens and visit small exhibits on the reunification of Vietnam. You'll also have the chance to see the various wartime rooms housed in the Palace, including bunkers and the commander's office. While it's not the most in-depth tour on our list, it's worth a stop simply because its front gates were seen by millions across the globe in 1975.

How much: 40k Admission
Open: 7:30am – 11pm, 1pm - 4pm
Where: District 1

Chua Van Phat – The Temple of 10,000 Buddhas

I know, I know. If you've spent any more than a few days in Southeast Asia, then you've probably had your fill of temples! They seem to be everywhere and after a while they may all blur together. But I promise, Chua Van Phat will definitely stand out! It's a simple, charming pagoda in the middle of an extremely residential community. That alone makes it a great escape from the hustle and bustle of Saigon, allowing you to collect your thoughts before heading back into the madness. Even better, it boasts 10,000 small Buddha statues in a single room, which is truly a site to behold. Now used exclusively by local families, this Pagoda is as off-the-beaten-path as you can get!

Cost: Free
Open: Sunrise to Sunset
Where: District 5 (Corner of Cach Mang Thang Tam & Nguyen Dinh Chieu Street)

The Venerable Which Quang Duc Monument

During the Vietnam War, protest both within the country and internationally was common. Students picketed and walked out of class. Families boycotted certain protects. Politicians called on the United States to pull out of the war. But the most shocking and extreme protests came in the form of self-immolation. At this street corner, a Vietnamese Monk chose to douse himself in petrol before setting himself on fire to protest the treatment of Buddhist Monks at the time. This monument was later created in his honor and sits at the corner of two of Saigon's busy, bustling streets. The contrast between peace, history, and urban life is clearer here than anywhere else in the city.

How much: Free
Open: Always
Where: District 3 (Corner of Cach Mang Thang Tam & Nguyen Dinh Chieu Street)

Ho Chi Minh Square

Ho Chi Minh Square is in the dead-center of Saigon's busy District 1. Surrounded on all four sides by colonial buildings in the traditional French style, the square itself and a statue of its namesake are popular photo-ops for countless tourists. Historically, the square is home to Saigon's City Hall as well as the Rex Hotel, which housed international journalists throughout the Vietnam War. And once you've finished being a tourist, you can head on over to its modern shopping mall that comes equipped with a food court and the international stores you've come to love!

How much: Free
Open: Always
Where: District 1

Museum of Vietnamese History

When you think of Vietnam, you most likely think of its civil war that drew international outcry. And that's entirely fair. The country we know today was born out of the war. However, Vietnam has centuries of interesting history—everything from Chinese imperial rule to French colonization. All together, that history explains a variety of things that make Vietnam so amazing (including why it's the only Southeast Asian country with great bread)! Spending a few hours at the Museum of Vietnamese History will help you learn how Vietnam came to be prior to the Communist takeover.

How much: 15k Admission (+25k Fee to Photograph)
Open: 8am - 11:30am & 1:30pm – 5pm
Where: District 1

Where: District 3

Fun Things to Do in HCMC

Take a Cooking Class

It's one thing to eat your way through every dish in Vietnam. It's another to learn how to make them! Any good cooking class will walk you through every step of the process, from purchasing the ingredients to making the dish and of course, eating the food. You can find out just how much work goes into your bowl of Pho, and even bring some pointers back home! Cooking classes are a great introduction to Vietnamese cuisine and a great way to fill up an afternoon. Prices will vary depending on your class but check out M.O.M Cooking Class for a super tasty (and affordable) experience.

How Much: 500k - 1m
Open: Daily
Where: Anywhere

Day Trip Can Gio Islands (Monkey Island)

During the Vietnam War, the Can Gio Islands were heavily hit by Agent Orange. Despite countless forests being knocked out, a newly formed nature reserve allows crocodiles and monkeys to thrive. It's an awesome opportunity to wade through the mangroves and experience tropical wildlife. Even better, you can go relax on one of several gorgeous beaches when you've had enough adventure for the day!

How to Get There: Public Buses / Ferries – any tour company can get

you there!
Distance from HCMC: 25km

Visit the Water Puppet Show

Admittedly, this one sounds a bit lame – but I promise it's not! However, it makes for an awesome night and provides some insight into Vietnamese culture. This traditional show covers a variety of aspects of Vietnamese life, making it a great intro to Saigon. All of the puppets are controlled under the water, and they reveal the secret trick that makes it all work towards the end of the show.

How Much: 230k
Open: Shows at 6:30pm and 8:30pm
Where: District 1

Visit Bixteco Financial Tower

Unless you're a regular at sky bars, you probably haven't seen Ho Chi Minh City from the sky. On the street, it's easy to feel trapped in the moment. Cars and motorbikes combine with the humidity to overwhelm your senses, leaving you dazed and a bit confused. But with a quick elevator ride to an aerial viewpoint, you'll feel like those cars are just ants. It's nothing short of amazing to see the city's big picture for once! Better yet, you'll also get a quick cultural lesson thanks to a small exhibit on traditional Vietnamese dress.

How Much: 200k
Open: 9:30am – 9:30pm
Where: District 1

Hire a Moto-Taxi

Do I recommend driving in Ho Chi Minh City? Definitely not! Saigon boasts some of the craziest traffic in the world, boasting nearly as many motorbikes as people. However, you can't go through Saigon without hoping on the back of a motorbike at least once. Trust the pros to drive; it's such a thrilling experience. And with Grab Taxi, it's never been easier!

How Much: 10k-30k
Open: Always
Where: Anywhere (I recommend District 1)

Markets & Shopping in HCMC

Malls, markets, street vendors, and more! If you're a shopaholic, Saigon is the place for you. Ho Chi Minh City definitely doesn't have a shortage of shopping opportunities. From knock-off handbags at bargain prices to luxury goods at top-end retailers, you're sure to find what you're looking for. Why not get some holiday shopping done while you're in town? Put that VAT refund to good use!

Ben Thanh Market

The OG of hawker markets. You can find literally everything and anything in Ben Thanh. It's the most popular market in HCMC because of its central location in District 1 and it's abundance of goodies. Just be prepared for lots of women vendors shouting "Buy something, lady" around every corner with their calculator in hand. Haggle, shop around, and don't feel pressured to buy shit if you don't' want to.

Open: Early morning – 7pm (then the outside turns into a night market)
Where: District 1
Address: Ben Thanh Market, Lê Lợi, Phường Bến Thành, Quận 1

Vincom Center

The Vincom Center is possibly Saigon's most popular shopping mall. If you've had your fill of outdoor markets, the air-con and brand name stores will be a pleasant change of pace. You'll find everything from cell phone accessories to clothing. Once you've shopped your heart out, be sure to check out the food court. Even though you'd imagine food courts are unchanged internationally, the Vietnamese have added their own twists at every corner!

Open: 9am-10pm
Where: District 1
Address: 72 Lê Thánh Tôn

L'Usine

This shopping hot spot is entirely unique to Ho Chi Minh City. L'Usine houses a variety of boutique stores, all stocked with contemporary Vietnamese fashion and modern styles. Even if you aren't looking to buy, window shopping is an adventure in itself here. Be sure to check out their coffee shop on the second floor, which doubles as a lunch spot and a place to drop off uninterested friends! This complex as a whole truly pays homage to Vietnamese style and offers a great glance into what modern Vietnamese people consider fashionable.

Open: 10am- 9pm
Where: District 1
Address: 70B Le Loi Street

Street Shopping

Saigon is home to countless streets solely dedicated to shopping. There are too many to list them all, but three destinations definitely stand out. First off, Le Van Sy Street is home to endless street vendors selling everything from clothes to bed sheets at insanely low prices. Next, Nguyen Trai Street boasts one of the busiest shopping districts in town, with countless boutique stores and haggle-friendly vendors. Lastly, Nguyen Dinh Chieu Street is locally known as the place to purchase great and affordable shoes (just keep in mind that Western sizes won't always be available).

Hanh Thong Tay Night Market

Unlike many other night markets, Hanh Thong Tay doesn't boast a lot of food. Instead, it's the perfect stop to find cheap bags, clothes, cosmetics, and more. It's especially popular with Saigon's university students, giving it a uniquely youthful vibe. This market is essentially your one-stop shop—I promise you'll be able to find anything you're looking for! And while it's not the best spot for food, the portions are big and the prices low.

Open: 6pm – 11pm
Where: Go Vap District

Spas in HCMC

My Spa

Owned by a badass boss babe named My, you will be pampered from the moment you walk through the door. My has set out to create a spa experience more luxurious than any other spa in Saigon- but at a reasonable price. Enjoy a welcome drink in a large, velvet chair as you choose your massage service.

The standard massage here is lavish. The 90-minute massage starts out with you lying on your back as a cool cucumber mask is applied to your face. Enjoy the massage as it finishes with a hot stone treatment. All of this for less than $25.

Open: Daily 10am - 11:30pm (last booking at 10:00 pm)
Starts at: $18 USD / 420k VND
Where: District 1
Location1: 15C4 Thi Sách Street (if one entrance in closed, go round' the corner)
Location 2: 29b Le Thanh Ton, Ben Nghe Ward, Distric 1

How to Get around HCMC

Walk

You can walk everywhere during the day in Ho Chi Minh City, as long as you're mindful of traffic. However, please be cautious at night – particularly in District 1. There are bag snatchers, often on motorbikes looking for easy targets. Wear a cross-shoulder bag, especially when you're drinking.

Grab Taxi

Grab Bikes and taxis are everywhere! Grab Bike costs around $1-$2 and Grab Cars typically cost $2-$3 depending where you're going. Install this app ASAP.

Taxis

I do not recommend getting in a taxi here. It's common for a taxi for charge you 100k for the same journey that a Grab Taxi would charge just 30K for. 3x the price, ya'll. If you have no choice, go with **Mai Linh Taxi** – they are the most trustworthy of the bunch.

Chapter 18: Off the Beaten Path from Ho Chi Minh City

Saigon can be a lot to handle. All the things that make it great—endless options, busy streets, and constant nightlife—can also make it exhausting. Luckily, there are a variety of day trips you can take from Ho Chi Minh City that require little to no extra effort! A beach escape may be exactly what you need, and it's a great chance to see a part of South Vietnam that many tourists miss out on.

Nguyen Shack - Can Tho

Come see "The Real Vietnam" along the Mekong River. Down here, life moves slower, fruit tastes juicer, prices are cheaper, and the smiles are bigger.

Experience floating markets in the morning where vendors row their boat alongside yours, selling morning coffee, hot soup, and fresh coconuts.

Ride your bicycle along newly paved jungle roads to discover centuries-old Buddhist pagodas and stunning vistas.

Go fishing for squid and fresh water fish and then grill them up for dinner.

Nguyen Shack, a riverside jungle homestay and tree house resort, is literally the #1 place to experience Can Tho. There's simply no other place like it and staying here is worth the trip (I once flew to Vietnam just to spend a week at Nguyen Shack- it's that amazing).

Staying at Nguyen Shack feels like staying with family and friends...on a sprawling piece of jungle property. Because its so far off the beaten path, the staff and guests all hang out together like they're the last people on earth. Here, you have access to free bicycles, free fishing gear, every tour possible...and best of all...free Chinese Cupping sessions! The food is amazing, the beer is cheap, and the experience in unforgettable.

How to Get to Nguyen Shack – Can Tho

You have 3 options...

Option 1 – by Bus

Bus Company: Phuong Trang or Chau Doc

How Much: $5 to Can Tho bus station
Duration: 4 hours

From Can Tho Bus Station: Take a green Mai Linh Taxi for about 80 000vnd or a Motorbike Taxi for 50 000vnd
Ask the driver to go to Ong Tim Bridge and follow the river down to Nguyen Shack – you'll see signs.

Option 2- By Private Car

You can arrange your transport beforehand for ultra-convenience.

How Much: $90
Duration: 3 Hours
Booking: info@nguyenshack.com

Option 3- By Boat

How Much: $12.50
Duration: 3.5 Hours
Booking: transmekong.com
How to Get There: From the pier in Can Tho, you can take a taxi to Nguyen Shack or message them at the email above to arrange pick up.

Chapter 19: Dalat

Even the beachiest of babes need a break from hot & humid days in the sun! Escape the city buzz and head for the hills to take in the cool mountain air and possibly, drink your body weight in coffee.

Dalat is a quaint little town snuggled into Vietnam's Central Highlands, surrounded by beautiful pine forests, lakes and rolling hills.

The area is famed for its cooler climate (it can actually get pretty chilly here in the evening), its robust coffee and its wonderful day trips to waterfalls, palaces and monasteries. Take a moment to chill out in one of Dalat's ubiquitous coffee houses and plan your adventure with a cup of regionally grown coffee and tropical treats. Motorbike tours and days exploring the forest hills await those looking to get off of the normal Vietnam travel trail.

Areas to Explore in Dalat

Dalat is broken down into Wards (or "Phuongs" in Vietnamese) and unlike most cities the wards do not have names and are simply know as Ward 1, Ward 2, Ward 3, etc. The system is relatively simple to understand, with Ward 1 being the most central and then the numbers going up as you get further away from the city center. For frame of reference Bui Thi Xuan is fairly centrally located within Ward 1 and all of the guest houses and restaurants mentioned in this guide have the Ward number attached so you can see where they are in relation to the city center.

Dalat city center is pretty small, so most of the Wards are within easy walking distance of each other.

Bui Thi Xuan Street

Bui Thi Xuan (Ward 1) is ground zero for travelers in Dalat, dripping with reasonably priced local restaurants, bars and coffee houses. It's also the link to the maze of hostel streets and fun little souvenir shops. Bui Thi Xuan's central location within Dalat makes it a great base for those looking to spend a few days exploring the town without having to bus or cab around the city. It is also a great spot to organize those famous adventure tours that lure you up here, with multiple tour shops lining the street ready to take you to far flung corners of the countryside.

Xuan Huong Lake

This large man-made lake is just a short walk from Bui Thi Xuan Street. The lake is surrounded by beautiful flower gardens, a large golf course and Dalat's famous Palace Hotel. It's a great place to wander, smell the flowers and enjoy the regions cooler, spring-like climate with a cup of coffee in hand.

Tuyen Lam Lake

This large lake is a fifteen-minute walk downhill from Truc Lam Pagoda and offers peace and relaxation, plus boats for hire and quaint local restaurants. There's often a local man offering to show you his classic car collection at the bottom of the walk (basically a Cadillac and an old Vespa rickshaw) but he's very sweet and is keen to practice his English. His cars are normally parked up outside one of the lake's restaurants for your viewing pleasure.

Accommodation in Dalat

Dalat offers everything in terms of accommodation and the region offers such great value that even the most budget conscious traveler will probably be able to stretch to a private room. Most guesthouses are family run, cozy as hell and generally, just great places to hang your head. For a truly local homestay, don't be afraid to wander on your own in the back alleys to find a tiny family guest- so small that they don't advertise on the internet.

Pro Tip

In the summer, Vietnam's honeymooning couples come to town, so it pays to book ahead during this high season.

Dalat Backpackers Hostel

There's a reason that Dalat Backpackers Hostel is often booked up...because they're the best in terms of comfort, hospitality, and fun. Once you get to Ho Chi Minh City and start planning your trip up to Dalat, get online and book a bed. You'll be glad you did.

Located right by Xuan Huong Lake, this hostel is a great base for exploring both the city and the surrounding countryside. The beds are cozy, the breakfast is complimentary, and the staff can assist with airport shuttles, tours and laundry.

Style: Privates & Dorms
Starts at: $5 USD / 114k VND
Where: Ward 3
Address: 1 Ha Huy Tap, Phường 3

Smiley Backpackers Hostel

When Dalat Backpacker Hostel is booked up or you want just 80% of the social vibes, Smiley Backpackers is the next best thing. This hostel has comfy beds, an onsite souvenir shop, a shared kitchen for cooking with fresh ingredients from the market and complimentary breakfasts. They have a knowledgeable tour desk able to help you plan your next adventure and the staff are always on hand to help you out. It's a one stop shop.

Style: Privates & Large Shared Rooms (Max 4 people)
Starts at: $12 USD / 274k VND
Where: Ward 1
Address: 71 Thu Khoa Huan, Phuong 1

The Lake House

Wake up on the lake. Yes...ON. Cozy rooms with big windows that offer unobstructed views of the water and rolling hills is the epitome of travel goals. This cozy, peaceful guesthouse is located on Tuyen Lam Lake and offers up a far more secluded side of Dalat – while not being too far from the city center. You're just a short walk from monasteries, waterfalls and lakes- allowing you to take advantage of life off the beaten path. When you're in the mood for night markets and shopping, just hop in a free shuttle to town.

Style: Privates and Dorms
Starts at: $16 USD / 365 VND
Where: Ward 3
Address: Next to the boat dock, Tuyen Lam Lake, Phuong 3

Banyan House

Rustic, boho and contemporary all at the same time, Banyan House is exactly what you picture when you think of a tropical mountain vacation. Like you've stepped into one of your Pinterest boards, this place screams 'gorgeous' from the bright teal window shutters to the bedside lanterns. Located close to Xuan Huong Lake in a beautiful, secluded garden, Banyan House is the place to treat yourself; I highly recommend booking a room with garden views!

Style: Privates
Starts at: $55 USD / 1.25 million
Where: Ward 2

Address: 94 Ly Tu Trong, Phuong 2

Dreams Hotel

This large and fairly modern hotel is owned and run by a friendly, uber-helpful local family and offers large rooms and even bigger breakfasts. The place is super clean, conveniently located and has a hot tub and sauna for when it just gets that little bit too cold to venture out. Don't expect luxury...but when you want some privacy on a budget, it's a smart option.

Style: Privates
Starts at: $22 USD / 500k VND
Where: Ward 2
Address: 141 Phan Dinh Phung, Phuong

Coffee Houses in Dalat

No trip to Dalat would be complete without a buzz from the region's locally grown coffee. Dalat is so dense in coffee shops that you can barely move without falling into one.

La Viet

Dalat's extra famous coffee mecca is a little out of the way; but well worth the trip; some reviews even have this place pegged as one of the best coffee shops in the world! A bold claim that you must confirm for yourself. The coffee is tasty, the staff is knowledgeable, and the decor is pretty trendy (think East London + Melbourne + New York and you'll be right on track). They also offer really great coffee tours to local farms and then let you brew your own blend at the end.

Open: 7:30am-9:30pm
Where: Ward 8
Address: 200 Da Lat, Nguyen Cong Tru, Phuong 8

Bicycle Up Cafe

I'm about to make a controversial statement...Bicycle Up Cafe might be even better than La Viet in terms of atmosphere. It's cozier, the decor is whimsical, baristas have this cheerful Disneyland vibe to them and damn, that coffee is good. Not to mention, the food here is always on point! Plus, you don't have to haul your ass all the way over to the other side of town and back just to get you caffeine fix.

Open: 7am-10:30pm
Where: Ward 1
Address: 82 Truong Cong Dinh, Phuong 1

Me Linh Coffee Garden

You've never seen a coffee shop with a view like this before; I guarantee it. Me Linh Coffee Garden sits overlooking the area's bright green coffee farms, rolling hills, and reservoir- showing off where these pretty little beans come from. This coffee shop is fast becoming a mandatory stop on Dalat's tourist trail, so get here early to grab a table with a full view.

Open: 7am-6:30pm
Where: Ta Nang Commune
Address: To 4, Ta Nang Commune, La Ham District

Where to Eat in Dalat

With reasonably price food everywhere you turn, Dalat is a foodie paradise
Be it hot pots, incredible local produce or the sweet and juicy Dalat
strawberries- the eating never ends! So, pull up a seat on Bui Thi Xuan or
travel slightly further afield for your fill, because dinner every meal is a
memorable meal in Dalat.

One More Cafe

Ignore the slightly odd decor (it's like going for tea at your nan's house) and
jump into the amazing breakfasts at One More Cafe. It's mainly western
fare only, but the chefs here know how to whip up a smashed avocado on
toast & a healthy Chia seed parfait just like you'd expect at a fancy
schmancy brunch spot. The place is always full (a great sign) and you get to
sit and eat your breakfast in an armchair. The whole experience is quirky
(unintentionally, I think) and delicious. How can you pass this up?

Open: 8am-9pm
Where: Ward 6
Address: 77 Hai Ba Trung, Phuong 6

Oz Burgers

Burgers and beers in this tiny little eatery hidden in an alley give you a nice
break from broth noodles and hit the spot after a few beers (even a breakfast
beer). Stop by for their huge, filling brunch or their famous burgers. If there
aren't enough places to sit, grab your burgers to go and eat by the lake for
dinner and a show.

Open: 9am-9pm
Where: Ward 1
Address: 61 Ba Tháng Hai, Phường 1

Pho Pho Everywhere!

With such a chilly mountain climate, you can find a pho spot on every street
corner to warm your soul. Pull up a metal or plastic chair, use the good old
'point and order' tactic and wait for a massive bowl to be brought over.
Garnish with lime, chili, and soy sauce and enjoy. Warning: these mom &
pop bowls of pho tend to be ridiculously big and ridiculously cheap.

Nightlife in Dalat

Nightlife in Dalat doesn't carry on much past midnight. But have no fear, hostels in the area pick up the slack. So, start drinking early with happy hours and sunset views at some of the best bars in town...

B21 Beer

B21 Beer is a large and busy bar with a 2 for-1 happy hour every day of the week, except for Saturdays. This is one of the bigger bars in Dalat and always has something to offer, whether it be live sports, live music or DJs- it's nice to just sit back and melt into the atmosphere. The bar caters mainly to westerners, and a traveler crowd. It's no surprise then that B21 Beer tends to get pretty lively most nights. Throw yourself in the new mix and you'll surely meet some new people and make some new friends.

Open: 3pm-1am
Where: Ward 1
Address: 68 Truong Cong Dinh, Phuong 1

100 Roofs Cafe

If hobbits wanted a beer this is where they'd hang out. This place is part bar / part art installation and the weirdest beer experience you'll ever have. Happy hour is cheap, and the bar has multiple nooks and crannies to hide yourself away from the chilly night air while also providing the perfect place for a Tinder date (even in the mountains). While you're here, be sure to check out the surreal rooftop garden!

Open: 8:30am-12am
Where: Ward 1
Address: 57 Phan Boi Chau, Phuong 1

Goc Ha Thanh

Goc Ha Thanh is the place to go to experience a Vietnamese obsession: hotpot. Here, you can dine on flavorful hotpots (they are one of the few places to offer a vegetarian hotpot), great curries and heaping plates of noodles! This place is so popular that it's always full. Located close to Dalat's night market, try to get there in the early evening.

Open: 12pm-8pm
Where: Ward 1
Address: 53 Trương Công Định, Phường 1

Ca Ri Vit

There's not method to the madness here. This local spot cooks what they want, when they want. Sometimes its pork, sometimes chicken, but most often than not, it's a duck and noodle dish that will change your life (Vegetarians and Vegans need not apply). You might have no idea what's being served up, but get in line either way and prepare for a culinary adventure. Locals literally cue round the block just to get a bowl.

Open: Whenever they want (cause Vietnam) - If it's open you'll see the cue
Where: Ward 1
Address: Wander down the alley next to Tra Khiep supermarket, Duong Phan Dinh, Phuong 1

Street Beers

One of the most common ways to enjoy the nightlife in Dalat is to buy a beer from a street vendor and just have a wander. Walk through the markets, people watch in the park, or snack as you go. Consider it a nightlife walking tour…

Fun Vietnam Fact

Vietnam is home to the world's fastest-growing population of ultra-rich individuals with 5,900 millionaires and 260 multimillionaires to date.

Fun Things to Do in Dalat

Go Canyoning & Rappelling

Spreadthewings.com

The main attraction in Dalat is canyoning and rappelling! Hike up a rocky mountain, repel down a water fall, swim in cool pools of fresh mountain water and slide down natural rock waterslides. You'll set off on a group tour (expect others from your hostel to have come to Dalat for this exact tour) and have a wet and wild day full of adrenaline. You'll get tons of badass photos, as well, all of which will scare the shit out of your mom. You can these tours with your hostel or hotel.

Pro Tip

If you're staying at a private hotel but want to meet some people on your Canyoning adventure, walk into Dalat Backpackers or Smiley Hostel and book your tour there.

Starting at: About $50 USD (and worth every penny)

Adventure Tours

Dalat has an adventurous side and with multiple tours and adventure activities to keep even the hungriest adrenaline junkie well fed you won't be disappointed.

There are some great hikes through the mountains and hills surrounding Dalat and many companies offering to show them to you.

There's the beautiful hike to Lang Biang Mountain and the slightly challenging yet rewarding hike to Elephant Falls with a trip to Nam Ban Village.

Groovy Gecko Adventure Tours is your one stop shop for adventure activities ranging from rock climbing and canyoning to multi-day treks.

Staring at: $35 USD / 800k VND
Open: 7am-7pm
Where: Ward 1
Address: 65 Truong Cong Dinh, Phuong 1

Pro Tip

Avoid booking tours with the infamous scamming company called "Trung Tam Dich Vu Lu Hanh Da Lat" and tour companies that offer elephant rides such as Dalat Passion Tours

Royal Palaces
Check out the collection of 3 royal palaces, formerly home to Emperor Bao Dai. Don't expect glitz and glamour, these palaces have seen better days and are in need of some TLC – but in terms of architecture and history, they are pretty cool and provide a glimpse into Vietnam's opulent imperial past.

Entrance Fee: $1 USD/ 22k VND
Open: 7am-4pm (closed from 11am-1:30pm for lunch)
Where: Ward 4
Address: Trieu Viet Vuong street, Phuong 4

Hang Nga Crazy House
Home to one of Vietnam's most avantgarde architects, this ever-evolving wonderland has been growing and manifesting for many years as the designer's dreams are brought to life in front of your eyes. The house is a surreal and utterly outrageous- much like a scene out of Alice in Wonderland. You can wander around the house as you wish, easily spending a good few hours exploring it's never ending corners.

Bonus: Hang Nga Crazy House also doubles as a mind-blowing hotel, with future plans to build a restaurant and under the sea nightclub here, too.

Entrance Fee: $2 USD / 45k VND
Open: 8:30am-7pm

Where: Ward 4
Address: 3 Huynh Thuc Khang Street, Phuong 4

Easy Rider Tours

Also, not to be missed are Dalat's famous Easy Rider tours (but watch out, there are plenty of imitators that claim to be "Easy Riders" – everyone wants to be like the best). These tours involve hopping on the back of a motorbike and being whisked through Dalat's scenic and beautiful countryside.

There are plenty of routes that you can take that vary with waterfalls, mountains, distance, etc. Check em' out at the shop and agree the price upfront. Once you are ready, hop on and prepare for what may well be the most enjoyable day of your trip!

Starting at: $25 USD / 570k VND
Open: 7am-7pm
Where: Ward 2
Address: 181 Phan Dinh Phung, Phuong 2

Truc Lam Pagoda

This truly serene working monastery is a short cab ride from the city center and well worth a day's visit. Wander through the beautiful gardens to the sound of windchimes and monks chanting; you are even able to join in meditation classes if that's your jam. The pagoda's hilltop location offers staggering views of the surrounding area and can be reached by cable car (by far the best way to get to the pagoda) taking you over coffee farms and local villages as you go.

Roller Blade in the Park at Night

Taking it back to the 90's, ya'll. When you're in Dalat, check out Dalat City Centre at night. There's a cement park full of teenagers and young 20-somthings roller skating along and doing tricks. They'll ride up alongside you and ask if you'd like to try for a small fee (you can always haggle this price).

Where: Near the Night Market

Shopping in Dalat

You'll find tons of little souvenir shops in Dalat alongside plenty of shops selling coffee of all kind. But if you want the big-ticket items, check out Dalat's markets...

Day Market

Ever wanted to up your swag game with some Abidas or Lewis Vuitton? No, those aren't typos...these are the awesome imitation brands that you can find at Dalat's Day Market. If you can put it on your body, you can buy it at this local friendly market and much more! Haggle hard; but with a smile.

Night Market

Come evening time, Dalat's evening traders swap places with Dalat's day traders as Dalat's Day Market turns into Dalat's Night Market. Mainly concentrating on street food and entertainment, the streets around the crowded market become abuzz with locals and travelers alike. Lights, sounds, toys, and treasures- grab a walking beer and explore.

How to Get around Dalat

Walk

Dalat is small and mountainous. You can walk just about everywhere!

Motorbike Taxi

There will be a man on just about every corner saying, "Hey, mo-to-bike". These guys are pretty cheap and can take you just about anywhere in the city.

Rent a Scooter

Da Nang is pretty spread out, so if you want to cover a lot of ground, rent a motorbike for your visit. The roads are relatively wide, and the traffic isn't too chaotic- especially once you get out of the city center. The coastal roads are quite peaceful.

Chapter 20: Mui Ne

Just 180 kilometers east of Ho Chi Minh City is Mui Ne- the famous coastal town of southeastern Vietnam. Beautiful beaches, sand dunes, busy fishing villages, and fresh seafood are the main highlights of this area.

Tourism has been booming these past decades, which is why you'll find resort after resort and bar after bar in the area. The forces of nature are strong here as it creates powerful winds perfect for kitesurfing and ever-shifting sands. This crazy wind pattern has given life to Arabian-esque sand dunes just waiting for you to play in!

Fun Vietnam Fact
29.6% of the country does not practice any religion.

Areas to Explore in Mui Ne

Mui Ne Ward

Mui Ne Ward is the fishing town of Binh Thuan. Though the entire area is generally called Mui Ne, it's actually the port area where all the fishing boats are. Marvel at the everyday activity of the local people and watch how they catch the country's most popular seafood.

Phan Thiet City

Resort City! The capital of the Binh Thuan Province is basically a 57.4-kilometers of coastline, beaches, and fishing areas! Water sports and seafood of all kind is what attracts the tourists here. It's famous for all their international and Vietnamese bars and restaurants as well as their cheap hostels! Ho Chi Minh and Hanoi is also a short drive away. Enjoy dragon and seafood as you watch the waves.

Ham Tien Ward

It's a little confusing, but what most people call Mui Ne is actually Ham Tien. It's actually the place between Mui Ne and Phan Thiet. This is where the massive kitesurfing craze began. The best time to go is from October to March, and the peak season is December to January. Aside from that, there's also tons of sailing, windsurfing, and kayaking rentals in this area.

Phu Hai Ward

(Remainder of the Ancient Cham Culture)

On the hill just northeast of Phan Thiet is Phu Hai, and remnants of the ancient Cham culture can be found here. They were an ethnic group that have Austronesian origins. You can also find the most amazing sand sculptures in the area.

Accommodation in Mui Ne

Long Son Mui Ne Campground Resort $

Alone and on a budget? No problem! This super social beach resort for budget travelers will give you more than your money's worth! Rent a tent and camp out on the private beach without worrying about crowded shores. You'll have access to all of the necessities: showers, bathrooms, and a 24-hour bar and restaurant; plus, beachy activities like surfing and volley ball. There's always something fun going on at the campground whether it be a chilled-out bonfire or massive pool party with all of the shots. Talk about the perfect summer getaway!

Style: Tents & Dorms
Starts at: $5 USD/ 114k VND
Where: Between the White and Red Sand Dunes

Mui Ne Backpacker Village $

The most legendary hostel in Mui Ne – and for good reason. This place is the most social hostel there is with an opportunity to interact with other travelers 24/7. You've got the gorgeous pool where you can tan or play pool volley ball. There's their poolside bar and restaurant with amazing drink specials. A billiards table is the perfect place to challenge a stranger to a game. And the hostel offers day time tours where you can link up with other guests for some adventure time. Active during the day and a bit wild at night. Winning all around.

PS. Not to be confused with all the copy cats like 'Mui Ne Hills Backpacker Backpackers' or 'Mui Ne Hills Budget Hotel'. These places are fine if Option A is booked up…but option A might be booked up for a good reason.

Style: Dorms & Privates
Starts at: $5 USD / 114k VND
Where: Ham Tien Ward

Lotus Village Resort

Get a feel traditional Vietnamese architecture with Lotus Village. The vibe and aesthetic of the place gives of a distinct feeling. It'll feel like you're in some exotic location rather than just the regular tropical hotel. Enjoy the sea breeze as you relax with their spa and massage treatments. You'll feel so at peace you'd never want to leave!

Style: Privates
Starts at: $60
Where: Phan Thiet City

Mui Ne Ocean House

415

Looks can be deceiving. While Mui Ne Ocean House looks like your standard budget hotel, it is so much more! Yes, it's incredibly clean, extremely well priced, and just a short walk to the beach – but the extra special touches are what really stand out. You get freebies like free breakfast, free water & coffee, a free washing machine and free bicycles for hire. You get incredible hospitality from staff that offer to drive you to the bus station or book tours. You get the perfect pool for tanning. And you get a view of the ocean from the balcony! Best value for money!

Style: Privates
Starts at: $16 USD / 365k VND

Sunsea Resort

Their world-class food and drinks is definitely one of the things guests love about this resort. International and Thai cuisine is the specialty in their restaurant Sukhothai. You can also enjoy a wide range of beer, wine, cocktails, and other beverages in their Beach bar. All the rooms are designed to your liking with TVs and DVDs. There's even hot tubs and Jacuzzis if you ask for it!

Style: Privates
Starts at: $57 USD / 1.3 million VND
Where: Nguyen Dinh Chieu Street

Four Oceans Resort

Beachfront access? Yes, please. Stay in luxury rooms equipped with a beach view or wake up with views of colorful flowers in the garden. Either way, you'll be surrounded by a tropical themed paradise that you'll never want to leave. Oh, and the pool...incredible.

Style: Privates
Starts at: $70 USD / 1.6 million VND
Where: Ham Tien Ward

The Cliffs Resort & Residence

It really doesn't get any more Kardashian than this. The Cliffs is one of those resorts that you see on TV, with Jacuzzis overlooking the water and sexy swimming pools meant for slow motion diving, but without the celebrity price tag. It's not a total guilt-free spend but at $165, it's a bucket list sleepover that every solo girl should experience once in her life. Live a little!

Style: Privates, Bungalows & Condominiums
Starts at: $165 USD / 3.75 million VND
Where: 25-minute drive away from the White Sand Dunes

Where to Eat in Mui Ne

BiBo

Watch out seafood lovers! The place may not look like those fancy fine dining restaurants, but the food is the best around. Made with the freshest ingredients, you can find cheap and delicious clams, oysters prawns, and fish of all kinds. If you're not the seafood type, it'll surely change your mind.

Open: Daily 10am - 11pm
Where: Nguyen Dinh Chieu Street
Address: 191 Nguyen Dinh Chieu Street, Ham Tien Ward

Surfing Bird's WOK

Your Asian experience isn't complete without noodles and here in Mui Ne, this is the place to go. They specialize in Asian and Chinese dishes all cooked on the wok. Fried noodles with mushroom and black pepper beef are a must-try! They also have great homemade lemonade and cheesecake. It's the equivalent of Asian soul food all under one roof.

Open: Daily 12pm - 10:30pm
Where: Dong Vui Food Court
Address: 246/2B Nguyen Dinh Chieu, Mui Ne, Phan Thiet

El Cafe Vegetarian Food

You think finding good vegan food is hard in Vietnam? Well, the owner of this restaurant thought so, too! Try a wide range of international cuisine made vegan and vegetarian. Their food is moderately priced and packed with spices that you've probably never heard of. Take note of their vegan cheese and sauce as it was made by the owner himself!

Open: Daily 9am - 11pm
Where: Dong Vui Food Court
Address: 246/2B, Nguyen Dinh Chieu, Mui Ne, Phan Thiet

Karlito's Way Pasta Bar

I bet you didn't expect to find handmade pasta in this corner of the world, did you? Get a taste of Italy with professional pasta makers right here in Mui Ne. Each dish is made with the freshest ingredients from nearby fishing villages and picked from local farms You can order right off the menu or customize your past dish by picking the sauce and goodies to go with.

Open: Daily 5pm - 10pm
Where: Nguyen Dinh Chieu Street

Address: 246 Nguyen Dinh Chieu | Khu Pho 3, Mui Ne

Pho Bo and Sandwiches

Looking for a late-night snack? There aren't a lot of places open but luckily, Pho Bo and sandwiches serves late in the night! Have one of Vietnam's most popular comfort food after a long day of touring and sightseeing. You still need to make a few turns to get to it, so be mindful of your surroundings!

Open: 4pm - 11pm
Where: Bo Ke Street
Address: 138 Nguyen Dinh Chieu Street, Mui Ne

Dong Vui Food Court

Crowded and fun is what the name says, and it's definitely true when you get there. This food park has practically every cuisine you're hoping to try, and some of the best restaurants in the area can be found here too. Local, international, vegan, and more! You'll probably going to have to come back a second time if you want to try all their stalls.

Note: Opening hours vary per season. Individual stalls also have their own opening hours so if you're looking for one store in particular, better check in advance.

Open: Daily 7:30am - 11pm
Where: Nguyen Dinh Chieu Street
Address: 246/2B Nguyen Dinh Chieu Street, Mui Ne

Sightseeing & Culture in Mui Ne

Reclining Buddha on Ta Cu Mountain

Ta Cu Mountain is said to be the home of the largest reclining Buddha in the country. To get to the top of the mountain, tourists can either take a cable car or traverse the easy hike through an enjoyable jungle path. Once you reach the top, you'll be welcomed by a beautiful viewing deck that overlooks Mui Ne and the Linh Son Truong Tho Pagoda built in 1879. Behind the pagoda complex lies the impressive 49-meter long & 11 -meter high white Buddha named 'Thich Ca Nhap Niet Ban '(Buddha entering Nirvana) surrounded by lush green jungle. Stunning. Breathtaking. So worth the visit.

Price: (Cable car- Round-trip) 160,000 VND
Open: Daily 8am – 5pm
Location: Ta Cu Mountain
Address: National Route 1A, 649m, Ham Thuan Nam

Check out Mui Ne Fishing Village

If you want to experience local life, Mui Ne Fishing Village should be included in your holiday. This small village has a very impressive coastline that is colored with fishing boats of all shapes and sizes. There are food carts and restaurants along the coast, serving Vietnamese signatures at an affordable price. If you want to visit without battling the huge tours visiting the village or walk under the scorching sun, it is best to visit in the early morning or in the afternoon.

Van Thuy Tu Temple

In 1762, this temple was built in memory of a legendary whale known as Ca Ong (Lord Whale), whom many fishermen believe protected them from bad weather while at sea. The temple houses many cultural relics from the Nguyen dynasty, as well as a 22-meter long whale skeleton that weight over 65 tons when it was still alive. Every June, the people of Phan Thiet and nearby areas host the Cau Ngu Festival (Whale Worshipping Festival) to pray for a good fishing haul, good weather and smooth sailing for the entire year.

Open: Daily 7:00 am to 5:00 pm

Poshanu Tower

One of the most precious cultural landmarks of the Cham Kingdom that remains can be found in Phan Thiet. It was built over a millennium ago as a temple of worship for Shiva, but only three towers are what's left of it now. This is the only architectural work of the Cham left in Phan Thiet and occasionally, Cham people from nearby areas conduct religious ceremonies here.

Open: Daily 7:30am - 11.30am; 1pm - 4:30pm
Location: 7km northeast of Phan Thiet
Address: Ong Hoang Hill, Phan Thiet

Fun Things to Do in Mui Ne

Slide on the Red Sand Dunes

Right down the road from Sand Dunes Beach Resort near central Mui Ne lies a big rolling hill of red sand. When you drive by, there will be Vietnamese kids on the side of the road, waving your down to give you plastic slides where you can sled down the sand dune. It's a fun little detour before or after the beach.

Pro Tip: Don't leave your bags with these kids. They're sneaky.
Location: Mui Ne Town
Address: South of Sand Dunes Beach Resort

ATV on the White Sand Dunes

When you arrive at this place, you may find yourself asking "Did I just teleport to the Sahara?" The White Sand Dunes are about 35 minutes north of Mui Ne and covers a vast expanse of land that stretches as far as you can see. Locals call these dunes the Bau Trang or "the White Lake". In the monsoon season, they say the winds changes the location of the sandhills scattered in the dunes, making for fresh adventures.

Sign up for a tour and pile into a big ass jeep that can handle the rolling roads. When you get there, you'll hop on an ATV to zoom around or grab a sand surfing board and shred.

Open: All day
Location: 35 Minutes North of Mui Ne
How to Get There: Hotel Pick Up

Walk the Fairy Stream

Peaceful and adventurous, this little stream is nothing more than a small ankle-to-knee deep river that travels through forests, sand dunes and rock formations- but is beyond enjoyable. The 'fairy' name comes from the blue, red, white, and green sands mixing in with the stream, creating a whimsical piece of heaven. Kick your shoes off and enjoy the cool, clean water rushing over your skin.

Pro Tip: The tour to the White Sand Dunes usually includes a detour to the stream. You can get this as a package deal

Markets & Shopping in Mui Ne

Oyster heaven, Mui Ne is full of pearl shops everywhere you turn. You can get glossy white peals and rare black pearls of every quality in this city, usually in peal boutique shops that all seem to sell around the same price.

And if you're not in the market for pearls, head to a local market for some of the best shopping around.

Ham Tien Market

As far as markets are concerned, Ham Tien's is relatively small, but the goods there are just as diverse. Around 6 to 9 in the morning is their busiest because everyone is buying stuff for their own homes. Native food and packaged desserts are plenty here! Make sure to get some mangosteens and custard apples while you're at it.

Open: 5:30 am - 9pm
Address: Nguyen Dinh Chieu Street, Phan Thiet

Phan Thiet Central Market

With hundreds of markets, this market is largest of its kind in Mui Ne and holds a ton of handicrafts. Paintings, bags, scarves, and ceramics made in ancient Cham styles can also be found here. There aren't a lot of places where you'll see Cham anything, so this is definitely a treat worth going for. Make sure you bring enough money!

Open: 5am - 6pm
Address: Intersection between Ly Thuong Kiet and Nguyen Hue Streets, Phan Thiet

Fun Vietnam Fact

Lizard Fishing is one of Vietnam's most widespread hobbies. Ask a local and maybe they'll take you.

How to Get around Mui Ne

Walk

There's not much to see via walking, but you can easily reach some restaurants and beach bars if you're hotel is on the main strip.

Local Bus

To go into Phan Thiet Town, hop on a cheap bus. Blue Bus (#1) and Red Bus (#9) go from Mui Ne to Phan Thiet city center every 15-20 minutes. No bus stops; just go on to the closest main street in front of your resort or hostel and wave your hand when one passes by. Tickets are around 20k ($1).

Motorbike Taxi

Motorbike Taxis hustle up and down the tourist area offering rides to the train station, bus station, restaurants, etc. Expect to pay $1-4 per ride.

Rent a Scooter

Instead of signing up for tours to the sand dunes or the beach, rent your own motorbike and drive along the chilled out coastal road to create your own tour!

Important Note

The traffic police in Mui Ne are constantly pulling western tourists over to check for a Vietnamese or International Driver's License. If don't have ID to show, you might be shaken down for as much a $50. On that note, don't travel with any illegal greens on your person!

Chapter 21: Nha Trang

The coastal city of Nha Trang is the capital city of Khanh Hoa Province-popular with backpackers, for good reason. Nha Trang, one of the most famous beaches in Vietnam, boasts miles of beautiful sand, colorful scuba diving spots, affordable boat trips and a cosmopolitan nightlife.

With its range of accommodation from budget to fancy pants, Nha Trang attracts both Southeast Asia Backpackers and more affluent vacationers. It doesn't matter how big your bank account, you can make a fun little beach holiday in Nha Trang with plenty to do besides soak up the sun. There are Buddhist temples, scenic hikes, natural hot springs, breathtaking waterfalls, and an unlimited supply of fresh seafood!

Areas to Explore in Nha Trang

Downtown Nha Trang

Relax on the beach or party downtown? In Nha Trang, you don't have to choose! The city of Nha Trang is essentially a beachside city with all the action just a quick walk from the shore.

Nha Trang Beach

Picturesque turquoise waters and golden sands combine to make a truly unforgettable beach experience. Located near downtown, this beach is perfect for swimming, kayaking, and home to a vibrant nightlife. Nha Trang beach stretches around 5 kilometers long and is also known as "Tourist Beach."

Super Fun Vietnam Fact

Vietnam is one of the most progressive LGBT countries in Asia, recently uplifting the ban on Gay Marriage.

Accommodation in Nha Trang

iHome Nha Trang $

IHOME is the #1 party hostel in Nha Trang. Specially designed for backpackers who seek a vibrant social scene- making friends here is easy. Not to mention, IHOME is pretty friendly to a traveler's budget: they offer free breakfast, free unlimited beer for 1 hour per night, a rooftop bar so you don't have to spend nightclub prices, and organized activities for guests.

Style: Dorm Beds
Starts at: $10
Where: Thành phố
Address: 31E2, Biệt Thự, Tân Lập

Vivid Seaside Homestay $

When it comes to value for money in Nha Trang, it really doesn't get any better than this. $25 for a quaint private room and $35 for that same quaint private room with a seaside view from your balcony- it's worth the $10 upgrade just to wake up to the ocean. While situated right on the main road, you'll hear the buzzing of motorbikes during the day (fun for watching) but they quiet down at night. Walk to the beach or hop on the local city bus that stops right outside of the hotel. The owners are extremely helpful and will show you exactly how to navigate the city to make the most of your visit. This is the adventure-girl's ideal hotel.

Style: Privates
Starts at: $27 USD / 615k VND
Where: Downtown
Address: 3/37 Pham Van Dong Street

The Summer Hotel $

Located just 400 meters from Nha Trang Beach, The Summer Hotel is a comfy and affordable option for ladies seeking a more private experience where you can take in some 'Me' time. This 3-star hotel offers all the amenities you need to slip into vacation-mode including a rooftop pool with a poolside bar, fast Wifi, and a lounge area to enjoy a drink or shoot a game of billiards...while possibly chatting up some eligible male travelers with a nice smile or scruffy beard (just sayin').

Style: Privates
Starts at: $30 USD / 684k VND
Where: Tran Phu Beach district

Address: 34 C-D Nguyen Thien Thuat Street, Nha Trang, Vietnam

BonJour Nha Trang $$

Fit for a queen with an upscale 1960's New York style feel, any glam-packing girl will appreciate the comforts at Bonjour Nha Trang. This snazzy hotel is just a short 6-minute walk from the beach with plenty of food and drink options along the way for a hassle-free stay. Bonjour offers prioritizes comfort with beds that feel like you're floating on a cloud, rooms that make you feel like you're in an episode of 'Gossip Girl', and an outdoor pool that gets plenty of sun for you to get that sun-kissed glow.

Style: Privates
Starts at: $47 USD / 1 million VND
Where: Nha Trang
Address: 17/2A Nguyen Thi Minh Khai, Nha Trang, Vietnam

Havana Nha Trang Hotel $$$

Listen, if you often pinch pennies and stay in dorms...then you can totally justify treating yourself to a fancy 5-star hotel for at least one night, don't you think? Switch things up with Havana Nha Trang- a chic, but not ridiculously expensive, luxury hotel. This gorgeous oasis overlooks the beautiful Nha Trang Bay with glistening turquoise water and beautiful sunrises. Havana offers a skyrise rooftop pool with ridiculous views of the ocean, a well-equipped fitness center with free cardio classes, and 4 restaurants (some on rooftop overlooking the ocean) specializing in international cuisine to complete the whole glam-packing experience.

Style: 5 Star Hotel, Privates
Starts at: $100 USD / 2.28 million VND
Where: Nha Trang Bay
Address: 38 Tran Phu, Nha Trang, Vietnam

Where to Eat in Nha Trang

Nha Trang Street Food Tour

Although wandering around Nha Trang in search for the next source of delicious cuisine can be an immensely enjoyable experience, it could take you hours to find the best little hidden spots. Solution: The Nha Trang Street Food Tour. Hop on a scooter and follow your guide around the city to sample the best culinary treats this city has to offer- along with some local history along the way!

How Much: Starting around $30 USD / 700k VND
Time: 3 hours
Contact: Nhatrangstreetfood.com

Rainforest

WTF is this? A treehouse? A tree city? Rainforest is a wild wooden & bamboo structure with multiple levels, little nooks, and birdcage-esque dining areas that are 100% worth a visit. IF that wasn't enough to spark your curiosity, their food is local, organic, and cheap. Come detox your body while you detox your brain. Rainforest aims to create a relaxing, whimsical experience all around with fresh eats, with a calming music and ambient rain sounds. Ps. This place is the fabulous for breakfast (try the quail eggs).

Open: Daily, 7am-10:30pm
Where: Nha Trang City Center
Address: 146 Vo Tru

Lac Canh

Lac Can is a local favorite for expats and Vietnamese in Nha Trang. This social Vietnamese style BBQ is an interactive experience that starts with teamwork and ends with melt-in-your-mouth eats. First, order your meat. It will be brought to your table to cook over a charcoal grill - kind of like you'd find at a Korean BBQ joint. So, when the crew at the hostel doesn't know where to eat, you have the perfect place to suggest.

Open: Daily, 10am-9pm
Where: Cai River area
Address: 44 Nguyen Binh Khiem

BBQ Un In

Southern BBQ using local ingredients with a view of the Cai River...have I got your attention yet? Take advantage of Vietnam's red meat culture and head over to BBQ Un In where you can sink your teeth into a juicy rack of ribs, gourmet sausages, and finger-licking chicken. They also serve up a mean seafood platter! Plus, the beer is cheap, and the staff are friendly. PS. Try to score a spot on the balcony for the best views.

Open: Daily, 11:30am-10:30pm
Where: Cai River area
Address: 206/66 Xom Con Street

BOGOSOV Pizza & Grill

If you think you can't find good pizza in Southeast Asia, think again. Often voted the #1 restaurant in Nha Trang, Bogosov's menu will make any pizza lovers' dreams come true. Each pizza is made with the freshest ingredients from local markets, topped with imported buffalo mozzarella, and laid out on hand-tossed dough. Go with a classic Margherita pizza to really appreciate those fresh flavors or get a little adventurous with their CrocoPizza cooked with...smoked crocodile.

Open: Daily, 12pm-10pm
Where: Nha Trang beach
Address: Lot 1 Pham Van Dogn

Pita GR Restaurant

You can only eat so many bowls of Pho in one week! Eventually, you'll need a break from Vietnamese cuisine and that's when you turn to Pita GR! This authentic Greek restaurant offers up classic dishes like the famed kebab for only 50,000 dong, plus tzatziki and hummus dips that are to die for!

Pro Tip: Pita GR place is open late and makes for the perfect drunk food stop on your way home from the bars.

Open: Daily, Closed Mondays, 8am-11pm
Where: Nha Trang beach
Address: 7G/3 Hung Vuong

Bars & Nightlife in Nha Trang

Skylight Skydeck & Rooftop Beach Club

Views of the ocean, mountains, and city all in one place. Sounds like the perfect place to have a beer, eh? Chilled out during the day and full of energy at night, come watch this peaceful skydeck transform from a bird's nest to nightclub complete with a DJ and dance floor as the sun goes down.

Open: Daily, 9am-2pm, 4:30pm-12am
Where: Nha Trang Beach
Address: 38 Tran Phu Street

The Sailing Club

As the sun starts to set, the party starts to kick off at the Sailing Club, Nha Trang's most prized nightlife spot. On any given night, patrons are treated to killer DJs, live dance performances, fire shows, and even some trippy magicians. Each month, Sailing Club also hosts a full-moon party featuring international DJs and stays open until at least 2am. Oh, and the cocktails? Ridiculously good. The kind you always imagined grownups drink on vacation…

Open: Daily, 7:30am-1:30am
Where: Nha Trang beach
Address: 72-74 Tran Phu Street

Rooftop Lounge

Offering a chill vibe with a friendly staff, the Rooftop Lounge offers a more laid-back option for those seeking to avoid the typical nightclub scene but still like the ideas of shisha and cocktails. Perched atop the fifth floor of Havana Hotel, this rooftop bar is run by expats and therefore, is very expat friendly. The is a great spot to gather with other backpackers where you can actually afford the food and drinks, while getting a pretty cool view of the city.

Open: Daily, 5pm-3am
Where: Nha Trang beach
Address: 73/6 Tran Quang Khai

Fun Things to Do in Nha Trang

Diep Son Island

One of the appealing things about visiting Nha Trang is the accessibility to nearby islands that can be reached inexpensively and quickly from town. Diep Son is a beautiful island with a unique and natural 800-meter sandbar that takes you from little island to the other. If you've never walked a sandbar, it's a surreal experience. With ocean on both sides of the sandy path, you'll feel like Moses splitting the sea. Magical Mystery Tour Nha Trang does a nice tour that will pick you up from Nha Trang and take you to Diep Son, leaving at 08:30 and returning at 15:30.

How Much: $35 USD / 800k VND
Contact: MagicalMysteryTourNhaTrang.com

Po Nagar Cham Towers

Ancient architecture with Angkor Wat style features, Po Nagar Cham Towers are the most magnificent complexes built by the Cham people back in the 8th and 11th century. Over centuries, the towers have endured battles and the elements, yet are still standing is impressive form- with the exception of the Golden Dome (which was robbed by pirates).

Pro Tip

When planning your trip, keep in mind that one of the best times to visit the Po Nagar Cham Towers is at the end of April to first week of May when annual Thap Ba Festival is held in Nha Trang.

Entrance Fee: $1 USD / 22k VND
Open: Daily 6:00am - 6:00pm
Location: Citadel

Fairy Spring Waterfalls

Got a motorbike? Ride the 20km south of Nha Trang to the Fairy Spring Waterfalls consisting of a gentle waterfall and swimming hole in the middle of the jungle. Local teens come here on the weekends to do teen stuff, but during the weekdays- you won't find much of a crowd. At the time of this writing, it tends to be a peaceful place to swim and enjoy natural scenery, however, plans are being made to further develop the area for tourism. Get there before it's too late.

How to Get There: Drive 10km west of Nha Trang to Diên Khánh. You'll go through the old citadel (Thành Cổ Diên Khánh) to Diên Phước village (5km) and then turn left for a 4km drive to Suoi Tien Village. After

1km, you'll turn right to find the stream. If you get lost, just keep showing locals a picture or translation of where you want to go.

Ba Ho Waterfalls
An even more spectacular waterfall and swimming hole, Ba Ho is a must-visit nature destination if you've got a bike! Similar to Fairy Spring, Ba Ho Waterfalls offers an alternative to lying on the local beaches by getting deep into the jungle. Made up of 3 waterfalls and 1 large swimming hole surrounded by big massive boulders- you could spend all day here just lounging around, tanning, and cooling off in the water. That is...after the 20-minute hike/boulder scramble that it takes to get there. There's no admission fee but to find this fall, it's best to hire a local guide or sign up for a full-day tour with a tourist company that often includes a stop off here.
Where: Ninh Ich, Ninh Hoa District

Thap Ba Hot Springs and Mud Baths
After long bus rides and miles of exploring, your body will be in need of a little TLC. Thap Ba Hot Spring, about 6 km away from downtown Nha Trang, provides mud baths for you to cover yourself in soothing clay. Locals believe that the hot mineral spring and mud have healing properties and can aid in detoxification. First, you'll soak in the mud for 15 minutes, and then transfer into the mineral bath for 30 minutes, and finish with a hydrotherapy session with warm or cold water. The baths are communal, and you wear your clothes- making it a silly yet gratifying experience.
How Much: $6.50 USD / 150k VND
Open: Daily 7am-7pm

Long Son Pagoda
Immerse yourself in a serene escape from the busy streets to an elevating experience. Overlooking the city of Nha Trang, Long Son Pagoda is a magnificent compound featuring state-of-the-art Taoist architecture exemplified by intricately designed sculptures and engravings of mythical creatures and Taoist deities. While strolling, listen to the refreshing chants of monks and nuns echoing through the halls for a spiritual aura. Climb the 152 steps from the entrance that lead you to the breathtaking 24-meter towering white Buddha sitting on a lotus blossom.

Entrance Fee: Free
Open: Daily 7:30-11:30am & 1:30-5:30pm
Location: Thai Nguyen Street (400m west of Nha Trang train station)

Shopping in Nha Trang

Thap Ba Street

As a traveler in Nha Trang it is inevitable that you will come across delicious seafood more than once. Thap Ba Street is a place where you can get fresh seafood at street food prices. The typical process involves you choosing the seafood you want (which is often still living) and instructing the vendor how you would like it cooked (fried, grilled, with rice). This is where you'll master the art of pointing and miming.

Open: Daily
Where: Thap Ba Street

Nha Trang Market, AKA Dam Market

Pure Vietnamese chaos kicks off bright and early at Dam Market, the most popular market in Nha Trang. With three stories and one main center floor- you can find anything and everything at this market. The morning is an especially popular time to visit. This is when all of the local descend onto the market to buy their ingredients for their shops and restaurants for the day.

Ps. If you're not in the market for anything particular but just want some surreal people watching, this is where to go.

Open: Daily, 7am-6pm
Where: Van Thanh

Vinh Luong Market

Fresh seafood is plentiful at many of the markets in Nha Trang, but Vinh Luong promises the most varied selection of fresh fish caught by local fisherman. The fishermen lug in their haul of shellfish, crustaceans, colorful fish, squid, oysters, and creatures you've never even seen before. It's kind of like going to an aquarium but free...and knowing that all the animals have merely 24 hours to live....it's fascinating.

Open: Daily, 5am-7pm
Where: 20-minute drive from Nha Trang city center

Nha Trang Night Market

Grab a walking beer and prepare for an evening of pure shopping and eating bliss. Nha Trang Night Market, located smack dab in the middle of Phu Dong Park, will loosen up your pocket book real quick; first with yummy street food and causal sit-down stalls, and then with all of the shopping! From cute clothes for the beach, dried fruit for the road, and Vietnamese souvenirs for home – there's no way you're going home empty-handed.. Not to mention, the people watching here is beyond amazing with European families and Russian couples that give this spot a quirky international feel.

Open: Daily, 6pm-12am
Where: Phu Dong Park

Fun Vietnam Fact
Vietnam is the world's largest exporter of black pepper.

How to Get around Nha Trang

Grab Taxi

Grab Taxi is Southeast Asia's answer to Uber, and offers westerners a familiar look and feel to the incredibly popular Uber app. In addition to being a convenient way to find local taxi drivers within your local area, Grab Taxi also reduces the risk of a taxi driver overcharging you or getting lost. Get a Grab Car or a Grab Bike.

Walking

Enjoy the scenery! Nha Trang is a very walkable city with a pretty safe community. Just don't walk on the beach alone at night. This will open you up for pick pockets and bag snatchers.

Fun Vietnam Fact

Nguyen is the most common family name in Vietnam.

Chapter 22: Hue

Hue is right in the center of Vietnam. Vietnam, a country which was once divided with the Communist Party in the North, and the freedom fighters in the South. It is no surprise, that during the conflict of the Vietnam War, that Hue was literally caught in the middle.

The Viet Cong conquered and held Hue captive for 24 days during the Vietnam War. In attempts to further their position south, they killed anyone who was educated beyond a high school degree, and anyone who sympathized with the US. In just 24 days, 3,000 Vietnamese were killed before the US forces came to their aid.

Generally, in order to preserve ancient buildings during the Vietnam war, the US Military avoided air bombings and artillery while fighting the Vietnamese communist party- but they had to make an exception to stop the amount of violence happening in Hue and as a result, a large portion of the city was ruined- but not all.

Hue is still home to some of the most gorgeous historic sites and relics in the country. There have been massive preservation efforts, historical reconstruction, and a few lucky sites that were spared.

You only need a couple days in Hue, all of which will be spent soaking up surreal ancient history and understanding the travesties that occurred during one the most violent wars the world has ever seen. Each temple, tomb, and historical site left standing makes this city come alive with stories and secrets waiting to be discovered.

I'm tellin' ya, Hue is not to be skipped.

Areas to Explore in Hue

Imperial Citadel
The main attraction of Hue, home of ancient Emperors and some of the most historic sites in Vietnam.

The Imperial Tombs
To the north of the Imperial Citadel lies the seven imperial tombs of Hue honor of the ancient Emperors and transport you back in time to the 17th century.

The New City
Across the bridge from the Imperial Citadel, lies the New City with modern buildings, restaurants, hotels, and nightlife.

Historical Outskirts of Town
You can find even more tombs, temples, and historic bridges outside of the main attractions in Hue. If you've got a 3rd day to spare in Hue- sign up for a tour or rent a motorbike to go exploring.

Fun Vietnam Fact
Vietnam's unemployment rate is one of the lowest among all developing countries.

Accommodation in Hue

Amy 2 Hostel Hue $

Arriving late? Sometimes your bus gets in to Hue after midnight…and that's stressful. No problem when you book at Amy 2 – they will sort you out with their 24-hour reception. This place is quickly becoming a backpacker favorite for solo female travelers for how Amy 2 goes above and beyond for the safety of their guests. Close to the train station and bus station, this place is as convenient as it gets.
Style: Dorms (they have all-female dorms, too).

Starts at: $4.50 USD / 102k VND
Where: Hue Town
Address: 10/26 Võ Thị Sáu, Phú Hội

New Life Homestay $

Not in the mood for the party scene but still want to get a little social? New Life Homestay offers you a sanctuary where you can relax! Chill out on their amazing rooftop terrace with a few beers and take in the sites of the city. Located in a side street alley, you can expect peace and quiet at night (something that can be hard to come by on the backpacker path). Everything from the beds to the facilities are relatively new for a great night's sleep. As if all of that weren't enough…your host family are very friendly and will go above and beyond to make you feel comfortable and even offers rental bikes for you to get around.

Style: Dorms and Privates
Starts at: $6 & $12
Where: Near the Trang Tien Bridge and Chieu Ung Pagoda
Address: 35 Lane 10 Chu Van An, Hue

Vietnam Backpackers Hostel – Hue $

They've done it again. VBH just never quits when it comes to throwing good parties and amazing tours in every city they touch! They offer countless tours of the city. Instead of touring solo, you can link up with other travelers for some fun company! Afterwards, come back for free beer hour and then head out with the gang for some street food. Oh, and after you've seen all the historical sites in Hue…consider seeing a different kind of history with this epic abandoned waterpark on the outskirts of the city. VBH offers an epic Motorbike Tour finishing at the abandoned water park…go go go.

Style: Dorms

Starts at: $6.50 USD / 148k VND
Where: New City
Address: 10 Pham Ngu Lao St

Rosaleen Boutique Hotel $$

Did you say pool AND sauna? Sign me up! Stay at Rosaleen where you can sunbathe next to their outdoor pool while ordering from a pool-side menu. The rooms here are spacious and luxurious- some with their own breezy balcony. One of the best things about it is that it's located at the heart of Hue and just a short distance away from popular tourist spots. Not sure where to start going? The friendly staff would help you out with that!

Style: Privates
Starts at: $55 USD / 1.25 million VND
Where: 5 minutes from the Perfume River
Address: 36 Chu Van An, Phu Hoi Ward, Hue

Why Not? Hostel $

Looking for local nightlife? Why Not Hostel is all about the social backpacker experience! Conveniently located on one of wildest streets in town, you'll find bars, restaurants, and touristy shops right outside your door. Why Not Hostel offers a sure-fire way to make friends with two of its own bars AND a popular Mexican restaurant. When you're not eating, drinking, or partying…kick it in the cozy rooms that have this Old Western theme to them, giving off a laid-back vibe- perfect for hangovers.

Style: Dorms and Privates
Starts at: $4 - $20
Where: Pham Ngu Lao street
Address: 26 Pham Ngu Lao, Hue

Pilgrimage Village Boutique Resort & Spa $$

Bask in a rustic and secluded resort away from the center of this bustling city. Hand-crafted bungalows surrounded by lush gardens where you can just lay around and take in nature in all its glory. Pilgrimage Village is the perfect place for an intimate getaway. Aside from their pool and spa, you can also sign up for yoga and Tai Chi classes. Don't worry about being too far from the city center, this resort offers private tours and a shuttle service into town. Then, when you're done exploring, you can come back and snuggle into nature.

Style: Private Rooms, Bungalow and Huts
Starts at: $76 USD / 1.73 million VND
Where: 20 minutes away from the Hue airport
Address: 130 Minh Mang Road, Hue

Ana Mandara Hue Beach Resort $$$

There's only thing you need to know about this resort to fall in love: it's literally on the beach! The white sands of Thuan An Beach are just outside your window. When you get tired of the sand, they also have an equally amazing pool, spa, sports facilities, and children's playground, so you'll never run out of things to do here. It's a few ways off the main city, but you can always check out the nearby fishing village at the Tam Giang Lagoon to get a feel of the local culture. What are you even waiting for? Treat yo' self.

Style: Privates
Starts at: $113 USD / 2.58 million VND
Where: 1 minute away from Thuan An Beach
Address: 131 Nguyen Van Tuyet, Thua Thien

Where to Eat in Hue

Bun Bo Hue

Of course, your Hue food trip isn't complete without Bun Bo Hue, and this little eatery is the best place to have them. And yes, it is named after the very dish it specializes in, so don't even bother asking for directions (follow the address below). When you do find it, you'll see that it's actually a modest little restaurant packed with people. For as low as $2, you can get a generous bowl of soup with beef that just melts in your mouth. Experience eating like a local with the locals.

Open: Daily 5am - 7pm
Where: A few streets down the Perfume River
Address: 11B Ly Thuong Kiet

Nina's Café

Tucked away in some obscure backstreet is a quaint family restaurant that specializes in Western, Vietnamese, and local Hue cuisine. They offer cheap dishes made with the freshest ingredients picked and caught that very day! Get a taste of the local Banh Beo and Hue Banh Khoai alongside a selection of refreshing drinks- perfect for a hot day! And don't worry, they also have a vegan and vegetarian menu!

Open: Daily 8am - 10:30pm

Where: A few streets down the Perfume River, near the Hung Vuong main road
Address: 16/34 Nguyen Tri Phuong | Laneway 34, Hue

Cafe on Thu Wheels

Fast-food with local ingredients! Burgers, sandwiches, or rice meals, this place is all about casual dining for the active traveler! Tons of backpackers stop by here all the time to grab a quick meal or to just mingle. Here, you can share your experience with a couple of drinks and at the end of your stay, leave your mark on the walls. Don't worry! Graffiti is encouraged! It's a pretty small place- not suited for big groups - just radiating 'chill'.

Open: Breakfast: 6am - 10:30am; Lunch & Dinner: 11:30am - 11:00pm
Where: 500m down the Perfume River
Address: 3/34 Nguyen Tri Phuong Street, Hue

Hue Street Food Tour

Southeast Asian culture is street food culture and your trip just isn't complete without trying the food of the masses! Of course, mindlessly going around town in hopes of finding them would take up too much time. Luckily, you can sign up for a tour that lets you try out all of the best street food spots in just a few hours. Yes, you heard that right, a tour just for food (#AlwaysHungry). Here, you'll be riding around in a cyclo with a guide taking you to the best street food stalls around. Don't be shy...bring a beer for the ride.

How Much: $49 USD / 1.1 million VND
Time: 9:00am or 2:00pm (each tour will last approximately 4 hours)
Contact: (+84) 0932 420 099

Mandarin Café

There's a reason why backpackers and travelers go all out in trying to find this place and keep coming back for second and third visits, too! Photographs showing the everyday life of sampan villagers line the walls of the café, adding an authentic touch. The beauty and simplicity of the village lifestyle and culture are perfectly captured and represented here by the cultured café owner, Mr. Cu. The cafe specializes in traditional Vietnamese and Western dishes made by the owner's wife, and you can even ask for the recipe to take home if you like your dish that much! Oh, and make sure you try their banana pancake and noodles while you're here!

Open: Daily 6am - 10pm
Where: Across the Imperial Hotel Hue

Address: 24 Tran Cao Van St. | South Bank, Hue

Hanh Restaurant

Also called 'Le Hanh' or 'Quan Hanh', this traditional Vietnamese restaurant is famous in Hue! Try their Chao Tom (shrimp around sugar cane stick) & Banh Khoai (crispy fried potato cake). This place is always busy during high season which is always a great sign of a high-quality establishment. The service is on point, food comes out hot, and the beers are always cold. The perfect place for a true Vietnamese cuisine experience.

Open: Daily 10am – 9pm
Where: New City
Address: 11 Pho Duc Chinh

Fun Vietnam Fact

Vietnam borders Cambodia, Laos and China

Bars & Nightlife in Hue

Brown Eyes Bar

The party ends you when you pass out; that's the rule in this bar! In a city that sleeps early, this is one of the few bars that's still alive late into the night. I mean, with a drink selection that's probably the most extensive that you'll find in Hue PLUS a dance floor and DJ, it's no surprise that Brown Eyes Bar is so popular among tourists and locals. Catch them at happy hour and get 2 drinks for the price of 1! During happy hours, you're even greeted with a free drink and snack!

Open: Daily 5pm - late
Where: 5 minutes away from the Night Market
Address: 56 Chu Van An, Hue

Secret Lounge Hue

Casual drinking without the loud music in an open-air tropical garden designed with a traditional Vietnamese spice. Secret Lounge is worth a visit. They're also got a Foosball table, a pool table, and a big ass TV to keep you entertained!

Open: Daily 7AM - 2:30AM
Where: 10-minute drive from Hue Imperial City
Address: 15/42 Nguyen Cong Tru, Hue

The DMZ Bar

Want lots of food choices to go with your night of drinking? The DMZ offers a mix of foreign and local alcohol alongside Italian, Western, and Vietnamese cuisine. Enjoy it in their upstairs garden terrace that overlooks the Perfume River! There's also happy hour promos on the daily!

Open: Daily 5pm and 9pm
Where: By the Perfume River, Near the Hotel Century Riverside
Address: 60 Le Loi Street, Hue

Sightseeing & Culture in Hue

Tombs of the Emperors

Scattered near the Perfume River, you can find seven individual, uniquely designed imperial tombs made to comfort the Emperors of the Nguyen Dynasty in the afterlife. Among these, there are three that are more popular and accessible to tourists.

The Tomb of Tu Duc, which is considered the most beautiful tomb, was made for the longest reigning Emperor of his time. Because this Emperor never had a child, he had to write his epitaph himself.

The Tomb of Minh Mang is seen as the most elegant and regal one because of its architectural design. Classical Chinese style with impeccable symmetry made a structure that blends so perfectly with the landscape you'd think it was part of nature.

Taking in a mix of French and Eastern design, the Tomb of Khai Dinh is the last emperor on the list. The architecture is more complex and is perched in an ideal location with a nice view on a hill.

Thien Mu Pagoda

On top a hill overlooking the Perfume River, you can find this iconic 7-storey pagoda. Thien Mu is the stuff of folk rhymes and literature since it's basically the oldest religious building in Vietnam. Inside, you'll find various Buddha statues, representing different stages of his life. The legend behind the name is that there was once a mysterious old lady who showed up on the hill and foretold that a Lord would pass by and build something important. Sometimes, you might even find monks praying or practicing calligraphy here.

Thanh Toan Bridge

'Simple yet picturesque' has to be the best way to describe this iconic Hue bridge. As you bike through the countryside, you'll find this bridge east of the Thuy Thanh Commune. It was made to facilitate transportation and communication between the two villages on each side of the canal. One of its unique traits is that it's built with architectural details that are similar to the Japanese Bridge in Hoi An. For generations, the community has always repaired and maintained their beloved bridge.

Within the Imperial Citadel

The Imperial Citadel is a walled fortress that lies at the center of Hue. It was added to the list of UNESCO's World Heritage Site in 2010 because it holds centuries of history and culture. For a thousand years, it was the center for military and political power. Stepping into the gates feels like going back in time to a place of grand and beautiful structures where emperors of Vietnam's past once walked. There's not much left of the royal palaces and structures because of years of war, but ancient architecture and relics still remains

Within the Imperial Citadel, here are the main attractions…

- **Hue Jungle Crevice**

This place has a pretty… morbid backstory actually. Here, the Viet Cong imprisoned 3,000 citizen and officials and, in attempts to slow down the opposition, all 3,000 citizens were pushed off cliff to their death.

- **Forbidden Purple City**

You've heard of China's Forbidden City, right? Well, this is conceptually the same thing. This citadel in citadel was made solely for the emperor and a handful of royals and servants.

- **Trường Sanh Residence**

Also called the Palace of Longevity, these buildings were built to house the Grand Empress Tu Du, mother of Emperor Tu Duc of the Nguyen

Dynasty. Restoration was completed back in 2007 so now, you visit it at the northern part of the citadel.

- **Thái Hòa Palace**

Among all the structures in the citadel, the Thai Hoa palace is the most important one in every way. It's the most majestic place in all the city and its architecture has deep philosophical, cultural, historical, and artistic meaning. At the heart of it lies the Emperor's throne where the most important ceremonies and coronations happened.

The Demilitarized Zone (DMZ)

Much like North Korea and South Korea created a DMZ border during the Korean War, the Vietnamese did the same during the Vietnam War. This Demilitarized Zone was the forefront for intense battles and bloodshed. It is also home to the fascinating Vinh Moc tunnels, where hundreds of people lived for 2.5 years during these battles.

Important to note: the DMZ is about 150km north of Hue. If you take a day trip (around $12 USD / 273k NVD), you can go by bus which will take you on a full 6am-6pm adventure. But if you're motorbike savvy, this is a popular stop on the way from Hue as you continue up north. The DMZ is located in the town of Dong Ha. Consider spending the night there and continuing on your motorbike journey after you explore.

Pro Tip for Sightseeing in Hue

As mentioned before, you can find tours offering a balanced 1-2 days adventure that hits up all of these lovely spots! There are a plethora of tour companies in Hue, all of which have similar prices and standards of English. While you can just sign up for a tour when you arrive in Hue, either at your hotel or compare tours by walking around the city and popping into a couple of tourism offices.

Great Tour Companies

- ✓ Beebee Travel
- ✓ Cafe On Thu Wheels
- ✓ I Love Hue Tours

Fun Things to Do in Hue

My An Hot Spring and Spa

Thinking of going to Hue in the summer? Beat the heat at this resort! The name says hot spring and spa, but there's way more things to do there than that! It's actually a water park with pools and everything, so you can bring the kids or the whole family even. The mineral water that make up the place is said to have therapeutic qualities, too. My An's hot spring is world-class, and many can vouch that it's one of the best.

Abandoned Water Park

You hear 'water park' and you're probably thinking of refreshing pools and exhilarating waterslides…but there will be no swimming here- just a crazy dystopian adventure. What was intended to be a large tourist attraction never picked up traction and is now just a wasteland for adventurous tourists. Nobody really knows what happened. All we know is that millions were spent…all to be forgotten after a couple of years.

Now, you can have this whole creepy park to yourself and during the rainy season…you can CAREFULL climb the stairs up to the water slides and get dirty as you slide down these dirty tracks. It's so much fun.

You won't find it in a lot of itineraries or maps, so directions are more on word of mouth. Either sign up with the 'I love Hue' Tour, or go with a buddy on this one…cause ya know…abandoned stuff is creepy on your own.

Pro Tip

Make sure you wear some comfortable hiking clothes and closed shoes for this area because it's pretty muddy and swampy.

Free Hanging Zipline

If you're feeling adventurous, head to Thanh Tan Hot Springs to enjoy the free-hanging zipline and high wire.

They have the longest zipline in the country, with a length of 560 meters. Stay suspended 45m up the Ma Yen Mountain and land all the way down to the lake! All the equipment and facilities are safe and secure! The best way to experience it all is to sign up with a day tour with eOasia. They take care of all the planning and you just hang out and enjoy the ride!

Contact: eoasia.com
Starting at: $83 USD / 1.9 million VND

Beach Day at Thuan An Beach

Don't worry about being stuck in the city and missing out the beach. Thuan An Beach is just within reach of the area. On the way, you can stop by the many temples, pagodas, and commune villages. Rent a tent and camp out overnight! It isn't as developed as some of Vietnam's other beaches, but there are still some restaurants that take advantage of the tourists going there. Eat fresh seafood and enjoy true isolation!

Beebee Travel Walking Tour

Discover Vietnam's vast history via a walking excursion through Hue! Stories from 700 years ago, monuments from the French War, and remnants from the bloody Battle of Hue, you can explore all these in a 3-hour walking tour.

For a starting price of $10/227k, you can go to Vietnam War memorials, old bunkers, and weapons museums across Hue. Their friendly and attentive guides speak English and can answer any questions you might have.

Hue Countryside Cycling Tour

Another fun and relaxing way to see the area is through bike! Go through the countryside and see rice paddies, hills, duck farms, fishing farms, and so much more! You'll also get to see some villages and communities along the way! Make sure you pass by Thanh Toan and check out the handicrafts in their local market.

Contact: Ilovehuetour.com

Markets & Shopping in Hue

Dong Ba Market

More than a place for tourists to get cheap goods, Dong Ba Market is kind of like the heart and center of Hue. It's the biggest and oldest market, that stretches from the Trang Tien Bridge to Gia Hoi Bridge. Hundreds of people go here to make a living or buy goods for their everyday lives. You can find anything here: food, souvenirs, and even cultural gifts that you can't find anywhere else. Make sure to keep a good eye on your stuff, though, as pickpockets are just lurking around. Also, don't forget to bargain, bargain, bargain!

Open: Daily 6am - 8pm
Address: Tran Hung Dao street, Hue

Hue Walking Street

Take a break from all the fast-paced touring and unwind in the new and improved Walking Street. You're now greeted with better pavements and beautiful scenery! They've even made it so that no vehicles would pass by on weekends and holidays. If you're lucky, you can catch street performances and festivals on this street.

Open: All day - Every day
Address: Nguyen Dinh Chieu

How to Get around Hue

Taxi

Taxis are usually more reliable in their fees, but make sure you keep watch on that meter! It starts at 15k VND for the first 2 kilometers and goes up 11,500 VND per kilometer. It's best to ask your hotel about the estimate fee, so you'll have an idea of how much you should be paying.

Motorbike

Whether you're touring within town or in the countryside, motorcycles are the most ideal way to get around. Fast and accessible, hotels and restaurants all around Hue offer motorcycle rentals and even tours for as low as $10 / 228k.

Bicycle

For a quick ride within the city, bicycles are the way to go! You can easily go through all those small alleys and inner streets to get to those hidden restaurants. There are tons of bike shops and tours that rent a bike for at least $2 a day.

Cyclo

Where there are tourists, there are cyclo drivers. It's actually a fun and unique way to get around! Sure, it's not as fast and traffic is bad, but sitting in your own little covered chair as someone pushes you to your destination is an experience in itself. You can choose to go on cyclo tours or find one walking around offering rides. Be careful when you're around an empty street at night, though. Make sure you ask for their price before picking one as some tend to up the cost for obvious tourists. For cyclos, it would usually cost roughly $5 /114k for an hour's trip. Of course, the price is less if it's just one nearby stop. Also, bring a notepad with you to write down prices as miscommunication tends to happen sometimes.

Scams Particularly in Hue

✓ **Bus Ticket Scams**

When it comes to booking a bus to HCMC, shop around! Hotels and tourism offices often try to increase the price to keep the difference. Let them know you're shopping around and don't be afraid to walk away. The price will magically drop. Bus tickets to HCMC should be around $20-$30.

Avoid 'Adin's Café Booking Office' and 'Moon Travel'. They are infamous for jacking up prices – no matter how friendly they may seem...

✓ **Recommendations from your Hotel**

Everyone is trying to make a dime in Hue- including hotel receptionists. Be weary when you ask for massage, tour, or restaurant recommendations from your hotel. Everyone is looking to make a little commission and might give you a less-than-amazing recommendation. Good thing you have this book, ya?

✓ **Ordering food at the Market**

When you order your meal...only eat when you've specifically ordered. The vendors can be tricky and bring you an extra plate of food. If you eat it...you buy it.

How to Get to Hue

> **By Bus**
> When: About 6 buses per day from 9am – 2:30pm
> Duration: 3 hours
> Cost: $6

> **By Train**
> When: 20 Trains per day, 3am – 11pm
> Duration: 2.5-3.5 hours
> Cost: $6-$10

> **By Motorbike**

This is a very popular stretch of coastal highway for those who want to experience a motorbike adventure but don't want to traverse the whole damn country on 2 wheels.

You can sign up for a tour, where you'll have a guide that leads the way. You can also opt to ride on the back of their bike while you take in the views. You'll stop by waterfalls and do some little hikes along the way!

The entire journey is 165km which can be completed in 1-3 days...depending on how many stops you want to make.

Know that you can do this journey in 4 different sequences:
- ✓ Hoi An to Hue
- ✓ Da Nang to Hue
- ✓ Or flip those two around and go the other direction.
- ✓ Just ask around in Hue, Hoi An, or Da Nang and you can find this tour being offered!

Chapter 23: Da Nang

Da Nang is the 3rd biggest city in Vietnam, home to tall sky scraper condos, a busting middle-class population, a few universities, and a decent sized expat + digital nomad community. Despite all of this, Da Nang is quiet a sleepy little city with not too much to offer tourists outside of a couple viewpoints.

Oh…except beaches. Did I mention beaches?

Da Nang IS home to some of the most gorgeous beaches in Vietnam. Long stretches of white sand with resorts, condos, and tour agencies lining their perimeter offer a fun few days in the sun.

You'll need no more than 1-2 days in Da Nang – lounging on the beach and exploring the winding streets to find plastic-table restaurants with authentic central-Vietnamese cuisine!

The 2 days spent here will be worth your time, but there isn't too much to do beyond that. Da Nang is a nice stop over before you hit up the ancient town of Hoi An (my favorite city in all of Vietnam).

Areas to Explore in Da Nang

Hai Chua

Hai Chua is known as the commercial center of Da Nang. This is where urban activity happens, and you can find their main theatre and shopping center here.

An Thuong

Hai Chua may be where the market is, but An Thuong has all the best cafes. You'll have tons of variety, and it's a great place to ask around if you're still figuring out where to go.

Bach Dang

At night, Bach Dang just lights up, and not in a wild party way! The side of the city near the river gives off a really chill vibe with all its lights and cafes.

My Khe Beach

Along this beach is where all the seafood restaurants are! If you're looking to hang around the beach or just eat good food, this is the place to go.

Accommodation in Da Nang

Rom Casa Da Nang $

Rom Casa is like Peter Pan meets Alice in Wonderland. Made from refurbished shipping containers and recycled wood– all painted brightly and whimsically, this is a fairytale getaway. Despite the DIY feel, rooms here are pretty cozy and equipped with air conditioning and comfy beds. Hang out in the garden surrounded by twinkly lights, relax in the library, or cool off in the pool. If you can bring yourself to leave this magical little place, the beach is just a short walk away.

Style: Privates & Dorms
Starts at: $7 & $15 / 160k & 342k
Where: 300 meters from My An Beach
Address: 26 An Thuong 4 street, Ngu Hanh Son District, Da Nang

Da Nang Backpackers Hostel $

When it comes to budget travel in Da Nang, there's no competition! After you tally up all the freebies at Da Nang Backpackers- your entire stay is practically free. For $5 per night, you get free breakfast, 1 free bottle of beer per night, 1 free bottle of water, a free walking tour every night, and free foosball & pool table. All of these freebies bring guests together, as does the food tour, pub crawl, movie night, and karaoke night.

Style: Dorms & Privates
Starts at: $5 /114k
Where: Hai Chua
Address: 106 Nguyen Chi Thanh St, Hai Chau

Mai Boutique Villa $

Simple and clean is most people would describe this place, but what really gets people talking is the attentive and friendly staff! The staff are always at your service, and they're a big help when it comes to information about the area. The on-f bar and restaurant serves some of the best Vietnamese food and drinks, too. Get a taste of Da Nang specialties along with extensive wine options.

Style: Privates
Starts at: $25 /570k
Where: Past the Song Han Bridge
Address: Lot I-09 Pham Van Dong, Da Nang

The Herriott Hotel & Suite $

Pool on the terrace, anyone? No question, this hotel has some of the finest looking rooms in Da Nang. Aside from the nice interior, it has everything you'll need that it seems like a mini apartment than a hotel room. Units complete with a kitchen, oven, and TV is what you'll find. A breakfast buffet is included, too!

Style: Privates
Starts at: $39 / 888k
Where: 1.3 km from the Love Lock Bridge Da Nang
Address: Lot I-09 Pham Van Dong, Da Nang

Pavilion Hotel $$

Looking for a place to stay that has the familiar amenities from back home and within walking distance of one of the most beautiful beaches in Asia? Look no further than Pavilion Hotel. This beachfront beauty is located directly along the My Khe Beach district and offers its guests free WiFi, free use of bicycles, restaurant with complimentary breakfast, fitness center, hot tub, rooftop pool with views of the city and the ocean, and much more. Language barriers are no barrier at Pavilion, the staff speaks English!

Style: Privates, Beachfront
Starts at: $60 /1.37 million
Where: My Khe Beach district
Address: 35 Vo Van Kiet,

Where to Eat in Da Nang

Tamarind Tree Restaurant Da Nang

Never had food with tamarind before? Well, this restaurant will change that. With a diverse menu that even includes vegetarian-friendly food, you can get a taste of traditional Vietnamese food here. Everything is made with fresh ingredients and tastes so good that you'd want to eat there for breakfast, lunch, and dinner! Try their spring rolls and Morning Glory, and you'll see what I mean!

Open: Daily 9am - 10pm
Where: Along Nguyen Phan Vinh
Address: My Khe 4, Phuoc My, Da Nang, Vietnam

Market's

Barbecued food and cold beer is definitely Market's specialty. They have a wide choice of meat, seafood, and vegetables that's all cooked right in front of you! A small grill is placed beside you, so you can experience flipping and booking your own food, too. Of course, the friendly and attentive staff is willing to help you out.

Open: 10am - 10pm
Where: A side Street at 59 Ho Xuan Huong Street
Address: 29 Luu Quang Thuan, Da Nang, Vietnam

Pizza 4 P's

Yes, I've already talked about it in the Ho Chi Minh section…but the moment you need a break from Vietnamese food, Pizza 4P's is here for the most heavenly pizza experience ever. Don't leave this country without trying Pizza 4 P's in one of the big cities. Any pizza that comes with a fresh ball of mozzarella on top, just to be rolled out at the table is worth an order! You haven't lived until you've tried it!
Open: Daily 10am-10:30pm
Where: Near the Cau Rong Bridge
Address: 8 Hoàng Văn Thụ, Phước Ninh, Hải Châu

Mi Total

Chinese food with Vietnamese ingredients makes for a must-try Asian fusion meal cooked by the same Chinese family that opened this spot 30 years ago! Have Pho Ap Chao (deep fried pho) served with veggies and gravy for dirt cheap prices! With a beer of course.

Open: Evening-Late
Where: Corner of Thai Phien and Nguyen Chi Thanh

Pho 75

Staying loyal to the Southern way of making Pho, tender pieces of raw beef are placed in hot clear broth where they cook right before your eyes. The broth is very light, waiting for you to spice it up to your liking with chili sauce, soy, lime, and hot sauce. This street food stall is the OG of Pho in Da Nang.

Open: Friday-Wednesday 8am-8pm
Where: Thành Phố Đà Nẵng
Address: 91 Ngo Gia Tu, Đà Nẵng

Street Food Galore!
Just explore, sit, eat and repeat!

Sightseeing & Culture in Da Nang

Marble Mountain

On the Son Tra Peninsula of Da Nang lies the Indiana Jones style Marble Mountains that look more like a cluster of skyscrapers than rock formations. There are 5 mini "mountains" in total, made of marble and limestone. On your Marble Mountain adventure, you can explore mysterious caves tucked into the mountains and visit the 220-foot-high marble Bodhisattva statue resting in the Ling Ung Buddhist Pagoda.

At the base of Marble Mountain is Non Nuoc Stone Carving Village, a centuries-old craft village here with impressive stone carved statues of Buddhist figures, dragons, and more

Rent a motorbike and visit on your own or sign up for a half-day tour that includes mini detours around the peninsula.

My Son Sanctuary

In a valley surrounded by two mountain ranges and picturesque countryside, lies My son sanctuary. This place is a cluster of ruined Hindu temples dating back to as early as the 4th century and is a magnificent display of unique architecture that bears witness to an ancient civilization that is now extinct.

Here, you will find a complex of 70 edifices crafted from sandstone and reinforced with red bricks. Back in the day, this was a place of worship for the Cham people as well as a burial ground for their royalty. Now regarded as a Unesco World Heritage site, this little haven gives you a glimpse into a civilization long forgotten.

Entrance Fee: 100k VND
Open: All day but best to visit early to avoid the hot afternoons
Location: DuyXunen District
Address: 70km southwest of Danang and 40km from Hoi An

Fun Things to Do in Da Nang

Bach Ma National Park
Part of the Annamite Mountain Range and the wettest region in Vietnam, Bach Ma National Park is the place to go if you want to get off the beaten path. A paradise for nature lovers, there's plenty to see including wildlife, lagoons and waterfalls. Adventurers can enjoy climbing, camping and hiking, most notably, the Summit Hike. The park is about 55km from Hue and you have a few options to get there. Hire a motorbike or car and drive yourself there or take a bus or one of the many guided tours that leave from the city.

Beach Day
Thanh Binh Beach: The main strip of beach in Da Nang, you'll have instant access to Thanh Binh Beach when your bus pulls into town or when you drive in from the airport. It's decent for a day of sun tanning, but not extremely impressive in terms of beauty.

Non Nuoc Beach: 20 minutes from Da Nang is the most beautiful beach in the area. With soft white sand, jet skiing, and surfing – it's definitely worth the drive.

My Khe Beach: Once listed in Forbes Magazine as one of the 'World's Most Luxurious Beaches, My Khe Beach is now home to upscale resorts like the Hyatt and smaller boutique resorts. Amazing area to stay!

Scuba Dive
Right off the coast of Da Nang, you can find a colorful collection coral and shoals of fish, as well as abundant marine life. Sign up for some fun dives or get your Open Water Certification in Da Nang. Most of your dives will be done 18km off the coast near the Cham islands where the best underwater sites can be found.

Try **Da Nang Scuba**. They're reputable, fun and PADI certified.

Open Water Course Price: $260 / 6 million
Length of Course: 3 Days

Cham Island Tour

Known by locals as 'Cu Lao Cham', this island is home to Vietnamese Fishing Villages who make their living off the land, the sea, and a little bit of tourism. There are plenty of day tours being offered from Da Nang (and Hoi An) that will whisk you away to snorkel in crystal clear waters, hike through unspoiled jungles, and sample some of the freshest sea food dishes in Vietnam. Sign up with **Vietnam Typical Tours** for a 5.5-hour tour that includes lunch, snorkel gear, and a village trek for $35/ 800k per person.

If you're really feeling some island vibes, you can stay overnight by booking a basic bungalow on the island – nothing too fancy here. There are boats that leave every day from both Da Nang and Hoi An to the islands.

Dragon Bridge at Night

Photographers, get your camera ready. The Dragon Bridge over the Han River is designed to look like a fire-breathing dragon that lights up at night, reflecting off of the water below. Take a walk along the riverside, buy some snacks from vendors, and take some great Instagram-worthy shots of the 666-meter long beast.

Location: Phuoc Ninh
Address: Nguyễn Văn Linh, An Hải T

Day Trips from Da Nang

Hai Van Pass

How do you feel on a Motorbike? Good? Great. Because you're going to want to see this...

Hai Van Pass is a mountain road that also straddles the coast line. You've got lush green jungle on one side and deep blue water on the other. The road is windy yet wide, making for a fun day of pure adventure.

The whole trip takes about 3.5 hours and there are plenty of little snack bars and cafes along the way. If you want to get hyped up about this drive, it was featured on an episode of Top Gear and is every bit as amazing in real life as it is on screen. And trust me, photos could never do this one justice...

Drive to Hue

This is a very popular stretch of coastal highway for those who want to experience a motorbike adventure but don't want to traverse the whole damn country on 2 wheels.

You can sign up for a tour, where you'll have a guide that leads the way. You can also opt to ride on the back of their bike while you take in the views. You'll stop by waterfalls and do some little hikes along the way! The entire journey is 165km which can be completed in 1-3 days...depending on how many stops you want to make.

Note that you can do this journey in 4 different sequences:
- ✓ Hoi An to Hue
- ✓ Da Nang to Hue
- ✓ Or flip those two around and go the other direc

Markets & Shopping in Da Nang

Han Market

Rise and shine, kiddos! Han Market opens early. The locals descend on the market while it's still cool outside to pick up their goodies for the day. Han Market follows the template for one of those massive 'all of the above' markets in Vietnam: huge multi-leveled building with sections dedicated to fresh fruit, dried fruit, fabrics, baby gear, random trinkets and more. I love this place for the cheap spices and tea that make for amazing gifts to bring back home. And don't forget that haggling is always allowed!

Open: Daily 5am -7pm
Address: 119, Tran Phu Street, Hau Chai District

Con Market

This huge stadium-style market in the center of Da Nang has literally every item you could ever want to buy while on vacation. Need sunglasses? They have hundreds. In the market for a knock-off NBA cap? They're reppin' every team. Looking for children's clothes to send back to your niece and nephew? Outfit them like an adorable Vietnamese kid. You could easily spend hours wandering this market as Con Market is the biggest wholesale market in the city.

When you get hungry, you can find row after row of Vietnamese food stalls selling fresh fruit, meat on a stick, and all of the Bahn Mi!

Open: Daily 8am-8pm
Address: 18, Ong Ich Khiem Street, Hai Chau District

How to Get around Da Nang

Walk

You'll find more sidewalks in Da Nang than other parts of Vietnam. There is lots to see on foot and the area is generally pretty safe.

Grab Taxi

Grab Bikes and taxis are everywhere! Grab Bike costs around $1-$2 and Grab Cars typically cost $2-$3 depending where you're going. Install this app ASAP.

Rent a Scooter

Da Nang is pretty spread out, so if you want to cover a lot of ground, rent a motorbike for your visit. The roads are relatively wide and the traffic isn't too chaotic- especially once you get out of the city center. The coastal roads are quite peaceful.

Fun Vietnam Fact

With 6 different tones and dozens of dialects, Vietnamese is considered one of the most difficult languages in the world...which is why you will not see a "Vietnamese Language Guide" in this section...

Chapter 24: Hoi An

Hoi An is magic. You'll see it and feel it the moment you arrive, and it will leave a dreamlike imprint on your mind even after you leave. This ancient town is located in the middle of Vietnam holds over 2,000 years history, which have been preserved to an impressive standard. Hoi An is incredibly picturesque with winding alleys between bright yellow French style buildings that look like illustrations come to life. The incredible ancient French architecture can be seen all over Hoi An- perfectly preserved with historical buildings turned into coffee shops and Bahn Mi stalls. The town glitters with brightly painted window shutters and rusty red tiled roofs- all begging to be photographed. By day, the town is full of bicyclists and coffee shops. By night, the entire town lights up with colorful lanterns hanging from lamp posts or floating in the river canal. This place is magical. Truly, sincerely magical.

To get there, you'll start in Da Nang and drive 30 minutes along the coastal highway, passing beach resorts and secret beach roads that you wouldn't even know were there (until I tell you about them later). You'll then turn off the coastal road towards Hoi An where you'll pass long stretches of bright green rice paddies with water buffalo and cow farmers working the day away.

Now, you're in Hoi An. Prepare to be dazzled.

Areas to Explore in Hoi An

Old Town

Come admire the beautiful heritage buildings dating back to the 16th and 17th century. This well-preserved towns architecture includes a mix of Chinese, Japanese, Vietnam and French colonial designed buildings. Grab something traditional to eat as you wander the streets of Hoi An at night, admiring the history and small beautifully decorated tourist shops, governed by locals with friendly smiles on their faces. One will not fail to notice the traditional lanterns which light up the streets, providing a very colorful and magical experience.

Cua Dai Beach

The most popular stretch of beach and for good reason. Cua Dai Beach is the biggest and has plenty of restaurant options that provide lounge chairs and umbrellas with full beer and food service.

Oh, and it is consistently listed as one of best beaches of Vietnam for its pristine white sand, turquoise water and gentle waves. Despite being the most popular, the beach remains relatively unspoiled and clean.

Hidden Beach

It really is hidden. From the main road in Hoi An, you take a right when you get to the coastal highway. About 5 minutes up the road, there is a tiny jungle road that leads to a small stretch of beach where you can enjoy more privacy than Cua Dai Beach.

Look for signs that says, "Hidden Beach Bungalow". This tiny 5-bunalow resort offers a beach front restaurant with yummy pizza and cold beer! Next door is Wild Beach Restaurant also offering some delicious food and drinks.

Take your pick- both have lounge chairs and umbrellas for guests where you can sink your toes in the sand and soak up the sun. Some days the waves here are too intense to swim and others, they are perfect. Fingers crossed.

The Rice Fields

Bright green rice fields line the main road that connects the beach to the ancient town. With little cement paths that wind in-between bright green pastures, this makes for a surreal adventure. You'll pass herds of cattle, farmers, locals, and the famous 'old man posing with a water buffalo for $1'. Don't be afraid to pedal past the fields and into the neighborhoods for a sneaky peak of local life.

Accommodation in Hoi An

Sunshine Hotel $

I planned to stay at Sunshine Hotel for 2 nights…but I accidentally stayed for 1 month. I'm not kidding. The breakfast buffet is incredible, the pool is gorgeous with full sun for tanning and your room is cleaned every day!

Not to mention, the balcony with views of bright green rice paddies in the distance is the perfect way to start your day. Located smack dab between the beach and Old Town, you've got easy access to every single area worth visiting in Hoi An.
Take a free bicycle for a spin and explore. Go right on the main road and you'll ride through bright green rice fields; go left and you're 5 minutes from the city center. Sunshine Hotel also offers free shuttles to the beach and Old Town all day long. This place is THE BEST value for money and is a fabulous way to see and do it all!

Style: Privates
Starting at: $23 /524k
Where: Between the beach and Old Town/Ancient Town
Address: 02 Phan Đình Phùng, Cẩm Sơn

Tribee Ede $

Relax and recharge in this peaceful hostel. They have all the facilities you'll need to unwind from individual bath tubs, outdoor pools, to a garden restaurant. All the beds are super comfortable, too! If you feel like going out, the Cua Dai Beach is just a hike away, or you can take the 30-minute drive to Marble Mountain.

Style: Privates & Dorms
Starting at: $8 & $20 / 182k & 455k
Where: 5-minute walk from the Ancient Town
Address: 30 Ba Trieu street, Hoi An

The Seaside Bungalow $

If beach getaway is your style, this homestay is just for you. It's conveniently located Ha My Beach, which isn't the most popular beach, but that just means less people! A near isolated white sand, blue seas beach is great for those who want time for themselves. They have private rooms for couples and families that are fully equipped with a fridge, TV, and air condition.

Style: Privates & Dorms
Starting at: $7 & $30 / 169k & 684k
Where: 3-minute walk from Ha My beach
Address: Ha My Beach, Ha My Village, Quang Nam Province

Hidden Beach Bungalow Hoi An $$

These bungalows are literally hidden. The turn off to Hidden Beach Bungalow feels like you're encroaching on some rich family's hidden piece of land. As you drive down the steep-dip back road, you'll see the ocean right at the foot of this tiny resort. There are only about 5 private bungalows, which means you get top tier service. Staff will take your breakfast order the night before and ask what time you'd like to eat. Eat in your room or at a private table overlooking the water.

As the sun emerges, lounge on the sandy beach while ice cold beers are delivered right to you. During the day, hang out in their beachfront restaurant where you're sure to meet some fellow travelers or tan on their beach lounge chairs with a cold coconut.

Style: Private Bungalows
Starting at: $60 / 1.36 million
Where: Cam An Beach
Address: Lac long Quan street Tan Thinh Group

470

Lasenta Boutique Hotel Hoian $$$

As far as high-end hotels in Hoi An are concerned, this one is one of the best. Their spacious and well-designed rooms are fully equipped with a TV, bathroom, and kettle. The thing that sold me on these rooms are the amazing rice field views! Their restaurant is equally classy too plus you can get access to their spa, gym, and yoga classes. What more are you looking for?

Style: Privates
Starting at: $90 / 2 million
Where: 1 km from Hoi An Ancient Town
Address: 57 Ly Thuong Kiet Street, Hoi An

Hoi An Beach Resort $$$

This place has a private beach, 2 pools (one of which is an infinity pool overlooking the river), a riverside restaurant where you can watch ducks swimming about while you eat from an incredible gourmet buffet breakfast, and the rooms come with gorgeous garden or riverside balconies. Some of the best restaurants are just across the street and there's plenty of shopping, nail salons, and waxing to be done nearby. It's like they knew you were coming....

Style: Privates
Starting at: $120 USD/ 2.74 million VND
Where: Cua Dai Beach
Address: 1 Cua Dai Street

Cafes and Coffee Shops in Hoi An

Hoi An Roastery

The OG of coffee in Hoi An, Hoi An Roastery is an iconic coffee experience you'll never forget- I mean it. Nestled at the bottom of Hai Ba Trung Street, it's hard to miss this gem. Staring at bright yellow walls and old shuttered windows, it feels as if you've gone back in time just to enjoy the perfect cup of coffee. Don't forget to grab a bag of beans to take home.

Open: Daily 7am-10pm
Where: Old Town
Address: 685 Hai Bà Trưng, Phường Minh An

Reach Out Tea House

When you first visit Reach Out Tea House, you'd notice nothing out of the ordinary. It's quaint, it's cute, and it has a great selection of drinks and munchies. However, when you order, you'll notice the staff are all hearing impaired. Order by writing on paper what you'd like and viola. Besides serving a wonderful cause to provide work opportunities to the hearing impaired, Reach Out Tea also has some of the best local teas and blends in the city. Win-win.

Open: Monday-Friday 8:30am-9pm/Saturday-Sunday 10am-8pm
Where: Old Town

Address: 131 Trần Phú, Phường Minh An

3A Cafe

Sit outside under shady trees or take a seat upstairs where you can look down onto the cafe; any seat at 3A Cafe is a good one. This place has some of the cheapest AND most delicious blended coffee in town...because it's local. Local but trendy and chic. Located on the road that connects the beach and old town, this is the perfect place to stop after pedaling for an hour.

Open: Early-Late
Where: 5-minute bike ride north of Old Town
Address: Corner of Hai Ba Trung & Ly Thai Tho

Fun Vietnam Fact

Vietnam is the world's second largest producer of coffee, right behind Brazil.

Where to Eat in Hoi An

Minh Hiển Vegetarian Restaurant

You don't have to be veggie to eat like a ravenous carnivore here. What started as a small local restaurant many years ago steadily picked up popularity amongst westerners over the years. Dishes like Sautéed Pumpkin and Peanuts, Grilled Eggplant with Lemongrass and the 'Mien Hein Special' noodle dish keeps this place packed. They got tons of fresh juices, smoothies, and homemade beer...all for super cheap.

Open: Daily 9am-10pm
Where: Northern Old Town in a small alley off of Hai Ba Trung Street
Address: 30A Dinh Tien Hoang

Banh Mi Phuong

2-minutes of airtime on Anthony Bourdain's episode of 'No Reservations' back in 2012 was enough to put Banh Mi Phuong on the map for all of eternity. There is so much hype around this little hole in the wall with lines literally out the door all day every day...that it's enough to roll your eyes at if you've never tried it.

Like, how good can a sandwich actually be? But I'm telling you, one bite and your world will be changed forever. I can confirm- this is the BEST BANH MI in all of Vietnam. Even better...they've never changed their prices. You pay 25k Dong for a mind-blowing Grilled Chicken Bahn Mi (which I insist you try).

Open: Sunday-Friday 6:30am-9:30pm / Saturday 7am-9:30pm
Where: Old Town
Address: 2B Phan Chau Trinh

Jim's Snack Bar

The best burger I've had in South East Asia EVER is the Blue Cheese Burger at Jim's Snack Bar. Dripping with cheese, this place does not skimp on ingredients. Every burger is served on super fresh buns that pull apart and juicy imported beef. Order with a side of thick cut fries and a craft beer, and you've got the perfect meal after a long day of bicycling around town. Plus, prices are pretty damn reasonable.

Open: Tuesday-Sunday 11am-9pm
Where: Northern Old Town
Address: 552 Hai Ba Trung

Khoai Tay Va Ca - Chips N' Fish

Head up to the second-floor balcony where you can watch boats float down the river and tourists from all over the world have a wander as you sip on cold, homemade beer and British-boyfriend approve Fish n' Chips served with tartar sauce. Also, super yummy is anything wrapped and steamed in banana leaf. This place specializes in local seafood like squid, shrimp, and of course, fish. Cheap prices but high-quality flavors.

Open: Daily all day
Where: Old City, cross the bridge and head all the way to the left, slightly around the corner (you'll see).
Address: 1 Nguyen Phuc Chu Street

Street Food in the Old City

Since the beginning of time, women have been selling snacks on the street in Hoi An. Each vendor has a specialty from Banh Mi to Chicken & Rice. These dishes tend to be super cheap. You can grab and go, take a seat on the sidewalk, or pull up a plastic chair.

Quite convenient for a day of exploring, don't ya think?

Culture & History

Old City
The Old City is a cultural and historical sight in itself. The buildings, the bridges, the shutters, the family transitions- walk or bicycle around and soak it all up during the day. In the evening, the old city comes to life with bright lanterns, toy hawkers, and live music.

Japanese Covered Bridge
While remaining one of the most iconic sights of Hoi An tourism, the Japanese Covered Bridge, or "Chùa Cầu" in Vietnamese, is actually a product of Japanese merchants who sought easier means of trade with surrounding communities. Although Constructed in the 17th century, the Earthquake-proof bridge still displays many of the ornate details of its time. The warm waters of the Thu Bon River flow beautifully beneath the bridge, allowing many photo ops to be had showcasing the artwork of an ancient culture. Adorned with a sacred pagoda, Japanese Covered Bridge is said to dedicate this space for a guardian who will bless the people with happiness and well-being. A timeless must-see!

Entrance Fee: $5 USD/ 120,000 VND
Location: At the end of Tran Phu Street in Hoi-An, Vietnam
Address: Nguyễn Thị Minh Khai, Phường Minh An

Fukian Assembly Hall (Phuc Kien)

A visit to Vietnam is incomplete without experiencing the spectacular Fukian Assembly Hall (Phuc Kien) located in Hoi An's Ancient Town.

In 1697, ethnic traders coming from China settled in Hoi An and established this largest and most intricate architectural Chinese Assembly hall. Avoid the street chaos and take a moment to admire the Buddhist Iconography and classic architecture. Throughout the hall, there are statues, bronze bells, horizontal lacquered boards having Chinese characters and bronze drums. It's exciting to see a very large and impressive dragon statue made of porcelain tiles affixed at the back side of the Hall.

Bonus: Nowadays Fukien Assembly Hall is more popular for amazing activities and events for celebrating Chinese festivals.

Entrance Fee: 120,000 VND (approx. 5 USD)
Open: Daily from 08.00AM to 05.00PM
Location: Old Quarter
Address: 46 Tran Phu, Phuong Minh An

Fun Things to Do in Hoi An

Have a Dress Made

Hoi An is the mecca for tailored clothing. See a dress you like? Or a playsuit that you have to have? Literally every shop will tailor that exact piece just for you- sometimes within 2 hours. They've got all the fabrics you need!

Have a particular design in mind? There are tons of tailors who are eager to make it for you...but that's the tricky part.

Pro Dress Making Tips

- ✓ The tailors in Hoi An are hustlers. They will never tell you 'no'. Some tailors are patient and will work with you to customize your dream dress....and some tailors want to slap something together and hurry your ass out of town, so they can keep your money.

- ✓ Remember that these women are tailors, not designers. Keep your concepts simple.

- ✓ Make sure to allot three days in Hoi An in case you need to return to the shop for adjustments (which you almost certainly will).

Highly Recommended Tailor: Anh Silk Shop
Contact: Facebook.com/mit.mitmap

Coconut Basket Boat Tour

When in Hoi An, experience life as locals do. Learn from the locals how to paddle a wooden boat through narrow steams lined with palm trees and catch little crabs without falling from the boat. Sounds simple enough? Guess again! When you've finished catching your crabs, join the locals back at their home for some refreshments and look into the life of local fishermen. These tours are offered through many companies- I recommend 'Hoi An Eco Green Tours'.
Starting at: $26 USD/ 600k VND

Lanterns in the Canal

When the sun goes down, head towards the canal where you'll find women selling bright lanterns. You light a candle and realize it into the water while making a wish. Even if you don't participate, it's quite the sight to see; a canal full of brightly colored lanterns glowing in the darkness. Prices vary from lady to lady, so ask around to find the cheapest price.

Night Life Hoi An

Outside of hostel parties, there is only elements to nightlife in
Hoi An...

Hoi An Night Market
The Night Market is the perfect place to grab a walking beer and start your
night. Do some buzzed shopping with lanterns and jewelry. Eat some fresh
mango roti made right in front of you. Or sit down at a plastic table and
people watch as you sip $1 beers.

Bars Along the River
Just skip away is the boardwalk along the river, lined with bars of all kinds.
There are bars with live music, bars with a rasta vibe, bars for the younger
travelers to mingle and do shots...have a wander and pick a bar that suits
your fancy.

How to Get Around Hoi An

Bicycle
Bikes are the way to go in Hoi An! The streets are mellow and drivers are constantly cautious of the dozens of bicyclists that surround them at any given time. You can bike through the entire ancient city and down to the beach within 1 hour- taking your time for snacks, fresh coconuts and rice fields along the way.

Ps. Hoi an is so safe. You don't even need to chain your bicycle up when you park.

Walk
Hoi An is a walking city! Winding alleys and little bridges are best when you just walk and get lost amongst it all. Sidewalks are safe and street crossing are respected by drivers here (a rare thing for Vietnam).

Motorbike
Rent a motorbike and get even further off the beaten path. Explore neighborhoods, islands, deeper into the rice fields and go all around the beach roads. Motorbikes aren't great for the Ancient City as there is so much foot traffic, but everywhere else is an open road!

Grab Taxi
At night, opt for a grab taxi that will cost you no more than $2-3 to get anywhere in the city.

How to Get to Hoi An

Make your way to Da Nang.

From there, you can hire a taxi to drive you to Hoi An or arrange with your hotel to pick you up.

I prefer to use a private driver – the same one every time.

His name is Kieu Peck.
He offers the cheapest price: 200k from Da Nang to Hoi An
Write him on Facebook here: Facebook.com/hai.kieu.52

Chapter 25: Phong Nha Ke-Bang National Park

Travel to another planet when you step inside the realm of Phong Nha Ke-Bang National Park. This vortex of nature is unlike anything you've ever experienced...

Officially a UNESCO World Heritage Site, Phong Nha Ke-Bang is heavily protected and preserved. Here lie millions of years of unspoiled, virgin Earth.

With such preservation, it's no surprise that there are still mysteries to be discovered within this National Park. Take for example... Son Doong Cave.

Son Doong Cave is the biggest cave in the world. Yes, the biggest cave in the world is right here in Vietnam. Even crazier...this cave was only discovered back in 2009 (and opened to tourists in 2014) by a local farmer just doing his thang.

Along with a collection of additional cave systems, you can explore the limestone forest, go on mystical rainforest hikes, and camp overnight on underground beaches next to underground rivers (yea, you heard that right).

In order to keep Phong Nha Ke-Bang National Park totally protected, you can't just tra-la-la through. Instead, there are a handful of tours that will guide you to protect you and the park.

Let's get into it...

The Caves of Phong Nha

We're starting out with the fun stuff, ya'll.

This national park is home to a collection of caves that can only be described as "geomorphic", representing millions of years of transformation through the Earth's crust.

Many of the caves are open to the public. And while you can rent a motorbike and trek these caves on your own, signing up for a tour is the most efficient way to fill your day with the most exciting caves. To name a few...

Hang Thien Duong
The longest dry cave in South East Asia, Paradise Cave spans a mind boggling 31.4km. Visitors can embark on a 7km hike through the cave, with or without a tour guide, as they marvel under cathedral ceilings and sculpture-esque formations.

Hang Toi
Unleash your inner Indiana Jones as you zip-line across the cave river, swim through the cool water, trek through the muddy riverbeds, and then kayak back to safety- all in the dark! Don't worry; you'll have a head lamp and adrenaline to guide you. This is a trek that can be done on your own or with a tour guide...and I definitely recommend a tour guide.

Hang Voi
Also known as Elephant Cave, this dry cave feels magical with sunbeams peeking through holes in the cave's ceilings like Aliens about to beam you up! These sunbeams have also given life to jungle that has grown inside of this cave creating a spectacular juxtaposition of million-year-old rock and lush green jungle. This cave is often incorporated in 1 or 2-day treks where you also get to experience amazing jungle wilderness hikes.

Hang En
One of the largest caves in the world – just being Son Doong- Hang En is mesmerizing and massive. Exploring this cave involves a 1-day trek through jungles and valleys, through an ethnic village and then an overnight stay at "The Entrance to Neverland" where you'll camp on a riverside beach inside the cave. Hang En is as close as you can get to the Son Doong caving experience without dropping a whole month's paycheck. Highly recommended!

Hang Son Doong

The worlds largest cave! Discovered in 2009 and opened to tours in 2014, Son Doong is so big that a whole Manhattan city block - with skyscrapers and all -could fit inside. To preserve this magnificent phenomenon, tours are carefully measured, allowing just 60 people per day to enter. Furthermore, only one tour company is allowed to operate.

The 4-day trek is pricey. It costs $3,000 USD per person but is fully inclusive with some amazingly delicious meals offered – this isn't your run of the mill camping trip. Porters carry these ingredients in the cave, along with camping gear and cooking gear. This is a once in a lifetime experience.

Pro Tip

Anyone who says they can take you into the Hang Son Doong for cheap or on a private tour is a scam. The Hang Son Doong cave is government regulated and so, you must go with a licensed company if you want to explore.

For all of the caving tours and adventures, check out my favorite tour company, **Jungle Boss**....

There is so much more to see in this National Park that I could literally write an entire encyclopedia...but then you'd be stuck with your nose in a book reading about otherworldly experiences that can only really be devoured in person.

Jungle Boss has expertly bundled tours so that no matter which tour fits your budget and time schedule- you'll be able to absorb the maximum amount of literal awesomeness. Check out their website at Jungle-Boss.com

Accommodation in Phong Nha

Nguyen Shack - Phong Nha Central Town $

Ready to rough it? But with a gorgeous view and cheap cheap prices? Nguyen Shack offers a range of room styles to choose from- none of which are fancy- but all of which give you unique access the prehistoric limestone cliffs that surround the area. Relax on the roof in a chilled-out hammock and you enjoy the view of the mountains and surrounding forests. After all this, you'll feel like a new person when you check out!

Style: Dormitory
Starts at: $5 /114k
Where: Phong Natural Heritage Area
Address: Phong Nha Town, Son Tien Village, Son Trach Commune, Dong Hoi

Phong Nha Coco House $

Not a fan of big crowds and excessive tourists? Well, this place is perfect for you! They offer a more intimate set-up with private rooms and a scenic view of the Son River just outside your window. Rooms are equipped with air condition, kitchen, TV, and internet, too! It's great for those who aren't super social and need some time alone every once in a while.

Style: Privates
Starts at: $18 USD / 410k VND
Where: Phong Nha-Ke Bang National Park
Address: Phong Nha Village, Son Trach Commune, Bo Trach District

Heritage By Night Hotel $

Have you ever gone swimming in a pool surrounded by cliffs and forests? The view from the outdoor pool is so surreal and the best thing about this place. With its own bar, garden, and sun terrace, it just screams 'vacation'! For all those adventurous types, the caves are just nearby!

Style: Dorms & Privates
Starts at: $8 USD / 182 VND
Where: Phong Nha-Ke Bang National Park
Address: Son Trach Commune, Bo Trach District

Jungle Boss Homestay $

If you want to bring your whole family to experience nature, then make sure you check in at Jungle Boss Homestay. Their garden and organic farm are a great way to teach the kids about the value of nature and living off the land! Though it's in a pretty far off part of the park, the homestay can easily arrange taxis for you. Adventure tours of all kinds are also offered here, so you can go cave exploring or valley climbing!

Style: Privates
Starts at: $12 USD / 274k VND
Where: Phong Nha-Ke Bang National Park
Address: Phong Nha Village, Son Trach Commune, Bo Trach District

Where to Eat in Phong Nha

Listen, Phong Nha is a tiny little town. When it comes to food, the good stuff is usually right in front of your face. Here, the guest houses and hostels have mastered the art of 'yum'. But if you're really in the mood for some foodie adventures...here you go.

A Little Vietnam

Some people know this place as 'Why Not?', but don't worry because they're exactly the same place. This quaint little bar, restaurant, and cafe has a simple but tasty menu. Pho here is great and reasonably price, perfect for those working on a budget. The portion may be way bigger than what you're used to, so bring a friend to share with!

Open: Daily 6am - 10pm
Where: Phong Nha-Ke Bang National Park
Address: Phong Nha Village, Son Trach Commune

The Pub with Cold Beer

Across rocky hills in the middle of nowhere, you'll find a great pub owned by a humble farming family. Naturally, they grow their own ingredients, so you get to experience firsthand how your food, which includes killing your own chicken. For all those concerned, you can choose not to and yes, the chicken died humanely. If anything, their cook on it is amazing along with their delicious peanut sauce!

Open: Daily 6am - 12am
Where: On the edge of Phong Nha-Ke Bang National Park
Address: Ho Chi Minh Highway, Phong Nha-Ke Bang National Park

Easy Tiger - Jungle Bar

This bar is definitely the place to go if you're looking for a fun and exciting night. As one of the few bars in Son Trach, they have live music, pool tables, and cheap beer! Food and cocktails are one of the best around, too. The owner, Hai, is really friendly and willing to help you out in picking the best tours for your trip.

Open: Daily 7am - 12MN
Where: Easy Tiger Hostel
Address: Son Trach Village, Phong Nha-Ke Bang National Park

Getting Around Phong Nha

Motorbike
If you know how to ride a motorbike, this is a MUST. With a bike, you get access to the most off-the-grid locations, explore farm lands, and go on your own mini tours through the park. Plus, this is a great way to explore the town. Most places rent bikes for 150k.

Pro Tip: Take photos of your bike before you leave the shop. Document any existing scratches or dents. This is standard practice for South East Asian bike rentals

Bicycle
Rent a bicycle and you can get around town very easily. You can also explore nearby rice paddies!

Taxi
Both car and motorbike taxis can take you and drop you at the mouth of any cave or the entrance to a trail. This will involve some haggling. It's best to ask your hotel about a suitable price, and then go haggle a taxi driver on the street for slightly lower than the price which your (commission making) hotel gave you.

Chapter 26: Ninh Binh

You have now left Earth. Welcome to the planet of Ninh Binh.

Nguyen Shack

Often referred to as "Ha Long Bay on land," Ninh Binh is a bucket list
destination that is a jaw-dropper and a life-changer.
If I could stress one place that you should absolutely visit in all of Vietnam,
this would be it.

Just a few years ago, Ninh Binh was nothing more than an undiscovered
paradise where farmers and fishermen worked the day away in the fields
surrounded by Avatar-esque limestone cliffs in the middle of nowhere.

Steeped in history, Ninh Binh is also an incredibly spiritual place with
pagodas, statues and Buddhist prayer sites around every corner.

Somehow, days spent in Ninh Binh are equally sleepy as they are adventurous. You'll hike up a 300-step mountain just to sit in silence at the top for an hour. You'll bicycle down to the river, just to lounge in a boat pedaled through caves while sipping coffee. Here is where you come to reflect on life and walk away with a totally refreshed perspective.

Fun Vietnam Fact

Vietnam is officially a "Tropical Country"

Areas to Explore in Ninh Binh

Tam Coc

A short distance from Ninh Binh city, Tam Coc is where the action is. Famous for its limestone hils and foot-pedal boat tours, Tam Coc is an ideal location to base your stay in Ninh Binh. The ancient town is the main hub for tourists visiting the area, as most of the accommodation, amenities and tours run from here. There's a large selection of restaurants, coffee places and shops selling great little souvenirs, and the town still houses loads of friendly locals with great English. There's one or two great little convenience stores here which are super useful for picking up practical things like toothpaste, snacks and toiletries if you're backpacking.

Bich Dong

Around a 20-minute cycle/bike ride from Tam Coc town is Bich Dong, which is most famous for the iconic ancient pagoda. There's a really great hike up the mountain side to the pagoda which takes you through some lovely caves and has breathtaking views. There's a little path to the right of the entrance to the pagoda which leads down to an amazing little lake and up to some more caves. It's common to see some wild mountain goats here as well as hundreds, if not thousands, of dragonflies and butterflies.

Hang Mua

This area is famous for the Mua Caves and Dragon Mountain, but the roads around this area are great for cycling and biking. There's so much untouched countryside, rolling rice paddies and beautiful lakes filled with lily pads to see. There isn't really a better place for a road trip, as most of the roads are relatively safe and easy to drive on, and the area is 20 minute drive max from Tam Coc.

Accommodation in Ninh Binh

Nguyen Shack Ninh Binh

Waking up here feels surreal; like you're still dreaming. With bamboo huts covered by palm leaf thatched roofs, there is no back door- just a wide-open wall with a stunning view of tall limestone cliffs that encase your entire world. Enjoy the view from bed or lay on your private dock over the water, swaying in a hammock as you spot goats expertly climbing up and down the steep rockface.

Breakfast at Nguyen Shack is an 'all you can order' feast; the eggs are made from duck eggs and will blow your mind. Rent bikes from Nguyen Shack to adventure in the village or walk to the Mua Caves next door. Afterwards, come back and stroll around the property as you try to decipher, "Is this real life?". Words literally cannot serve justice to this jaw-dropping experience.

Pro Tip: Nguyen Shack does offer private rooms for $25 but with no waterfront view. It's worth the splurge, even just for 1 night, to stay in a waterfront Bungalow.

Style: Private Bungalows
Starts at: $55 USD / 1.25 million VND

Where: Next to the Mua Caves
Address: Hang Mua Road, Khe Ha Village, Ninh Xuan Commune

The Long Hotel

The Long Hotel is perfect when you're looking for a warm and comfortable room on a budget. The hotel is basic but clean with super helpful staff and breakfast included in the price. The hotel is well equipped with a bar and restaurant, as well as lots of opportunities to book tours and bikes through reception.

But what makes this place really special is the location! It's situated right in the center of Tam Coc, directly opposite one of the main boat ports that offer the famous boat tours through the caves. The Long Hotel is also near the main pagoda in Tam Coc that is still used regularly by the locals, so you get the amazing sounds of prayer ceremonies daily- just adding to the peaceful nature of this quaint little town.

Style: Privates & Dorms
Starts at: $5.5 $ 9.5 USD / 125k & 217k VND
Where: Tam Coc
Address: Bich Dong Road (opposite the boat port)

Xuan Lai Right View

This homestay is ideal for a more authentic experience. It's a short distance away from the center of Tam Coc, great if you're driving a motorbike but still a manageable distance to walk into town. The owner is so friendly and knowledgeable about every tour offered- this guest house is a one stop shop for adventure. As an added bonus, the owner is also as an ex-chef who is passionate about great tasting, fresh food (that means breakfast is amazing). He also owns two restaurants in Tam Coc which are both worth a visit- just ask him!

Style: Homestay
Starts at: $14.5 USD / 330k VND
Where: Tam Coc
Address: 37 Luong Van Thang, Group 4, Van Lam, Ninh Hai, Hoa Lu, Ninh Binh, Ninh Binh, Vietnam

Where to Eat in Ninh Binh

Eat at your homestay! Your homestay or guest house undoubtedly cooks authentic regional dishes using local duck eggs and fresh picked veggies. Some even offer cooking classes.

If you've like to get out and explore, however, here are a few suggestions.

Orchid

Feeling some homemade Vietnamese cuisine? Much like you'd find in a Vietnamese mama's kitchen, Orchid offers up the classic dishes such as Pho, Bun Cha and fresh spring rolls. While their prices are just a tad bit higher than what you'd expect in rural Vietnam- you can still totally afford it, even on a budget. Treat yourself to a $5 meal! And if you're not in the mood for Vietnamese, like any well-rounded restaurant, there are a few western options for picky eaters.

Open: 8am -11pm
Where: Tam Coc
Address: Bich Dong Road

Chookies

Just a 10-minute walk north from the center of Tam Coc is Chookies – a great little spot for eating, drinking and chilling out (especially when the weather is chilly). They offer a really tasty selection of Vietnamese and western food with some clean vegan and gluten free options. Oh, and they also have authentic wood fired pizzas! The atmosphere here is super relaxed with a mix of backpackers and families. In the evening Chookies turns into a relaxing place to have a drink, offering amazing cocktails AND local beer at just 10k VND ($0.43) per glass.

Open: 9am -10pm
Where: Tam Coc
Address: Bich Dong Road

Sunflower

A close second to Chookies, Sunflower is brilliant if you're looking for some western food on a budget, with most dishes coming in at under 50,000VND. Sunflower is so easy to find (just a few doors up from the main boat port in Tam Coc) and is consistent in service and quality. Just make sure to leave plenty of time, as most dishes are made fresh!

Open: 8am -11pm
Where: Tam Coc
Address: Bich Dong Road

Sightseeing & Culture in Ninh Binh

Bai Dinh Pagoda

Wander through Vietnam's biggest Buddhist temple complex and enjoy its breathtaking landscapes of the mainland's answer to Halong Bay. Cruise on the calm waters to have a glimpse of caves, grottoes, and karst cliffs of Trang An. Experience the tranquility and sereneness of the landscapes of Ninh Binh on the countryside before reaching the Pagoda. This all-in journey is complete with a savory Vietnamese lunch of local delicacies such as goat meat.

Adorned with statues, artifacts, and buddhas, the temples of Bai Dinh Pagoda ooze with splendor and sophistication. Touch the knee of monk statues for good luck and see the wonderful interiors of the complex in awe.

Entrance Fee: Free
Open: 7am-5:45pm
Location: Gia Viễn District
Address: Gia Sinh, Ninh Bình Province 432449, Vietnam

Bich Dong Pagoda

Built in 1428, this Pagoda is one of those 'If walls could talk" sites that has seen centuries of change and growth in this tiny town. After you walk through the pagoda, you'll be taken to a square with a couple smaller pagodas where monks still live today (so dress appropriately).

While the exact history of this Pagoda seems to be rather low-key, the intricacies of the carvings, architecture, and location and absolutely fascinating. Take your time to soak up the little details.

Entrance Fee: per person
Open: Daily from 8: 00 am - 5: 00 pm
Location: Ngu Nhac Son Mountains

Lying Dragon Mountain

A short drive from Tam Coc, Lying Dragon Mountain is well worth a visit. It's one of the top attractions in Ninh Binh, and it's easy to see why – the view from the top of the mountain is truly stunning. The ancient Lying Dragon statue is paired with a beautiful buddha statue and stands opposite a smaller mountain with a mini pagoda, which is also available to walk up. The climb up is a tough one, with around 300 super steep steps, but it's definitely worth it for the views. The mountain is near the ancient Mua Caves which are also worth a visit, so it's worth keeping aside the better part of a day for this.

Entrance Fee: $4.5 USD / 100k VND
Open: 8am – Late
Location: Hang Mua

Fun Things to Do in Ninh Binh

Visit and Hike the Mua Caves

It's only 300 steps to the top of the world! Hike up the mountain where you can see all on Ninh Binh and its rivers that look like veins running through rice fields. You can see boat tours, mountain goats, and waves of mountains in the distance. When you're done, take a right at the bottom of the stairs (as you're coming down) and venture off to find the caves. You'll walk through dark caves with watery pools below. The water is fresh, clean, and free of monsters – so feel free to take your shoes off and splash about.

Where: Right next to Nguyen Shack

Cuc Phuong National Park

Rent a motorbike and explore the jungle roads that weave and wind through this gorgeous national park. When you hire a guide, he'll lead the pack through the dense forest, taking you to see the majestic 1000-year-old tree, explore a prehistoric cave system, visit a turtle & primate conservation center, the delicate observation tower and if you wish- go on a 2 hour hike!

All in all, you'll drive about 60km for the whole trip. Pack water, snacks and a flash light for the cave!

Boat Tours
Boat tours are a must if you're visiting Ninh Binh!
There are two boat piers to choose from: one in Trang An and one in Tam Coc.

Trang An Boat Tour
Just outside of Tam Coc in an area called Trang An which is a quick taxi ride away. At this boat port you will embark on a 3- hour tour around a labyrinth of floating pagodas, limestone caves and stunning landscapes. You get the chance to hop off the boat to explore at least 3 of the incredible ancient temples, which the locals still use for prayer.

These stopovers allow you to see the stunning biodiversity and architecture of Ninh Binh up close and personal, and the individual islands are full of wild dragonflies and birds.

As the tour continues, you drift through the narrow caves, thanks to the steady hand of your tour guide. Be prepared to duck to avoid jutting stone formations and look out for bats!

The last stop on the tour is to the movie set of King Kong – Skull Island, which was primarily filmed around Ninh Binh. A large part of the set still remains and tourists are encourage to visit and experience them, with some locals in costume as the natives of Skull Island. It's delightfully strange. As you make your way back to the boat port, you pass the most astonishingly beautiful parts of Ninh Binh, including shines and Buddhist burial grounds.

PS. This is seriously an incredible experience! Don't skip it.

Starting at: $11 USD / 250k VND

Tam Coc Boat Tour
If you don't have the time or energy to lug yourself to the other side of town, the Tam Coc Boat Tour is a delightful second choice. You can head down to the boat pier in Tam Coc Town via bicycle, where dozens of little boats and their captains are waiting to take you on a magical ride through caves, jungle, wetlands, and mountains. You'll see locals in the water digging for clams or fishing for their family. Even more awesome…the boat captains row the entire way with their feet. It's quite the spectacle and yet, makes total sense. The entire ride lasts about an hour; maybe more if you stop and buy some coffee or snacks from the boat vendors along the way.

499

How to Get around Ninh Binh

Motorbike or Bicycle
By far the best way to get around in Ninh Binh is by motorbike. If you're a confident driver, there's plenty of places to rent bikes in Tam Coc for around $5 per day, and most also have bicycles (around $1.50 per day) for those that prefer to cycle. The whole of Ninh Binh is spread across a 30km, so walking isn't really a great option if you want to see anything outside the main town.

When you first arrive in Ninh Binh, whether you've travelled by bus or train, its likely that you will find yourself in Ninh Binh city - a taxi ride from Tam Coc town and most of the pagodas/attractions.

Taxi
A taxi from the outskirts of the city to Tam Coc will set you back around 150,000VND if you're using a metered one (always recommended) and more if you're paying a set price. Look out for Mai Linh taxis, as these are available all over Vietnam and are usually metered.

Chapter 27: Hanoi

The capitol of Vietnam and the former communist headquarters during the

Vietnam war, Hanoi is a beautiful juxtaposition of old vs. new.

Most of this city… isn't trying to be anything that it's not. The locals are chill and life moves at quite a slow pace for such a big city. The neighborhoods seem quite content with their old school buildings that crumble away, revealing red bricks and years of layered paint and graffiti. There's always a winding alley to get lost in, street food to be had, temples to be explored, and locals offering you some fresh Bia Hoi.

Then, scattered amongst the old Hanoi, you'll find pockets of expat areas with shiny hotels and western food to hit the spot. You get a little bit of everything in Hanoi – it's the best of both words.

From the Airport into Hanoi

Hanoi has an international airport that you can fly into from just about any location in Vietnam and outside of Vietnam.
Easy.

Otherwise, you'll be taking the train or the bus…which by now you've mastered so we're not going to waste precious pages.
Let us, however, discuss what to do once you land.

Option 1: Grab Taxi

Once you're outside the airport, order a grab. They'll take you anywhere you need to go and help you with your bags.

How Much: Around $9 USD / 200k VND
Duration: 30-40 minutes

Option 2: The Bus

Outside of Terminal 2 (T2), you can hop on a very cheap bus to the Old Quarter. Look for bus #17.

You board, tell the driver "Old Quarter" like 3x, and he'll tell you when to get off. Your stop is one of the last stops, called "Long Bien".

Once you're off the bus, it's a 5 to 10-minute walk to the Old Quarter. This is where having a SIM card comes in handy. Either order a Grab Taxi/Bike from the bus station to your hotel or walk it.

How Much: $1.5 USD / 30k VND
Duration: 55 minutes depending on traffic
Where: Right outside of Terminal 2

Areas to Explore in Ha Noi

Old Quarter
All the fast-paced action happens in the Old Quarter. It's a shopping dream, a party paradise and a foodie heaven. There are hotels, bars, and stores for all ages, price ranges, and purposes. You could easily stay in Old Quarter for your whole vacay while still seeing the nearby temples and sights.

Hoan Kiem Lake
Starting at the south end of the Old Quarter, Hoan Kiem Lake a great place to wander during the day and night. Home to little islands with ancient pagodas, parks with beer vendors, and Hanoi's only McDonalds on the south end, Haon Kiem has a fun perimeter to wander. There are tons of upscale hotels in this area with nice restaurants to go along with them.

Tay Ho & Truc Bach
These expat areas as low-key and picturesque versions of a bustling city. Tons of western food, lots of little parks, lake views, and western amenities. Get your laptop, find a café, and blend in with the expats.

Accommodation in Hanoi

Chien Hostel $

This super chill hostel in the heart of Hanoi is 100% female approve. It's clean, it's safe, and the vibes are social but not too crazy. Spend your day walking around Hoan Kiem Lake to see the sights, and the evenings on the rooftop bar overlooking the historic catholic cathedral. They've got bikes for rent and breakfast is included- making for a cozy hostel stay with minimal hangovers in Hanoi.

Style: Dorms and Private Rooms
Starts at: $5 USD/ 114k VND
Where: In the Old Quarter, just to the left of Hoan Kiem Lake
Address: 12&14 Au Trieu, Hang Trong Ward

Vietnam Backpackers – Hanoi Downtown $

If boozy and wild is the kind of vacation you're looking for...girl, you've just found it. Vietnam Backpackers Hanoi is a massive party spot where it is impossible not to make friends. In other words, perfect for solo girl travelers!

This place is huge, easily fitting up to 50 guests at a time...all of which mingle in downstairs the bar at night, spilling onto the streets of the Old Quarter- often to the 10k street beer spots across the street.
Minus the nightly shit show, the beds are cozy, there is tight security to handle drunk slobs, and for the sober daylight hours- the tour desk inside will take care of all your needs.

Pro Tip: They also have an "original location" nearby which is much more lowkey and easy to mix up. Make sure you book the downtown property if you're looking to party.

Style: Dorms, Female Dorms, and Private Rooms
Starts at: $8.50 USD/ 194k VND
Where: Old Quarter
Address: 9 Ma May, Hoan Kiem, Hanoi

Babylon Garden Hotel $$

The Babylon Garden Hotel is a new four-star hotel in Hanoi's Old Quarter. It offers luxurious rooms with plenty of space to relax during the mid-day heat. Located in the center of the city it's just walking distance from the famous Hoan Kiem Lake. Also, near the hotel you will find the busy streets of the old city that every weekend boasts one of the most famous night markets in South East Asia.

If you're looking to expand your travels beyond Hanoi, the hotel offers numerous trips outside the city. If you desire comfort and a central location, the Babylon Garden is perfect.
Style: Private Rooms
Starts at: $40 USD / 912k VND

Where: Old Quarter
Address: 25-27 Lo Lu Street, Hoan Kiem

Hanoi Gratitude Hotel $

For the travel girl who likes her space, craves a touch of that posh lifestyle, but also loves a good deal- it just doesn't get any better than Hanoi Gratitude Hotel. While the rooms aren't massive, and the views are nothing to write home about, the décor is bright and fresh, the staff goes above and beyond to help newbie travelers feels extra comfortable, and the location is perfect for galivanting around town. Plus, breakfast is on point. This is the perfect place to unwind after a long day of sightseeing.

Style: Private Rooms
Starts at: $30 USD / 684k VND
Where: In the Old Quarter, just to the left of Hoan Kiem Lake
Address: 106 Hang Bong, Hoan Kiem

Sunline Paon Hotel & Spa $$

Hanoi gets hot in the spring and summer. Really hot. After a day of wandering the sweaty city, sometimes all you want is a pool. The rooftop pool at Sunline Paon Hotel will do the trick. There's not much in terms of lounge chairs but throw a towel down and you've got the perfect tanning spot. Plus, the glittering view of the city at night is gorgeous. Located right in Old Quarter with cozy beds, free breakfast, and friendly reception, this place is a steal.

Style: Privates
Starts at: $40 USD / 912k VND
Where: Old Quarter
Address: 27 Hang Thung Str, Hoan Kiem District, Hoan Kiem

Artisan Boutique Hotel $$$

The location doesn't get any better than Artisan Boutique Hotel. Located right next to the main round-about at the top of Hoan Kiem Lake, you're nearby all the western food, the upscale Vietnamese food, the best happy hours, and literally on the edge of Old Quarter. At night, the park around the lake come alive with street food and entertainers. When you're all tuckered out, crawl back into your dreamy bed with chic design and maybe have a night cap on your private balcony. This place is beyond perfect for a solo girl.

Style: Chic Privates
Starts at: $100 USD / 2.28 million VND
Where: Top of Hoan Kiem Lake
Address: 24 Hang Hanh

Cafes in Hanoi

Hanoi has the best coffee culture in the world. Not only is the coffee strong and flavorful but the cafes are so mysterious and full of character. Upon arrival, straight-up Google "hidden cafes" for some of the best spots. Sometimes you'll find a coffee vendor down a discrete alleyway or in the courtyards of someone's house.

Coffee in Hanoi is often served with milk- but the super sweet condensed milk. This means that the coffee is very thick and rich with a unique flavor.

If you want your cup a bit more specialized, check out these cafes below…

Cup of Tea

Pull up a seat at this quaint 4-story café overlooking the lake and the skyline of Tay Ho. Cup of Tea has beautiful natural lighting that makes for a lovely afternoon sipping Mexican Hot Chocolate or a pot of Early Grey. Each floor is staffed by an attentive and trendy young Vietnamese girl who is excited to interact with the foreign girl. Afterwards, take a walk along the lake and keep an eye out for fisherman pulling in the day's catch.

Open: Daily 7am-10:30pm
Where: Ba Dinh – South of West Lake
Address: 109 Nguyễn Đình Thi, Thuỵ Khuê, Tây Hồ

Café Giảng 39 - Egg Coffee Lane

The OG of egg coffee, this family-run coffee spot is as local as it gets with dad handwriting each transition in his daily register while mom makes the coffees and his older kids run the drinks to customers. You'll sit up stairs on little floor stools about a foot tall with a matching table. You can order the classic egg coffee (like a sweet egg whipped cream latte) or try egg beer where you're brought a can of beer with a side of egg whipped cream. Order some sunflower seeds and throw the shells on the floor, this is the Vietnamese way!

Open: Daily 7am-10pm
Where: North East Old Quarter
Address: 39 Nguyễn Hữu Huân, Hàng Bạc

Where to Eat in Hanoi

Bún Bò Nam Bô

Alert: My favorite restaurant in Vietnam!

There's something special about a restaurant that ONLY makes one dish…and they make it to utter perfection. A beefy broth with crunchy veggies, tender meat and gorgeous noodles- you won't know whether to call this a soup or a salad. Bún bò nam bộ is both and neither at the same time. It arrives on your table as a gorgeous, artistically displayed bowl of beauty- and then it's your job to mix it up into a schmorgesborg of yum. Such a specialty, that you've likely never heard of this dish in your home country and good luck trying to find it.

Open: Daily 7:30am-10:30pm
Where: North West Old Quarter
Address: 12-76 Hàng Điếu, Hàng Gai

Bánh Mỳ Phố Cổ

The 2nd best Bahn Mi I've had in all of Vietnam (after Hoi An)! This small establishment is hidden in plain sight. No sign. Just a hole in the wall with 5 tables. Banh My Pho Co caters to locals which means that their quality is high, and the prices are low! Get the roasted chicken Banh Mi with generous portions of chicken, veggies and a mayo sauce that is to die for. Order a beer or a milk tea to complete the experience.

Open: Daily 9am-6pm
Where: Old Quarter
Address: 38 Dinh Let

Hong Hoai Restaurant

Hungry foodies flock to Hong Hoai Restaurant in Hanoi for one dish in particular: Bun Cha. But this Bun Cha is special – it is made with a delicious western twist. Rather than ground pork patties, you are served glistening pieces of grilled pork on top of savory veggies with a side of lettuce, noodles, and Bun Cha broth. Hong Hoai calls themselves "Vietnamese Fusion" for putting a western spin on all their dishes…in other words, nothing weird. You can get your favorites like spring rolls, pho, and western dishes too. Clean eating with no surprises!

Open: Daily 10am-11pm
Where: Old Quarter
Address: 20 Bát Đàn, Hàng Bồ, Hoàn Kiếm

Quan An Ngon

A businessman had the idea of gathering all of the best food vendors in town and placing them together under one roof. This idea turned into a restaurant known as Quan An Ngon (they have one in Saigon aka Southern Vietnam as well), attracting both locals and tourists. For some of the most popular dishes, try the Banh Xiao (savory pancake taco) or Banh Beo (steam rice cake dumplings).

Open: Daily 6:45am-10pm
Where: South Western Corner of Old Quarter
Address: 18 Phan Bội Châu, Cửa Nam

Bun Cha Huong Lien aka "Obama Bun Cha"

When former US President Barack Obama came to Hanoi, Anthony Bourdain took him to a local Bun Cha restaurant to enjoy some of the best Bun Cha in town. This was a HUGE deal and so…the restaurant is now referred to by locals as "Obama Bun Cha". This place is so extra that they memorialized the actual table and plates that the pair used by encasing them in glass and have hung framed photos of Obama all around. This spot is always bustling with locals and tourists often ordering "The Obama Combo". If this Bun Cha good enough for Obama, it's certainly good enough for you.

Open: 10am-7pm
Where: North Hai Ba Trung

Address: 24 Le Van Huu

Chim Sao

Representing the northing ethnic minorities of Vietnam Chim Sao has some unique flavors to bring to the table...the table that is on the floor with floor pillows beneath contemporary Hanoi art in a refurbished French Style building. The food is inexpensive, served on banana leaves and great for sharing or a super hungry girl. Try the mustard beef and the pumpkin greens with a side of sticky rice for a true culinary experience.

Open: 10am-8pm
Where: Hai Ba Trung
Address: 65 Ngõ Huế, Ngô Thì Nhậm

Luk Lak

This breezy open-air European-style bistro is a bit on the fancier side with swanky décor and plates starting at $6 a pop. Luk Lak offers an elevated take on classic Vietnamese dishes plus, mountain specialties that incorporate delicacies like Water Buffalo, Snail and Pigeon. Portions are huge, culinary quality is gourmet and the service is very attentive. If you just want to pop in for a quick meal rather than a feast, their Bun Cha is to die for!

Open: Daily 7am-11pm
Where: South East of Hoàn Kiem Lake
Address: 4A Le Thanh Tong

Pizza 4 P's

I'm never going to stop talking about Pizza 4 P's. Ever. It's the most authentic pizza outside of Italy in...Vietnam of all places! There is a 4ps in Ho Chi Minh City, Da Nang, and Hanoi – all of which serve mind-blowing pizza with gobs of fresh mozzarella, hand tossed crust, and gourmet toppings. Some pizzas come served with a full fist-sized ball of fresh mozzarella which is unrolled to cover each slice of pizza at the table. For an extra special experience, call ahead to get a table at the wood fired oven where you can watch the pizzas being made to order.

Pro Tip: Make a reservation or just call ahead 1 hour to make sure they've got room!
Open: Daily 10am-10:30pm
Where: District 1
Address: 8/15 Lê Thánh Tôn, Bến Nghé, Quận 1

The Hung Snake Restaurant

Before you freak out, let me tell you that even the pickiest of eaters enjoy their meal and experience here at The Hung Snake Restaurant, an establishment that has managed to turn an old-school tradition into a gourmet experience. The restaurant is actually located in Hanoi's Snake Village where the family raises their own snakes, giving you plenty of options when it comes to what kind of snake you want to eat. Come with a couple people from your hostel, as snake meals are meant for sharing...plus you'll need moral support when it's time to take a shot of snake blood. The host, Mr. Hung, is lovely and will make you feel like a part of the snake family! Oh, and beer is free to give you a little liquie courage.

Open: Daily 9am-11pm
Where: North East Hanoi – About a 20-minute drive from Old Quarter
Address: 33 Lệ Mật, Việt Hưng, Long Biên
Contact: Facebook 'The Hung Snake Restaurant"

Street Food Tour

Food tour by motorbike, anyone? Hanoi Food Tasting Tours offers this tour where you can either drive a motorbike or hop on the back of a staff motorbike (with a beer, of course) as you visit all the best street food in the city. This takes the wondering ang guessing out of everything for you, as your guide explains exactly how each dish is made and why each particular stall is so special.

Starting at: $50 per person
Contact: HanoiFoodTastingTours.com

511

Nightlife in Hanoi

Night life seemingly never ends in Hanoi. You could be out all-night drinking, dancing, and bullshitting. Then order a Grab Taxi back home. It's a pretty safe city, so go for it.

Bia Hoi or Street Beer

You'll find Bia Hoi offered all over Vietnam; sometimes in a restaurant, sometimes at a hole in the wall…or best of all, just on the side of the road.

Most often, you can pull up a little plastic stool on the sidewalk, where you'll drink from the keg…. for around 25-50 cents per glass. Bia Hoi is the homemade brew that you'll find all over Vietnam- especially in Hanoi. Also called "fresh beer", there are no preservatives in this brew, so it must be consumed the same day that it's brewed.

While it only contains about 3% alcohol content – it goes down way too easy, so keep track of how many you knock back. Otherwise, the infamous 'Bia Hoi Hangover' awaits.

The best place to drink Bia Hoi in Hanoi? Head to the Old Quarter and right across from Vietnam Backpacker Hostel, you'll find the cutest little lady with the biggest smile excited for you to pull up a seat. This is also a great place to meet other travelers as sometimes you're just thrown together by mama.

Open: Late afternoon-mid morning
Where: Old Quarter – Vietnam Backpacker Hostel Downtown
Address: 9 Mã Mây, Hàng Buồm, Hoàn Kiếm

Old Quarter
Old Quarter is filled with bars that go late into the night. Most people don't really go into it with a plan. They start with a bia hoi, mingle with others and then end up doing one of the following….

- ✓ Dance at Dragonfly Lounge.
- ✓ Sip cocktails at Polite & Co.
- ✓ Drink til 4am at The Porch.
- ✓ Join the pub crawl at Vietnam Backpackers.
- ✓ Or just follow the crowd and see what happens.

Beer Street

Ta Hien Street is one narrow alley lined with Vietnamese restaurants selling food…and cheap beer. On warm weekend nights, this alley fills up with locals and expats alike. Mingling, eating, drinking, and buzzing with noise. It's worth a visit and some photos.

Not so Fun Vietnam Fact

Especially in Hanoi, dog meat is still sold in the markets. It's very unlikely, however, to wind up on your plate.

Sightseeing in Hanoi

Are you ready for all the temples? Because Hanoi has all the temples!

Pro Tip

Ladies, cover your shoulders and knees when entering any temple or pagoda in order to show respect for Buddhist culture and the monks wandering the grounds.

Ho Chi Minh Mausoleum

This 21-meter high granite building houses the body of Vietnam's most iconic and influential leader, Ho Chi Minh, despite him specifically saying that he wanted to be cremated. Inspired by Lenin's own mausoleum, this building also contains elements of Vietnamese architecture. Tourists and locals alike go here to pay their respects to this leader. Be mindful of how you act as many Vietnamese consider this an important place to visit their beloved grandfather.

Because of its historical value, security is tight, and rules are strictly followed. A dress code is followed too, so don't go here wearing shorts, skirts, or tank tops. Lines usually stretch out pretty long, but don't get discouraged as it normally flows quickly and with no delay.

Entrance Fee: $1 USD / 20k VND
Open: Every day except Monday & Friday, 8:00am - 11:30am and 4:00pm - 16:30pm
Location: Ba Dinh Square

Bach Ma Temple

A small building with yellow walls and a red gate, you could easily miss this beautiful temple, located in the heart of the old quarter. Built in the 11th century by Emperor Ly Thai To, Bach Ma or White Horse Temple, is the oldest temple in the city. Inside, there are glorious shrines and decorations, brightly-colored flags, and richly-painted columns. It's the perfect place for some peace and quiet with only the local's whispering their prayers and the smell of incense floating through the air.

Entrance Fee: Free
Open: Tuesday-Sunday 8.00am-11.00am; 2.00pm-5.00pm
Location: Hanoi

Temple of Literature - Van Mieu

A Temple of Confucius built almost a thousand years ago, the Temple of Literature is an astonishingly well-preserved piece of Vietnamese history. As the name might have given away, the Temple has been a place of learning for over 700 years. In fact, the Imperial Academy it houses was Vietnam's first national university. Today, it is one of Hanoi's most visited tourist attractions.

Explore the grounds that Confucius scholars and, on occasion, royalty, roamed centuries ago and experience the intricate Hanoi style architecture that Vietnam is known for. Divided into five courtyards, each section represents an era of Vietnamese architecture.

Entrance Fee: $1.3 USD / 30k VND
Open: Monday to Friday, 7.30am — 5.30pm; Weekend, 7:30am — 8.30pm
Location: P Quoc Tu Giam

Address: 58 Quoc Tu Giam, Van Mieu, Dong Da

Vietnam Military History Museum

Notable as the Military Museum or Army Museum, Vietnam Military History Museum commemorates Vietnam's victories over the U.S. and French forces during the 20th century. The museum serves as one of the seven national museums in the country and one of the oldest museums located in Hanoi. Its wide collection of distinctive original artifacts makes it a cultural center for the Vietnamese military history.

Spotting the museum is made easy with the display of a huge weaponry collection at the front. It also displays the U.S. and French weapons and the Chinese and Soviet equipment captured during warfare.

Entrance Fee: $1.75 USD / 40k VND
Open: 8-11:30am & 1-4:30pm Tuesday-Thursday, Sat & Sunday
Location: 28a P Dien Bien Phu
Address: Hanoi, Vietnam

Hoa Lo Prison (The Hanoi Hilton)

The French built the Hao Lo prison in the late 19th century to house political prisoners and revolutionaries during the colonization of Vietnam. This prison is known as one of the most inhumane prisons in all of Asia, as you'll discover during your tour of tiny cells where Vietnamese were kept like animals, torture chambers, guillotines and more. You'll also see parts of the narrow pipe by which some prisoners were lucky enough to use as they fled from this hellhole.

But, instead of tearing down this monstrosity once the French abandoned post, the Vietnamese decided to continue the tradition of heinous torture within these walls- but on the Americans.

During the Vietnam War, Hoa Lo Prison became known as the "Hanoi Hilton" by American soldiers who were captured, held, and tortured by the communists. It's a gruesome yet poignant part of Vietnamese history, representing the battles, struggles, and revolutions that this country has endured and participated in.

The museum itself is not very big and you can tour the entire place within 30 minutes- which is probably all you can stomach anyways as some tourists report that they can actually feel heavy dread with every step.

Entrance Fee: $1.3 USD / 30k VND
Open: Daily 8:00am – 5:00pm (including festivals and holidays)

Location: Hoa Lo Street, French Quarter
Address: No. 1 Hoa Lo, Tran Hung Dao, Hoan Kiem District, Hanoi

Tran Quoc Pagoda

The oldest pagoda in Hanoi, Tran Quoc Pagoda is over 1,405 years old. Built during the sixth century during the reign of Emperor **Lý Nam Đế**, this masterpiece is more than a piece of art; it is also the place of rest for many revered monks whose ashes lie inside. The pagoda is adorned with Buddhist symbolism with tranquil statues of buddha resting within the pagoda and lotus flower statues all around the property.

A true vision, this rusty red pagoda stands 15 meters tall or 11 stories high. Set between two large lakes, the pagoda reflects its image off the water, offering stunning mirror images that photographers will adore, especially in the mid-afternoon.

Entrance Fee: Free
Open: 7:30am-6pm
Location: Truc Bach area, on a tiny island floating on Westlake, connected by a walkable bridge.
Address: Thanh Nien, Truc Bach, Ba Dình

Quán Thánh Temple

Classic. Historical. Unforgettable. Quán Thánh Temple is easily the most beautiful ancient architectural structure in all of Hanoi.
With grey stone walls, adorned with intricate carvings, details, and elephant statues, utter silence seems appropriate as you absorb the peaceful history within these grounds.

Enter through the majestic archway into an outdoor square lined with centuries old trees, leading to a traditional Buddhist shrine.

Located right across the street, at the south end of the Tran Quoc Pagoda road, these two places make for a great back-to-back sightseeing trip.

Pro Tip: Right outside of Quán Thánh Temple are a couple coffee shops selling coconut coffee and fresh coconuts which will round out your adventure perfectly.

Entrance Fee: $.50 USD / 10k VND
Open: Daily 5am-7pm
Location: Ba Dinh, across from the park at the south end of Thanh Nien Street

Ngoc Son Temple

Situated on a small islet in the middle of **Hoan** Kiem Lake of Hanoi, Ngoc Son Temple (also known as Temple of the Jade Mountain) is one of the prime tourist attractions. The temple was built in 19th century and is dedicated to 13th Century Vietnamese military national hero General Tran Hung Dao. The temple is accessed via a quaint red wooden bridge named as The Huc Bridge meaning the Bridge of the Rising Sun. This is a perfect place to start your day watching a spectacular sunrise in quiet environment. The bridge leads to Dac Nguyet Lau meaning the "Moon Light tower" and Ngoc Son shrine.

The temple has 3 entrance gates in a series, depicting various Taoist symbols like tiger and Vietnamese dragon. There is a side room on left of the main temple which has a preserved body of a giant soft backed turtle which was found in 1968. The temple grounds offer lovely views of the lake and the Turtle Pagoda. Together with Hoan Kiem Lake and the Tortoise Tower, Ngoc Son Temple is definitely a must visit place to enjoy Hanoi's age-old culture.

Pro Tip

The red bridge is accessible without needing to buy a ticket. The rest you'll need to pay the entrance fee.

Entrance Fee: $1.3 USD / 30k VND
Open: Daily 8:00am – 6:00pm
Location: Hoan Kiem Lake
Address: Đinh Tiên Hoàng, Hàng Trống

Fun Things to Do in Hanoi

History. Food. Shopping.
This is basically what Hanoi is all about.

But there are a couple extra fun activities worth checking out...

Walk the Train Tracks

As if a post card came to life, the train tracks that run through Hanoi are picturesque AF. Lines with local Vietnamese people's homes, you see laundry hanging, chickens roaming, and old men squatting in their underwear eating noodles from a bowl like they are in their own little private bubble (more power to you, dudes). A couple of these locals have caught on to the opportunity and have turned their homes into coffee houses, egg coffee houses, or tiny restaurants. Walk on the tracks and snap a few super cool vintage-style photos. Oh, and trains actually do still use these tracks 2x per day: around 3pm and 7:30pm. Watch as everyone scrambles out of the way!

Where: East of Old Quarter – "Train Street"
How to Get There: Located between Lê Duẩn and Khâm Thin Street

Take a Cooking Class

Want to take some of your favorite Vietnamese dishes back home? The ultimate souvenir is learning how to recreate a classic Vietnamese meal once you get back home. Take a Vietnamese Cooking Classes that often starts by shopping for ingredients in the morning market, which you then bring back to the kitchen and learn to prepare step-by-step.

Check Out: Rose Kitchen Hanoi
Starting at: $40 USD / 910 VND

Go to a Park in the Morning

Hanoi at 6am is a totally different world. There are community Zumba classes, badminton games, old people doing Tai Chi, chess games, speed walkers, and of course...retired men sipping Vietnamese coffee while reading the newspaper. By 8am, everyone disappears like nothing ever happened.

Check out google maps, find the biggest park near you and you're bound to stumble upon fascinating old people activities.

Markets & Shopping in Hanoi

All of Old Quarter

Old Quarter is dense with stores selling knock off Under Armor and North Face gear alongside legit brand stores like Converse and Adidas. You'll find lots of souvenir knick knacks, shops selling bags of tea and coffee, and traditional Vietnamese dresses for humans of all ages. Just be ready to haggle. Any price you're given, counter with half the price. Never buy the first dress you like. Shop around and see what the average going rate is so that you get a good idea where your price point should be.

Dong Xuan Market

Hanoi's biggest indoor market offers 4-stories of everything from dried fruit to traditional Vietnamese dresses. As you wander around you'll notice that each section has its specialty: fabrics, baby clothes, shoes, and more. This market caters to both Vietnamese and Tourists – so even if you're not in the market for a wooden set of chopsticks, it's still fun to come and watch the madness. Located in Old Quarter, you can mosey on over here for a leisurely gander.

Open: Daily 7am-6pm
Where: Old Quarter

Hanoi Weekend Night Market

In terms of trinkets and souvenirs, the Hanoi Weekend Market is pretty standard. The cool part, however, is that the entire street is closed off to traffic, so you can wander and shop as you please. The ambiance is relaxing with glowing lights, while exhilarating with crowds of people as far as you can see. You'll definitely have one of those mental photo moments that you'll never forget. Plus, more street food vendors pop up, allowing for an unofficial food tour. If you're in the area, why not?

Open: Friday-Sunday 6pm- Midnight
Where: Old Quarter – Starts Hang Dao Street towards Dong Xuan Market

Cho Hom Market

This 3-story market is a colorful playground for photographers and a fresh foodie's dream! The entire ground floor is packed with exotic fruit that you can buy and eat on the spot. Head upstairs to fabric heaven where several tailors have set up shop, ready to make you a classic Vietnamese dress or modern jacket. Just remember to haggle!

Open: Daily 6am-5pm
Where: Hai Ba Trung
Address: 293 Tran Nhan Tong, Hai Ba Trung District

Quang Ba Flower Market

While you may not have a practical use for fresh flowers while you're traveling through Hanoi, that doesn't mean that you don't have time to stop and smell the roses! Especially if you're an early riser. This place opens at 2am, featuring flowers from all across the country. Bring your camera!

Open: 2am-Noon
Where: Tay Ho
Address: Au Co Street

Royal City Mall

If you've worn your clothes down to holey rags, head on over to Royal City Mall where you can pop into stores like H&M, Levi's, Mangos, and Nike to freshen up that wardrobe. You'll find some coveted Korean Beauty stores here too like Skin Food and The Face Shop. This mall also has a decent food court and a gym if you want to make a day of it.

Open: Daily 10am-10pm
Where: Royal City (20-30 minutes South West of Old Quarter)
Address: Ngách 190/7, Thượng Đình, Thanh Xuân

Spas in Hanoi

Omanori Spa – Visually Impaired

An amazing spa with an amazing cause. All of the massage therapists at Omanori Spa are visually impaired. I say 'massage therapists' with emphasis, because these girls are professionally trained - a qualification that 90% of massage shops in Vietnam do not require. Omanori is run by a reputable non-profit whose goal is to empower those with disabilities.

Also, amazing: the 'no tipping policy' means no haggling and no shakedowns. These girls are compensated by commission AND profits by this amazing non-profit organization that is empowering the disabled while providing the most reputable and trustworthy spa services out there.

Starting at: 300k for a 60-minute massage (plus no tip, this ends up being one of the cheapest places for a massage in Hanoi).
Open: Daily 9am-10pm
Where: Old quarter
Address: 52A Hàng Bún, Quán Thánh, Ba Đình

Genkiland Onsen and Spa

Detox your system by spending the day hopping from one hot bath to another in a calming, warmly lit atmosphere.

There is a spa menu that offers different massage sets ranging from a 1-hour Thai Massage at 350k to a 2-hour body scrub, massage, and herbal compression for 750k. Of course, you could just come to use the Onsen baths for 180k, where you can soak for hours. You also get access to the heavenly Himalayan Salt sauna! If you aren't familiar, an Onsen is a traditional Japanese bath house that is communal- but separated by gender. I promise, it's not as awkward as it sounds. It's actually a very luxurious and pampering experience.

Open: Daily 9am-11pm
Where: 10 Minutes South of Old Quarter
Address: 5 Phan Ke Binh, Ba Dinh District

Salon Blonde

Blondes, Mitch is your man. This American artist turned Hanoi expat is king when it comes to blonde hair. He does gorgeous highlights, seamless touch ups…and most importantly, he is the man that girls run to when someone else has dyed their hair orange or cat piss yellow. He's got the magic touch, and in Asia- that is worth every god damn penny. Plus, his salon is just a lot of fun. Order delivery while you process, have a beer, join in on the gossip, and get some restaurant recommendations. And even if you're not in the market for color, treat yourself to a shampoo scalp massage and blow out.

Where: Truc Bach (gorgeous area for a stroll along the water)
Address: 104 A2 Luc Chính Truc Bach
Facebook: Mitch Brookman

Hue Beauty House Calls

The most popular way to get waxed in Hanoi? Have your wax girl make a house call. Hue Pham is Hanoi's waxing extraordinaire! She comes to your hotel or house with all of her super clean waxing equipment in toe. She's got fresh Australian hot wax and accessories to wax any and everything. She'll lay a mat on the floor and clean you up for half the price of a salon. This was the most pain free Brazilian I've ever had. Also, important to note, when you get waxed at a salon, the girls who do the waxing only 5-10% of the service price. The boss takes the rest. Home waxers in Hanoi are entrepreneurs who love what they do, take pride in what they do and can actually make a living wage.

Where: House/Hotel Calls
Price for Brazilian: $11
Phone: 01682757993
Facebook: Facebook.com/hue.pham.73594

Australian Dental Clinic

Okay, it's not a spa- BUT you can get your teeth cleaned by professionals for $12. They also do teeth whitening, cavity care, and even more intense procedures like full porcelain crowns and root canals. This is the place that expats from all around the world trust with their teeth and their wallet. Take advantage!

Open: Wednesday-Saturday 8:30am-7pm/Sunday 8:30am-5pm
Where: Hai Ba Trung
Address: No 3 Nguyễn Du, Bùi Thị Xuân

How to Get around Hanoi

Walk
Here's the trick to mastering the art of walking through traffic and crossing the street in Vietnam: keep a slow and steady pace but keep moving. This allows the bikes and cars to predict your speed so that they can move around you. Never take your eyes off the cars and make eye contact or put your hand out like you're God stopping traffic with your hand. This actually works.

Grab Taxi
Grab Bike is massively popular here! You can get just about anywhere in the city for $1-$2 on the back of a Grab Bike. Grab Cars are typically $2-$3 depending where you're going. Definitely install this app.

Taxis
I **do not** recommend getting in a taxi here. It's common for a taxi for charge you 100k for the same journey that a Grab Taxi would charge just 30K for. 3x the price, ya'll.

Chapter 28: Off the Beaten Path – Hanoi

Cat Ba Island

Get here and get here quick. Cat Ba Island is having a moment. With the island's ever-expanding transport links including new express ferries and more boat tours, Cat Ba is becoming everyone's favorite Vietnamese paradise playground.

This small island is about 50km from Hai Phong (a town just north of Hanoi), offering an experience rich in biodiversity, culture and history.

With amazing limestone cliffs, a huge national park and tons of cheap options for accommodation, consider Cat Ba in the Top 5 places to visit when traveling Vietnam.

The island has an amazing history dating back to Vietnam's dynasty period, when the island was used as an important base for the army during both the French and Vietnam Wars.

A super important thing to note about Cat Ba: is that this island is the most convenient way to access Ha Long Bay and Lan Ha Bay. Going this route saves you the trouble of dealing with the hustle and bustle Ha Long City from Hanoi, it's super easy to organize both long and short tours from Cat Ba, plus- you have even more incentive to get your cute but up here.

Before we get ahead of ourselves, you can expect your time on Cat Ba to be spent kayaking, hiking or just relaxing on the beach. Go girl, go.

Ha Long Bay

Considered as one of the country's most popular tourist destinations, Ha Long Bay is a must-see when you are in Vietnam...but you won't need long. 2-3 days max. That's it, really.

You'll set off on a boat cruise that takes you on a tour between tall cliffsides and limestone mountains that are absolutely stunning. Intermittently, the boat will dock at little bays where you can kayak and explore. Spend the rest of the days lounging on the deck with a cold beer and soaking up some sun.

There are plenty of fancy boats to choose from, but one of the more fun and social options is the **Halong Bay Castaway Tour.**

Here are the highlights of **Halong Bay CastAway Tour**

- ✓ Epic Party Boat with a super social crowd
- ✓ Sun deck where you can jump off into the water
- ✓ Free booze all night for the 1st night
- ✓ Kayaking excursions
- ✓ Cozy cabins
- ✓ Transportation and all meals included

Starts at: $115 for 2 days + 1 Night
Contact: HalongBayCastAwayTour.com
Beware: There are so many copycats. Book directly from the source or with Vietnam Backpackers

Ps. You don't need to spend time in Ha Long Town. Ya just don't. You can get to Ha Long Bay from Hanoi or even better- from Cat Ba or Hai Phong.

Drive the Ha Giang Loop

One of the most remote regions on Earth, Ha Giang is region where time seemingly stands still. Isolated villages that are a 3-days drive into the mountains, mind-blowing valleys where few humans have ever stood, and human connections so pure that your heart will grow 3 sizes. Ha Giang is a once in a lifetime trip. And to access it, you need two wheels.

The "Ha Giang Loop" is typically a 5-day motorbiking adventure through windy mountain hills where each day your only goal is to make it to the next village for a warm bed, homecooked meals, and rice wine shared with new friends.

Not many people know about this loop. It's like Sapa 20 years ago, before tourism swooped in. For this trip you will need:
- ✓ A freshly-tuned motorbike and helmet
- ✓ A poncho
- ✓ Warm clothing
- ✓ Ideally, a travel partner
- ✓ A Waterproof bag is a good idea, too.

You can take 5-days to drive this loop or more – depending on how much of local life and planet earth you want to soak up. And because I could never do this trip as much justice as Lana, the badass female traveler from the Czech Republic has done … I'm leaving the itinerary details up to her.

Visit her Ha Giang Guide at miles-smilesaway.com/ha-giang-loop-itinerar/

To Get to Ha Giang, you'll start in Hai Phong and take an 11-hour night bus. Head over to QT Hostel and they'll sort you out with a bike.

Chapter 29: Sapa

Sapa.
For years, this region represented the mystical fairytales that we only believed to exists in fairytales (or before the invention of plastic).

With winding mountain roads, lush tropical rainforests, rolling hills for miles, and not a skyscraper in sight, Sapa is the epitome of pure nature. The land before time.

Only until the past 15 years or so, Sapa has been a town isolated from the rest of the world. Located in the Hoang Lien Son mountain range near the Chinese border, this northwestern Vietnamese region is full of locals living off the land and children who make a living by hauling rocks up the mountain roads instead of going to school.
Representing ethnic minorities, life in Sapa has always been more primitive than the rest of Vietnam. Homestays, treks, cooking over fire- this is what attracted westerners from near and far to come and marvel at a world once forgotten. And marvel they did.

The bittersweet result is that this sudden influx of tourism has transformed Sapa. Before tourism, the locals desperately struggled with poverty. And now...they still struggle with poverty but have come to rely on money from tourism.

You'll be introduced to five of Vietnam's ethnic minority tribes here: Black Hmong, Red Dzao, Tay, Giáy, Thai, and Phù Lá.
These locals have started setting up more homestays, more treks, and are selling more weed. For a while, this was manageable with a happy medium. But you'll notice that in the center of town, the locals are literally money hungry.

The Sapa tourist scene can be a bit overwhelming, at first. To reach the unspoiled nature treks and to get totally of the grid, you first must battle hawkers tugging on your clothes trying to sell you a tour or guest houses giving you misleading information that sways you to sign up with their bus company.

The innocence is gone. But the beauty remains.
That is why this chapter is particularly important as it's filled with trust-worthy guest houses, money-saving tours, and 'what to expect' advice. Because once you make it past the 'wall of sales', there's no denying how magical Sapa really can be.

Also, make sure you pack for the weather as thick fogs are known to block tourists in their trails. Their billboard "Four seasons in one day" is no joke as it can literally go from freezing winters to tropical summers within the day. Do a bit of research before you come so that you can dress accordingly.

Areas to Explore in Sapa

The Main Village of Sapa
The base camp for all of your adventures!

If you've ever been to Pai, Vietnam- that's kind of what to expect in the Main Village of Sapa. The main road is called Pho Cau May, where you'll find plenty of guest houses, and a couple upscale hostels surrounded by little restaurants and brightly colored souvenir shops. All of this dropped right in the middle rolling green mountains and lush rainforest. There's even a big lake where you can take a little boat out for a little paddle.

There are tour offices, places to drink, and locals always selling a service or a trinket. While the main village is a sight in itself.... this is just the beginning.

The Main Trekking Destinations

Sapa is the adventure capital of the north and offers lots of interesting trekking options, giving you an insight into local villages, valleys and rice fields. Grab a guide and head for the hills, it's time to explore Sapa's remotest regions.

Cat Cat Village
Home to the Black Hmong, Cat Cat Village is a beautiful village located about 3km from Sapa and presents an easy and rewarding trek to visit a village famed for its traditional handicrafts. The Black Hmong are weavers and you will be able to see numerous craftspeople at work throughout the village. You can also purchase these goods at the numerous stores dotted around the village.

Ta Phin Village
Located 17km from Sapa, Ta Phin is the village of the Red Dao people and has remained unchanged for centuries. The Red Dao are famed for their textile work and the village is known to supply most of the shops in Hanoi and Ho Chi Minh with brocade work dresses and silks. The workers do not stop and will negotiate prices and sales with you whilst still weaving, a tradition that goes back centuries to ensure they remain productive at all times. Ta Phin is a challenging trek from Sapa due to the condition of the roads but can be easily accomplished by motorbike.

Lao Chai Village

Flickr @ ronan crowley

Lao Chao is another village made up almost exclusively of Black Hmong people and serves as a great resting spot for those on the longer trek to Tavan. The village has become famous as a great place to get a little downtime on the challenging trek to Tavan and offers some great local foods and the opportunity to purchase the weaved handicrafts the Black Hmong are famous for. Lao Chai Village is roughly 7 km from Sapa.

Ban Ho Village

Ban Ho is home to the Tay people and is known for its scenic beauty and slightly warmer climate than Sapa. The Muong Hoa river runs through the valley that the Tay people call home and helps them irrigate their farmland, the Tay are known to be great farmers and grow crops of rice and beans that they trade with the other local tribes. The beautiful scenic route to Ban Ho valley is roughly 25 km from Sapa, but makes for a rewarding trek due to the nature of the lush valley that Ban Ho Village sits in.

Ta Van Village

Tavan is located at the bottom of the valley just along from Lao Chai and is known for being best accessed by jeep due to the nature of the narrow, dirt roads leading to the bottom of the valley. Tavan is home to the Giay people who are the areas main rice farmers and supply a number of the regions towns and cities. The Giay are also famed for their silver crafts and for the quaint stilt houses that are dotted around their village.

Heaven's Gate

Take a drive breathtaking drive along the mountain road called Tram Ton Pass, which is the highest mountain pass in all of Vietnam at 1900 meters. On your journey, you'll zoom by bright green rice fields, vast valleys, and rolling hills along the way until you get to what the locals call "Heaven's Gate"- a gorgeous rock face with a unique window that when light shines through, looks like a portal to another world. You'll either need to rent a motorbike to her here or hire a guide and hop on the back of his bike.

Accommodation in Sapa

The whole allure of Sapa is to have a local experience in a local homestay. Go on a trekking tour and you'll be led to a local's homestay where you'll eat homecooked meals and get a glimpse into local life.

I've also thrown in a couple luxury retreats to soothe those legs of yours after all that trekking...

Mountain River Homestay Sapa $

Surrounded by rice fields and nature, this peaceful homestay has great dorms and large privates with terraces. This is the perfect compromise between homestay and guesthouse- while not skimping on the breathtaking scenery. This place is seriously relaxing and offers free bicycles and a barbecue, so you can get you grill on! A Booking.com score of 9.7 and its easy access to the local treks and tours make this place hard to beat.

Style: Dorms & Privates
Starts at: $6
Where: Sapa
Address: Ta Van Dzay, Ta Van, Lao Cai

ZiZi Mekhoo Sapa Homestay $

Located on the mountainside 8km from Sapa this cute and spotlessly clean homestay drops you right into the mix with the local hill-tribes and is superbly located for trekking around Sapa's valleys. They also offer you the opportunity to participate in volunteer classes to improve the education of the local people and can put you in touch with local guides and can organize some longer-term treks into the forests. They also whip up incredible family style meals at the end of the day while you rest up those weary "trekked out" legs!

Style: Dorms & Privates
Starts at: $5 USD / 114k VND
Where: Hau Thao
Address: Hau Thao Village, Ban Pho

Luckydaisy Buffalo House $

A stay a Luckydaisy's feels akin to a detox retreat for the mind, body, and soul. Cozy wooden cabins surrounded by green rolling hills and fresh air is just what you need to press the restart button on life! This local run homestay offers functional rooms with great terraces or balconies, plus beautiful gardens to wander in after a hard day trekking.

Style: Privates
Starts at: $25 USD / 569k VND
Where: Ta Van
Address: Tan Van, Sapa, Lao Chai

The Little Hmong House $

This ever popular Sapa mainstay scores highly on all fronts and seems perennially booked up, so get in early! The property offers incredible vegetarian breakfasts and a huge terrace with incredible valley views. The staff are super helpful and are happy to go out of their way to give you local tips on where to go and what to see.

Style: Dorms & Privates
Starts at: $5 USD / 114k VND
Where: Ben Den Village
Address: Giang Ta Chai Mong, Km5, Ban Den Village, Lao Cai

Topas Ecolodge $$$

Excuse my language, but holy fucking shit. No budget? GET IT, GIRL. This frankly stunning hotel nestled in the mountains rocks your world with clean, design focused rooms, friendly staff and quite possibly one of the most gorgeous infinity pools you will ever come across. Just go here, love it and then tell everyone you know that you went there; making people jealous isn't just confined to social media, right?

Style: Privates
Starts at: $255 USD/ 5.8 million VND
Where: Outside Sapa – The Ecolodge will arrange transport
Address: 21 Muong Hoa, Sa Pa

Where to Eat in Sapa

You'll find tons of restaurants lining Pho Cau May, the main road in Sapa's central village. There are plenty of places for coffee, Vietnamese food, local dishes, and pizza! Prices are reasonable and portions generally huge, so roll up your sleeves and dive in!
Here are some of the favorites…

Little View Restaurant

This welcoming little eatery has bright and fun decor, is warm and cozy and serves up heaping plates of those local dishes you just can't get enough of. From crispy spring rolls and huge plates of fried rice, to more traditional western fair, every plate that lands on your table really hits the spot. Try their fresh salads and sensational Vietnamese hot pots they are to die for.

Open: 8am-9:30pm
Where: Sapa
Address: So 042 Ngo Cau May, Sapa

Moment Romantic Restaurant

The views of the Hoang Lien Mountain are breathtaking and complement this restaurant's slightly more upmarket vibe. The restaurant is small, but really well laid out and the staff (who speak excellent English) really seem to care about your meal. It's a little pricey than elsewhere but when those plates drop you'll understand why. The care and attention to detail at Moment Romantic is spot on. Always full and always tasty; fuel up here and you won't be disappointed. Their fried spring rolls are beyond incredible.

Open: 8am-10pm
Where: Sapa Town
Address: 026 Muong Hoa Street, TT. Sa P

Good Morning Vietnam Restaurant

Huge portions and lots of laughs at this family run favorite. Good Morning Vietnam is an ever present when it comes to Sapa's "top eats" list and it's easy to see why at this place. The service is incredible; with friendly staff happy to make suggestions and great value to be had all round. The menu is extensive and takes in traditional Vietnamese favorites and more local

Hmong specialties. The Coconut Curry is their specialty and order after order seems to stream from the kitchen doors.

Open: 8:30am-10:30pm
Where: Sapa Town
Address: 063 B Fanxipan

The Hill Station Signature Restaurant

Great food and they offer cooking classes, this Sapa staple is a must! Try your hand at cooking like the locals at this fun for all restaurant. The English-speaking Hmong chefs will put you through your paces as you whip you some local specialties. Wash the lot down with some rice wine and you'll soon be on your way to cooking like a local.

Open: 7am-10pm
Where: Sapa Town
Address: 37 D Phan Si, Sapa

Nightlife in Sapa

With most visitors hunkered down in homestays and getting drunk of rice wine with the locals – there isn't a huge nightlife scene here...except for these rare gems...

Sapa Street Bar and Shisha

Sapa's Highland Cafe was renamed and rebranded into what is now one of Sapa's best bars. Offering great price spirits and beers, plus shisha to warm you up on those cold nights I'd definitely recommend it. It's also a great spot to meet people and get some tips on treks and activities in the surrounding area.

Open: Might as well be 24/7
Where: Sapa
Address: 036 Pho Cau May, TT

The H'mong Sisters

This relaxed and fun pub serves up great cocktails and ice-cold beer. The atmosphere is a lot more relaxed than some of the other bars on this list and is a good place to unwind after a hard day on the trails. Locals like to come here and swap stories about their monster hikes too, so it's fun to grab a seat and listen in. They also have a pool table and a great buy-one-get-one free happy hour (4pm-7pm) every day.

Open: 4pm-1am
Where: Sapa Town
Address: 31 Muong Hoa

Mountain Bar and Pub

This place serves up incredibly strong cocktails, super cheap beers and really gets the place rocking with table football tournaments most nights. Mountain Bar seems to always be buzzing with something going on and tends to score pretty highly on Sapa's "go to nightlife" list. Grab a seat and join the fun!

Open: 2pm-11:30 (open till 2am on Saturday and Sunday)
Where: Sapa
Address: 02 Muong Hoa Road

Fun Things to Do in Sapa

Go on a Trek

The heavenly valleys, the unspoiled wildlife, the isolated villages, the clean air...trekking in Sapa is a humbling and life-changing experience. There are so many treks that you can sign up for; some of which last for 4 hours and some of which last for 4 days.

Flickr @ TJTAK

<u>Here's the Trick to Trekking in Sapa</u>

Look through the trekking options at your hotel or a local tourist office. Take a picture of the page, if you'd like. And then.... go find a local to take you on that very same trek. Why? Here's a little scenario....

Let's say you get a local guide named Lek via your hotel. Your hotel hires Lek to take you on a 4-hour trek for the price of $60, BUT the hotel will most likely pay Lek just $15.

Alternatively, you can go find Lek on your own and haggle your price down to $45. Lek gets to keep every penny and is happy as a clam. You can even ask Lek to take you back to his family's home for lunch!

Just make sure you work out a round-trip deal, whether that is your guide trekking back with you or a taxi coming to pick you back up.

Pro Tip

Sapa is extremely safe in terms of crime. Trust is inherent and there are no reports of violence towards travelers. You're okay to hire a local to trek into the wilderness with. If you feel uncomfortable, ask around for some other travelers who are interested in a group trek.

Bring School Supplies to Village Schools

The most rewarding day that you'll ever have in Vietnam is when you get to deliver pencils, notepads, erasers, or even toothbrushes to the isolated ethnic minority schools. Hire a motorbike driver to take you or seek out a trekking tour that will take you past a school that is a 3-day hike away from town. These schools need all the help they can get.

Do a Home Stay

Homestay sleeps can actually be quite comfortable with big heavy blankets to keep you warm during the night and incredible views to wake up to. An overnight homestay usually includes all of your meals, a trekking guide, local village tours, and an all around memorable experience.

To choose a homestay, either pick a trekking distance you can handle, a village that seems extra interesting, or a guide who you just have a good feeling about- and go. I've also listed a few popular homestays in our 'accommodation' section.

If you come across the opportunity, the Red Dao Village is a cool experience as this community specializes in herbal medicine, with some homestays offering herbal baths and treatments.

Typical Standard for Homestays in Sapa

Style: Shared living quarters
Starts at: $20-$45 USD/ 455k – 1 million

Pro Tip

These homestays are run by ethnic minorities, whom the mainstream Vietnamese don't have much compassion for. Keep in mind, when you buy a homestay trek from a Vietnamese company (rather than a local minority), the Vietnamese company gives the bare minimum to the local guide who houses you, feeds you, and cares for you.

Fansipan Mountain

The highest peak in Indochina, Fansipan Mountain is 3,143 meters of pure Earth just waiting for you to climb it...or cable car it.

You can either trek up the mountain with a guided tour or take an exhilarating cable car ride up to the top. The cable car ride is a better idea if rigorous trails and hiking gear don't appeal to you.
No matter how you get there, once at the top, you'll be greeted with 'top of the world' views along with crisp air and an unforgettable sense of accomplishment.

For the cable car, you'll be riding with Sun World Fansipan Legend. Get a motor taxi to the cable car platform from town.

Entrance Fee: $30 USD /700k VND Round Trip
Where: Includes the "Finicular" train takes you to the Fanispan Terminal so that you can avoid walking up 600 steps to the cable car platform.
Address: Nguyen Chi Thanh Street

Sapa Culture Museum

Learn about the history and mythology of the local tribes at this free to enter cracker of a museum. The exhibits aim to help you understand the differences between the hill-tribes and showcases local handicrafts.

Entrance Fee: Free, but donations are appreciated (and needed)
Open: Daily, 7:30am-11:30am, 1:30pm-5pm
Address: TT. Sa Pa, Lao Cai

Hmong Cooking Classes

How does smoked buffalo sound to you? What about tofu from scratch? When you take a Hmong cooking class, you'll learn how to make a 5-course meal using fresh ingredients from the region. Sign up for the 7am cooking class, where you'll join your Hmong chef on an errand to the market. You'll collect all your ingredients and return to a beautifully clean kitchen to learn how to cook like a Hmong step-by-step. After you cook, sit down and enjoy your meal like a mountain queen, wine and all. You'll find these classes being offered by local Hmong people and guesthouses. Take your pick.

Markets & Shopping in Sapa

Buy local! If you see something you like in the shops, you can ask a local to take you to the source. Not only does this make a better story, but you are giving 100% of the profits to the local handicraftsman.

Sapa Market

Tribespeople from the local area converge on Sapa daily to sell their handicrafts and warm clothing. The prices are tourist focused, but haggling is expected. The food stalls are open for breakfast and lunch and offer hearty, filling trekker friendly local cuisine. Saturday tends to be the busiest day so get there early for the best bargains.

Open: 6am-6pm
Address: QL4D, TT. Sa Pa, Lao Cai

Pro Tip

Any fabric or trinket made with blue dye will stain your fingers and clothes. You'll actually see local women with blue fingers. Take note from them.

Crime and Safety in Sapa

Sapa is very safe. Attacks, assaults, and robberies are rare.
There are, however, a couple things to watch out for.

✓ Renting a Motorbike from Locals

They will ask for your Passport or $250 deposit...which are usually fine in bigger cities but when you're renting from a local, you have no real terms of action if something goes wrong.

✓ Petty Theft

Kids are sneaky. Keep your purse zipped while out and about. Bring a lock and key to keep your big backpack impenetrable when you leave it at a homestay while you play with chickens and cows.

✓ Rugged Terrain

Walking and riding a motorbike on Rocky Mountains and muddy hills presents the opportunity for slipping. Wear appropriate shoes and don't trek drunk!

Say it with me, now... "Travel Insurance".

Worldnomads.com

Insider Tips for Sapa

Bring Clothes made for Mountain Weather
The higher elevation offers colder temperatures, especially at night. Bring a poncho or a jacket. Don't have one? You can buy one in Sapa. If you plan to go trekking, bring hiking shoes or rubber boots. You can also rent these from trekking offices.

Buy from Adults, Not Kids
Kids are cute, and the local families have caught on that tourists agree! Because tourists have big hearts, they often can't say no when a child comes up to them selling trinkets. But you must say no. Do not encourage the practice of children begging. Do not incentivize these families to pull their children from school in order to make a living on the street.

Don't Say "Maybe Later"
This is as good as "Yes, please" when trying to get hawkers to leave you alone. On your treks, you'll be followed by kids trying to sell you things. They can be relentless little hustlers, so "maybe later" is just more incentive to keep trying.

Do Not Give Kids Candy

You'll see signs around the town in English that encourage locals not to give the children sugary treats. The kids here have terrible dental health which is perpetuated by the casual import of sugar by good-intentioned tourists. Instead, bring stickers!

Do Buy from Old Ladies

Like grandmas everywhere, you'll find old women from ethnic minority tribes who have kept the tradition of hand weaving alive. These women sell blankets, scarves, and bags made with their own two hands. You'll come across these women in town, in the villages, along local paths- it's all good.

Buy Local

Buy trinkets from local hands instead of the shops. And go on treks by hiring your own guide on the street, rather than a trek from your hotel which typically gives the guides just 20% of the profits for their hard days work.

Accidents Happen

Muddy hills can lead to falls and scraps and sprains. The hospitals around here are very basic. The hospitals around here can provide temporary care, but for bigger accidents, head to Lao Cai Hospital (38kms away).

Tag me in your Instagram photos @SoloGirlsTravelGuide

How to Get to Sapa

From Hanoi

Hanoi is the most convenient jumping off point for Sapa, unless you're driving a motorbike.

➤ By Bus

The bus is very windy as it goes up twisting mountain roads, but also very scenic. If you get motion sickness, ask sit in the front seat and bring motion sickness pills. There is no toilet on the bus, but it will make stops along the way.

Point of Departure:
When: Multiple times per day but it's best to take a morning bus around 7am.
Duration: 5.5-6 Hours
Cost: $12-$17

Pro Tip

If you book with Sapa Express Bus, they will pick you up directly from your hotel or hostel in the Old Quarter of Hanoi.

➤ By Sleeper Train

*You are traveling from Hanoi to Lao Cai Station.

The sleeper train is comfortable with sleeper beds, a dining car, and bathrooms. It will take you to Lao Cai Station, which is 35 kilometers from Sapa. Once you get into Lao Cai Station, there will be multiple shuttle buses waiting to take you into Sapa for less than 100k VND.

Point of Departure: Hanoi Station to Lao Cai Station
When: There are multiple night trains that leave around 9:30-10pm
Duration: 8-9 hours
Cost: $40-$80

Pro Tip

Buy your train ticket from the train station or 12Go.Asia a few days in advance so you can avoid paying marked up tourist office prices. Ask for a top bunk. As you'll be sharing a car with 3 other strangers, the top bunk will make you feel a bit safer as your slumber.

Itineraries for Vietnam

The first thing you should realize about visiting Vietnam is that Vietnam is HUGE.

With a length of 3,260 km from top to bottom, you need at least 3 weeks to travel the entire country, with MANY bus legs taking around 11 hours from one city to the next.

If you're going to properly backpack around Vietnam, then you must **budget 3 weeks minimum.** If you're going to fly around to a few different cities, you can certainly see quite a bit **within 1-2 weeks.**

While there are SO many ways to explore Vietnam, here are just a few of the most popular itineraries…

1 Week: Ho Chi Minh & Hoi An

Day 1: Ho Chi Minh City
- Fly into HCMC
- Check into your hotel
- Explore Bui Vien Street
- Eat street food for dinner

Day 2: Ho Chi Minh City
- Wake up at 6am and go to Da'an Park
- Eat breakfast at Propaganda Bistro Restaurant
- Visit the War Remnants Museum
- Shop at Ben Thanh Market
- Kick your feet up at the hotel
- Eat dinner on Tran Khac Chan Street
- Finish your night at Mary Jane's Bar

Day 3: Ho Chi Minh City
- Go have some Egg Coffee
- Sign up for a day tour to the Chu Chi Tunnels
- Treat yourself to a massage at My Massage
- Go to dinner at Den Long - Home Cooked Vietnamese Restaurant
-

Day 4: Fly to Da Nang
- Take a taxi from Da Nang to Hoi An
- Stay at Sunshine Resort
- Hop on a bicycle and explore the old city
- Pop into a clothing shop to have a dress or playsuit made
- Have dinner at Minh Hiển Vegetarian Restaurant
- Explore the riverside and the Japanese Bridge

Day 5: Hoi An
- Ride your bicycle around the rice fields and stop for a little photoshoot
- Take a cooking class in the afternoon
- Wander the night market for some shopping and street food
- Have a drink by the river

Day 6: Hoi An Beach
- Go pick up your clothing made at the tailor
- Head to the beach and check into your hotel
- Spend the day in the sun on the sand
- Have dinner at your hotel

Day 7: Bangkok
- Have breakfast on the beach – make sure you get a fresh coconut
- Head to the airport and fly back to HCMC for your connecting flight.

1 Week: Hanoi and Ha Long Bay

Day 1: Hanoi
- Fly into Hanoi and check into your hotel
- Walk around the Old Quarter for shopping and street food
- Visit the Military Museum and Ho Chi Minh's Mausoleum
- Go to Bún Bò Nam Bô for dinner
- Drink Bia Hoi in the Old Quarter

Day 2: Hanoi
- Take a cooking class in the morning
- Visit Tran Quoc Pagoda and walk around Truc Bach lake
- Treat yourself to Omanori Spa
- Time for dinner at Obama Bun Cha

Day 3-5: Ha Long Bay
- Sign up for a 2-night tour on Ha Long Bay
- They'll take care of everything – transport, food, kayaks, and adventure.

Day 5: Hanoi
- Once you've returned to Hanoi, go to the Hung Snake Restaurant or sign up for the Street Food Tour

Day 7: Railay
- Visit any street market you've missed and drink all the coffee possible before you journey home.

2 Weeks: Hanoi, Ha Long Bay, Hoi An and HCMC

The perfect amount of time to see the best Vietnam has to offer. Combine the two 1-Week Itineraries above with a little extra trip to Ninh Binh...if you can swing it!

4 Weeks: Bus Along the Whole Country

Alright ladies, when you sign-up for a 'Hop On/Hop Off' Bus Ticket, you can take your time hitting up the main spots in Vietnam. **Spend 2-3 days** in each place and enjoy the spontaneous journey.

You get a fun little packet of tickets. Tear off your ticket and present it to the bus station or your hotel reception when you're ready to book.

The most popular route is **Bus Route #11 for $60 total.**

Route # 11 goes like this...

1. Ho Chi Minh City
2. Dalat
3. Mui Ne
4. Nha Trang
5. Hoi An
6. Hue
7. Ninh Binh
8. Hanoi

From Hanoi, you can then arrange transport to

9. Ha Long Bay
10. Sapa

Stay as long or as little as you'd like! This is the best way to see the country on your time.

Want me to plan your trip for you?
Hotels, flights, and itinerary – I got you, girl.
Visit **TheSoloGirlsTravelGuide.com** to start planning.

Vietnamese Food Guide

Travel is just an excuse to eat…

Okay, for your reading pleasure! You don't have to know how to pronounce these words- but it's so helpful to be able to identify them on a menu.

Pork: Thịt lợn
Beef: Thịt bò
Chicken: Gà
Lamb: Tôm
Shrimp: Thịt cừu
Fish: Cá
Vegetarian: Tiếng Việt

Keep an eye out for these favs.

Pho

Pronounced 'Fuh', this is the most well-known Vietnamese dish within the Western world. Deep broth with tender chicken, beef, pork, or seafood along with freshly made rice noodles, Pho is the ultimate comfort food. Season to your liking with soy sauce, chili, and lime on the side.

Bun Cha

Freshly grilled and perfectly seasoned pork is served in a tangy broth with pickled veggies. With your chopsticks, grab a mouthful of sticky noodles, mint, lettuce and mix together in one bite. Watch the locals around you to figure it out.

Fried Spring Rolls – Nem Ran (in the North) / Cha Gio (in the South)

Crispy deep-fried spring rolls typically filled with pork, shrimp or kept vegetarian. Often, served with Bun Cha in the North. They're not always pretty…but they're always delicious.

Fresh Spring Rolls- Goi Cuon

Shrimp, lettuce, and cilantro wrapped in rice paper and served with a sweet & sour fish sauce- this is a classic.

Bahn Mi

Vietnamese sandwich made with fresh French baguettes, typically filled with chicken, pork, or pattee and garnished with cilantro, pickled veggies and mayonnaise.

Bún Bò Nam Bộ

Not a soup; yet not a salad- Bún bò nam bộ mixes a little bit of everything in one savory bowl. Rice noodles, beef, peanuts, lettuce, crispy dried shallots, and a deep broth collide to create my favorite dish in Vietnam.

Bún Bò Hue

A specialty from the town of Hue, Bun Bo Hue is a bowl of spicy beef noodle soup made with rice vermicelli noodles and seasoned beef patties, garnished with chilies, chopped cilantro and lime.

Grilled Shrimp - Tôm Nướng

Whole shrimp grilled on a stick and served with a side of dipping sauce, the trick is to remove the head first and suck out the sweet, creamy brains.

Cao Lau

A specialty of Hoi An, this bowl of pork or beef broth and meat is distinct when it comes to its thick noodles, fried lard and tangy sauce that you mix all together.

Xoi Xeo

A sweet sticky rice with mung bean paste, fried shallots, fried egg, stewed pork and shredded pork is about as close to soul food as it gets in Vietnam.

Bánh Xèo

"A Vietnamese Pancake" looks more like a taco as it wraps up a mixture of protein, usually shrimp or pork, with crunchy veggies, scallions and tangy sauce.

Broken Rice - Cơm Tấm

Literally, broken pieces of rice, this grain tastes more like couscous. Served as the working-class lunch staple, Com Tam is dished up with your choosing of sides like sweet grilled chicken or sautéed veggies. Look out for Com Tam places on the side of the road with a 'point & choose' display case.

Hot Pot

Vietnamese love a good Hot Pot; not just for the vibrant flavors but for the social aspect of cooking meat and veggies in one communal simmering pot of broth. When it comes to Hot Pot, you've got option: Vit Nau Chao (Duck hot pot), Lau Hai San (seafood hot pot), Lau Ca Keo (fish hot pot with small fish that look similar to eel), Lau Chua (sweet & sour hot pot with river fish.

Drinks

Street Beer - Bia Hoi

Homemade street beer that is typically served out of family run establishments or just a keg on the side of the road, this beer is sold for as low as 4,000 dong and has a slight buttery taste to it.

Sugar Cane Juice- Nước Mía

No refined sugar here, just pure organic sugar cane juice full of electrolytes. You'll see little stands on the side of the road with fresh sugar cane juice that is crushed as it's ran through a machine, with it's pure juice poured over ice.

Iced Black Coffee – Ca Fe Da

Strong drip coffee, black. But make a point to ask for no sugar.

Sweetened Iced Coffee- Ca Fe Sua Da

The most popular style of coffee in Vietnam is this iced coffee that is sweetened with condensed milk, creating a thick, slow-drinking treat.

Coconut Coffee - Cà Phê Dừa

Instead of milk or sweetened cream, add coconut cream to your iced coffee for an exotic texture and flavor.

Egg Coffee - Cà Phê Trứng

For ages, when I heard "Egg Coffee" I imagined a raw egg being dropped into a cup of coffee – but I was so wrong. Egg Coffee is a sweet whipped cream made of egg and sugar that is added into a black coffee to make a thick and tasty coffee that resembles a dense latte.

Vietnamese Festivals and Holidays

Tet Holiday - January/February

Tet is the Vietnamese equivalent of Chinese New Year. It's, by far, the country's most important holiday. Locals make their back to their hometowns to spend time with their families and honor their ancestors. In addition to endless family meals, you can expect beating drums, firecrackers, and elaborate costumes.

Perfume Pagoda Festival - February/March

Near Hanoi, the Perfume Pagoda is the most famous site for Buddhist pilgrims in Vietnam. Each year—immediately following the Tet Holiday—hundreds of thousands of Vietnamese visit a sacred cave to pray for the new year. The pilgrims travel through a series of caves both on foot and by boat prior to reaching the Pagoda.

Hung Festival - April

Vietnam's first monarchs—known as the Hung Vuong—are celebrated during this festival. Legend has it that these kings were born when a mountain princess and sea dragon joined together. The one hundred eggs laid turned into one hundred children, with half returning to the sea and half learning to rule. Each year, the Vietnamese gather outside of Hanoi to make offerings, beat drums, and enjoy traditional entertaining arts.

Mui Ne Street Food Festival - July

Are you visiting Mui Ne in January, April or July? If you are and go food tasting, you should join the Mui Ne Street Food Festival. The festival is held 3x a year for two days and held along the beach fronts of Blue Ocean Resort and Coco Beach Resort. When you join in the fun, you can select from a variety of local dishes famous in Phan Thiet and even some of the national and international signatures. Aside from the selection of dishes, there is also music and dancing included in the festivities to bring everyone together.

Autumn Festival - September/October

Known in Vietnamese as Tet Trung Thu, this festival celebrates the moon. Elaborate lanterns are placed across Vietnam to help guide moon spirits back to Earth. Children particularly love this time of year because there more toys, candy, and fruit than you can count! Be sure to try traditional cakes in the shapes of fish and the moon, and don't miss the lion dancers that travel house to house.

The Best Ways to Travel Around Vietnam

Vietnam is so unique as a backpacker destination in that there is no central hub. Thailand has Bangkok, Cambodia has Phnom Penh, and Malaysia has Kuala Lumpur. But with Vietnam...this S-shaped country has got 2 main hubs at opposite ends of the country with bonus destinations spread out north-to-south within a distance of 1,650 kilometers. So, when it comes to covering ground, you've got options.

Option 1: The 'Hop On / Hop Off Bus'

An open bus ticket. How genius!

When you buy your Open Bus Ticket package, you'll receive a little notepad of tickets.

There are multiple packages you can buy, with options to start in Hanoi or Ho Chi Minh City.

Let's say you get to Mui Ne. Stay for a few days and then decide, "Tomorrow, I'm ready to head to my next destination." Bring your ticket to reception, they'll call the bus station, book you a seat, and you're off.

The two most popular companies are Viet Nhat and Hanh Cafe.

The Full Route Typically looks like this....

1. Ho Chi Minh > Mui Ne = 4.5 Hours
2. Mui Ne > Da Lat = 4 hours
3. Da Lat > Nha Trang = 3.5 hours
4. Nha Trang > Hoi An = 10 hours (overnight sleeper bus)
5. Hoi An > Hue = 3 hours
6. Hue > Hanoi = 14 hours (overnight sleeper bus)

Expect to pay anywhere from 900k VND to the 1,230,000 VND.

The Benefits
✓ 1 Flat Fee
✓ Discounted price
✓ Utterly convenient
✓ The cheapest option

- ✓ Trusted Bus Company
- ✓ Easy way to cover the must-see destinations
- ✓ Removes the stress and headache of planning.

The Annoyances

- ✓ Most backpackers buy this ticket, so expect to see the same people. On the bus. In the next town. At your popular hostel. You're all kind of moving at the same pace. This is great if you like them...annoying if you don't.
- ✓ Sleeper buses can get old after you've spent 25 hours laying there – bring entertainment and sleeping pills.

Ps. Avoid Moon Travel (Nguyen Tri Phuong) Tour Bus Company. They've got a bad reputation round' these parts.

Option 2: Fly

If you've got the budget, flying is such a convenient way to get around Vietnam. While the bus from Ho Chi Minh to Nha Trang is 10.5 hours...the plane is only 1 hour.
Flying is a great option to cover the country quickly but expect to pair this mode of transport with couple train and buses here and there.

The Benefits

- ✓ Fast
- ✓ Convenient
- ✓ Comfortable

The Annoyances

- ✓ More expensive
- ✓ Consider transportation costs to and from the airport
- ✓ Some of the best off-the-beaten path areas have no airport

Option 3: Train

The train is one of the most comfortable ways to travel Vietnam! There is always a bathroom, the sleeper trains are comfy, and the train takes some seriously scenic routes.

Here's what a sleeper train carriage looks like (Hue to Hanoi route).

- ✓ More leg room
- ✓ Comfortable for long distances
- ✓ Available for most destinations

The Annoyances
- ✓ Less trains per day than buses and planes
- ✓ Train stations are sometimes a few kilometers away from your final destination town/city

Option 4: Motorbike

Driving the length of Vietnam via motorbike is a lifetime bucket list adventure. The memories you make, the people you meet, and the motorbike gang you collect along the way is a once in a lifetime experience...if you are confident on a motorbike.

The Benefits
- ✓ Get off-the-beaten path with scenic highways and isolated villages
- ✓ You have instant access to the "Real Vietnam" with detours that other travelers will never get to see
- ✓ Link up with other motorbike drivers along the way
- ✓ Train stations are sometimes a few kilometers away from your final destination town/city

The Annoyances
- ✓ Rainy Weather, Hot Weather, Sweaty Weather
- ✓ Your ass will get numb and some days will be long
- ✓ You'll need a Vietnamese or International Drivers License
- ✓ Motorbikes come with a level of danger and risk – absolutely do not ride without travel insurance
- ✓ Your bike **will** break down and you will have to get it fixed along the way – it's just a fact of life that makes the adventure a bit more fun and spontaneous.

Plan to spend at least 5 weeks driving from Ho Chi Minh City to Hanoi. Alternatively, you can always rent a bike and just drive scenic areas for a few days such as the Ha Giang Loop up north.

To get your hands on a motorbike, you'll buy one in Ho Chi Minh and sell it in Hanoi (or the other way around).
Pro Tip: Bring a cup of noodles (there's free hot water on most trains), snacks, and a big water for your journey. There will be a snack car but with rip-off prices.

Where to Buy a Bike

1. In Ho Chi Minh, head to the neighborhood of Pham Ngu Lao, where there will be countless people trying to sell you a bike. Compare prices and quality. You're essentially choosing a boyfriend, so consider all variables here.
2. The Facebook Group 'Vietnam Backpackers Travel and Sales
3. A Backpacker Finishing a Trip: Ask around in your hostel or look for signs that resemble 'Missing Cat' posters posted around the backpacker area. You can buy direct from a backpacker.

Ps. Every single bike must come with a blue registration card – don't buy without one.

The Best Manual Bike for this trip: **Honda Win** (around $175 depending on condition)

The Best Automatic Bike for this trip: Any automatic scooter -but make sure it has good breaks and decent kick for those uphill mountain roads (around $300 depending on condition).

Pro Tip

f you're unsure about 5 weeks on the road, then come on over to Vietnam, rent a motorbike for a few days and see how it feels. THEN make a decision because girl, once you commit to this wild and crazy adventure, you've really got to commit. It takes a badass.

Pro Tip 2

There are more factors to consider when planning this trip like clothing, food, gasoline- do some deep dive research, first.

You'll find plenty of blogs with bike tips and suggested routes that make this experience so much fucking fun.

Tourist Visas for Vietnam

Before you come to Vietnam, you must apply for a tourist visa or an "E-Visa".

It's a simple process and can be done within 2 days or 2 hours - depends on how rushed you feel.

The Visa Allowances for Vietnam are as follows:

- 1 Month Single Entry
- 1 Month Multiple Entry
- 3 Months Single Entry
- 3 Months Multiple Entries

The Single Entry means that if you leave Vietnam in that time frame, you'll have to apply for another visa if you want to come back in. The Multiple Entry means that you can come and go as you please.

So, if you plan on coming to Vietnam then going to Cambodia then back to Vietnam in a span of 3 months –you should get the 3 Month Multiple Entry Visa. Make sense?

There are two ways to obtain a Vietnamese Visa:

Option 1: Apply Online

Step 1: Visit the website 'Vietnam Visa Pro' and choose your visa.
Step 2: Fill out the online form.
Step 3: Make your payment for the Visa Approval Letter.
Step 4: Receive your Visa Approval Letter via email and print it out.
Step 5: At the airport or border crossing in Vietnam, present your Visa Approval Letter to the visa counter and pay the Official Visa Fee.
Step 6: Receive your Visa Sticker in your passport (yep, a full-page sticker – not a stamp).

So, the fee that you pay to the agency is for the Visa Approval Letter and the fee that you pay the airport is for the actual Visa.

The entire visa can cost anywhere from $31 - $70, depending on how long you stay + Single vs. Multiple entry.

What You'll Need when Receiving a Visa at Immigration:

- ✓ 1 Passport Photo
- ✓ Visa Fee in US Cash
- ✓ Visa Approval Letter
- ✓ 1 Full Blank Page in your Passport

Option 2: Go to a Visa Agency in Person

If you're already traveling in Cambodia, Thailand, Laos or other nearby South East Asian countries, you'll see plenty of visa agencies offering Vietnamese Visa services. They do the visa entire process for you by going to the Vietnamese Embassy and getting the actual Visa put in your passport so that you can enter Vietnam straight away.

This option is fine. But not necessarily any more convenient than applying online + you will pay a small fee to the agency. Also, you'll be without your passport for a few days while the visa is being processed.

But if you want to breeze through customs at the border in Vietnam, this option will help you do that. Here's how it works…

Step 1: Visit a visa agency and fill out the paperwork for your Vietnamese Visa.

Step 2: Pay the agency fee and the visa fee.

Step 3: Entrust your passport to the agency. They will personally take your passport to the Vietnamese Embassy to process your visa.

Step 4: Pick up your passport (usually 3-5 days, sometimes quicker depending on location).

Step 5: Now you have your visa and can pass through Vietnamese customs with no letter needed.

What You'll Need when Applying with an Agency:
- ✓ 2 Passport Photos
- ✓ Visa Fee
- ✓ 1 Full Blank Page in your Passport

Technically, you can come and go into Vietnam as many times as you want. Once your visa expires, just make a trip to the border. Cross into the bordering country and re-enter same day.

What to Expect at Immigration

When you fly into the airport, you'll need:

- Your visa letter printed out
- 2 Passport Sized Photos
- $25 USD

You'll hand these documents to the immigration counter, they'll process them on the spot and return your passport with a fancy full-page sticker visa.

Crime and Safety in Vietnam

The scams, the tricks, the dangers – and how to avoid them all…

Rule of Thumb: Vietnam gets safer and safer the further north you travel.

The most crime-ridden city is Ho Chi Minh. The biggest crime? Street theft. Watch your pockets, wear a cross should purse, and don't leave your purse or phone out in the open.

Besides pickpockets, here's what else you need to know…

Learn How to Cross the Street
Crossing the street in Vietnam is a skill. Once you must master.
Stop lights are sparse and even when they are present, they aren't always followed. So, you must learn to be one with the traffic!

You'll notice quickly that when driving, motorbikes will weave around each other in an organized form of chaos. This chaos means that you can't predict their path. Instead, let the motorbikes predict yours.
You'll cross the street in 2 phases, pausing in the middle of the road.

Wait until you see a slight pocket in the traffic and keep your eyes on the bikes while walking a steady pace to the middle of the road. Then repeat while watching the other direction. All the while, be aware of rogue drivers that may be driving the wrong way on the side that you're not watching.

Do not stop or jump or jerk or run. Walk at a consistent pace so bikes can move around you.

To get the hang of this, simply wait for a local to cross the street and follow their lead.

Motorbikes and Car Crashes
Man oh man. There are far too many traffic accidents in Vietnam. You have monster 16-wheel trucks next to tiny motorbikes passing each other on dirt roads. You have cows in the road. You have drunk drivers galore.

Where: Particularly in Hanoi and Ho Chi Minh city.
What to do: Always wear your seatbelt in a car and always secure your helmet tightly when riding a motorbike. Don't ride or drive with someone

you have an uneasy feeling about. Practice riding your motorbike in rural areas before driving in the city or on main roads.

Donut Ladies

Don't trust their "free donut" gimmick. Once you take a bite, they'll follow you and relentlessly hassle you to buy buy buy.

Vietnam Directory

Police: 113
Fire: 114
Ambulance – First Aid: 115

British Embassy Hanoi
Phone: 024 3936 0500
Address: 4 Central Building, 31 Hai Bà Trưng, Tràng Tiền, Hoàn Kiếm,
Hà Nội

British Consulate Ho Chi Minh City
Phone: 028 3825 1380
Address: 25 Lê Duẩn, Bến Nghé, District 1, Hồ Chí Minh

US Embassy Hanoi
Phone: 024 3850 5000
Address: Chợ Dừa, 7 Láng Hạ, Chợ Dừa, Ba Đình, Hà Nội

US Consulate Ho Chi Minh
Phone: 028 3520 4200
Address: 4 Lê Duẩn, Bến Nghé, Quận 1, Hồ Chí Minh

Canadian Embassy Hanoi
Phone: 024 3734 5000
Address: 31 Hùng Vương, Điện Bàn, Ba Đình, Hà Nội

Canadian Consulate Ho Chi Minh
Phone: 028 3827 9899
Address: The Metropolitan, 235 Đồng Khởi, Bến Nghé, Quận 1, Hồ Chí
Minh

South African Embassy Hanoi
Phone: 024 3936 2000
Address: 31 Hai Bà Trưng, Hàng Bài, Hoàn Kiếm, Hà Nội

South African Consulate Ho Chi Minh
Phone: 028 3823 8556
Address: 80 Võ Văn Tần, Phường 6, Quận 3, Hồ Chí Minh

Australian Embassy Hanoi
Phone: 024 3774 0100

Address: Đào Tấn, Cống Vị, Ba Đình, Hà Nội

Australian Consulate Ho Chi Minh
Phone: 028 3521 8100
Address: 45 Lý Tự Trọng, Bến Nghé, Quận 1, Hồ Chí Minh

German Embassy Hanoi
Phone: 024 3267 3335
Address: 25 Tran Phu, Dien Ban, Ba Dinh, Hanoi

German Consulate Ho Chi Minh
Phone: 028 3829 1967
Address: 126 Nguyễn Đình Chiểu, phường 6, quận 3, Ho Chi Minh City, Hồ Chí Minh

For Broken Apple Products

Professional Computer Care & IT Services (ProCare Hanoi)
Phone: 098 301 10 81
Address: No 10 lane, 12 Đặng Thai Mai, Tây Hồ, Hanoi, Hà Nội 100000

IKNOW-ITM | Apple & Microsoft Experts (Ho Chi Minh)
Phone: 028 6252 4141
Address: 94 Xuan Thuy, Thao Dien Ward, 2 District, Thảo Điền, Quận 2, Hồ Chí Minh 713385

Need help finding something?
Reach out to me on Instagram @SoloGirlsTravelGuide

Gynecology Services & Female Stuff

Birth Control Pills

You can buy birth control pills and contraception over the counter in Vietnam. The word for birth control is Vietnamese is "thuốc tránh thai".

Some of the most popular brands include HN Choice, Rigevidon, Marvelon, and Microgynon – you can do an easy search of these pills online.

Morning After Pill

All pharmacies carry the Morning After Pill for around $2. There are at least 9 different brands, all of which you can take within a 120-hour window after unprotected sex.

Depo Shot / IUDs

You can get the Depo shot for as low as $15 and the IUD for $150-$350…without insurance. For these, you can visit one of the gynecologists we've listed below.

Women's Health Centers in Hanoi

Hanoi Family Program
The French Vietnamese Hospital
International SOS
Family Medical Practice

Women's Health Centers Ho Chi Minh
Family Medical Practice
International SOS

If you find yourself in an "accidental fertility situation" then visit Family Medical Practice Vietnam (Hanoi or Ho Chi Minh) to receive "Unwanted Pregnancy Pills". You'll have a consultation with a Women's Health Doctor, who will provide an exam and the pill for around $230 total.

Abortions are legal in Vietnam, up to 22 weeks. Check out France-Vietnam Hospital in HCMC or Family Medical Practice in both Hanoi and HCMC.

For more information, check out gynopedia.org/Vietnam

The Vietnam Bucketlist

- ✓ Visit the War Museum in HCMC
- ✓ Ride on the back of a Grab Taxi
- ✓ Drink Egg Coffee (or Egg Beer)
- ✓ Ride in a Boat of Some Form
- ✓ Learn 3 words in Vietnamese
- ✓ Eat an authentic bowl of Pho
- ✓ Make a Vietnamese Friend
- ✓ Take a Cooking Class
- ✓ Drink Bia Hoi
- ✓ Get a Massage
- ✓ Visit a Temple
- ✓ Get Lost

What to Pack for Southeast Asia

First. Don't stress. As long as you have your passport, bank card and a decent backpack- you can get your cute but on that plane.

Anything you need or forget at home can be found in Thailand, Cambodia and Vietnam- just at a slightly more expensive price.

So, let's get organized now. It's taken me years to perfect packing for Asia, but I've finally got it down. This list will teach you in 3 minutes what I learned in 6 years!

The Perfect Backpack

Yes, backpack! Not a rolley suitcase. With sandy beaches, the absence of sidewalks, and dirt roads with potholes, you want a bag you can easily carry. Even more important, there is no free checked baggage on short flights – you need an overhead compartment sized bag.

My go-to backpack is the **Osprey Farpoint 55** or 40-liter bag. I've gone through several backpacks over the years, and this one is my golden child.

Walking Shoes

Bring 3 pairs of shoes
- ✓ 1 Pair of Flip Flops
- ✓ 1 Pair of Cute Walking Sandals
- ✓ 1 Pair of Hiking / Running Shoes

This is my magical trifecta of shoes. Through rain, up mountains, and on long sweaty walks, they've never failed me. I replace the same pairs of shoes every year – find them in my travel store. Link below.

Tampons or a Vaginal Cup

Southeast Asian women prefer sanitary pads over tampons. Which means that tampons aren't sold everywhere. You **can** find them in Western drugstores in the bigger cities – but if you start bleeding on a bus in the middle of nowhere, you need your own stash. Pack some **OB tampons** - they are the most compact. Or try a vaginal cup like the Diva Cup.

Electric Adapter

Your phone, laptop and computer might not fit into electrical sockets out here. But more importantly, you need to regulate the voltage so that you don't fry your electronics. REI, Target, and Amazon have **Universal adapters** that every traveling girl should own.

Quick Dry Towel

Hostel girls! Hostels don't always provide towels so it's nice to bring a **travel towel** of your own. Not a total necessity, but a quick dry (usually some kind of microfiber) towel is nice to have- especially during rainy season when the heat isn't there to dry things quickly. Plus, it can double as your beach towel!

Normal towels are too bulky and take forever to dry- so don't bother bringing one.

Emergency Money Source/ $100 Cash US

Have a secret stash of cash or a backup credit card in case you get in a sticky situation. Keep this emergency money source separate from your other cards and cash- so that if you lose your wallet, you won't lose the secret stash, too.

Bank Cards

Travel with 2 cards. In the case that your bank flags one card with fraud and disables it, you'll want to have a backup. If the machine eats a card, if a card gets stolen, or if you lose your purse on a night out, a backup card will make all the difference between having mom fly you home and you continuing your travels.

If you're **moving** abroad, Charles Schwab pays your overseas ATM fees! Just sayin…

Passport with at Least 6 Months Validity

Some countries enforce it and some countries don't- but to play it safe, you need to have at least 6 months validity on your passport. For example, if it's January 1st, 2018 and your passport expires before June 1st, 2018, immigration might not let you in the country and you'll have to return home immediately.

Travel Insurance

Better safe than sorry. From minor bouts of food poisoning to helicopter medevac off a mountain, a standard travel insurance policy is a nonnegotiable in my (literal) book. Check out a company called **World Nomads** which offers full-coverage plans for extremely reasonable prices.

Empty Space in Your Bag

The less stuff you have, the more free you are. You are free to pick up and move around, free to shop for souvenirs, and free from relying on porters and taxis to help you carry your luggage.

Want to see what I travel with?
All of my favorite travel gear can be found in my **Travel Store** at
TheSoloGirlsTravelGuide.com

Behind every badass woman is a tribe of other badass women who have her back.

Coming to Southeast Asia want some tips or have a question that I didn't cover? Reach out to me on Instagram @ SoloGirlsTravelGuide

No seriously. Message me. I'd love to hear from you and stalk your trip.

And ya'll, if you liked this book- **please leave me a review on Amazon.com!**

Be wild. Be safe. Message me if you need me.

Stressing about planning such a huge trip?

Let me help you.

Second-guessing your itinerary?

✦ Email me your itinerary for suggestions and advice.

Want help planning best vacation ever?

✦ 30-minute Skype Itinerary Consultations

Trust me to plan the whole trip for you?

✦ Full-on Itinerary Planning with your Bucket List

Don't want to lift a finger?

✦ Total Itinerary Planning including Reservations and Flights, plus 24-hour concierge service while you travel.

Visit **TheSoloGirlsTravelGuide.com** for trip planning help!